CONSTITUTION

OF THE

UNITED STATES OF AMERICA,

WITH THE

AMENDMENTS THERETO:

TO WHICH ARE ADDED

JEFFERSON'S MANUAL OF PARLIAMENTARY PRACTICE,

THE

STANDING RULES AND ORDERS

FOR CONDUCTING BUSINESS IN

THE HOUSE OF REPRESENTATIVES AND SENATE OF THE UNITED STATES,

AND

BARCLAY'S DIGEST.

WASHINGTON:
GOVERNMENT PRINTING OFFICE.
1ST SESS. 43D CONG.

CONSTITUTION

OF

THE UNITED STATES OF AMERICA.

IN THE HOUSE OF REPRESENTATIVES UNITED STATES,
March 15, 1871.

Resolved, That there be printed after the close of each session, and on the same terms as heretofore, the usual edition of the Constitution, Manual, Rules, and Barclay's Digest for the use of the members of the House at the next session thereafter.

CONSTITUTION.

Preamble

We, the people of the United States, in order to form a more perfect union, establish justice, insure domestic tranquility, provide for the common defence, promote the general welfare, and secure the blessings of liberty to ourselves and our posterity, do ordain and establish this Constitution for the United States of America.

ARTICLE I.

SECTION I.

Congress.

All legislative powers herein granted shall be vested in a Congress of the United States, which shall consist of a Senate and House of Representatives.

SECTION II.

Representatives, how chosen.

The House of Representatives shall be composed of members chosen every second year by the people of the several States, and the electors in each State shall have the qualifications requisite for electors of the most numerous branch of the State legislature.

Qualification of representatives.

No person shall be a Representative who shall not have attained the age of twenty-five years, and been seven years a citizen of the United States, and who shall not, when elected, be an inhabitant of that State in which he shall be chosen.

Apportionment of representatives and direct taxes.

Representatives and direct taxes shall be apportioned among the several States which may be included within this Union, according to their respective numbers, which shall be determined by adding to the whole number of free persons, including those bound to service for a term of years, and excluding Indians not taxed, three-fifths of all other persons. The actual enumeration shall be made within three years after the first meeting of the Congress of the United States, and within every subsequent term of ten years, in such manner as they shall by law direct. The number of Representatives shall not exceed one for every thirty thousand, but each State shall have at least one Representative; and until such enumeration shall be made, the State of *New Hampshire* shall be entitled to choose three, *Massachusetts* eight, *Rhode Island and Providence Plantations* one, *Connecticut* five, *New York* six, *New Jersey* four, *Pennsylvania* eight, *Delaware* one, *Maryland* six, *Virginia* ten, *North Carolina* five, *South Carolina* five, and *Georgia* three.

Census every ten years.

Vacancies, how filled.

When vacancies happen in the representation from any State, the executive authority thereof shall issue writs of election to fill such vacancies.

Representatives choose officers and bring impeachments.

The House of Representatives shall choose their Speaker and other officers; and shall have the sole power of impeachment.

SECTION III.

Senate, how chosen.

The Senate of the United States shall be composed of two Senators from each State, chosen by the legislature thereof, for six years; and each Senator shall have one vote.

Immediately after they shall be assembled in consequence of the first election, they shall be divided as equally as may be into three classes. The seats of the Senators of the first class shall be vacated at the expiration of the second year; of the second class, at the expiration of the fourth year, and of the third class, at the expiration of the sixth year, so that one-third may be chosen every second year; and if vacancies happen by resignation or otherwise, during the recess of the legislature of any State, the executive thereof may make temporary appointments until the next meeting of the legislature, which shall then fill such vacancies. Senators classed. Vacancies, how filled.

No person shall be a Senator, who shall not have attained to the age of thirty years, and been nine years a citizen of the United States, and who shall not, when elected, be an inhabitant of that State for which he shall be chosen. Qualification of Senators.

The Vice President of the United States shall be President of the Senate, but shall have no vote, unless they be equally divided. Vice President to preside.

The Senate shall choose their other officers, and also a President *pro tempore* in the absence of the Vice President, or when he shall exercise the office of President of the United States. Officers of Senate.

The Senate shall have the sole power to try all impeachments. When sitting for that purpose, they shall be on oath or affirmation. When the President of the United States is tried, the Chief Justice shall preside: and no person shall Trial of impeachments.

be convicted without the concurrence of two-thirds of the members present.

Judgment in impeachments.

Effect of.

Judgment in cases of impeachment shall not extend further than to removal from office, and disqualification to hold and enjoy any office of honor, trust or profit under the United States: but the party convicted shall nevertheless be liable and subject to indictment, trial, judgment, and punishment, according to law.

SECTION IV.

Elections, when and how held.

The times, places, and manner of holding elections for Senators and Representatives shall be prescribed in each State by the legislature thereof; but the Congress may at any time by law make or alter such regulations, except as to the places of choosing Senators.

Congress assemble annually.

The Congress shall assemble at least once in every year, and such meeting shall be on the first Monday in December, unless they shall by law appoint a different day.

SECTION V.

Elections, how judged.

Quorum.

Absent members.

Each house shall be the judge of the elections, returns, and qualifications of its own members, and a majority of each shall constitute a quorum to do business; but a smaller number may adjourn from day to day, and may be authorized to compel the attendance of absent members, in such manner, and under such penalties, as each house may provide.

Rules.

Expulsion.

Each house may determine the rules of its proceedings, punish its members for disorderly behavior, and with the concurrence of two-thirds, expel a member.

Each house shall keep a journal of its proceedings, and from time to time publish the same, excepting such parts as may in their judgment require secrecy, and the yeas and nays of the members of either house on any question shall, at the desire of one-fifth of those present, be entered on the journal.

Journals to be kept and published.

Yeas and nays.

Neither house, during the session of Congress, shall, without the consent of the other, adjourn for more than three days, nor to any other place than that in which the two houses shall be sitting.

Adjournments.

SECTION VI.

The Senators and Representatives shall receive a compensation for their services, to be ascertained by law, and paid out of the Treasury of the United States. They shall in all cases except treason, felony and breach of the peace, be privileged from arrest during their attendance at the session of their respective houses, and in going to and returning from the same ; and for any speech or debate in either house, they shall not be questioned in any other place.

Compensation.

Privileges.

No Senator or Representative shall, during the time for which he was elected, be appointed to any civil office under the authority of the United States, which shall have been created, or the emoluments whereof shall have been increased during such time ; and no person holding any office under the United States, shall be a member of either house during his continuance in office.

Members not appointed to office.

Officers of government cannot be members.

SECTION VII.

Revenue bills.

All bills for raising revenue shall originate in the House of Representatives; but the Senate may propose or concur with amendments as on other bills.

Bills to be presented to the President.

Every bill which shall have passed the House of Representatives and the Senate, shall, before it become a law, be presented to the President

His powers over them.

of the United States; if he approve he shall sign it, but if not he shall return it, with his objections to that house in which it shall have originated, who shall enter the objections at

Proceedings on his veto.

large on their journal, and proceed to reconsider it. If after such reconsideration two-thirds of that house shall agree to pass the bill, it shall be sent, together with the objections, to the other house, by which it shall likewise be reconsidered, and if approved by two-thirds of that house, it shall become a law. But in all cases the votes of both houses shall be determined by yeas and nays, and the names of the persons voting for and against the bill shall be entered on the journal of each house respectively. If

Bills to be laws if not returned in ten days.

any bill shall not be returned by the President within ten days (Sundays excepted) after it shall have been presented to him, the same shall be a law, in like manner as if he had signed it, unless the Congress by their adjournment prevent its return, in which case it shall not be a law.

Joint orders or resolutions to be approved by the President.

Every order, resolution, or vote to which the concurrence of the Senate and House of Representatives may be necessary (except on a question of adjournment) shall be presented to the

President of the United States; and before the same shall take effect, shall be approved by him, or being disapproved by him, shall be repassed by two-thirds of the Senate and House of Representatives, according to the rules and limitations prescribed in the case of a bill.

SECTION VIII.

The Congress shall have power to lay and collect taxes, duties, imposts and excises, to pay the debts and provide for the common defence and general welfare of the United States; but all duties, imposts and excises shall be uniform throughout the United States; Power of Congress to lay taxes —pay debts. General welfare. Duties uniform.

To borrow money on the credit of the United States; Borrow money.

To regulate commerce with foreign nations, and among the several States, and with the Indian tribes; Commerce.

To establish an uniform rule of naturalization, and uniform laws on the subject of bankruptcies throughout the United States; Naturalization. Bankruptcy.

To coin money, regulate the value thereof, and of foreign coin, and fix the standard of weights and measures; Coin money. Weights and measures.

To provide for the punishment of counterfeiting the securities and current coin of the United States; Counterfeiting.

To establish post offices and post roads; Post roads.

To promote the progress of science and useful arts, by securing for limited times to authors and inventors the exclusive right to their respective writings and discoveries; Promote arts and science.

Inferior courts. To constitute tribunals inferior to the Supreme Court;

Piracies, &c. To define and punish piracies and felonies committed on the high seas, and offences against the law of nations;

Declare war and make captures. To declare war, grant letters of marque and reprisal, and make rules concerning captures on land and water;

Raise armies. To raise and support armies, but no appropriation of money to that use shall be for a longer term than two years;

Navy. To provide and maintain a navy;

Rules and articles of war. To make rules for the government and regulation of the land and naval forces;

Call out militia. To provide for calling forth the militia to execute the laws of the Union, suppress insurrections and repel invasions;

Organize and govern militia. To provide for organizing, arming, and disciplining the militia, and for governing such part of them as may be employed in the service of the United States, reserving to the States respectively, Officers of militia. the appointment of the officers, and the authority of training the militia according to the discipline prescribed by Congress;

Exclusive legislation over seat of government. To exercise exclusive legislation in all cases whatsoever, over such district (not exceeding ten miles square) as may, by cession of particular States, and the acceptance of Congress, become the seat of the government of the United States, and to exercise like authority over all places purchased by the consent of the legislature of the State in which the same shall be, for the And over forts, arsenals, docks, &c. erection of forts, magazines, arsenals, dock-yards, and other needful buildings;—and

To make all laws which shall be necessary and proper for carrying into execution the foregoing powers, and all other powers vested by this Constitution in the Government of the United States, or in any department or officer thereof. To make general laws to carry powers into effect.

SECTION IX.

The migration or importation of such persons as any of the States now existing shall think proper to admit, shall not be prohibited by the Congress prior to the year one thousand eight hundred and eight, but a tax or duty may be imposed on such importation, not exceeding ten dollars for each person. Importation of slaves allowed till 1808.

The privilege of the writ of habeas corpus shall not be suspended, unless when in cases of rebellion or invasion the public safety may require it. Habeas corpus.

No bill of attainder or ex post facto law shall be passed. Attainder and ex post facto laws.

No capitation, or other direct tax shall be laid, unless in proportion to the census or enumeration hereinbefore directed to be taken. Direct taxes.

No tax or duty shall be laid on articles exported from any State. No exportation duty.

No preference shall be given by any regulation of commerce or revenue to the ports of one State over those of another: nor shall vessels bound to, or from, one State, be obliged to enter, clear, or pay duties in another. Commerce between the States.

No money shall be drawn from the treasury, but in consequence of appropriations made by law; and a regular statement and account of the Money, how drawn from the treasury.

To be published. receipts and expenditures of all public money shall be published from time to time.

No nobility. No title of nobility shall be granted by the United States; and no person holding any office of profit or trust under them, shall, without the consent of the Congress, accept of any present, emolument, office, or title, of any kind whatever, from any king, prince, or foreign State.

Foreign presents and titles.

SECTION X.

Powers denied to the States.

No State shall enter into any treaty, alliance, or confederation; grant letters of marque and reprisal; coin money; emit bills of credit; make anything but gold and silver coin a tender in payment of debts; pass any bill of attainder, ex post facto law, or law impairing the obligation of contracts, or grant any title of nobility.

Other powers denied to States.

No State shall, without the consent of the Congress, lay any imposts or duties on imports or exports, except what may be absolutely necessary for executing its inspection laws: and the net produce of all duties and imposts, laid by any State on imports or exports, shall be for the use of the Treasury of the United States; and all such laws shall be subject to the revision and control of the Congress.

Further denial of powers to States.

No State shall, without the consent of Congress, lay any duty of tonnage, keep troops, or ships of war in time of peace, enter into any agreement or compact with another State, or with a foreign power, or engage in war, unless actually invaded, or in such imminent danger as will not admit of delay.

ARTICLE II.

SECTION I.

The executive power shall be vested in a President of the United States of America. He shall hold his office during the term of four years, and together with the Vice President, chosen for the same term, be elected as follows: President of the United States.

Each State shall appoint, in such manner as the legislature thereof may direct, a number of electors, equal to the whole number of Senators and Representatives to which the State may be entitled in the Congress: but no Senator or Representative, or person holding an office of trust or profit under the United States, shall be appointed an elector. Electors, how appointed.

The electors shall meet in their respective States, and vote by ballot for two persons, of whom one at least shall not be an inhabitant of the same State with themselves. And they shall make a list of all the persons voted for, and of the number of votes for each; which list they shall sign and certify, and transmit sealed to the seat of the government of the United States, directed to the President of the Senate. The President of the Senate shall, in the presence of the Senate and House of Representatives, open all the certificates, and the votes shall then be counted. The person having the greatest number of votes shall be the President, if such number be a majority of the whole number of electors appointed; and if there be more than one Electors to meet and to elect a President and Vice President. Their votes counted in Congress.

who have such a majority, and have an equal number of votes, then the House of Representatives shall immediately choose by ballot one of them for President; and if no person have a majority, then from the five highest on the list the said House shall in like manner choose the President. But in choosing the President, the votes shall be taken by States, the representation from each State having one vote; a quorum for this purpose shall consist of a member or members from two-thirds of the States, and a majority of all the States shall be necessary to a choice. In every case, after the choice of the President, the person having the greatest number of votes of the electors, shall be the Vice President. But if there should remain two or more who have equal votes, the Senate shall choose from them by ballot the Vice President.*

Representatives to choose if electors fail.

Votes by States.

Vice President.

Election and meeting of electors.

The Congress may determine the time of choosing the electors, and the day on which they shall give their votes; which day shall be the same throughout the United States.

Qualifications of President.

No person except a natural-born citizen, or a citizen of the United States, at the time of the adoption of this Constitution shall be eligible to the office of President; neither shall any person be eligble to that office who shall not have attained to the age of thirty-five years, and been fourteen years a resident within the United States.

Removal, death, &c., of President.

In case of the removal of the President from office, or of his death, resignation, or inability to

* This clause of the Constitution has been amended. See twelfth article of the amendments, page 31.

discharge the powers and duties of the said office, the same shall devolve on the Vice President, and the Congress may by law provide for the case of removal, death, resignation, or inability, both of the President and Vice President, declaring what officer shall then act as President, and such officer shall act accordingly, until the disability be removed, or a President shall be elected.

Compensation of President.

The President shall, at stated times, receive for his services a compensation, which shall neither be increased nor diminished during the period for which he shall have been elected, and he shall not receive within that period any other emolument from the United States, or any of them.

Before he enter on the execution of his office, he shall take the following oath or affirmation:—

Oath.

"I do solemnly swear (or affirm) that I will faithfully execute the office of President of the United States, and will to the best of my ability preserve, protect, and defend the Constitution of the United States."

SECTION II.

Powers and duties of the President.

The President shall be Commander-in-chief of the army and navy of the United States, and of the militia of the several States, when called into the actual service of the United States; he may require the opinion, in writing, of the principal officer in each of the executive departments, upon any subject relating to the duties of their respective offices, and he shall have power to grant reprieves and pardons for offences against the United States, except in cases of impeachment.

He shall have power, by and with the advice and consent of the Senate, to make treaties, provided two-thirds of the senators present concur; and he shall nominate, and, by and with the advice and consent of the Senate, shall appoint ambassadors, other public ministers and consuls, judges of the Supreme Court, and all other officers of the United States, whose appointments are not herein otherwise provided for, and which shall be established by law; but the Congress may by law vest the appointment of such inferior officers, as they think proper, in the President alone, in the courts of law, or in the heads of departments.

Appointment of public officers.

The President shall have power to fill up all vacancies that may happen during the recess of the Senate, by granting commissions which shall expire at the end of their next session.

Vacancies in office.

SECTION III.

He shall from time to time give to the Congress information of the state of the Union, and recommend to their consideration such measures as he shall judge necessary and expedient; he may, on extraordinary occasions, convene both houses, or either of them, and in case of disagreement between them, with respect to the time of adjournment, he may adjourn them to such time as he shall think proper; he shall receive ambassadors and other public ministers; he shall take care that the laws be faithfully executed, and shall commission all the officers of the United States

Further powers and duties of the President.

SECTION IV.

The President, Vice President, and all civil officers of the United States, shall be removed from office on impeachment for, and conviction of treason, bribery, or other high crimes and misdemeanors. Impeachment

ARTICLE III.

SECTION I.

The judicial power of the United States shall be vested in one Supreme Court, and in such inferior courts as the Congress may from time to time ordain and establish. The judges, both of the Supreme and inferior courts, shall hold their offices during good behavior, and shall, at stated times, receive for their services a compensation which shall not be diminished during their continuance in office. Judiciary and tenure of judges.

SECTION II.

The judicial power shall extend to all cases, in law and equity, arising under this Constitution, the laws of the United States, and treaties made, or which shall be made, under their authority;—to all cases affecting ambassadors, other public ministers, and consuls; to all cases of admiralty and maritime jurisdiction; to controversies to which the United States shall be a party; to controversies between two or more States; between a State and citizens of another Power of the judiciary.

State; between citizens of different States; between citizens of the same State claiming lands under grants of different States, and between a State, or the citizens thereof, and foreign States, citizens or subjects.

Jurisdiction of the Supreme Court.

In all cases affecting ambassadors, other public ministers and consuls, and those in which a State shall be party, the Supreme Court shall have original jurisdiction. In all the other cases before mentioned, the Supreme Court shall have appellate jurisdiction, both as to law and fact; with such exceptions, and under such regulations as the Congress shall make.

Trials by jury.

And where held.

The trial of all crimes, except in cases of impeachment, shall be by jury; and such trial shall be held in the State where the said crimes shall have been committed; but when not committed within any State, the trial shall be at such place or places as the Congress may by law have directed.

SECTION III.

Treason.

Treason against the United States shall consist only in levying war against them, or in adhering to their enemies, giving them aid and comfort. No person shall be convicted of treason unless on the testimony of two witnesses to the same overt act, or on confession in open court.

No corruption of blood.

The Congress shall have power to declare the punishment of treason, but no attainder of treason shall work corruption of blood or forfeiture except during the life of the person attainted.

ARTICLE IV.

SECTION I.

Full faith and credit shall be given in each State to the public acts, records, and judicial proceedings of every other State. And the Congress may by general laws prescribe the manner in which such acts, records and proceedings shall be proved, and the effect thereof. Acts of States accredited.

SECTION II.

The citizens of each State shall be entitled to all privileges and immunities of citizens in the several States. Privileges of citizenship.

A person charged in any State with treason, felony, or other crime, who shall flee from justice, and be found in another State, shall, on demand of the executive authority of the State from which he fled, be delivered up, to be removed to the State having jurisdiction of the crime. Fugitives from justice to be delivered up.

No person held to service or labor in one State, under the laws thereof, escaping into another, shall, in consequence of any law or regulation therein, be discharged from such service or labor, but shall be delivered up on claim of the party to whom such service or labor may be due. Fugitive slaves to be delivered up.

SECTION III.

New States may be admitted by the Congress into this Union; but no new State shall be formed or erected within the jurisdiction of any other State; nor any State be formed by the New States.

junction of two or more States, or part of States, without the consent of the legislatures of the States concerned as well as of the Congress.

Territory and other property of United States.

The Congress shall have power to dispose of and make all needful rules and regulations respecting the territory or other property belonging to the United States; and nothing in this Constitution shall be so construed as to prejudice any claims of the United States, or of any particular State.

SECTION IV.

Republican form of government.

Protection of States.

The United States shall guaranty to every State in this Union a republican form of government, and shall protect each of them against invasion, and on application of the legislature, or of the executive, (when the legislature cannot be convened,) against domestic violence.

ARTICLE V.

Amendments of this Constitution.

The Congress, whenever two-thirds of both houses shall deem it necessary, shall propose amendments to this Constitution, or, on the application of the legislatures of two-thirds of the several States, shall call a convention for proposing amendments, which in either case, shall be valid to all intents and purposes, as part of this Constitution, when ratified by the legislatures of three-fourths of the several States, or by conventions in three-fourths thereof, as the one or the other mode of ratification may be proposed by the Congress; provided that no amendment which may be made prior to the year one thousand eight hundred and eight, shall in any manner affect the first and fourth clauses in the ninth section of the first article; and that no State, without its consent, shall be deprived of its equal suffrage in the Senate.

ARTICLE VI.

All debts contracted and engagements entered into, before the adoption of this Constitution, shall be as valid against the United States under this Constitution, as under the confederation. Debts of former government recognized.

This Constitution, and the laws of the United States which shall be made in pursuance thereof, and all treaties made, or which shall be made, under the authority of the United States, shall be the supreme law of the land; and the judges in every State shall be bound thereby, anything in the Constitution or laws of any State to the contrary notwithstanding. What constitutes the supreme law.

The Senators and Representatives before mentioned, and the members of the several State legislatures, and all executive and judicial officers, both of the United States and of the several States, shall be bound by oath or affirmation, to support this Constitution; but no religious test shall ever be required as a qualification to any office or public trust under the United States. Oath of public officers. No religious test.

ARTICLE VII.

The ratification of the conventions of nine States shall be sufficient for the establishment of this Constitution between the States so ratifying the same. Ratification.

Done in convention by the unanimous consent of the States present the seventeenth day of September in the year of our Lord one thousand seven hundred and eighty-seven and of the Independence of the United States of America the twelfth. In witness whereof we have hereunto subscribed our names.

GEO WASHINGTON—
Presid't and deputy from Virginia.

NEW HAMPSHIRE.
John Langdon,
Nicholas Gilman.

MASSACHUSETTS.
Nathaniel Gorham,
Rufus King.

CONNECTICUT.
Wm. Saml. Johnson,
Roger Sherman.

NEW YORK.
Alexander Hamilton.

NEW JERSEY.
Wil: Livingston,
David Brearley,
Wm. Paterson,
Jona. Dayton.

PENNSYLVANIA.
B. Franklin,
Thomas Mifflin,
Robt. Morris,
Geo: Clymer,
Tho: Fitzsimons,
Jared Ingersoll,
James Wilson,
Gouv: Morris.

DELAWARE.
Geo: Read,
Gunning Bedford, jun'r,
John Dickinson,
Richard Bassett,
Jaco: Broom.

MARYLAND.
James McHenry,
Dan: of St. Thos: Jenifer,
Danl. Carroll.

VIRGINIA.
John Blair,
James Madison, jr.

NORTH CAROLINA.
Wm. Blount,
Rich'd Dobbs Spaight,
Hu. Williamson.

SOUTH CAROLINA.
J. Rutledge,
Charles Coatesworth Pinckney
Charles Pinckney,
Pierce Butler.

GEORGIA.
William Few,
Abr. Baldwin.

Attest: WILLIAM JACKSON, *Secretary*

PROCEEDINGS

OF THE

CONVENTION WHICH FORMED THE CONSTITUTION

IN CONVENTION.

MONDAY, *September* 17, 1787.

Resolved, That the preceding Constitution be laid before the United States in Congress assembled: and that it is the opinion of this Convention that it should afterwards be submitted to a convention of delegates, chosen in each State by the people thereof, under the recommendation of its legislature, for their assent and ratification; and that each convention assenting to and ratifying the same should give notice thereof to the United States in Congress assembled.

Resolved, That it is the opinion of this Convention that, as soon as the conventions of nine States shall have ratified this Constitution, the United States in Congress assembled should fix a day on which electors should be appointed by the States which shall have ratified the same, and a day on which electors should assemble to vote for the President, and the time and place for commencing proceedings under this Constitution; that after such publication, the electors should be appointed, and the Senators and Representatives elected; that the electors should meet on the day fixed for the election of the President, and should transmit their votes, certified, signed, sealed, and directed, as the Constitution requires, to the Secretary of the United States in Congress assembled; that the Senators and Representatives should convene at the time and place assigned; that the Senators should appoint a President of the Senate, for the sole purpose of receiving, opening, and counting the votes for President; and that, after he shall be chosen, the Congress, together with the President, should, without delay, proceed to execute this Constitution.

By the unanimous order of the Convention:

GEO: WASHINGTON, *President.*

WILLIAM JACKSON, *Secretary.*

LETTER OF THE CONVENTION TO THE OLD CONGRESS.

IN CONVENTION

SEPTEMBER 17, 1787.

SIR: We have now the honor to submit to the consideration of the United States in Congress assembled, that Constitution which has appeared to us the most advisable.

The friends of our country have long seen and desired that the power of making war, peace, and treaties; that of levying money, and regulating commerce, and the correspondent executive and judicial authorities, should be fully and effectually vested in the General Government of the Union; but the impropriety of delegating such extensive trust to one body of men is evident; hence results the necessity of a different organization.

It is obviously impracticable in the federal government of these States to secure all rights of independent sovereignty to each, and yet provide for the interest and safety of all. Individuals entering into society must give up a share of liberty to preserve the rest. The magnitude of the sacrifice must depend as well on situation and circumstance as on the object to be obtained. It is at all times difficult to draw with precision the line between those rights which must be surrendered and those which may be reserved; and on the present occasion, this difficulty was increased by a difference among the several States as to their situation, extent, habits, and particular interests.

In all our deliberations on this subject, we kept steadily in our view that which appears to us the greatest interest of every true American—the consolidation of our Union—in which is involved our prosperity, felicity, safety, perhaps our national existence. This important consideration, seriously and deeply impressed on our minds, led each State in the Convention to be less rigid on points of inferior magnitude than might have been otherwise expected; and thus the Constitution which we now present is the result of a spirit of amity, and of that mutual deference and concession which the peculiarity of our political situation rendered indispensable.

That it will meet the full and entire approbation of every State is not, perhaps, to be expected; but each will doubtless consider that, had her interest been alone consulted, the consequences might have been particularly disagreeable or injurious to others. That it is liable to as few exceptions as could reasonably have been expected, we hope and believe. That it may promote the lasting welfare of that country so dear to us all, and secure her freedom and happiness, is our most ardent wish.

With great respect, we have the honor to be, sir, your excellency's most obedient, humble servants.

By unanimous order of the Convention:

GEO: WASHINGTON, *President.*

His Excellency the PRESIDENT OF CONGRESS.

PROCEEDINGS IN THE OLD CONGRESS.

UNITED STATES IN CONGRESS ASSEMBLED.

FRIDAY, *September* 28, 1787

Present.—New Hampshire, Massachusetts, Connecticut, New York, New Jersey, Pennsylvania, Delaware, Virginia, North Carolina, South Carolina, and Georgia; and from Maryland, Mr. Ross.

Congress having received the report of the Convention lately assembled in Philadelphia—

Resolved, unanimously, That the said report, with the resolutions and letter accompanying the same, be transmitted to the several legislatures, in order to be submitted to a convention of delegates chosen in each State by the people thereof, in conformity to the resolves of the Convention made and provided in that case.

CHARLES THOMPSON, *Secretary.*

AMENDMENTS.

ARTICLE I.

Congress shall make no law respecting an establishment of religion, or prohibiting the free exercise thereof; or abridging the freedom of speech, or of the press; or the right of the people peaceably to assemble, and to petition the government for a redress of grievances.

ARTICLE II.

A well regulated militia, being necessary to the security of a free State, the right of the people to keep and bear arms shall not be infringed.

ARTICLE III

No soldier shall, in time of peace, be quartered in any house, without the consent of the owner, nor in time of war, but in a manner to be prescribed by law.

ARTICLE IV.

The right of the people to be secure in their persons, houses, papers, and effects, against unreasonable searches and seizures, shall not be violated, and no warrants shall issue, but upon probable cause, supported by oath or affirmation, and particularly describing the place to be searched, and the persons or things to be seized.

ARTICLE V.

No person shall be held to answer for a capital, or otherwise infamous crime, unless on a presentment or indictment of a grand jury, except in cases arising in the land or naval forces, or in the militia, when in actual service in time of war or public danger; nor shall any person be subject for the same offence to be twice put in jeopardy of life or limb; nor shall be compelled in any criminal case to be a witness against himself, nor be deprived of life, liberty, or property, without due process of law; nor shall private property be taken for public use, without just compensation.

ARTICLE VI.

In all criminal prosecutions, the accused shall enjoy the right to a speedy and public trial, by an impartial jury of the State and district wherein the crime shall have been committed, which district shall have been previously ascertained by law, and to be informed of the nature and cause of the accusation; to be confronted with the witnesses against him; to have compulsory process for obtaining witnesses in his favor, and to have the assistance of counsel for his defence.

ARTICLE VII.

In suits at common law, where the value in controversy shall exceed twenty dollars, the right of trial by jury shall be preserved, and no fact tried by a jury shall be otherwise re-examined in any court of the United States, than according to the rules of the common law.

ARTICLE VIII.

Excessive bail shall not be required, nor excessive fines imposed, nor cruel and unusual punishments inflicted.

ARTICLE IX.

The enumeration in the Constitution, of certain rights, shall not be construed to deny or disparage others retained by the people.

ARTICLE X.

The powers not delegated to the United States by the Constitution, nor prohibited by it to the States, are reserved to the States respectively, or to the people.

ARTICLE XI.

The judicial power of the United States shall not be construed to extend to any suit in law or equity, commenced or prosecuted against one of the United States by citizens of another State, or by citizens or subjects of any foreign State.

ARTICLE XII.

The electors shall meet in their respective States and vote by ballot for President and Vice President, one of whom, at least, shall not be an inhabitant of the same State with themselves; they shall name in their ballots the person voted for as President, and in distinct ballots the person voted for as Vice President, and they shall make distinct lists of all persons voted for as President, and of all persons voted for as Vice President, and of the number of votes for each; which lists they shall sign and certify, and transmit sealed to the seat of government of the United States, directed to the President of the Senate. The President of the Senate shall, in the presence of the Senate and House of Representatives, open all the certificates and the votes shall then be counted;—the person having the greatest number of votes for President, shall be the President, if such number be a majority of the whole number of electors appointed; and if no person have such majority, then from the persons having the highest numbers not exceeding three on the list of those voted for as President, the House of Representatives shall choose immediately, by ballot, the President. But in choosing the President, the votes shall be taken by States, the representation from each State having one vote ; a quorum for this purpose shall consist of a member or members from two-thirds of the States, and a majority of all the States shall be necessary to a choice. And if the House of Representatives shall not choose a President whenever the right of choice shall devolve upon them, before the fourth day of March, next following, then the Vice-President shall act as President, as in the case of the death or other constitutional disability of the President.

The person having the greatest number of votes as Vice-President shall be the Vice-President, if such number be a majority of the whole number of electors appointed; and if no person have a majority, then from the two highest numbers on the list the Senate shall choose the Vice-President ; a quorum for the purpose shall consist of two-thirds of the whole number of Senators, and a majority of the whole number shall be necessary to a choice. But no person constitutionally ineligible to the office of President shall be eligible to that of Vice-President of the United States.

ARTICLE XIII.

SECTION 1. Neither slavery nor involuntary servitude, except as a punishment for crime whereof the party shall have been duly convicted, shall exist within the United States, or any place subject to their jurisdiction.

SECTION 2. Congress shall have power to enforce this article by appropriate legislation.

ARTICLE XIV.

SECTION 1. All persons born or naturalized in the United States, and subject to the jurisdiction thereof, are citizens of the United States and of the State wherein they reside. No State shall make or enforce any law which shall abridge the privileges or immunities of citizens of the United States; nor shall any State deprive any person of life, liberty, or property, without due process of law; nor deny to any person within its jurisdiction the equal protection of the laws.

SECTION 2. Representatives shall be apportioned among the several States according to their respective numbers, counting the whole number of persons in each State, excluding Indians not taxed. But when the right to vote at any election for the choice of electors for President and Vice-President of the United States, Representatives in Congress, the executive and judicial officers of a State, or the members of the legislature thereof, is denied to any of the male inhabitants of such State, being twenty-one years of age, and citizens of the United States, or in any way abridged, except for participation in rebellion, or other crime, the basis of representation therein shall be reduced in the proportion which the number of such male citizens shall bear to the whole number of male citizens twenty-one years of age in such State.

SECTION 3. No person shall be a Senator or Representative in Congress, or elector of President and Vice-President, or hold any office, civil or military, under the United States, or under any State, who, having previously taken an oath, as a member of Congress, or as an officer of the United States, or as a member of any State legislature, or as an executive or judicial officer of any State, to support the Constitution of the United States, shall have engaged in insurrection or rebellion against the same, or given aid or comfort to the enemies thereof. But Congress may, by a vote of two-thirds of each house, remove such disability.

SECTION 4. The validity of the public debt of the United States, authorized by law, including debts incurred for payment of pensions and bounties for services in suppressing insurrection or rebellion, shall not be questioned. But neither the United States nor any State shall assume or pay any debt or obligation incurred in aid of insurrection or rebellion against the United States, or any claim for the loss or emancipation of any slave ; but all such debts, obligations and claims shall be held illegal and void.

SECTION 5. The Congress shall have power to enforce, by appropriate legislation, the provisions of this article.

ARTICLE XV.

SECTION 1. The right of citizens of the United States to vote shall not be denied or abridged by the United States or by any State on account of race, color, or previous condition of servitude.

SECTION 2. The Congress shall have power to enforce this article by appropriate legislation.

INDEX

TO

THE CONSTITUTION OF THE UNITED STATES.

A.

B.

C.

D.

J.

L.

M.

N.

O.

S.

T.

V.

MANUAL

OF

PARLIAMENTARY PRACTICE:

EXTRACT FROM THE RULES OF THE HOUSE OF REPRESENTATIVES OF THE UNITED STATES.

The rules of parliamentary practice comprised in Jefferson's Manual shall govern the House in all cases to which they are applicable, and in which they are not inconsistent with the standing rules and orders of the House and the joint rules of the Senate and House of Representatives.—(*Adopted September* 15, 1837.)

TABLE OF CONTENTS.

4

PREFACE.

The Constitution of the United States, establishing a legislature for the Union under certain forms, authorizes each branch of it "to determine the rules of its own proceedings." The Senate have accordingly formed some rules for its own government; but these going only to few cases, they have referred to the decision of their President, without debate and without appeal, all questions of order arising either under their own rules, or where they have provided none. This places under the discretion of the President a very extensive field of decision, and one which, irregularly exercised, would have a powerful effect upon the proceedings and determinations of the House. The President must feel, weightily and seriously, this confidence in his discretion, and the necessity of recurring, for its government, to some known system of rules, that he may neither leave himself free to indulge caprice or passion, nor open to the imputation of them. But to what system of rules is he to recur, as supplementary to those of the Senate? To this there can be but one answer. To the sytem of regulations adopted for the government of some one of the parliamentary bodies within these States, or of that which has served as a prototype to most of them. This last is the model which we have all studied, while we are little acquainted with the modifications of it in our several States. It is deposited, too, in publications possessed by many, and open to all. Its rules are probably as wisely constructed for governing the debates of a considerative body, and obtaining its true sense, as any which can become known to us; and the acquiescence of the Senate, hitherto, under the references to them, has given them the sanction of their approbation.

Considering, therefore, the law of proceedings in the Senate as composed of the precepts of the Constitution, the regulations of the Senate, and, where these are silent, of the rules of Parliament, I have here endeavored to collect and digest so much of these as is called for in ordinary practice, collating the Parliamentary with the Senatorial rules, both where they agree and where they vary. I have done this, as well to have them at hand for my own government, as to deposit with the Senate the standard by which I judge, and am willing to be judged. I could not doubt the necessity of quoting the sources of my information, among which Mr. Hatsel's most valuable book is pre-eminent; but as he has only treated some general heads, I have been obliged to recur to other authorities in support of a number of common rules of practice, to which his plan did not descend. Sometimes each authority cited supports the whole passage. Sometimes it rests on all taken together. Sometimes the authority goes only to a part of the text, the residue being inferred from known rules and principles. For some of the most familiar forms no written authority is or can be quoted; no writer having supposed it necessary to repeat what all were presumed to know. The statement of these must rest on their notoriety.

I am aware that authorities can often be produced in opposition to the rules which I lay down as parliamentary. An attention to dates will generally remove their weight. The proceedings of Parliament in ancient times, and for a long while, were crude, multiform, and embarrassing. They have been, however, constantly advancing towards uniformity and accuracy, and have now attained a degree of aptitude to their object beyond which little is to be desired or expected.

Yet I am far from the presumption of believing that I may not have mistaken the Parliamentary practice in some cases, and especially in those minor forms, which, being practised daily, are supposed known to everybody, and therefore have not been committed to writing. Our resources, in this quarter of the globe, for obtaining information on that part of the subject, are not perfect. But I have begun a sketch, which those who come after me will successively correct and fill up, till a code of rules shall be formed for the use of the Senate, the effects of which may be accuracy in business, economy of time, order, uniformity, and impartiality.

NOTE.—The rules and practices peculiar to the SENATE are printed between brackets, [ ]. Those of PARLIAMENT are not so distinguished.

MANUAL

OF

PARLIAMENTARY PRACTICE,

IMPORTANCE OF RULES.

SEC. I.—IMPORTANCE OF ADHERING TO RULES.

Mr. ONSLOW, the ablest among the Speakers of the House of Commons, used to say, "It was a maxim he had often heard when he was a young man, from old and experienced members, that nothing tended more to throw power into the hands of administration, and those who acted with the majority of the House of Commons, than a neglect of, or departure from, the rules of proceeding: that these forms, as instituted by our ancestors, operated as a check and control on the actions of the majority, and that they were, in many instances, a shelter and protection to the minority, against the attempts of power." So far the maxim is certainly true, and is founded in good sense, that as it is always in the power of the majority, by their numbers, to stop any improper measures proposed on the part of their opponents, the only weapons by which the minority can defend themselves against similar attempts from those in power, are the forms and rules of proceeding which have been adopted as they were found necessary, from time to time, and are become the law of the House; by a strict adherence to which, the weaker party can only be protected from those irregularities and abuses which these forms were intended to check, and which the wantonness of power is but too often apt to suggest to large and successful majorities. 2 *Hats.*, 171, 172.

And whether these forms be in all cases the most rational or not, is really not of so great importance. It is much more material that there should be a rule to go by, than what that rule is; that there may be a uniformity of proceeding in business, not subject to the caprice of the Speaker, or captiousness of the members. It is very material that order, decency, and regularity, be preserved in a dignified public body. 2 *Hats.*, 149.

SEC. II.—LEGISLATIVE.

[All legislative powers herein granted shall be vested in a Congress of the United States, which shall consist of a Senate and House of Representatives. *Constitution of the United States, Art.* 1, *Sec.* 1.]

[The Senators and Representatives shall receive a compensation for their services, to be ascertained by law, and paid out of the Treasury of the United States. *Constitution of the United States, Art.* 1, *Sec.* 6.]

[For the powers of Congress, see the following Articles and Sections of the Constitution of the United States. I, 4, 7, 8, 9. II, 1, 2. III, 3. IV, 1, 3, 5, and all the amendments.]

SEC. III.—PRIVILEGE.

The privileges of members of Parliament, from small and obscure beginnings, have been advancing for centuries with a firm and never yielding pace. Claims seem to have been brought forward from time to time, and repeated, till some example of their admission enabled them to build law on that example. We can only, therefore, state the points of progression at which they now are. It is now acknowledged, 1st. That they are at all times exempted from question elsewhere for anything said in their own House; that during the time of privilege, 2d. Neither a member himself, his* wife, nor his servants, (familiares sui,) for any matter of their own, may be† arrested on mesne process, in any civil suit: 3d. Nor be detained under execution, though levied before time of

* Order of the House of Commons, 1663, July 16.

† Elsynge, 217; 1 Hats., 21; Grey's Deb., 133.

privilege: 4th. Nor impleaded, cited, or subpœnaed in any court: 5th. Nor summoned as a witness or juror: 6th. Nor may their lands or goods be distrained: 7th. Nor their persons assaulted, or characters traduced. And the period of time covered by privilege, before and after the session, with the practice of short prorogations under the connivance of the crown, amounts in fact to a perpetual protection against the course of justice. In one instance, indeed, it has been relaxed by the 10 G. 3, c. 50, which permits judiciary proceedings to go on against them. That these privileges must be continually progressive, seems to result from their rejecting all definition of them; the doctrine being that "their dignity and independence are preserved by keeping their privileges indefinite; and that 'the maxims upon which they proceed, together with the method of proceeding, rest entirely in their own breast, and are not defined and ascertained by any particular stated laws.'" 1 *Blackst.*, 163, 164.

[It was probably from this view of the encroaching character of privilege that the framers of our Constitution, in their care to provide that the law shall bind equally on all, and especially that those who make them shall not exempt themselves from their operation, have only privileged "Senators and Representatives" themselves from the single act of "arrest in all cases except treason, felony, and breach of the peace, during their attendance at the session of their respective Houses, and in going to and returning from the same, and from being questioned in any other place for any speech or debate in either House." *Const. U. S., Art.* 1, *Sec.* 6. Under the general authority "to make all laws necessary and proper for carrying into execution the powers given them," *Const. U. S., Art.* 2, *Sec.* 8, they may provide by law the details which may be necessary for giving full effect to the enjoyment of this privilege. No such law being as yet made, it seems to stand at present on the following ground: 1. The act of arrest is void, ab initio.* 2. The member arrested may be

* 2 Stra., 989.

discharged on motion, 1 *Bl.*, 166; 3 *Stra.*, 990; or by habeas corpus under the Federal or State authority, as the case may be; or by a writ of privilege out of the Chancery, 2 *Stra.*, 989, in those States which have adopted that part of the laws of England. *Orders of the House of Commons*, 1550, *February* 20. 3. The arrest being unlawful, is a trespass for which the officer and others concerned are liable to action or indictment in the ordinary courts of justice, as in other cases of unauthorized arrest. 4. The court before which the process is returnable is bound to act as in other cases of unauthorized proceeding, and liable also, as in other similar cases, to have their proceedings stayed or corrected by the superior courts.]

[The time necessary for going to, and returning from, Congress, not being defined, it will, of course, be judged of in every particular case by those who will have to decide the case.] While privilege was understood in England to extend, as it does here, only to exemption from arrest, eundo, morando, et redeundo, the House of Commons themselves decided that "a convenient time was to be understood." (1580,) 1 *Hats.*, 99, 100. Nor is the law so strict in point of time as to require the party to set out immediately on his return, but allows him time to settle his private affairs, and to prepare for his journey; and does not even scan his road very nicely, nor forfeit his protection for a little deviation from that which is most direct; some necessity perhaps constraining him to it. 2 *Stra.*, 986, 987.

This privilege from arrest, privileges, of course, against all process the disobedience to which is punishable by an attachment of the person; as a subpœna ad respondendum, or testificandum, or a summons on a jury; and with reason, because a member has superior duties to perform in another place. [When a representative is withdrawn from his seat by summons, the 40,000 people whom he represents lose their voice in debate and vote, as they do on his voluntary absence: when a senator is withdrawn by summons, his State loses half its voice in debate and vote, as it does on his voluntary absence. The enormous disparity of evil admits no comparison.]

[So far there will probably be no difference of opinion as to the privileges of the two houses of Congress; but in the following cases it is otherwise. In December, 1795, the House of Representatives committed two persons of the name of Randall and Whitney, for attempting to corrupt the integrity of certain members, which they considered as a contempt and breach of the privileges of the House; and the facts being proved, Whitney was detained in confinement a fortnight, and Randall three weeks, and was reprimanded by the Speaker. In March, 1796, the House of Representatives voted a challenge given to a member of their House to be a breach of the privileges of the House; but satisfactory apologies and acknowledgments being made, no further proceeding was had. The editor of the Aurora having, in his paper of February 19. 1800, inserted some paragraphs defamatory of the Senate, and failed in his appearance, he was ordered to be committed. In debating the legality of this order, it was insisted, in support of it, that every man, by the law of nature, and every body of men, possesses the right of self-defence; that all public functionaries are essentially invested with the powers of self-preservation; that they have an inherent right to do all acts necessary to keep themselves in a condition to discharge the trusts confided to them; that whenever authorities are given, the means of carrying them into execution are given by necessary implication; that thus we see the British Parliament exercise the right of punishing contempts; all the State Legislatures exercise the same power, and every court does the same; that, if we have it not, we sit at the mercy of every intruder who may enter our doors or gallery, and, by noise and tumult, render proceeding in business impracticable; that if our tranquillity is to be perpetually disturbed by newspaper defamation, it will not be possible to exercise our functions with the requisite coolness and deliberation; and that we must, therefore, have a power to punish these disturbers of our peace and proceedings. To this it was answered, that the Parliament and courts of England have cognizance of contempts by the express provisions of their law; that the State Legislatures have equal authority, because their powers are plenary; they represent their constituents completely, and possess all their powers, except such as their constitutions have expressly denied them; that the courts of the several States have the same powers by the laws of their States, and those of the Federal Government by the same State laws adopted in each State, by a law of Congress; that none of these bodies, therefore, derive those powers from natural or necessary right, but from express law; that Congress have no such natural or necessary power, nor any powers but such as are given them by the Constitution; that that has given them, directly, exemption from personal arrest, exemption from question elsewhere for what is said in their House, and power over their own members and proceedings; for these no further law is necessary, the Constitution being the law; that, moreover, by that article of the Constitution which authorizes them "to make all laws necessary and proper for carrying into execution the powers vested by the Constitution in them," they may provide by law for an undisturbed exercise of their functions, e. g., for the punishment of contempts, of affrays or tumult in their presence, &c.; but, till the law be made, it does not exist; and does not exist, from their own neglect; that in the mean time, however, that they are not unprotected, the ordinary magistrates and courts of law being open and competent to punish all unjustifiable disturbances or defamations, and even their own sergeant, who may appoint deputies ad libitum to aid him, 3 *Grey*, 59, 147, 255, is equal to small disturbances; that in requiring a previous law, the Constitution had regard to the inviolability of the citizen, as well as of the member; as, should one House, in the regular form of a bill, aim at too broad privileges, it may be checked by the other, and both by the President; and also as, the law being promulgated. the citizen will know how to avoid offence. But if one branch may assume its own privileges without control, if it may do it on the spur of the occasion, conceal the law in its own breast, and after the fact committed, make its sentence both the law and the judgment on that fact; if the offence is to be kept undefined, and to be declared only ex re nata, and according to the passions of the moment, and there be no limitation either in the manner or measure of the punishment, the condition of the citizen will be perilous indeed. Which of these doctrines is to prevail, time will decide. Where there is no fixed law, the judgment on any particular case is the law of that single case only, and dies with it. When a new and even similar case arises, the judgment which is to make, and at the same time apply the law, is open to question and consideration, as are all new laws. Perhaps Congress, in the mean time, in their care for the safety of the citizen, as well as that for their own protection, may declare by law what is necessary and proper to enable them to carry into execution the powers vested in them, and thereby hang up a rule for the inspection of all, which may direct the conduct of the citizen, and at the same time test the judgments they shall themselves pronounce in their own case.]

Privilege from arrest takes place by force of the election; and before a return be made a member elected may be named of a committee, and is to every extent a member, except that he cannot vote until he is sworn. *Memor.*, 107, 108. *D' Ewes*, 642, *col.* 2; 643, *col.* 1. *Pet. Miscel. Parl.*, 119. *Lex. Parl.*, c. 23. 2 *Hats.*, 22, 62.

Every man must, at his peril, take notice who are members of either House returned of record. *Lex. Parl.*, 23; 4 *Inst.*, 24.

On complaint of a breach of privilege; the party may either be summoned or sent for in custody of the sergeant. *Grey*, 88, 95.

The privilege of a member is the privilege of the House. If the member waive it without leave, it is a ground for punishing him, but cannot in effect waive the privilege of the House. 3 *Grey*, 140, 222.

For any speech or debate in either House, they shall not be questioned in any other place. *Const. U. S.*, I, 6; *S. P. protest of the Commons to James I.*, 1621; 2 *Rapin*, No. 54, pp. 211, 212. But this is restrained to things done in the House in a parliamentary course. 1 *Rush.*, 663. For he is not to have privilege contra morem parliamentarium, to exceed the bounds and limits of his place and duty. *Com. p.*

If an offence be committed by a member in the House, of which the House has cognizance, it is an infringement of their right for any person or court to take notice of it, till the House has punished the offender, or referred him to a due course. *Lex. Parl.*, 63.

Privilege is in the power of the House, and is a restraint to the proceedings of inferior courts, but not of the House itself. 2 *Nalson*, 450; 2 *Grey*, 399. For whatever is spoken in the House is subject to the censure of the House; and offences of this kind have been severely punished by calling the person to the bar to make submission, committing him to the tower, expelling the House, &c. *Scob.*, 72; *L. Parl.*, c. 22.

It is a breach of order for the Speaker to refuse to put a question which is in order. 2 *Hats.*, 175–6; 5 *Grey*, 133.

And even in cases of treason, felony, and breach of the peace, to which privilege does not extend as to substance, yet in Parliament a member is privileged as to the mode of proceeding. The case is first to be laid before the House, that it may judge of the fact and of the grounds of the accusation, and how far forth the manner of the trial may concern their privilege; otherwise it would be in the power of other branches of the government, and even of every private man, under pretences of treason, &c., to take any man from his service in the House, and so as many, one after another, as would make the House what he pleaseth. *Dec. of the Com.*

on the King's declaring Sir John Hotham a traitor. 4 *Rushw.*, 586. So, when a member stood indicted for felony, it was adjudged that he ought to remain of the House till conviction; for it may be any man's case, who is guiltless, to be accused and indicted of felony, or the like crime. 23 *El.*, 1580; *D'Ewes*, 283, *col.* 1; *Lex. Parl.*, 133.

When it is found necessary for the public service to put a member under arrest, or when, on any public inquiry, matter comes out which may lead to affect the person of a member, it is the practice immediately to acquaint the House, that they may know the reasons for such a proceeding, and take such steps as they think proper. 2 *Hats.*, 259. Of which see many examples. *Ib.*, 256, 257, 258. But the communication is subsequent to the arrest. 1 *Blackst.*, 167.

It is highly expedient, says Hatsel, for the due preservation of the privileges of the separate branches of the legislature, that neither should encroach on the other, or interfere in any matter depending before them, so as to preclude, or even influence that freedom of debate, which is essential to a free council. They are therefore not to take notice of any bills or other matters depending, or of votes that have been given, or of speeches which have been held, by the members of either of the other branches of the legislature, until the same have been communicated to them in the usual parliamentary manner. 2 *Hats.*, 252. 4 *Inst.*, 15. *Seld, Jud.*, 53. Thus the king's taking notice of the bill for suppressing soldiers, depending before the House; his proposing a provisional clause for a bill before it was presented to him by the two Houses; his expressing displeasure against some persons for matters moved in parliament during the debate and preparation of a bill, were breaches of privilege; 2 *Nalson*, 743; and in 1783, December 17, it was declared a breach of fundamental privileges, &c., to report any opinion or pretended opinion of the king on any bill or proceeding depending in either House of Parliament, with a view to influence the votes of the members. 2 *Hats.*, 251, 6.

SEC. IV.—ELECTIONS.

[The times, places, and manner of holding elections for senators and representatives shall be prescribed in each State by the legislature thereof; but the Congress may at any time by law make or alter such regulations, except as to the places of choosing senators. *Const.*, I, 4.]

[Each house shall be the judge of the elections, returns, and qualifications of its own members. *Const.*, I, 5.]

SEC. V.—QUALIFICATIONS.

[The Senate of the United States shall be composed of two senators from each State, chosen by the legislature thereof for six years, and each senator shall have one vote.]

[Immediately after they shall be assembled in consequence of the first election, they shall be divided as equally as may be into three classes. The seats of the senators of the first class shall be vacated at the end of the second year; of the second class at the expiration of the fourth year; and of the third class at the expiration of the sixth year; so that one-third may be chosen every second year; and if vacancies happen, by resignation or otherwise, during the recess of the legislature of any State, the executive thereof may make temporary appointments until the next meeting of the legislature, which shall then fill such vacancies.]

[No person shall be a senator who shall not have attained to the age of thirty years, and been nine years a citizen of the United States, and who shall not, when elected, be an inhabitant of that State for which he shall be chosen. *Const.*, I, 3.]

[The House of Representatives shall be composed of members chosen every second year by the people of the several States; and the electors in each State shall have the qualifications requisite for electors of the most numerous branch of the State legislature.]

[No person shall be a representative who shall not have attained to the age of twenty-five years, and been seven years a citizen of the United States, and who shall not, when elected, be an inhabitant of that State in which he shall be chosen.]

[Representatives and direct taxes shall be apportioned among the several States which may be included within this Union, according to their respective numbers; which shall be determined by adding to the whole number of free persons, including those bound to service for a term of years, and excluding Indians not taxed, three-fifths of all other persons. The actual enumeration shall be made within three years after the first meeting of the Congress of the United States, and within every subsequent term of ten years, in such manner as they shall by law direct. The number of representatives shall not exceed one for every thirty thousand, but each State shall have at least one representative. *Constitution of the United States*, I, 2.]

The provisional apportionments of representatives made in the Constitution in 1787, and afterwards by Congress, were as follows:

STATES.	1787. (*a*)	1790. (*b*)	1800. (*c*)	1810. (*d*)	1820. (*e*)	1830. (*f*)
Maine (*g*)	..	..	..	..	7	8
New Hampshire	3	4	5	6	6	5
Massachusetts	8	14	17	20	13	12
Rhode Island	1	2	2	2	2	2
Connecticut	5	7	7	7	6	6
Vermont	..	2	4	6	5	5
New York	6	10	17	27	34	40
New Jersey	4	5	6	6	6	6
Pennsylvania	8	13	18	23	26	28
Delaware	1	1	1	2	1	1
Maryland	6	8	9	9	9	8
Virginia	10	19	22	28	22	21
North Carolina	5	10	12	13	13	13
South Carolina	5	6	8	9	9	9
Georgia	3	2	4	6	7	9
Kentucky	..	2	6	10	12	13
Tennessee (*h*)	..	..	3	6	9	13
Ohio (*i*)	..	..	..	6	14	19
Louisiana (*j*)	..	..	..	..	3	3
Indiana (*k*)	..	..	..	..	3	7
Mississippi (*l*)	..	..	..	..	1	2
Illinois (*m*)	..	..	..	..	1	3
Alabama (*n*)	..	..	..	..	3	5
Missouri (*o*)	..	..	..	..	..	2
Michigan (*p*)	..	..	..	..	..	..
Arkansas (*q*)	..	..	..	..	..	..

(*a*) As per Constitution.

(*b*) As per act of April 14, 1792, one representative for 33,000—first census.

[When vacancies happen in the representation from any State, the executive authority thereof shall issue writs of election to fill such vacancies. *Const.*, I, 2.]

[No Senator or Representative shall, during the time for which he was elected, be appointed to any civil office under the authority of the United States which shall have been created, or the emoluments whereof shall have been increased, during such time; and no person holding any office under the United States shall be a member of either house during his continuance in office. *Const.*, I, 6.]

SEC. VI.—QUORUM.

[A majority of each house shall constitute a quorum to do business; but a smaller number may adjourn from day to day, and may be authorized to compel the attendance of absent members, in such manner, and under such penalties as each house may provide. *Const.*, I, 5.]

[In general, the chair is not to be taken till a quorum for busi-

(*c*) As per act of Jan. 14, 1802, one representative for 33,000—second census.

(*d*) As per act of Dec. 21, 1811, one representative for 35,000—third census.

(*e*) As per act of Mar. 7, 1822, one representative for 40,000—fourth census.

(*f*) As per act of May 22, 1832, one representative for 47,700—fifth census.

(*g*) Previous to the 3d March, 1820, Maine formed a part of Massachusetts, and was called the ***District of Maine***, and its representatives are numbered with those of Massachusetts. By compact between Maine and Massachusetts, Maine became a separate and independent State, and by act of Congress of 3d March, 1820, was admitted into the Union as such—the admission to take place on the 15th of the same month. On the 7th of April, 1820, Maine was declared entitled to seven representatives, to be taken from those of Massachusetts.

(*h*) Admitted under act of Congress of June 1, 1796, with one representative

(*i*) Do........do........do.........April 30, 1802......do......do.

(*j*) Do........do........do.........April 8, 1812......do......do.

(*k*) Do........do........do.........Dec. 11, 1816......do......do.

(*l*) Do........do........do.........Dec. 10, 1817......do......do.

(*m*) Do........do........do.........Dec. 3, 1818......do......do.

(*n*) Do........do........do.........Dec. 14, 1819......do......do.

(*o*) Do........do........do.........Mar. 2, 1821......do......do.

(*p*) Do........do........do.........Jan. 26, 1837......do......do.

(*q*) Do........do........do.........June 15, 1836......do......do.

ness is present; unless, after due waiting, such a quorum be despaired of, when the chair may be taken and the House adjourned. And whenever, during business, it is observed that a quorum is not present, any member may call for the House to be counted, and being found deficient, business is suspended. 2 *Hats.*, 125, 126.]

[The President having taken the chair, and a quorum being present, the journal of the preceding day shall be read, to the end that any mistake may be corrected that shall have been made in the entries. *Rules of the Senate.*]

SEC. VII.—CALL OF THE HOUSE.

On a call of the House, each person rises up as he is called and answereth; the absentees are then only noted, but no excuse to be made till the House be fully called over. Then the absentees are called a second time, and if still absent, excuses are to be heard. *Ord. House of Commons*, 92.

They rise that their persons may be recognized; the voice in such a crowd, being an insufficient verification of their presence. But in so small a body as the Senate of the United States, the trouble of rising cannot be necessary.

Orders for calls on different days may subsist at the same time. 2 *Hats.*, 72.

SEC. VIII.—ABSENCE.

[No member shall absent himself from the service of the Senate without leave of the Senate first obtained. And in case a less number than a quorum of the Senate shall convene, they are hereby authorized to send the Sergeant-at-Arms, or any other person or persons by them authorized, for any or all absent members, as the majority of such members present shall agree, at the expense of such absent members, respectively, unless such excuse for non-attendance shall be made as the Senate, when a quorum is convened, shall judge sufficient: and in that case the expense shall be paid out of the contingent fund. And this rule shall apply as well to the first convention of the Senate, at the legal time of meeting, as to each day of the session, after the hour is arrived to which the Senate stood adjourned. *Rule* 8.]

SEC. IX.—SPEAKER.

[The Vice President of the United States shall be President of the Senate, but shall have no vote unless they be equally divided. *Constitution*, I, 3.]

[The Senate shall choose their officers, and also a President pro tempore in the absence of the Vice President, or when he shall exercise the office of President of the United States. *Ib.*]

[The House of Representatives shall choose their Speaker and other officers. *Const.*, I, 2.]

When but one person is proposed, and no objection made, it has not been usual in Parliament to put any question to the House; but without a question the members proposing him conduct him to the chair. But if there be objection, or another proposed, a question is put by the clerk. 2 *Hats.*, 168. As are also questions of adjournment. 6 *Grey*, 406. Where the House debated and exchanged messages and answers with the king for a week, without a Speaker, till they were prorogued. They have done it de die in diem for 14 days. 1 *Chand.*, 331, 335.

[In the Senate, a President pro tempore in the absence of the Vice President is proposed and chosen by ballot. His office is understood to be determined on the Vice President's appearing and taking the chair, or at the meeting of the Senate after the first recess.]

Where the Speaker has been ill, other Speakers pro tempore have been appointed. Instances of this are 1 *H.*, 4. Sir John Cheyney, and for Sir Wm. Sturton, and in 15 *H.*, 6 Sir John Tyrrell, in 1656, January 27; 1658, March 9; 1659, January 13.

Sir Job Charlton ill, Seymour chosen, 1673, February 18.

Seymour being ill, Sir Robert Sawyer chosen, 1678, April 15.

Sawyer being ill, Seymour chosen.

} Not merely pro tempore. 1 *Chand.*, 169, 276, 277.

Thorpe in execution, a new Speaker chosen, 31 *H.* VI. 3 *Grey*, 11; and March 14, 1694, Sir John Trevor chosen. There have been no later instances. 2 *Hats.*, 161; 4 *Inst.*; 8 *L. Parl.*, 263.

A Speaker may be removed at the will of the House, and a Speaker pro tempore appointed.* 2 *Grey*, 186; 5 *Grey*, 134..

SEC. X.—ADDRESS.

[The President shall, from time to time, give to the Congress information of the state of the Union, and recommend to their consideration such measures as he shall judge necessary and expedient. *Const.*, II, 3.]

A joint address of both Houses of Parliament is read by the Speaker of the House of Lords. It may be attended by both Houses in a body, or by a committee from each House, or by the two Speakers only. An address of the House of Commons only, may be presented by the whole House, or by the Speaker, 9 *Grey*, 473; 1 *Chandler*, 298, 301; or by such particular members as are of the privy council. 2 *Hats.*, 278.

SEC. XI.—COMMITTEES.

Standing committees, as of privileges and elections, &c., are usually appointed at the first meeting, to continue through the session. The person first named is generally permitted to act as chairman. But this is a matter of courtesy; every committee having a right to elect their own chairman, who presides over them, puts questions, and reports their proceedings to the House. 4 *Inst.*, 11, 12; *Scob.*, 9; 1 *Grey*, 122.

* RULE 23. The Vice President or President of the Senate *pro tempore*, shall have the right to name a member to perform the duties of the Chair; but such substitution shall not extend beyond an adjournment.

At these committees the members are to speak standing, and not sitting; though there is reason to conjecture it was formerly otherwise. *D' Ewes*, 630, *col.* 1; 4 *Parl. Hist.*, 440; 2 *Hats.*, 77.

Their proceedings are not to be published, as they are of no force till confirmed by the House. *Rushw.*, *part* 3, *vol.* 2, 74; 3 *Grey*, 401; *Scob.*, 39. Nor can they receive a petition but through the House. 9 *Grey*, 412.

When a committee is charged with an inquiry, if a member prove to be involved, they cannot proceed against him, but must make a special report to the House; whereupon the member is heard in his place, or at the bar, or a special authority is given to the committee to inquire concerning him. 9 *Grey*, 523.

So soon as the House sits, and a committee is notified of it, the chairman is in duty bound to rise instantly, and the members to attend the service of the House. 2 *Nals.*, 319.

It appears that on joint committees of the Lords and Commons, each committee acted integrally in the following instances: 7 *Grey*, 261, 278, 285, 338; 1 *Chandler*, 357, 462. In the following instances it does not appear whether they did or not: 6 *Grey*, 129; 7 *Grey*, 213, 229, 321.*

RULE 33. The following standing committees, to consist of five members each, shall be appointed at the commencement of each session, with leave to report by bill or otherwise:

A Committee on Foreign Relations.
A Committee on Finance.
A Committee on Commerce.
A Committee on Manufactures.
A Committee on Agriculture.
A Committee on Military Affairs.
A Committee on the Militia.
A Committee on Naval Affairs.
A Committee on Public Lands.
A Committee on Private Land Claims.
A Committee on Indian Affairs.
A Committee of Claims.
A Committee on the Judiciary.

SEC. XII.—COMMITTEE OF THE WHOLE.

The speech, messages, and other matters of great concernment, are usually referred to a committee of the whole house, (6 *Grey*, 311,) where general principles are digested in the form of resolutions, which are debated and amended till they get into a shape which meets the approbation of a majority. These being reported and confirmed by the House, are then referred to one or more select committees, according as the subject divides itself into one or more bills. *Scob.*, 36, 44. Propositions for any charge on the people are especially to be first made in a committee of the whole. 3 *Hats.*, 127. The sense of the whole is better taken in committee, because in all committees every one speaks as often as he pleases. *Scob.*, 49. They generally acquiesce in the chairman named by the Speaker; but, as well as all other committees, have a right to elect one, some member, by consent, putting the question. *Scob.*, 36; 3 *Grey*, 301. The form of going from the House into committee is for the Speaker, on motion, to put the question that the House do now resolve itself into a committee of the whole, to take under consideration such a matter, naming it. If determined in the affirmative, he leaves the chair and takes a seat elsewhere, as any other member; and the person appointed chairman seats himself at the clerk's table. *Scob.*, 36. Their quorum is the same as that of the House, and if a defect happens, the chairman, on a motion and question, rises, the Speaker resumes the chair, and the chairman can make no other report than to inform the House of the cause of their dissolution. If a message is announced during a com-

A Committee on the Post Office and Post Roads.

A Committee on Pensions.

A Committee on the District of Columbia.

A Committee, of three members, whose duty it shall be to audit and control the contingent expenses of the Senate.

And a Committee, consisting of three members, whose duty it shall be to examine all bills, amendments, resolutions, or motions, before they go out of the possession of the Senate, and to make report that they are correctly engrossed; which report shall be entered on the journal.

mittee, the Speaker takes the chair, and receives it, because the committee cannot. 2 *Hats.*, 125, 126.

In a committee of the whole, the tellers on a division differing as to numbers, great heats and confusion arose, and danger of a decision by the sword. The Speaker took the chair, the mace was forcibly laid on the table; whereupon, the members retiring to their places, the Speaker told the House "he had taken the chair without an order, to bring the House into order." Some excepted against it; but it was generally approved, as the only expedient to suppress the disorder. And every member was required, standing up in his place, to engage that he would proceed no further, in consequence of what had happened in the grand committee, which was done. 3 *Grey*, 128.

A committee of the whole being broken up in disorder, and the chair resumed by the Speaker without an order, the House was adjourned. The next day the committee was considered as thereby dissolved, and the subject again before the House; and it was decided in the House, without returning into committee. 3 *Grey*, 130.

No previous question can be put in a committee, nor can this committee adjourn as others may; but if their business is unfinished, they rise, on a question, the House is resumed, and the chairman reports that the committee of the whole have, according to order, had under their consideration such a matter, and have made progress therein; but not having had time to go through the same, have directed him to ask leave to sit again. Whereupon a question is put upon their having leave, and on the time the House will again resolve itself into a committee. *Scob.*, 38. But if they have gone through the matter referred to them, a member moves that the committee may rise, and the chairman report their proceedings to the House; which being resolved, the chairman rises, the Speaker resumes the chair, the chairman informs him that the committee have gone through the business referred to them, and that he is ready to make report when the House shall think proper to receive it. If the House have time to receive it, there is usually a cry of "now, now," whereupon he makes the report; but if it be late, the cry is "to-morrow, to-morrow," or "Monday," &c., or a motion is made to that effect, and a question put that it be received to-morrow, &c. *Scob.*, 38.

In other things the rules of proceedings are to be the same as in the House. *Scob.*, 39.

SECTION XIII.—EXAMINATION OF WITNESSES.

Common fame is a good ground for the House to proceed by inquiry, and even to accusation. *Resolution House of Commons*, 1 *Car.* 1, 1624; *Rush, L. Parl.*, 115; 1 *Grey*, 16–22, 92; 8 *Grey*, 21, 23, 27, 45.

Witnesses are not to be produced but where the House has previously instituted an inquiry, (2 *Hats.*, 102,) nor then are orders for their attendance given blank. 3 *Grey*, 51.

When any person is examined before a committee, or at the bar of the House, any member wishing to ask the person a question, must address it to the Speaker or chairman, who repeats the question to the person, or says to him, "you hear the question—answer it." But if the propriety of the question be objected to, the Speaker directs the witness, counsel, and parties, to withdraw, for no question can be moved or put, or debated while they are there. 2 *Hats.*, 108. Sometimes the questions are previously settled in writing before the witness enters. *Ib.*, 106, 107; 8 *Grey*, 64. The questions asked must be entered in the journals. 3 *Grey*, 81. But the testimony given in answer before the House is never written down; but before a committee, it must be, for the information of the House, who are not present to hear it. 7 *Grey*, 52, 334.

If either house have occasion for the presence of a person in custody of the other, they ask the other their leave that he may be brought up to them in custody. 3 *Hats.*, 52.

A member, in his place, gives information to the House of what he knows of any matter under hearing at the bar. *Jour. H. of C.*, *Jan.* 22, 1744–'45.

Either house may request, but not command, the attendance of a member of the other. They are to make the request by message to the other house, and to express clearly the purpose of attendance, that no improper subject of examination may be tendered to him. The House then gives leave to the member to attend, if he choose it; waiting first to know from the member himself whether he chooses to attend, till which they do not take the message into consideration. But when the peers are sitting as a court of criminal judicature, they may order attendance, unless where it be a case of impeachment by the Commons. There, it is to be a request. 3 *Hats.*, 17; 9 *Grey*, 306, 406; 10 *Grey*, 133.

Counsel are to be heard only on private, not on public bills, and on such points of law only as the House shall direct. 10 *Grey*, 61.

SECTION XIV.—ARRANGEMENT OF BUSINESS.

The Speaker is not precisely bound to any rules as to what bills or other matter shall be first taken up; but is left to his own discretion, unless the House on the question decide to take up a particular subject. *Hakew.*, 136.

A settled order of business is, however, necessary for the government of the presiding person, and to restrain individual members from calling up favorite measures, or matters under their special patronage, out of their just turn. It is useful also for directing the discretion of the House, when they are moved to take up a particular matter, to the prejudice of others having priority of right to their attention in the general order of business.

[In Senate, the bills and other papers which are in possession of the house, and in a state to be acted on, are arranged every morning, and brought on in the following order:]

[1. Bills ready for a second reading are read, that they may be referred to committees, and so be put under way. But if, on their being read, no motion is made for commitment, they are then laid on the table in the general file, to be taken up in their just turn.]

[2. After 12 o'clock, bills ready for it are put on their passage.]

[3. Reports in possession of the house, which offer grounds for a bill, are to be taken up, that the bill may be ordered in.]

[4. Bills or other matters before the house, and unfinished on the preceding day, whether taken up in turn or on special order, are entitled to be resumed and passed on through their present stage.]

[5. These matters being despatched, for preparing and expediting business, the general file of bills and other papers is then taken up, and each article of it is brought on according to its seniority, reckoned by the date of its first introduction to the house. Reports on bills belong to the dates of their bills.]

[The arrangement of the business of the Senate is now as follows :]

[1. Motions previously submitted.]

[2. Reports of Committees previously made.]

[3. Bills from the House of Representatives, and those introduced on leave, which have been read the first time, are read the second time; and if not referred to a committee, are considered in Committee of the Whole, and proceeded with as in other cases.]

[4. After twelve o'clock, engrossed bills of the Senate, and bills of the House of Representatives, on third reading, are put on their passage.]

[5. If the above are finished before one o'clock, the general file of bills, consisting of those reported from committees on the second reading, and those reported from committees after having been referred, are taken up in the order in which they were reported to the Senate by the respective committees.]

[6. At one o'clock, if no business be pending, or if no motion be called to proceed to other business, the special orders are called, at the head of which stands the unfinished business of the preceding day.]

[In this way we do not waste our time in debating what shall be taken up. We do one thing at a time; follow up a subject while it is fresh, and till it is done with, clear the house of business gradatim as it is brought on, and prevent, to a certain degree, its immense accumulation towards the close of the session.]

[Arrangement, however, can only take hold of matters in possession of the house. New matter may be moved at any time when no question is before the house. Such are original motions and reports on bills. Such are bills from the other house, which are received at all times, and receive their first reading as soon as the question then before the house is disposed of; and bills brought in on leave, which are read first whenever presented. So messages from the other house respecting amendments to bills are taken up as soon as the house is clear of a question, unless they require to be printed, for better consideration. Orders of the day may be called for. even when another question is before the house.]

SEC. XV.—ORDER.

[Each house may determine the rules of its proceedings; punish its members for disorderly behavior; and, with the concurrence of two-thirds, expel a member. *Const.*, I, 5.]

In Parliament, "instances make order," per Speaker Onslow. 2 *Hats.*, 141. But what is done only by one Parliament, cannot be called custom of Parliament; by Prynne. 1 *Grey*, 52.]

SEC. XVI.—ORDER RESPECTING PAPERS.

The clerk is to let no journals, records, accounts, or papers, be taken from the table or out of his custodv. 2 *Hats* 193, 194.

Mr. Prynne having at a committee of the whole amended a mistake in a bill without order or knowledge of the committee, was reprimanded. 1 *Chand.*, 77.

A bill being missing, the House resolved that a protestation should be made and subscribed by the members "before Almighty God, and this honorable House, that neither myself nor any other to my knowledge have taken away, or do at this present conceal a bill entitled," &c. 5 *Grey*, 202.

After a bill is engrossed, it is put into the Speaker's hands, and he is not to let any one have it to look into. *Town.*, *col.* 209.

SEC. XVII.—ORDER IN DEBATE.

When the Speaker is seated in his chair, every member is to sit in his place. *Scob.*, 6; *Grey*, 403.

When any member means to speak, he is to stand up in his place, uncovered, and to address himself, not to the House, or any particular member, but to the Speaker, who calls him by his name, that the House may take notice who it is that speaks. *Scob.*, 6; *D'Ewes*, 487, *col.* 1; 2 *Hats.*, 77; 4 *Grey*, 66; 8 *Grey*, 108. But members who are indisposed may be indulged to speak sitting. 2 *Hats.*, 75, 77; 1 *Grey*, 143.

[In Senate, every member, when he speaks, shall address the chair standing in his place, and when he has finished, shall sit down. *Rule* 3.]

When a member stands up to speak, no question is to be put, but he is to be heard, unless the House overrules him. 4 *Grey*, 390; 5 *Grey*, 6, 143.

If two or more rise to speak nearly together, the Speaker determines who was first up, and calls him by name; whereupon he proceeds, unless he voluntarily sits down and gives way to the other. But sometimes the House does not acquiesce in the Speaker's decision, in which case the question is put, "Which member was first up?" 2 *Hats.*, 76; *Scob.*, 7; *D'Ewes*, 434 *col.* 1, 2.

[In the Senate of the United States, the President's decision is without appeal. Their rule is in these words: *when two members rise at the same time, the President shall name the person to speak; but in all cases* the member who shall first rise and address the Chair shall speak first. *Rule* 5.]

No man may speak more than once on the same bill on the same day; or even on another day, if the debate be adjourned. But if it be read more than once in the same day, he may speak once at every reading. *Co.*, 12, 115; *Hakew.*, 148; *Scob.*, 58; 2 *Hats.*, 75. Even a change of opinion does not give a right to be heard a second time. *Smyth's Comw.*, *L.* 2, *c.* 3; *Arcan Parl.*, 17.

[The corresponding rule of the Senate is in these words: No member shall speak more than twice, in any one debate, on the same day, without leave of the Senate. *Rule* 4.]

But he may be permitted to speak again to clear a matter of fact, 3 *Grey*, 357, 416; or merely to explain himself (2 *Hats.*, 73) in some material part of his speech, *Ib.*, 75; or to the manner or words of the question, keeping himself to that only, and not travelling into the merits of it, *Memorials in Hakew.*, 29; or to the orders of the House, if they be transgressed, keeping within that line, and not falling into the matter itself. *Mem. Hakew.*, 30, 31.

But if the Speaker rise to speak, the member standing up ought to sit down, that he may be first heard. *Town.*, *col.* 205; *Hale Parl.*, 133; *Mem. in Hakew.*, 30, 31. Nevertheless, though the Speaker may of right speak to matters of order, and be first heard, he is restrained from speaking on any other subject, except where the House have occasion for facts within his knowledge; then he may, with their leave, state the matter of fact. 3 *Grey*, 38.

No one is to speak impertinently or beside the question, superfluous or tediously. *Scob.*, 31, 33; 2 *Hats.*, 166, 168; *Hale Parl.*, 133.

No person is to use indecent language against the proceed ings of the House; no prior determination of which is to be reflected on by any member, unless he means to conclude with a motion to rescind it. 2 *Hats.*, 169, 170; *Rushaw.*, *p.* 3, *v.* 1, *fol.* 42. But while a proposition under consideration is still in *fieri*, though it has even been reported by a committee, reflections on it are no reflections on the House. 9 *Grey*, 508.

No person, in speaking, is to mention a member then present by his name, but to describe him by his seat in the House, or who spoke last, or on the other side of the question, &c., *Mem. in Hakew.*, 3; *Smyth's Comw.*, *L.* 2, *c.* 3; nor to digress from the matter to fall upon the person (*Scob.*, 31; *Hale Parl.*, 133; 2 *Hats.*, 166) by speaking, reviling, nipping, or unmannerly words against a particular member. *Smyth's Comw.*, *L.* 2, *c.* 3. The consequences of a measure may be reprobated in strong terms; but to arraign the motives of those who propose to advocate it, is a personality, and against order. *Qui digreditur a materia ad personam*, Mr. Speaker ought to suppress. *Ord. Com.*, 1604, *Apr.* 19.

[When a member shall be called to order by the President or a Senator, he shall sit down; and every question of order shall be decided by the President, without debate, subject to an appeal to the Senate; and the President may call for the sense of the Senate on any question of order. *Rule* 6.]

[No member shall speak to another or otherwise interrupt the business of the Senate, or read any printed paper while the journals or public papers are reading, or when any member is speaking in any debate. *Rule* 2.]

No one is to disturb another in his speech by hissing, coughing, spitting, (6 *Grey*, 332; *Scob.*, 8; *D'Ewes*, 332, *col.* 1, 640, *col.* 1,) speaking or whispering to another, (*Scob.*, 6; *D'Ewes*, 487, *col.* 1;) nor stand up to interrupt him, (*Town.*, *col.* 205; *Mem. in Hakew.*, 31;) nor to pass between the Speaker and the speaking member, nor to go across the House, (*Scob.*, 6,) or to walk up and down it, or to take books or papers from the table, or write there. (2 *Hats.*, 171.)

Nevertheless, if a member finds that it is not the inclination of the House to hear him, and that by conversation or any other noise they endeavor to drown his voice, it is his most prudent way to submit to the pleasure of the House, and sit down; for it scarcely ever happens that they are guilty of this piece of ill manners without sufficient reason, or inattentive to a member who says anything worth their hearing. 2 *Hats.*, 77, 78.

If repeated calls do not produce order, the Speaker may call by his name any member obstinately persisting in irregularity; whereupon the House may require the member to withdraw. He is then to be heard in exculpation, and to withdraw. Then the Speaker states the offence committed, and the House considers the degree of punishment they will inflict. 2 *Hats.*, 167, 7, 8, 172.

For instances of assaults and affrays in the House of Commons, and the proceedings thereon, see 1 *Pet. Misc.*, 82; 3 *Grey*, 128; 4 *Grey*, 328; 5 *Grey*, 382; 6 *Grey*, 254; 10 *Grey*, 8. Whenever warm words or an assault has passed between members, the House, for the protection of their members, requires them to declare in their places not to prosecute any quarrel, (3 *Grey*, 127, 293; 5 *Grey*, 280;) or orders them to attend the Speaker, who is to accommodate their differences, and report to the House, (3 *Grey*, 419;) and they are put under restraint if they refuse, or until they do, 9 *Grey*, 234, 312.

Disorderly words are not to be noticed till the member has finished his speech. 5 *Grey*, 356; 6 *Grey*, 60. Then the person objecting to them, and desiring them to be taken down by the clerk at the table, must repeat them. The Speaker then may direct the clerk to take them down in his minutes; but if he thinks them not disorderly, he delays the direction. If the call becomes pretty general, he orders the clerk to take them down, as stated by the objecting member. They are then part of his minutes, and when read to the offending member, he may deny they were his words, and the House must then decide by a question whether they are his words or not. Then the member may justify them, or explain the sense in which he used them, or apologize. If the House is satisfied, no further proceeding is necessary. But if two members still insist to take the sense of the House, the member must withdraw before that question is stated and then the sense of the House is to be taken. 2 *Hats.*, 199; 4 *Grey*, 170; 6 *Grey*, 59. When any member has spoken, or other business intervened, after offensive words spoken, they cannot be taken notice of for censure. And this is for the common security of all, and to prevent mistakes which must happen if words are not taken down immediately. Formerly they might be taken down at any time the same day. 2 *Hats.*, 196; *Mem. in Hakew.*, 71; 3 *Grey*, 48; 9 *Grey*, 514.

Disorderly words spoken in a committee must be written down as in the House; but the committee can only report them to the House for animadversion. 6 *Grey*, 46.

[The rule of the Senate says: If the member be called to order by a senator for words spoken, the exceptionable words shall immediately be taken down in writing, that the President may be better enabled to judge of the matter. *Rule* 7.]

In Parliament, to speak irreverently or seditiously against the King is against order. *Smyth's Comw.*, *L.* 2, *c.*3; 2 *Hats.*, 170.

It is a breach of order in debate to notice what has been said on the same subject in the other house, or the particular votes or majorities on it there; because the opinion of each house should be left to its own independency, not to be influenced by the proceedings of the other; and the quoting them might beget reflections leading to a misunderstanding between the two houses. 8 *Grey*, 22.

Neither house can exercise any authority over a member or officer of the other, but should complain to the house of which he is, and leave the punishment to them. Where the complaint is of words disrespectfully spoken by a member of another house, it is difficult to obtain punishment, because of the rules supposed necessary to be observed (as to the immediate noting down of words) for the security of members. Therefore it is the duty of the House, and more particularly of the Speaker, to interfere immediately, and not to permit expressions to go unnoticed which may give a ground of complaint to the other house, and introduce proceedings and mutual accusations between the two houses, which can hardly be terminated without difficulty and disorder. 3 *Hats.*, 51.

No member may be present when a bill or any business concerning himself is debating; nor is any member to speak to the merits of it till he withdraws. 2 *Hats.*, 219. The rule is, that if a charge against a member arise out of a report of a committee, or examination of witnesses in the House, as the member knows from that to what points he is to direct his exculpation, he may be heard to those points before any question is moved or stated against him. He is then to be heard, and withdraw before any question is moved. But if the question itself is the charge, as for breach of order or matter arising in the debate, then the charge must be stated, (that is, the question must be moved,) himself heard, and then to withdraw. 2 *Hats.*, 121, 122.

Where the private interests of a member are concerned in a bill or question, he is to withdraw. And where such an interest has appeared, his voice has been disallowed, even after a division. In a case so contrary, not only to the laws of decency, but to the fundamental principle of the social compact which denies to any man to be a judge in his own cause, it is for the honor of the House that this rule, of immemorial observance, should be strictly adhered to. 2 *Hats.*, 119, 121; 6 *Grey*, 368.

No member is to come into the House with his head covered, nor to remove from one place to another with his hat on, nor is to put on his hat in coming in or removing, until he be set down in his place. *Scob.*, 6.

A question of order may be adjourned to give time to look into precedents. 2 *Hats.*, 118.

In Parliament, all decisions of the Speaker may be con trolled by the House. 3 *Grey*, 319.

SEC. XVIII.—ORDERS OF THE HOUSE.

Of right, the doors of the House ought not to be shut, but to be kept by porters, or sergeants-at-arms, assigned for that purpose. *Mod. Ten. Parl.*, 23.

[By the rules of the Senate, on motion made and seconded to shut the doors of the Senate on the discussion of any business which may, in the opinion of a member, require secrecy, the President shall direct the gallery to be cleared; and during the discussion of such motion the doors shall remain shut. *Rule* 18.]

[No motion shall be deemed in order to admit any person or persons whatever within the doors of the Senate chamber to present any petition, memorial, or address, or to hear any such read. *Rule* 19.]

The only case where a member has a right to insist on anything, is where he calls for the execution of a subsisting order of the House. Here, there having been already a resolution, any person has a right to insist that the Speaker, or any other whose duty it is, shall carry it into execution; and no debate or delay can be had on it. Thus any member has a right to have the House or gallery cleared of strangers, an order existing for that purpose; or to have the House told where there is not a quorum present. 2 *Hats.*, 87, 129. How far an order of the House is binding, see *Hakew.*, 392.

But where an order is made that any particular matter be taken up on a particular day, there a question is to be put, when it is called for, whether the House will now proceed to that matter? Where orders of the day are on important or interesting matter, they ought not to be proceeded on till an hour at which the House is usually full, [*which in Senate is at noon.*]

Orders of the day may be discharged at any time, and a new one made for a different day. 3 *Grey*, 48, 313.

When a session is drawing to a close, and the important bills are all brought in, the House, in order to prevent interruption by further unimportant bills, sometimes come to a resolution that no new bill be brought in, except it be sent from the other house. 3 *Grey*, 156.

All orders of the House determine with the session; and one taken under such an order may, after the session is ended, be discharged on a habeas corpus. *Raym.*, 120; *Jacob's L. D. by Ruffhead; Parliament*, 1 *Lev.*, 165 (*Pritchard's case.*)

[Where the Constitution authorizes each house to determine the rules of its proceedings, it must mean in those cases (legislative, executive, or judiciary) submitted to them by the Constitution, or in something relating to these, and necessary towards their execution. But orders and resolutions are sometimes entered in the journals, having no relation to these, such as acceptances of invitations to attend orations, to take part in processions, &c. These must be understood to be merely conventional among those who are willing to participate in the ceremony, and are therefore, perhaps, improperly placed among the records of the House.]

SEC. XIX.—PETITION.

A petition prays something. A remonstrance has no prayer. 1 *Grey*, 58.

Petitions must be subscribed by the petitioners, (*Scob.*, 87; *L. Parl.*, c. 22; 9 *Grey*, 362,) unless they are attending; (1 *Grey*, 401,) or unable to sign, and averred by a member, (3 *Grey*, 418.) But a petition not subscribed, but which the member presenting it affirmed to be all in the handwriting of the petitioner, and his name written in the beginning, was on the question (Mar. 14, 1800) received by the Senate. The averment of a member, or of somebody without doors, that they know the handwriting of the petitioners, is necessary, if it be questioned. 6 *Grey*, 36. It must be presented by a member, not by the petitioners, and must be opened by him, holding it in his hand. 10 *Grey*, 57.

[Before any petition or memorial addressed to the Senate shall be received and read at the table, whether the same shall be introduced by the President or a member, a brief statement of the contents of the petition or memorial shall verbally be made by the introducer. *Rule* 24.]

Regularly a motion for receiving it must be made and seconded, and a question put, whether it shall be received? but a cry from the House of "received," or even its silence, dispenses with the formality of this question. It is then to be read at the table and disposed of.

SEC. XX.—MOTIONS.

When a motion has been made, it is not to be put to the question or debated until it is seconded. *Scob.*, 21.

[The Senate say, No motion shall be debated until the same shall be seconded. *Rule* 9.]

It is then, and not till then, in possession of the House, and cannot be withdrawn but by leave of the House. It is to be put into writing, if the House or Speaker require it, and must be read to the House by the Speaker as often as any member desires it for his information. 2 *Hats.*, 82.

[The rule of the Senate is, when a motion shall be made and seconded, it shall be reduced to writing, if desired by the President or any member, delivered in at the table, and read by the President, before the same shall be debated. *Rule* 10.]

It might be asked, whether a motion for adjournment or for the orders of the day can be made by one member while another is speaking? It cannot. When two members offer to speak, he who rose first is to be heard, and it is a breach of order in another to interrupt him, unless by calling him to order if he departs from it. And the question of order being decided, he is still to be heard through. A call for adjournment, or for the order of the day, or for the question, by gentlemen from their seats, is not a motion. No motion can be made without rising and addressing the Chair. Such calls are themselves breaches of order, which though the member who has risen may respect, as an expression of impatience of the House against further debate; yet if he chooses, he has a right to go on.

SEC. XXI.—RESOLUTIONS.

When the House commands, it is by an "order." But fact, principles, and their own opinions and purposes, are expressed in the form of resolutions.

[A Resolution for an allowance of money to the clerks being moved, it was objected to as not in order, and so ruled by the Chair; but on an appeal to the Senate, (i. e., a call for their sense by the President, on account of doubt in his mind, according to Rule 16,) the decision was overruled. *Jour. Sen.*, *June* 1, 1796. I presume the doubt was, whether an allowance of money could be made otherwise than by bill.]

SEC. XXII.—BILLS.

[Every bill shall receive three readings previous to its being passed; and the President shall give notice at each whether it be first, second, or third; which readings shall be on three different days, unless the Senate unanimously direct otherwise. *Rule* 26.]

SEC. XXIII.—BILLS, LEAVE TO BRING IN.

[One day's notice, at least, shall be given of an intended motion for leave to bring in a bill. *Rule* 25.]

When a member desires to bring in a bill on any subject, he states to the House in general terms the causes for doing it, and concludes by moving for leave to bring in a bill entitled, &c. Leave being given on the question, a committee is appointed to prepare and bring in the bill. The mover and seconder are always appointed of this committee, and one or more in addition. *Hakew.*, 132; *Scob.*, 40.

It is to be presented fairly written, without any erasure or interlineation, or the Speaker may refuse it. *Scob.*, 41; 1 *Grey*, 82, 84.

SEC. XXIV.—BILLS, FIRST READING.

When a bill is first presented, the clerk reads it at the table, and hands it to the Speaker, who, rising, states to the House the title of the bill; that this is the first time of reading it; and the question will be, whether it shall be read a second time? then sitting down to give an opening for objections. If none be made, he rises again, and puts the question, whether it shall be read a second time? *Hakew.*, 137, 141. A bill cannot be amended on the first reading, (6 *Grey*, 286;) nor is it usual for it to be opposed then, but it may be done, and rejected. *D'Ewes*, 335, *col.* 1; 3 *Hats.*, 198.

SEC. XXV.—BILLS, SECOND READING.

The second reading must regularly be on another day. *Hakew.*, 143. It is done by the Clerk at the table, who then hands it to the Speaker. The Speaker, rising, states to the House the title of the bill; that this is the second time of reading it; and that the question will be, whether it shall be committed or engrossed and read a third time? But if the bill came from the other house, as it always comes engrossed, he states that the question will be, whether it shall be read a third time? and before he has so reported the state of the bill, no one is to speak to it. *Hakew.*, 143, 146.

[In the Senate of the United States, the President reports the title of the bill; that this is the second time of reading it; that it is now to be considered as in a Committee of the Whole; and the question will be, whether it shall be read a third time? or that it may be referred to a special committee?]

SEC. XXVI.—BILLS, COMMITMENT.

If on motion and question it be decided that the bill shall be committed, it may then be moved to be referred to Committee of the Whole House, or to a special committee. If the latter, the Speaker proceeds to name the committee. Any member also may name a single person, and the Clerk is to write him down as of the committee. But the House have a controlling power over the names and number, if a question be moved against any one; and may in any case put in and put out whom they please.

Those who take exceptions to some particulars in the bill are to be of the committee, but none who speak directly against the body of the bill; for he that would totally destroy will not amend it, (*Hakew.*, 146; *Town.*, *col.* 208; *D' Ewes*, 634, *col.* 2; *Scob.*, 47:) or, as it is said, (5 *Grey*, 145,) the child is not to be put to a nurse that cares not for it, (6 *Grey*. 373.) It is therefore a constant rule "that no man is to be employed in any matter who has declared himself against it." And when any member who is against the bill hears himself named of its committee, he ought to ask to be excused. Thus (March 7, 1606) Mr. Hadley was, on the question being put, excused from being of a committee, declaring himself to be against the matter itself. *Scob.*, 46.

[No bill shall be committed or amended until it shall have been twice read; after which it may be referred to a committee. *Rule* 27.]

[In the appointment of the standing committees, the Senate will proceed, by ballot, severally to appoint the chairman of each committee; and then, by one ballot, the other members necessary to complete the same; and a majority of the whole number of votes given shall be necessary to the choice of a chairman of a standing committee. All other committees shall be appointed by ballot, and a plurality of votes shall make a choice. When any subject or matter shall have been referred to a committee, any other subject or matter of a similar nature may, on motion, be referred to such committee. *Rule* 34.]

The Clerk may deliver the bill to any member of the committee, (*Town.*, *col.* 138;) but it is usual to deliver it to him who is first named.

In some cases the House has ordered a committee to withdraw immediately into the committee chamber and act on and bring back the bill, sitting in the House. *Scob.*, 48. A committee meet when and where they please, if the House has not ordered time and place for them, (6 *Grey*, 370;) but they can only act when together, and not by separate consultation and consent—nothing being the report of the committee but what has been agreed to in committee actually assembled.

A majority of the committee constitutes a quorum for business. *Elsynge's Method of Passing Bills*, 11.

Any member of the House may be present at any select committee, but cannot vote, and must give place to all of the committee, and sit below them. *Elsynge*, 12; *Scob.*, 49.

The committee have full power over the bill or other paper committed to them, except that they cannot change the title or subject. 8 *Grey*, 228.

The paper before a committee, whether select or of the whole, may be a bill, resolutions, draught of an address, &c., and it may either originate with them or be referred to them. In every case the whole paper is read first by the clerk, and then by the chairman, by paragraphs, (*Scob.*, 49,) pausing at the end of each paragraph, and putting questions for amending, if proposed. In the case of resolutions on distinct subjects, originating with themselves, a question is put on each separately, as amended or unamended, and no final question on the whole, (3 *Hats.*, 276;) but if they relate to the same subject, a question is put on the whole. If it be a bill, draught of an address, or other paper originating with them, they proceed by paragraphs; putting questions for amending either by insertion or striking out, if proposed; but no question on agreeing to the paragraphs separately; this is reserved to the close, when a question is put on the whole for agreeing to it as amended or unamended. But if it be a paper referred to them, they proceed to put questions of amendment, if proposed, but no final question on the whole, because all parts of the paper, having been adopted by the House, stand, of course, unless altered or struck out by a vote. Even if they are opposed to the whole paper, and think it cannot be made good by amendments, they cannot reject it, but must report it back to the House without amendments, and there make their opposition.

The natural order in considering and amending any paper is, to begin at the beginning, and .proceed through it by paragraphs, and this order is so strictly adhered to in Parliament, that when a latter part has been amended, you cannot recur back and make any alteration in a former part. 2 *Hats.*, 90. In numerous assemblies this restraint is doubtless important. [But in the Senate of the United States, though in the main we consider and amend the paragraphs in their natural order, yet recurrences are indulged; and they seem, on the whole, in that small body, to produce advantages overweighing their inconveniences.]

To this natural order of beginning at the beginning, there is a single exception found in parliamentary usage. When a bill is taken up in committee, or on its second reading, they postpone the preamble till the other parts of the bill are gone through. The reason is, that on consideration of the body of the bill, such alterations may therein be made as may also occasion the alteration of the preamble. *Scob.*, 50; 7 *Grey*, 431.

On this head the following case occurred in the Senate, March 6, 1800: A resolution which had no preamble having been already amended by the House so that a few words only of the original remained in it, a motion was made to prefix a preamble, which having an aspect very different from the resolution, the mover intimated that he should afterwards propose a correspondent amendment in the body of the resolution. It was objected that a preamble could not be taken up till the body of the resolution is done with; but the preamble was received, because we are in fact through the body of the resolution: we have amended that as far as amendments have been offered, and, indeed, till little of the original is left. It is the proper time, therefore, to consider a preamble; and whether the one offered be consistent with the resolution is for the House to determine. The mover, indeed, has intimated that he shall offer a subsequent proposition for the body of the resolution; but the House is not in possession of it; it remains in his breast, and may be withheld. The rules of the House can only operate on what is before them. [The practice of the Senate, too, allows recurrences backwards and forwards for the purposes of amendment, not permitting amendments in a subsequent to preclude those in a prior part, or *e converso.*]

When the committee is through the whole, a member moves that the committee may rise, and the chairman report the paper to the House, with or without amendments, as the case may be. 2 *Hats.*, 289, 292; *Scob.*, 53; 2 *Hats.*, 290; 8 *Scob.*, 50.

When a vote is once passed in a committee, it cannot be altered but by the House, their votes being binding on themselves. 1607, *June* 4.

The committee may not erase, interline, or blot the bill itself; but must, in a paper by itself, set down the amendments, stating the words which are to be inserted or omitted, (*Scob.*, 50,) and where, by references to the page, line, and word of the bill. *Scob.*, 50.

SEC. XXVII.—REPORT OF COMMITTEE.

The chairman of the committee, standing in his place, informs the House that the committee, to whom was referred such a bill, have, according to order, had the same under consideration, and have directed him to report the same without any amendment, or with sundry amendments, (as the case may be,) which he is ready to do when the House pleases to receive it. And he or any other may move that it be now received; but the cry of "now, now," from the House, generally dispenses with the formality of a motion and question. He then reads the amendments, with the coherence in the bill, and opens the alterations and the reasons of the committee for such amendments, until he has gone through the whole. He then delivers it at the Clerk's table, where the amendments reported are read by the Clerk. without the coherence; whereupon the papers lie upon the table till the House, at its convenience, shall take up the report. *Scob.*, 52; *Hakew.*, 148.

The report being made, the committee is dissolved, and can act no more without a new power. *Scob.*, 51. But it may be revived by a vote, and the same matter recommitted to them. 4 *Grey*, 361.

SEC. XXVIII.—BILL, RECOMMITMENT.

After a bill has been committed and reported, it ought not in an ordinary course to be recommitted; but in cases of importance, and for special reasons, it is sometimes recommitted, and usually to the same committee. *Hakew.*, 151. If a report be recommitted before agreed to in the House, what has passed in committee is of no validity; the whole question is again before the committee, and a new resolution must be again moved, as if nothing had passed. 3 *Hats.*, 131—*note.*

In Senate, January, 1800, the salvage bill was recommitted three times after the commitment.

A particular clause of a bill may be committed without the whole bill, (3 *Hats.*, 131;) or so much of a paper to one and so much to another committee.

SEC. XXIX.—BILL, REPORTS TAKEN UP.

When the report of a paper originating with a committee is taken up by the House, they proceed exactly as in committee. Here, as in committee, when the paragraphs have, on distinct questions, been agreed to *seriatim*, (5 *Grey*, 366; 6 *Grey*, 368; 8 *Grey*, 47, 104, 360; 1 *Torbuck's Deb.*, 125; 3 *Hats.*, 348,) no question needs be put on the whole report. 5 *Grey*, 381.

On taking up a bill reported with amendments, the amendments only are read by the Clerk. The Speaker then reads the first, and puts it to the question, and so on till the whole are adopted or rejected, before any other amendment be admitted, except it be an amendment to an amendment. *Elsynge's Mem.*, 53. When through the amendments of the committee, the Speaker pauses, and gives time for amendments to be proposed in the House to the body of the bill, as he does also if it has been reported without amendments, putting no questions but on amendments proposed; and when through the whole, he puts the question whether the bill shall be read the third time?

SEC. XXX.—QUASI-COMMITTEE.

If on motion and question the bill be not committed, or if no proposition for commitment be made, then the proceedings in the Senate of the United States and in Parliament are totally different. The former shall be first stated.

[The 28th rule of the Senate says: "All bills on a second reading shall first be considered by the Senate in the same manner as if the Senate were in Committee of the Whole before they shall be taken up and proceeded on by the Senate agreeably to the standing rules, unless otherwise ordered;" (that is to say, unless ordered to be referred to a special committee.) And when the Senate shall consider a treaty, bill, or resolution, as in Committee of the Whole, the Vice President or President *pro tempore* may call a member to fill the chair during the time the Senate shall remain in Committee of the Whole; and the chairman (so called) shall, during such time, have the powers of a President *pro tempore.*

[The proceedings of the Senate, as in a Committee of the Whole, or in Quasi-Committee, is precisely as in a real Committee of the Whole, taking no questions but on amendments. When through the whole, they consider the Quasi-Committee as risen, the House resumes without any motion, question, or resolution to that effect, and the President reports that "the House, acting as in a Committee of the Whole, have had under their consideration the bill entitled, &c., and have made sundry amendments, which he will now report to the House." The bill is then before them, as it would have been if reported from a committee, and questions are regularly to be put again on every amendment; which being gone through, the President pauses to give time to the House to propose amendments to the body of the bill, and, when through, puts the question whether it shall be read a third time?]

[After progress in amending the bill in Quasi-Committee, a motion may be made to refer it to a special committee. If the motion prevails, it is equivalent in effect to the several votes, that the committee rise, the House resume itself, discharge the Committee of the Whole, and refer the bill to a special committee. In that case, the amendments already made fall. But if the motion fails, the Quasi-Committee stands *in statu quo.*]

[How far does this 28th rule subject the House, when in Quasi-Committee, to the laws which regulate the proceedings of Committees of the Whole?] The particulars in which these differ from proceedings in the House are the following: 1. In a committee every member may speak as often as he pleases. 2. The votes of a committee may be rejected or altered when reported to the House. 3. A committee, even of the Whole, cannot refer any matter to another committee. 4. In a committee no previous question can be taken: the only means to avoid an improper discussion is to move that the committee rise; and if it be apprehended that the same discussion will be attempted on returning into committee, the House can discharge them, and proceed itself on the business, keeping down the improper discussion by the previous question. 5. A committee cannot punish a breach of order in the House or in the gallery. 9 *Grey*, 113. It can only rise and report it to the House, who may proceed to punish. [The first and second of these peculiarities attach to the Quasi-Committee of the Senate, as every day's practice proves, and seem to be the only ones to which the 28th rule meant to subject them; for it continues to be a house, and therefore, though it acts in some respects as a committee, in others it preserves its character as a house. Thus (3) it is in the daily habit of referring its business to a special committee. 4. It admits of the previous question. If it did not, it would have no means of preventing an improper discussion, not being able, as a committee is, to avoid it by returning into the house, for the moment it would resume the same subject there, the 28th rule declares it again a Quasi-Committee. 5. It would doubtless exercise its powers as a house on any breach of order. 6. It takes a question by yea and nay, as the House does. 7. It receives messages from the President and the other house. 8. In the midst of a debate it receives a motion to adjourn, and adjourns as a house, not as a committee.]

SEC. XXXI.—BILLS, SECOND READING IN THE HOUSE.

In Parliament, after the bill has been read a second time, if on the motion and question it be not committed, or if no proposition for commitment be made, the Speaker reads it by paragraphs, pausing between each, but putting no question but on amendments proposed; and when through the whole, he puts the question whether it shall be read a third time? if it come from the other house; or, if originating with themselves, whether it shall be engrossed and read a third time? The Speaker reads sitting, but rises to put questions. The Clerk stands while he reads.

[* But the Senate of the United States is so much in the

* The former practice of the Senate referred to in this paragraph has been changed by the following rule:

[The final question upon the second reading of every bill, resolution, constitutional amendment or motion, originating in the Senate, and requiring three readings previous to being passed, shall be, "Whether it shall be engrossed and read a third time?" and no amendment shall be received for discussion at the habit of making many and material amendments at the third reading, that it has become the practice not to engross a bill till it has passed—an irregular and dangerous practice, because in this way the paper which passes the Senate is not that which goes to the other house, and that which goes to the other house as the act of the Senate has never been seen in Senate. In reducing numerous, difficult, and illegible amendments into the text, the Secretary may, with the most innocent intentions, commit errors which can never again be corrected.]

The bill being now as perfect as its friends can make it, this is the proper stage for those fundamentally opposed to make their first attack. All attempts at earlier periods are with disjointed efforts, because many who do not expect to be in favor of the bill ultimately are willing to let it go on to its perfect state, to take time to examine it themselves and to hear what can be said for it, knowing that after all, they will have sufficient opportunities of giving it their veto. Its last two stages, therefore, are reserved for this—that is to say, on the question whether it shall be engrossed and read a third time? and lastly, whether it shall pass? The first of these is usually the most interesting contest, because then the whole subject is new and engaging; and the minds of the members having not yet been declared by any trying vote, the issue is the more doubtful. In this stage, therefore, is the main trial of strength between its friends and opponents, and it behooves every one to make up his mind decisively for this question, or he loses the main battle; and

third reading of any bill, resolution, amendment, or motion, unless by unanimous consent of the members present; but it shall at all times be in order before the final passage of any such bill, resolution, constitutional amendment, or motion, to move its commitment; and should such commitment take place, and any amendment be reported by the committee, the said bill, resolution, constitutional amendment, or motion, shall be again read a second time, and considered as in Committee of the Whole, and then the aforesaid question shall be again put. *Rule* 29.]

accident and management may and often do prevent a successful rallying on the next and last question, whether it shall pass?

When the bill is engrossed, the title is to be indorsed on the back, and not within the bill. *Hakew.*, 250.

SEC. XXXII.—READING PAPERS.

Where papers are laid before the House or referred to a committee, every member has a right to have them once read at the table before he can be compelled to vote on them; but it is a great though common error to suppose that he has a right, *toties quoties*, to have acts, journals, accounts, or papers on the table, read independently of the will of the House. The delay and interruption which this might be made to produce evince the impossibility of the existence of such a right. There is, indeed, so manifest a propriety of permitting every member to have as much information as possible on every question on which he is to vote, that when he desires the reading, if it be seen that it is really for information and not for delay, the Speaker directs it to be read without putting a question, if no one objects; but if objected to, a question must be put. 2 *Hats.*, 117, 118.

It is equally an error to suppose that any member has a right, without a question put, to lay a book or paper on the table, or have it read, on suggesting that it contains matter infringing on the privileges of the House. *Ib.*

For the same reason, a member has not a right to read a paper in his place, if it be objected to, without leave of the House. But this rigor is never exercised but where there is an intentional or gross abuse of the time and patience of the House.

A member has not a right even to read his own speech, committed to writing, without leave. This also is to prevent an abuse of time, and therefore is not refused but where that is intended. 2 *Grey*, 227.

A report of a committee of the Senate on a bill from the

House of Representatives being under consideration, on motion that the report of the committee of the House of Representatives on the same bill be read in the Senate, it passed in the negative. *Feb.* 28, 1793.

Formerly, when papers were referred to a committee, they used to be first read; but of late only the titles, unless a member insists they shall be read, and then nobodv can oppose it. 2 *Hats.*, 117.

SEC. XXXIII.—PRIVILEGED QUESTIONS.

[*While a question is before the Senate, no motion shall be received, unless for an amendment, for the previous question, or for postponing the main question, or to commit it, or to adjourn. *Rule* 8.]

It is no possession of a bill unless it be delivered to the Clerk to be read, or the Speaker reads the title. *Lex. Parl.*, 274; *Elsynge Mem.*, 85; *Ord. House of Commons*, 64.

It is a general rule that the question first moved and seconded shall be first put. *Scob.*, 28, 22; 2 *Hats.*, 81. But this rule gives way to what may be called privileged questions; and the privileged questions are of different grades among themselves.

A motion to adjourn simply takes place of all others, for otherwise the House might be kept sitting against its will, and indefinitely. Yet this motion cannot be received after another question is actually put, and while the House is engaged in voting.

Orders of the day take place of all other questions, except

* This rule has been modified so as to specify the questions entitled to preference. The rule is now as follows:

[When a question is under debate, no motion shall be received but to adjourn, to lay on the table, to postpone indefinitely, to postpone to a day certain, to commit, or to amend; which several motions shall have precedence in the order they stand arranged, and the motion for adjournment shall always be in order, and be decided without debate.]

for adjournment—that is to say, the question which is the subject of an order is made a privileged one, *pro hac vice*. The order is a repeal of the general rule as to this special case. When any member moves, therefore, for the order of the day to be read, no further debate is permitted on the question which was before the House; for if the debate might proceed, it might continue through the day and defeat the order. This motion, to entitle it to precedence, must be for the orders generally, and not for any particular one; and if it be carried on the question "Whether the House will now proceed to the orders of the day?" they must be read and proceeded on in the course in which they stand (2 *Hats.*, 83;) for priority of order gives priority of right, which cannot be taken away but by another special order.

After these there are other privileged questions, which will require considerable explanation.

It is proper that every parliamentary assembly should have certain forms of questions, so adapted as to enable them fitly to dispose of every proposition which can be made to them. Such are, 1. The previous question. 2. To postpone indefinitely. 3. To adjourn a question to a definite day. 4. To lie on the table. 5. To commit. 6. To amend. The proper occasion for each of these questions should be understood.

1. When a proposition is moved which it is useless or inexpedient now to express or discuss, the previous question has been introduced for suppressing for that time the motion and its discussion. 3 *Hats.*, 188, 189.

2. But as the previous question gets rid of it only for that day, and the same proposition may recur the next day, if they wish to suppress it for the whole of that session they postpone it indefinitely. 3 *Hats.*, 183. This quashes the proposition for that session, as an indefinite adjournment is a dissolution, or the continuance of a suit *sine die* is a discontinuance of it.

3. When a motion is made which it will be proper to act

on, but information is wanted, or something more pressing claims the present time, the question or debate is adjourned to such day within the session as will answer the views of the House. 2 *Hats.*, 81. And those who have spoken before may not speak again when the adjourned debate is resumed. 2 *Hats.*, 73. Sometimes, however, this has been abusedly used by adjourning it to a day beyond the session, to get rid of it altogether, as would be done by an indefinite postponement.

4. When the House has something else which claims its present attention, but would be willing to reserve in their power to take up a proposition whenever it shall suit them, they order it to lie on their table. It may then be called for at any time.

5. If the proposition will want more amendment and digestion than the formalities of the House will conveniently admit, they refer it to a committee.

6. But if the proposition be well digested, and may need but few and simple amendments, and especially if these be of leading consequence, they then proceed to consider and amend it themselves.

The Senate, in their practice, vary from this regular gradation of forms. Their practice comparatively with that of Parliament stands thus:

FOR THE PARLIAMENTARY,	THE SENATE USES:
Postponement indefinite,	Postponement to a day beyond the session.
Adjournment,	Postponement to a day within the session.
Lying on the table,	Postponement indefinite. Lying on the table.

In their eighth rule, therefore, which declares that while a question is before the Senate no motion shall be received, unless it be for the previous question, or to postpone, commit, or amend the main question, the term postponement must be understood according to their broad use of it, and not in the parliamentary sense. Their rule, then, establishes as privileged questions the previous question, postponement, commitment, and amendment.

But it may be asked, Have these questions any privilege among themselves? or are they so equal that the common principle of the "first moved first put" takes place among them? This will need explanation. Their competitions may be as follows:

1. Previous question and	postpone commit amend	In the first, second, and third classes, and the first member of the fourth class, the rule "first moved first put" takes place.
2. Postpone and	previous question commit amend	
3. Commit and	previous question postpone amend	
4. Amend and	previous question postpone commit	

In the first class, where the previous question is first moved, the effect is peculiar; for it not only prevents the after motion to postpone or commit from being put to question before it, but also from being put after it; for if the previous question be decided affirmatively, to wit, that the main question shall *now* be put, it would of course be against the decision to postpone or commit; and if it be decided negatively, to wit, that the main question shall not now be put, this puts the House out of possession of the main question, and consequently there is nothing before them to postpone or commit. So that neither voting for nor against the previous question will enable the advocates for postponing or committing to get at their object. Whether it may be amended shall be examined hereafter.

Second class. If postponement be decided affirmatively, the

proposition is removed from before the House, and consequently there is no ground for the previous question, commitment, or amendment; but if decided negatively, (that it shall not be postponed,) the main question may then be suppressed by the previous question, or may be committed or amended.

The third class is subject to the same observations as the second.

The fourth class. Amendment of the main question first moved, and afterwards the previous question, the question of amendment shall be first put.

Amendment and postponement competing, postponement is first put, as the equivalent proposition to adjourn the main question would be in Parliament. The reason is, that the question for amendment is not suppressed by postponing or adjourning the main question, but remains before the House whenever the main question is resumed; and it might be that the occasion for other urgent business might go by, and be lost by length of debate on the amendment, if the House had it not in their power to postpone the whole subject.

Amendment and commitment. The question for committing, though last moved, shall be first put; because, in truth, it facilitates and befriends the motion to amend. *Scobell* is express: "On motion to amend a bill, any one may notwithstanding move to commit it, and the question for commitment shall be first put." *Scob.*, 46.

We have hitherto considered the case of two or more of the privileged questions contending for privilege between themselves, when both are moved on the original or main question; but now let us suppose one of them to be moved, not on the original primary question, but on the secondary one, *e. g.*

Suppose a motion to postpone, commit, or amend the main question, and that it be moved to suppress that motion by putting a previous question on it. This is not allowed, because it would embarrass questions too much to allow them to be piled on one another several stories high; and the same result may be had in a more simple way, by deciding against the postponement, commitment, or amendment. 2 *Hats.*, 81, 2, 3, 4.

Suppose a motion for the previous question, or commitment or amendment of the main question, and that it be then moved to postpone the motion for the previous question, or for commitment or amendment of the main question. 1. It would be absurd to postpone the previous question, commitment, or amendment alone, and thus separate the appendage from its principal; yet it must be postponed separately from its original, if at all, because the eighth rule of Senate says that when a main question is before the house no motion shall be received but to commit, amend, or pre-question the original question, which is the parliamentary doctrine also, therefore the motion to postpone the secondary motion for the previous question, or for committing or amending, cannot be received. 2. This is a piling of questions one on another; which, to avoid embarrassment, is not allowed. 3. The same result may be had more simply by voting against the previous question, commitment, or amendment.

Suppose a commitment moved of a motion for the previous question, or to postpone, or amend. The first, second, and third reasons before stated, all hold good against this.

Suppose an amendment moved to a motion for the previous question. Answer: the previous question cannot be amended. Parliamentary usage, as well as the ninth rule of the Senate, has fixed its form to be, "Shall the main question be now put?"—*i. e.*, at this instant; and as the present instant is but one, it can admit of no modification. To change it to-morrow, or any other moment, is without example and without utility. But suppose a motion to amend a motion for postponement, as to one day instead of another, or to a special instead of an indefinite time. The useful character of amendment gives it a privilege of attaching itself to a secondary and privileged motion: that is, we may amend a postponement of a main question. So, we may amend a commitment of a main question, as by adding, for example, "with instructions to inquire," &c. In like manner, if an amendment be moved to an amendment, it is admitted; but it would not be admitted in another degree, to wit, to amend an amendment to an amendment of a main question. This would lead to too much embarrassment. The line must be drawn somewhere, and usage has drawn it after the amendment to the amendment. The same result must be sought by deciding against the amendment to the amendment, and then moving it again as it was wished to be amended. In this form it becomes only an amendment to an amendment.

[When motions are made for reference of the same subject to a select committee and to a standing committee, the question on reference to the standing committee shall be first put. *Rule* 35.]

[In filling a blank with a sum, the largest sum shall be first put to the question, by the thirteenth rule of the Senate,*] contrary to the rule of Parliament, which privileges the smallest sum and longest time. 5 *Grey*, 179; 2 *Hats.*, 8, 83; 3 *Hats.*, 132, 133. And this is considered to be not in the form of an amendment to the question, but as alternative or successive originals. In all cases of time or number, we must consider whether the larger comprehends the lesser, as in a question to what day a postponement shall be, the number of a committee, amount of a fine, term of an imprisonment, term of irredeemability of a loan, or the *terminus in quem* in any other case; then the question must begin *a maximo*. Or whether the lesser includes the greater, as in questions on the limitation of the rate of interest, on what day the session shall be closed by adjournment, on what day the next shall commence, when an act shall commence, or the *terminus a quo* in any other case where the question must begin *a minimo*: the object being not to begin at that extreme which, and more, being within every man's wish, no one could negative

[* In filling up blanks, the largest sum and longest time shall be first put. *Rule* 13.]

it, and yet, if he should vote in the affirmative, every question for more would be precluded; but at that extreme which would unite few, and then to advance or recede till you get a number which will unite a bare majority. 3 *Grey*, 376, 384, 385. "The fair question in this case is not that to which and more all will agree, but whether there shall be addition to the question." *Grey*, 365.

Another exception to the rule of priority is when a motion has been made to strike out or agree to a paragraph. Motions to amend it are to be put to the question before a vote is taken on striking out or agreeing to the whole paragraph.

But there are several questions which, being incidental to every one, will take place of every one, privileged or not, to wit, a question of order arising out of any other question must be decided before that question. 2 *Hats.*, 88.

A matter of privilege arising out of any question, or from a quarrel between two members or any other cause, supersedes the consideration of the original question, and must be first disposed of. 2 *Hats.*, 88.

Reading papers relative to the question before the House. This question must be put before the principal one. 2 *Hats.*, 88.

Leave asked to withdraw a motion. The rule of Parliament being that a motion made and seconded is in the possession of the House, and cannot be withdrawn without leave, the very terms of the rule imply that leave may be given, and, consequently, may be asked and put to the question.

SEC. XXXIV.—THE PREVIOUS QUESTION.

When any question is before the House, any member may move a previous question, "Whether that question (called the main question) shall now be put?" If it pass in the affirmative, then the main question is to be put immediately, and no man may speak anything further to it, either to add or alter. *Memor. in Hakew.*, 28 ; 4 *Grey*, 27.

The previous question being moved and seconded, the

question from the Chair shall be, "Shall the main question be now put?" and if the nays prevail, the main question shall not then be put.

This kind of question is understood by Mr. Hatsell to have been introduced in 1604. 2 *Hats.*, 80. Sir Henry Vane introduced it. 2 *Grey*, 113, 114; 3 *Grey*, 384. When the question was put in this form, "Shall the main question be put?" a determination in the negative suppressed the main question during the session; but since the words "now put" are used, they exclude it for the present only: formerly, indeed, only till the present debate was over, (4 *Grey*, 43,) but now for that day and no longer. 2 *Grey*, 113, 114.

Before the question "Whether the main question shall now be put?" any person might formerly have spoken to the main question, because otherwise he would be precluded from speaking to it at all. *Mem. in Hakew.*, 28.

The proper occasion for the previous question, is when a subject is brought forward of a delicate nature as to high personages, &c., or the discussion of which may call forth observations which might be of injurious consequences. Then the previous question is proposed; and in the modern usage, the discussion of the main question is suspended, and the debate confined to the previous question. The use of it has been extended abusively to other cases; but in these it has been an embarrassing procedure: its uses would be as well answered by other more simple parliamentary forms, and therefore it should not be favored, but restricted within as narrow limits as possible.

Whether a main question may be amended after the previous question on it has been moved and seconded? 2 *Hats.*, 88, says, if the previous question has been moved and seconded, and also proposed from the Chair, (by which he means stated by the Speaker for debate,) it has been doubted whether an amendment can be admitted to the main question. He thinks it may, after the previous question moved and seconded; but not after it has been proposed from the

Chair. In this case, he thinks the friends to the amendment must vote that the main question be not now put; and then move their amended question, which being made new by the amendment, is no longer the same which has been just suppressed, and therefore may be proposed as a new one. But this proceeding certainly endangers the main question, by dividing its friends, some of whom may choose it unamended, rather than lose it altogether; while others of them may vote, as Hatsell advises, that the main question be not now put with a view to move it again in an amended form. The enemies of the main question, by this manœuvre to the previous question, get the enemies to the amendment added to them on the first vote, and throw the friends of the main question under the embarrassment of rallying again as they can. To support his opinion, too, he makes the deciding circumstance, whether an amendment may or may not be made, to be, that the previous question has been proposed from the Chair. But, as the rule is that the House is in possession of a question as soon as it is moved and seconded, it cannot be more than possessed of it by its being also proposed from the Chair. It may be said, indeed, that the object of the previous question being to get rid of a question, which it is not expedient should be discussed, this object may be defeated by moving to amend, and, in the discussion of that motion, involving the subject of the main question. But so may the object of the previous question be defeated, by moving the amended question, as Mr. Hatsell proposes, after the decision against putting the original question. He acknowledges, too, that the practice has been to admit previous amendments, and only cites a few late instances to the contrary. On the whole, I should think it best to decide it ab inconvenienti, to wit: which is most inconvenient, to put it in the power of one side of the House to defeat a proposition by hastily moving the previous question, and thus forcing the main question to be put unamended; or to put it in the power of the other side to force on, incidentally at least, a discussion which would be better avoided? Perhaps the last is the least inconvenience; inasmuch as the Speaker, by confining the discussion rigorously to the amendment only, may prevent their going into the main question, and inasmuch also as so great a proportion of the cases in which the previous question is called for, are fair and proper subjects for public discussion, and ought not to be obstructed by a formality introduced for questions of a peculiar character.

SEC. XXXV.—AMENDMENTS.

On an amendment being moved, a member who has spoken to the main question may speak again to the amendment. *Scob.*, 23.

If an amendment be proposed inconsistent with one already agreed to, it is a fit ground for its rejection by the House, but not within the competence of the Speaker to suppress as if it were against order; for were he permitted to draw questions of consistence within the vortex of order, he might usurp a negative on important modifications, and suppress, instead of subserving the legislative will.

Amendments may be made so as totally to alter the nature of the proposition; and it is a way of getting rid of a proposition, by making it bear a sense different from what it was intended by the movers, so that they vote against it themselves. 2 *Hats.*, 79, 4, 82, 84. A new bill may be ingrafted by way of amendment, on the words "Be it enacted," &c. 1 *Grey*, 190, 192.

If it be proposed to amend by leaving out certain words, it may be moved, as an amendment to this amendment, to leave out a part of the words of the amendment, which is equivalent to leaving them in the bill. 2 *Hats.*, 80, 9. The parliamentary question is, always, whether the words shall stand part of the bill.

When it is proposed to amend by inserting a paragraph. or part of one, the friends of the paragraph may make it as perfect as they can by amendments before the question is put for inserting it. If it be received, it cannot be amended afterwards, in the same stage, because the House has, on a vote, agreed to it in that form. In like manner, if it is proposed to amend by striking out a paragraph, the friends of the paragraph are first to make it as perfect as they can by amendments, before the question is put for striking it out. If on the question it be retained, it cannot be amended afterwards, because a vote against striking out is equivalent to a vote agreeing to it in that form.

When it is moved to amend by striking out certain words and inserting others, the manner of stating the question is first to read the whole passage to be amended as it stands at present, then the words proposed to be struck out, next those to be inserted, and lastly the whole passage as it will be when amended. And the question, if desired, is then to be divided, and put first on striking out. If carried, it is next on inserting the words proposed. If that be lost, it may be moved to insert others. 2 *Hats.*, 80, 7.

A motion is made to amend by striking out certain words and inserting others in their place, which is negatived. Then it is moved to strike out the same words, and to insert others of a tenor entirely different from those first proposed. It is negatived. Then it is moved to strike out the same words and insert nothing, which is agreed to. All this is admissible, because to strike out and insert A is one proposition. To strike out and insert B is a different proposition. And to strike out and insert nothing is still different. And the rejection of one proposition does not preclude the offering a different one. Nor would it change the case were the first motion divided by putting the question first on striking out, and that negatived; for, as putting the whole motion to the question at once would not have precluded, the putting the half of it cannot do it.*

* In the case of a division of the question, and a decision against striking out, I advance doubtingly the opinion here expressed. I find no authority either way, and I know it may be viewed under a different aspect. It may be thought that, having decided separately not to strike out the passage, the same

But if it had been carried affirmatively to strike out the words and to insert A, it could not afterwards be permitted to strike out A and insert B. The mover of B should have notified, while the insertion of A was under debate, that he would move to insert B; in which case those who preferred it would join in rejecting A.

After A is inserted, however, it may be moved to strike out a portion of the original paragraph, comprehending A, provided the coherence to be struck out be so substantial as to make this effectively a different proposition; for then it is resolved into the common case of striking out a paragraph after amending it. Nor does anything forbid a new insertion, instead of A and its coherence.

In Senate, January 25, 1798, a motion to postpone until the second Tuesday in February some amendments proposed to the Constitution; the words "until the second Tuesday in February" were struck out by way of amendment. Then it was moved to add, "until the first day of June." Objected that it was not in order, as the question should be first put on the longest time; therefore, after a shorter time decided against, a longer cannot be put to question. It was answered that this rule takes place only in filling blanks for time. But when a specific time stands part of a motion, that may be struck out as well as any other part of a motion; and when struck out, a motion may be received to insert any other. In fact, it is not until they are struck out, and a blank for the time thereby produced, that the rule can begin to operate, by receiving all the propositions for different times, and putting the question successively on the longest. Otherwise it would be in the power of the mover, by inserting originally a short time, to preclude the possibility of a longer, for till the short time is struck out, you cannot insert a

question for striking out cannot be put over again, though with a view to a different insertion. Still I think it more reasonable and convenient to consider the striking out and insertion as forming one proposition; but should readily yield to any evidence that the contrary is the practice in Parliament.

longer; and if, after it is struck out, you cannot do it, then it cannot be done at all. Suppose the first motion had been made to amend by striking out "the second Tuesday in February," and inserting instead thereof "the first of June," it would have been regular, then, to divide the question, by proposing first the question to strike out and then that to insert. Now this is precisely the effect of the present proceeding; only, instead of one motion and two questions, there are two motions and two questions to effect it—the motion being divided as well as the question.

When the matter contained in two bills might be better put into one, the manner is to reject the one, and incorporate its matter into another bill by way of amendment. So if the matter of one bill would be better distributed into two, any part may be struck out by way of amendment, and put into a new bill. If a section is to be transposed, a question must be put on striking it out where it stands, and another for inserting it in the place desired.

A bill passed by the one house with blanks. These may be filled up by the other by way of amendments, returned to the first as such, and passed. 3 *Hats.*, 83.

The number prefixed to the section of a bill, being merely a marginal indication, and no part of the text of the bill, the clerk regulates that—the House or committee is only to amend the text.

SEC. XXXVI.—DIVISION OF THE QUESTION.

If a question contain more parts than one, it may be divided into two or more questions. *Mem. in Hakew.*, 29. But not as the right of an individual member, but with the consent of the House. For who is to decide whether a question is complicated or not?—where it is complicated?—into how many propositions it may be divided? The fact is, that the only mode of separating a complicated question is by moving amendments to it; and these must be decided by the House, on a question, unless the House orders it to be divided; as, on the question, December 2, 1640, making void the election of the knights for Worcester, on a motion it was resolved to make two questions of it, to wit: one on each knight. 2 *Hats.*, 85, 86. So, wherever there are several names in a question, they may be divided and put one by one. 9 *Grey*, 444. So, 1729, April 17, on an objection that a question was complicated, it was separated by amendment. 2 *Hats.*, 79.

The soundness of these observations will be evident from the embarrassments produced by the 12th rule of the Senate, which says, "if the question in debate contain several points, any member may have the same divided."

1798, May 30, the alien bill in quasi-committee. To a section and proviso in the original had been added two new provisoes by way of amendment. On a motion to strike out the section as amended, the question was desired to be divided. To do this it must be put first on striking out either the former proviso, or some distinct member of the section. But when nothing remains but the last member of the section and the provisoes, they cannot be divided so as to put the last member to question by itself; for the provisoes might thus be left standing alone as exceptions to a rule when the rule is taken away; or the new provisoes might be left to a second question, after having been decided on once before at the same reading, which is contrary to rule. But the question must be on striking out the last member of the section as amended. This sweeps away the exceptions with the rule, and relieves from inconsistence. A question to be divisible, must comprehend points so distinct and entire that one of them being taken away, the other may stand entire. But a proviso or exception, without an enacting clause, does not contain an entire point or proposition.

May 31.—The same bill being before the Senate. There was a proviso that the bill should not extend—1. To any foreign minister; nor, 2. To any person to whom the President should give a passport; nor, 3. To any alien merchant conforming himself to such regulations as the President shall prescribe; and a division of the question into its simplest elements was called for. It was divided into four parts, the 4th taking in the words "conforming himself," &c. It was objected that the words "any alien merchant" could not be separated from their modifying words, "conforming," &c., because these words, if left by themselves, contain no substantive idea—will make no sense. But admitting that the divisions of a paragraph into separate questions must be so made as that each part may stand by itself, yet the House having, on the question, retained the two first divisions, the words "any alien merchant" may be struck out, and their modifying words will then attach themselves to the preceding description of persons, and become a modification of that description.

When a question is divided, after the question on the 1st member, the 2d is open to debate and amendment; because it is a known rule that a person may rise and speak at any time before the question has been completely decided, by putting the negative as well as affirmative side. But the question is not completely put when the vote has been taken on the first member only. One-half of the question, both affirmative and negative, remains still to be put. See *Execut. Jour., June* 25, 1795. The same decision by President Adams.

SEC. XXXVII.—CO-EXISTING QUESTIONS.

It may be asked whether the House can be in possession of two motions or propositions at the same time? so that, one of them being decided, the other goes to question without being moved anew? The answer must be special. When a question is interrupted by a vote of adjournment, it is thereby removed from before the House, and does not stand ipso facto before them at their next meeting, but must come forward in the usual way. So, when it is interrupted by the order of the day. Such other privileged questions also as dispose of the main question, (*e. g.* the previous question, postponement, or commitment,) remove it from before the House. But it is only suspended by a motion to amend, to withdraw, to read papers, or by a question of order or privilege, and stands again before the House when these are decided. None but the class of privileged questions can be brought forward while there is another question before the House, the rule being that when a motion has been made and seconded, no other can be received, except it be a privileged one.

SEC. XXXVIII.—EQUIVALENT QUESTIONS.

If, on a question for rejection, a bill be retained, it passes, of course, to its next reading. *Hakew.*, 141; *Scob.*, 42. And a question for a second reading determined negatively, is a rejection without further question. 4 *Grey*, 149. And see *Elsynge's Memor.*, 42, in what cases questions are to be taken for rejection.

Where questions are perfectly equivalent, so that the negative of the one amounts to the affirmative of the other, and leaves no other alternative, the decision of the one concludes necessarily the other. 4 *Grey*, 157. Thus the negative of striking out amounts to the affirmative of agreeing; and therefore to put a question on agreeing after that on striking out, would be to put the same question in effect twice over. Not so in questions of amendments between the two houses. A motion to recede being negatived, does not amount to a positive vote to insist, because there is another alternative, to wit, to adhere.

A bill originating in one house is passed by the other with an amendment. A motion in the originating house to agree to the amendment is negatived. Does there result from this a vote of disagreement, or must the question on disagreement be expressly voted? The questions respecting amendments from another house are—1st, to agree; 2d, disagree; 3d, recede; 4th, insist; 5th. adhere.

1st. To agree. 2d. To disagree.	Either of these concludes the other necessarily, for the positive of either is exactly the equivalent of the negative of the other, and no other alternative remains. On either motion amendments to the amendment may be proposed; *e. g.*, if it be moved to disagree, those who are for the amendment have a right to propose amendments, and to make it as perfect as they can, before the question of disagreeing is put.
3d. To recede. 4th. To insist. 5th. To adhere.	You may then either insist or adhere. You may then either recede or adhere. You may then either recede or insist. Consequently the negative of these is not equivalent to a positive vote the other way. It does not raise so necessary an implication as may authorize the Secretary by inference to enter another vote; for two alternatives still remain, either of which may be adopted by the House.

SEC. XXXIX.—THE QUESTION.

The question is to be put first on the affirmative, and then on the negative side.

After the Speaker has put the affirmative part of the question, any member who has not spoken before to the question may rise and speak before the negative be put; because it is no full question till the negative part be put. *Scob.*, 23; 2 *Hats.*, 73.

But in small matters, and which are, of course, such as receiving petitions, reports, withdrawing motions, reading papers, &c., the Speaker most commonly supposes the consent of the House where no objection is expressed, and does not give them the trouble of putting the question formally. *Scob.*, 22; 2 *Hats.*, 87, 2, 87; 5 *Grey*, 129; 9 *Grey*, 301.

SEC. XL.—BILLS, THIRD READING.

To prevent bills from being passed by surprise, the House, by a standing order, directs that they shall not be put on their passage before a fixed hour, naming one at which the House is commonly full. *Hakew.*, 153.

[The usage of the Senate is, not to put bills on their passage till noon.]

A bill reported and passed to the third reading cannot on that day be read the third time and passed; because this would be to pass on two readings in the same day.

At the third reading the Clerk reads the bill and delivers it to the Speaker, who states the title, that it is the third time of reading the bill, and that the question will be whether it shall pass? Formerly the Speaker, or those who prepared a bill, prepared also a breviate or summary statement of its contents, which the Speaker read when he declared the state of the bill, at the several readings. Sometimes, however, he read the bill itself, especially on its passage. *Hakew.*, 136, 137, 153; *Coke*, 22, 115. Latterly, instead of this, he, at the third reading, states the whole contents of the bill, verbatim, only, instead of reading the formal parts, "Be it enacted," &c., he states that "preamble recites so and so—the 1st section enacts that, &c.; the 2d section enacts," &c.

[But in the Senate of the United States both of these formalities are dispensed with; the breviate presenting but an imperfect view of the bill, and being capable of being made to present a false one; and the full statement being a useless waste of time, immediately after a full reading by the Clerk, and especially as every member has a printed copy in his hand.]

A bill on the third reading is not to be committed for the matter or body thereof; but to receive some particular clause or proviso, it has been sometimes suffered, but as a thing very unusual. *Hakew.*, 126. Thus, 27 *El.*, 1584, a bill was committed on the third reading, having been formally committed on the second, but is declared not usual. *D' Ewes*, 337, *col.* 2; 414, *col.* 2.

When an essential provision has been omitted, rather than erase the bill and render it suspicious, they add a clause on a separate paper, engrossed and called a rider, which is read and put to the question three times. *Elsynge's Memorials*, 59; 6 *Grey*, 335; 1 *Blackst.*, 183. For examples of riders, see 3 *Hats.*, 121, 122, 124, 126. Every one is at liberty to bring in a rider without asking leave. 10 *Grey*, 52.

It is laid down as a general rule, that amendments proposed at the second reading shall be twice read, and those proposed at the third reading thrice read; as also all amendments from the other house. *Town. col.*, 19, 23, 24, 25, 26, 27, 28.

It is with great and almost invincible reluctance that amendments are admitted at this reading, which occasion erasures or interlineations. Sometimes a proviso has been cut off from a bill; sometimes erased. 9 *Grey*, 513.

This is the proper stage for filling up blanks; for if filled up before, and now altered by erasure, it would be peculiarly unsafe.

At this reading the bill is debated afresh, and for the most part is more spoken to at this time than on any of the former readings. *Hakew.*, 153.

The debate on the question whether it should be read a third time has discovered to its friends and opponents the arguments on which each side relies, and which of these appear to have influence with the House; they have had time to meet them with new arguments, and to put their old ones into new shapes. The former vote has tried the strength of the first opinion, and furnished grounds to estimate the issue; and the question now offered for its passage is the last occasion which is ever to be offered for carrying or rejecting it.

When the debate is ended, the Speaker, holding the bill in his hand, puts the question for its passage, by saying, "Gentlemen, all you who are of opinion that this bill shall pass, say ay;" and after the answer of the ayes, "All those of the contrary opinion, say no." *Hakew.*, 154.

After the bill is passed, there can be no further alteration of it in any point. *Hakew.*, 159.

SEC. XII.—DIVISION OF THE HOUSE.

The affirmative and negative of the question having been both put and answered, the Speaker declares whether the yeas or nays have it by the sound, if he be himself satisfied, and it stands as the judgment of the House. But if he be not himself satisfied which voice is the greater, or if before any other member comes into the House, or before any new motion made, (for it is too late after that,) any member shall rise and declare himself dissatisfied with the Speaker's decision, then the Speaker is to divide the House. *Scob.*, 24, 2 *Hats.*, 140.

When the House of Commons is divided, the one party goes forth, and the other remains in the House. This has made it important which go forth and which remain; because the latter gain all the indolent, the indifferent, and inattentive. Their general rule, therefore, is, that those who give their vote for the preservation of the orders of the House, shall stay in; and those who are for introducing any new matter or alteration, or proceeding contrary to the established course, are to go out. But this rule is subject to many exceptions and modifications. 2 *Hats.*, 134; 1 *Rush.*, *p.* 3, *fol.* 92; *Scob.*, 43, 52; *Co.*, 12, 116; *D'Ewes*, 505, *col.* 1; *Mem. in Hakew.*, 25, 29, as will appear by the following statement of who go forth:

Petition that it be received* . . .	Ayes.
Read	
Lie on the table	Noes.
Rejected after refusal to lie on table .	
Referred to a committee, for further proceeding	Ayes.
Bill, that it be brought in . . .	Ayes.
Read first or second time . . .	
Engrossed or read third time . .	
Proceeding on every other stage . .	
Committed	

* Noes. 9 Grey, 365.

To Committee of the Whole	Noes.	
To a select committee	Ayes.	
Report of bill to lie on table . . .	Noes.	
Be *now* read	Ayes.	
Be taken into consideration three months hence	30, P.	J. 251.
Amendments be read a second time · .	Noes.	
Clause offered on report of bill be read second time	Ayes.	
For receiving a clause		334.
With amendments be engrossed . .		395.
That a bill be *now* read a third time . .	Noes.	398.
Receive a rider	260.	
Pass		
Be printed	Ayes.	259.
Committees. That A take the chair .		
To agree to the whole or any part of report		
That the House do *now* resolve into committee	Noes.	291.
Speaker. That he now leave the chair, after order to go into committee .		
That he issue warrant for a new writ .		
Member. That none be absent without leave		
Witness. That he be further examined .	Ayes.	341.
Previous question	Noes.	
Blanks. That they be filled with the largest sum	Ayes.	
Amendments. That words stand part of .		
Lords. That their amendment be read a second time	Noes.	
Messenger be received		
Orders of day to be now read, if before 2 o'clock	Ayes.	
If after 2 o'clock	Noes.	

Adjournment. Till the next sitting day, if before 4 o'clock	Ayes.
If after 4 o'clock	Noes.
Over a sitting day, (unless a previous resolution)	Ayes.
Over the 30th of January	Noes.
For sitting on Sunday, or any other day . not being a sitting day	Ayes.

The one party being gone forth, the Speaker names two tellers from the affirmative and two from the negative side, who first count those sitting in the House and report the number to the Speaker. Then they place themselves within the door, two on each side, and count those who went forth as they come in, and report the number to the Speaker. *Mem. in Hakew.*, 26.

A mistake in the report of the tellers may be rectified after the report made. 2 *Hats.*, 145, *note.*

[But in both houses of Congress all these intricacies are avoided. The ayes first rise, and are counted standing in their places by the President or Speaker. Then they sit, and the noes rise and are counted in like manner.]

[In Senate, if they be equally divided, the Vice President announces his opinion, which decides.]

[The Constitution, however, has directed that "the yeas and nays of the members of either house on any question shall, at the desire of one-fifth of those present, be entered on the journal." And again: that in all cases of reconsidering a bill disapproved by the President, and returned with his objections, "the votes of both houses shall be determined by yeas and nays, and the names of the persons voting for and against the bill shall be entered on the journals of each house respectively."]

[By the 16th and 17th rules of the Senate, when the yeas and nays shall be called for by one-fifth of the members present, each member called upon shall, unless for special reasons he be excused by the Senate, declare openly, and without debate, his assent or dissent to the question. In taking the yeas and nays, and upon the call of the House, the names of the members shall be taken alphabetically.

[When the yeas and nays shall be taken upon any question in pursuance of the above rule, no member shall be permitted, under any circumstances whatever, to vote after the decision is announced from the Chair.]

[When it is proposed to take the vote by yeas and nays, the President or Speaker states that "the question is whether, *e. g.*, the bill shall pass—that it is proposed that the yeas and nays shall be entered on the journal. Those, therefore, who desire it, will rise. If he finds and declares that one-fifth have risen, he then states that "those who are of opinion that the bill shall pass, are to answer in the affirmative; those of the contrary opinion in the negative." The Clerk then calls over the names alphabetically, notes the yea or nay of each, and gives the list to the President or Speaker, who declares the result. In Senate, if there be an equal division, the Secretary calls on the Vice President and notes his affirmative or negative, which becomes the decision of the House.]

In the House of Commons, every member must give his vote the one way or the other, (*Scob.*, 24,) as it is not permitted to any one to withdraw who is in the House when the question is put, nor is any one to be told in the division who was not in when the question was put. 2 *Hats.*, 140.

This last position is always true when the vote is by yeas and nays; where the negative as well as affirmative of the question is stated by the President at the same time, and the vote of both sides begins and proceeds *pari passu.* It is true also when the question is put in the usual way, if the negative has also been put; but if it has not, the member entering, or any other member, may speak, and even propose amendments, by which the debate may be opened again, and the question be greatly deferred. And as some who have answered aye may have been changed by the new arguments the affirmative must be put over again. If, then, the member entering may, by speaking a few words, occasion a repetition of a question, it would be useless to deny it on his simple call for it.

While the House is telling no member may speak or move out of his place, for if any mistake be suspected it must be told again. *Mem. in Hakew.*, 26; 2 *Hats.*, 143.

If any difficulty arises in point of order during the division, the Speaker is to decide peremptorily, subject to the future censure of the House if irregular. He sometimes permits old experienced members to assist him with their advice, which they do sitting in their seats, covered, to avoid the appearance of debate; but this can only be with the Speaker's leave, else the division might last several hours. 2 *Hats.*, 143.

The voice of the majority decides; for the *lex majoris partis* is the law of all councils, elections, &c., where not otherwise expressly provided. *Hakew.*, 93. But if the House be equally divided, "*semper presumatur pro negante;*" that is, the former law is not to be changed but by a majority. *Towns.*, *col.* 134.

[But in the Senate of the United States the Vice President decides when the House is divided. *Const. U. S.*, I, 3.]

When from counting the House on a division it appears that there is not a quorum, the matter continues exactly in the state in which it was before the division, and must be resumed at that point on any future day. 2 *Hats.*, 126.

1606, May 1, on a question whether a member having said yea may afterwards sit and change his opinion, a precedent was remembered by the Speaker of Mr. Morris, attorney of the wards, in 39 *Eliz.*, who in like case changed his opinion. *Mem. in Hakew.*, 27.

SEC. XLII.—TITLES.

After the bill has passed, and not before, the title may be amended, and is to be fixed by a que tion; and the bill is then sent to the other house.

SEC. XLIII.—RECONSIDERATION.

[When a question has been once made and carried in the affirmative or negative, it shall be in order for any member of the majority to move for the reconsideration thereof; but no motion for the reconsideration of any vote shall be in order after a bill, resolution, message, report, amendment, or motion upon which the vote was taken shall have gone out of the possession of the Senate announcing their decision; nor shall any motion for reconsideration be in order unless made on the same day on which the vote was taken, or within the two next days of actual session of the Senate thereafter.* *Rule* 20.]

[1798, Jan. A bill on its second reading being amended, and on the question whether it shall be read a third time negatived, was restored by a decision to reconsider that question. Here the votes of negative and reconsideration, like positive and negative quantities in equation, destroy one another, and are as if they were expunged from the journals. Consequently the bill is open for amendment, just so far as it was the moment preceding the question for the third reading; that is to say, all parts of the bill are open for amendment except those on which votes have been already taken in its present stage. So, also, it may be recommitted.]

[†The rule permitting a reconsideration of a question affixing to it no limitation of time or circumstance, it may be asked whether there is no limitation? If, after the vote, the paper on which it is passed has been parted with, there can be no reconsideration: as if a vote has been for the passage of a bill, and the bill has been sent to the other house. But where the paper remains, as on a bill rejected, when, or under what circumstances, does it cease to be susceptible of reconsideration? This remains to be settled; unless a sense that the right of reconsideration is a right to waste the time of the House in repeated agitations of the same question, so that

* This part of the rule has been added since the Manual was compiled.

† The rule now fixes a limitation.

it shall never know when a question is done with, should induce them to reform this anomalous proceeding.]

In Parliament, a question once carried cannot be questioned again at the same session, but must stand as the judgment of the House. *Towns.*, *col.* 67; *Mem. in Hakew.*, 33. And a bill once rejected, another of the same substance cannot be brought in again the same session. *Hakew.*, 158; 6 *Grey*, 392. But this does not extend to prevent putting the same question in different stages of a bill; because every stage of a bill submits the whole and every part of it to the opinion of the House, as open for amendment, either by insertion or omission, though the same amendment has been accepted or rejected in a former stage. So in reports of committees, *e. g.* report of an address, the same question is before the House, and open for free discussion. *Towns.*, *col.* 26; 2 *Hats.*, 98, 100, 101. So orders of the house, or instructions to committees, may be discharged. So a bill, begun in one house, and sent to the other, and there rejected, may be renewed again in that other, passed and sent back. *Ib.*, 92; 3 *Hats.*, 161. Or if, instead of being rejected, they read it once and lay it aside, or amend it, and put it off a month, they may order in another to the same effect, with the same or a different title. *Hakew.*, 97, 98.

Divers expedients are used to correct the effects of this rule; as by passing an explanatory act, if anything has been omitted or ill expressed, 3 *Hats.*, 278, or an act to enforce, and make more effectual an act, &c., or to rectify mistakes in an act, &c., or a committee on one bill may be instructed to receive a clause to rectify the mistakes of another. Thus, June 24, 1685, a clause was inserted in a bill for rectifying a mistake committed by a clerk in engrossing a bill of supply. 2 *Hats.*, 194, 6. Or the session may be closed for one, two, three, or more days, and a new one commenced. But then all matters depending must be finished, or they fall, and are to begin de novo. 2 *Hats.*, 94, 98. Or a part of the subject may be taken up by another bill, or taken up in a different way. 6 *Grey*, 304, 316.

And in cases of the last magnitude, this rule has not been so strictly and verbally observed as to stop indispensable proceedings altogether. 2 *Hats.*, 92, 98. Thus when the address on the preliminaries of peace in 1782 had been lost by a majority of one, on account of the importance of the question, and smallness of the majority, the same question in substance, though with some words not in the first, and which might change the opinion of some members, was brought on again and carried, as the motives for it were thought to outweigh the objection of form. 2 *Hats.*, 99, 100.

A second bill may be passed to continue an act of the same session, or to enlarge the time limited for its execution. 2 *Hats.*, 95, 98. This is not in contradiction to the first act.

SEC. XLIV.—BILLS SENT TO THE OTHER HOUSE

[All bills passed in the Senate shall, before they are sent to the House of Representatives, be examined by a committee, consisting of three members, whose duty shall be to examine all bills, amendments, resolutions, or motions, before they go out of the possession of the Senate, and to make report that they are correctly engrossed; which report shall be entered on the journal. *Rule* 33.]

A bill from the other house is sometimes ordered to lie on the table. 2 *Hats.*, 97.

When bills, passed in one house and sent to the other, are grounded on special facts requiring proof, it is usual, either by message or at a conference, to ask the grounds and evidence; and this evidence, whether arising out of papers, or from the examination of witnesses, is immediately communicated. 3 *Hats.*, 48.

SEC. XLV.—AMENDMENTS BETWEEN THE HOUSES.

When either house, *e. g.* the House of Commons, send a bill to the other, the other may pass it with amendments.

The regular progression in this case is, that the commons disagree to the amendment; the lords insist on it; the commons insist on their disagreement; the lords adhere to their amendment; the commons adhere to their disagreement. The term of insisting may be repeated as often as they choose to keep the question open. But the first adherence by either renders it necessary for the other to recede or adhere also; when the matter is usually suffered to fall. 10 *Grey*, 148. Latterly, however, there are instances of their having gone to a second adherence. There must be an absolute conclusion of the subject somewhere, or otherwise transactions between the houses would become endless. 3 *Hats.*, 268, 270. The term of insisting, we are told by Sir John Trevor, was then (1679) newly introduced into parliamentary usage by the lords. 7 *Grey*, 94. It was certainly a happy innovation, as it multiplies the opportunities of trying modifications which may bring the houses to concurrence. Either house, however, is free to pass over the term of insisting, and to adhere in the first instance; 10 *Grey*, 146; but it is not respectful to the other. In the ordinary parliamentary course, there are two free conferences, at least, before an adherence. 10 *Grey*, 147.

Either house may recede from its amendment and agree to the bill; or recede from their disagreement to the amendment, and agree to the same absolutely, or with an amendment; for here the disagreement and receding destroy one another, and the subject stands as before the disagreement. *Elsynge*, 23, 27; 9 *Grey*, 476.

But the House cannot recede from, or insist on its own amendment, with an amendment; for the same reason that it cannot send to the other house an amendment to its own act after it has passed the act. They may modify an amendment from the other house by ingrafting an amendment on it, because they have never assented to it; but they cannot amend their own amendment, because they have, on the question, passed it in that form. 9 *Grey*, 363; 10 *Grey*, 240.

In Senate, March 29, 1798. Nor where one house has adhered to their amendment, and the other agrees with an amendment, can the first house depart from the form which they have fixed by an adherence.

In the case of a money bill, the lords' proposed amendments become, by delay, confessedly necessary. The commons, however, refused them, as infringing on their privilege as to money bills; but they offered themselves to add to the bill a proviso to the same effect, which had no coherence with the lords' amendments; and urged that it was an expedient warranted by precedent, and not unparliamentary in a case become impracticable, and irremediable in any other way. 3 *Hats.*, 256, 266, 270, 271. But the lords refused, and the bill was lost. 1 *Chand.*, 288. A like case, 1 *Chand.*, 311. So the commons resolved that it is unparliamentary to strike out, at a conference, anything in a bill which hath been agreed and passed by both houses. 6 *Grey*, 274; 1 *Chand.*, 312.

A motion to amend an amendment from the other house takes precedence of a motion to agree or disagree.

A bill originating in one house is passed by the other with an amendment.

The originating house agrees to their amendment with an amendment. The other may agree to their amendment with an amendment, that being only in the 2d and not the 3d degree; for, as to the amending house, the first amendment with which they passed the bill is a part of its text; it is the only text they have agreed to. The amendment to that text by the originating house, therefore, is only in the 1st degree, and the amendment to that again by the amending house is only in the 2d, to wit, an amendment to an amendment, and so admissible. Just so, when, on a bill from the originating house, the other, at its second reading makes an amendment; on the third reading this amendment is become the text of the bill, and if an amendment to it be moved, an amendment to that amendment may also be moved, as being only in the 2d degree.

SEC. XLVI.—CONFERENCES.

It is on the occasion of amendments between the houses that conferences are usually asked; but they may be asked in all cases of difference of opinion between the two houses on matters depending between them. The request of a conference, however, must always be by the house which is possessed of the papers. 3 *Hats.*, 31; 1 *Grey*, 425.

Conferences may be either simple or free. At a conference simply, written reasons are prepared by the house asking it, and they are read and delivered, without debate, to the managers of the other house at the conference; but are not then to be answered; 4 *Grey*, 144. The other house then, if satisfied, vote the reasons satisfactory, or say nothing: if not satisfied, they resolve them not satisfactory, and ask a conference on the subject of the last conference, where they read and deliver, in like manner, written answers to those reasons. 3 *Grey*, 183. They are meant chiefly to record the justification of each house to the nation at large, and to posterity, and in proof that the miscarriage of a necessary measure is not imputable to them. 3 *Grey*, 255. At free conferences, the managers discuss, viva voce and freely, and interchange propositions for such modifications as may be made in a parliamentary way, and may bring the sense of the two houses together. And each party reports in writing to their respective houses the substance of what is said on both sides, and it is entered in their journals. 9 *Grey*, 220; 3 *Hats.*, 280. This report cannot be amended or altered, as that of a committee may be. *Journal Senate, May* 24, 1796.

A conference may be asked, before the house asking it has come to a resolution of disagreement, insisting or adhering. 3 *Hats.*, 269, 341. In which case the papers are not left with the other conferees, but are brought back to be the foundation of the vote to be given. And this is the most reasonable and respectful proceeding; for, as was urged by the lords on a particular occasion, "it is held vain, and below the wisdom of Parliament, to reason or argue against fixed resolutions, and upon terms of impossibility to persuade." 3 *Hats.*, 226. So the commons say, "an adherence is never delivered at a free conference, which implies debate." 10 *Grey*, 137. And on another occasion the lords made it an objection that the commons had asked a free conference after they had made resolutions of adhering. It was then affirmed, however, on the part of the commons, that nothing was more parliamentary than to proceed with free conferences after adhering, (3 *Hats.*, 269,) and we do in fact see inferences of conference, or of free conference, asked after the resolution of disagreeing. 3 *Hats.*, 251, 253, 260, 286, 291, 316, 349; of insisting, *Ib.*, 280, 296, 299, 319, 322, 355; of adhering, 269, 270, 283, 300; and even of a second or final adherence. 3 *Hats.*, 270. And in all cases of conference asked after a vote of disagreement, &c., the conferees of the house asking it are to leave the papers with the conferees of the other; and in one case where they refused to receive them, they were left on the table in the conference chamber. *Ib.*, 271, 317, 323, 354; 10 *Grey*, 146.

After a free conference, the usage is to proceed with free conferences, and not to return again to a conference. 3 *Hats.*, 270; 9 *Grey*, 229.

After a conference denied, a free conference may be asked. 1 *Grey*, 45.

When a conference is asked, the subject of it must be expressed, or the conference not agreed to. *Ord, H. Com.*, 89; 1 *Grey*, 425; 7 *Grey*, 31. They are sometimes asked to inquire concerning an offence or default of a member of the other house. 6 *Grey*, 181; 1 *Chand.*, 304. Or the failure of the other house to present to the King a bill passed by both houses, 8 *Grey*, 302. Or on information received, and relating to the safety of the nation. 10 *Grey*, 171. Or when the methods of Parliament are thought by the one house to have been departed from by the other, a conference is asked to come to a right understanding thereon. 10 *Grey*, 148. So when an unparliamentary message has been sent, instead of answering it, they ask a conference. 3 *Grey*, 155. Formerly an address or articles of impeachment, or a bill with amendments, or a vote of the House, or concurrence in a vote, or a message from the King, were sometimes communicated by way of conference. 6 *Grey*, 128, 300, 387; 7 *Grey*, 80; 8 *Grey*, 210, 255; 1 *Torbuck's Deb.*, 278; 10 *Grey*, 293; 1 *Chandler*, 49, 287. But this is not the modern practice. 8 *Grey*, 255.

A conference has been asked after the first reading of a bill. 1 *Grey*, 194. This is a singular instance.

SEC. XLVII.—MESSAGES.

Messages between the houses are to be sent only while both houses are sitting. 3 *Hats.*, 15. They are received during debate without adjourning the debate. 3 *Hats.*, 22.

[In Senate the messengers are introduced in any state of business, except, 1. While a question is putting. 2. While the yeas and nays are calling. 3. While the ballots are counting. *Rule* 46. The first case is short; the second and third are cases where any interruption might occasion errors difficult to be corrected. So arranged June 15, 1798.]

In the House of Representatives, as in Parliament, if the House be in committee when a messenger attends, the Speaker takes the chair to receive the message, and then quits it to return into committee, without any question or interruption. 4 *Grey*, 226.

Messengers are not saluted by the members, but by the Speaker of the House. 2 *Grey*, 253, 274.

If messengers commit an error in delivering their message, they may be admitted or called in to correct their message. 4 *Grey*, 41. Accordingly, March 13, 1800, the Senate having made two amendments to a bill from the House of Representatives, their Secretary, by mistake, delivered one only, which being inadmissible by itself, that house disagreed, and notified the Senate of their disagreement. This produced a discovery of the mistake. The Secretary was sent to the other house to correct his mistake, the correction was received, and the two amendments acted on de novo.

As soon as the messenger, who has brought bills from the other house, has retired, the Speaker holds the bills in his hand, and acquaints the House "that the other house have by their messenger sent certain bills," and then reads their titles, and delivers them to the Clerk, to be safely kept till they shall be called for to be read. *Hakew.*, 178.

It is not the usage for one house to inform the other by what numbers a bill has passed. 10 *Grey*, 150. Yet they have sometimes recommended a bill, as of great importance, to the consideration of the house to which it is sent. 3 *Hats.*, 25. Nor when they have rejected a bill from the other house, do they give notice of it; but it passes sub silentio, to prevent unbecoming altercations. 1 *Blackst.*, 183.

[But in Congress the rejection is notified by message to the house in which the bill originated.]

A question is never asked by the one house of the other by way of message, but only at a conference; for this is an interrogatory, not a message. 3 *Grey*, 151, 181.

When a bill is sent by one house to the other, and is neglected, they may send a message to remind them of it. 3 *Hats.*, 25; 5 *Grey*, 154. But if it be mere inattention, it is better to have it done informally, by communication between the speakers or members of the two houses.

Where the subject of a message is of a nature that it can properly be communicated to both houses of Parliament, it is expected that this communication should be made to both on the same day. But where a message was accompanied with an original declaration, signed by the party to which the message referred, its being sent to one house was not noticed by the other, because the declaration, being original, could not possibly be sent to both houses at the same time. 2 *Hats.*, 260, 261, 262.

The King having sent original letters to the commons,

afterwards desires they may be returned, that he may communicate them to the Lords. 1 *Chandler*, 303.

SEC. XLVIII.—ASSENT.

The house which has received a bill and passed it may present it for the King's assent, and ought to do it, though they have not by message notified to the other their passage of it. Yet the notifying by message is a form which ought to be observed between the two houses from motives of respect and good understanding. 2 *Hats.*, 142. Were the bill to be withheld from being presented to the King, it would be an infringement of the rules of Parliament. *Ib.*

[When a bill has passed both houses of Congress, the house last acting on it notifies its passage to the other, and delivers the bill to the Joint Committee of Enrolment, who see that it is truly enrolled in parchment.] When the bill is enrolled, it is not to be written in paragraphs, but solidly, and all of a piece, that the blanks between the paragraphs may not give room for forgery. 9 *Grey*, 143. [It is then put into the hands of the Clerk of the House of Representatives to have it signed by the Speaker. The Clerk then brings it by way of message to the Senate to be signed by their President. The Secretary of the Senate returns it to the Committee of Enrolment, who present it to the President of the United States. If he approve, he signs, and deposits it among the rolls in the office of the Secretary of State, and notifies by message the house in which it originated that he has approved and signed it; of which that house informs the other by message. If the President disapproves, he is to return it, with his objections, to that house in which it shall have originated; who are to enter the objections at large on their journal, and proceed to reconsider it. If, after such reconsideration, two-thirds of that house shall agree to pass the bill, it shall be sent, together with the President's objections, to the other house, by which it shall likewise be reconsidered; and if approved by two-thirds of that house, it shall become a law. If any bill shall not be returned by the President within ten days (Sundays excepted) after it shall have been presented to him, the same shall be a law, in like manner as if he had signed it, unless the Congress, by their adjournment, prevent its return; in which case it shall not be a law. *Const. U. S.*, I, 7.]

[Every order, resolution, or vote, to which the concurrence of the Senate and House of Representatives may be necessary, (except on a question of adjournment,) shall be presented to the President of the United States, and before the same shall take effect, shall be approved by him; or, being disapproved by him, shall be repassed by two-thirds of the Senate and House of Representatives, according to the rules and limitations prescribed in the case of a bill. *Const. U. S.*, I, 7.]

SEC. XLIX.—JOURNALS.

[Each house shall keep a journal of its proceedings, and from time to time publish the same, excepting such parts as may, in their judgment, require secrecy. *Const.*, I, 5.]

[The proceedings of the Senate, when not acting as in a Committee of the Whole, shall be entered on the journals as concisely as possible, care being taken to detail a true account of the proceedings. Every vote of the Senate shall be entered on the journals, and a brief statement of the contents of each petition, memorial, or paper presented to the Senate, be also inserted on the journal. *Rule* 32.]

[The titles of bills, and such parts thereof, only, as shall be affected by proposed amendments, shall be inserted on the journals. *Rule* 31.]

If a question is interrupted by a vote to adjourn, or to proceed to the orders of the day, the original question is never printed in the journal, it never having been a vote, nor introductory to any vote; but when suppressed by the previous question, the first question must be stated, in order to introduce and make intelligible the second. 2 *Hats.*, 83.

So also when a question is postponed, adjourned, or laid

on the table, the original question, though not yet a vote, must be expressed in the journals; because it makes part of the vote of postponement, adjourning, or laying it on the table.

Where amendments are made to a question, those amendments are not printed in the journals, separated from the question; but only the question as finally agreed to by the House. The rule of entering in the journals only what the House has agreed to, is founded in great prudence and good sense; as there may be many questions proposed, which it may be improper to publish to the world in the form in which they are made. 2 *Hats.*, 85.

[In both houses of Congress, all questions whereon the yeas and nays are desired by one-fifth of the members present, whether decided affirmatively or negatively, must be entered in the journals. *Const.*, I, 5.]

The first order for printing the votes of the House of Commons was October 30, 1685. 1 *Chandler*, 387.

Some judges have been of opinion that the journals of the House of Commons are no records, but only remembrances. But this is not law. *Hob.*, 110, 111; *Lex. Parl.*, 114, 115; *Jour. H. C.*, *Mar.* 17, 1592; *Hale, Parl.*, 105. For the lords in their house have power of judicature, the commons in their house have power of judicature; and both houses together have power of judicature; and the book of the Clerk of the House of Commons is a record, as is affirmed by act of Parl., 6 *H.* 8, *c.* 16; 4 *Inst.*, 23, 24; and every member of the House of Commons hath a judicial place. 4 *Inst.*, 15. As records they are open to every person, and a printed vote of either house is sufficient ground for the other to notice it. Either may appoint a committee to inspect the journals of the other, and report what has been done by the other in any particular case. 2 *Hats.*, 361; 3 *Hats.*, 27—30. Every member has a right to see the journals, and to take and publish votes from them. Being a record, every one may see and publish them. 6 *Grey*, 118, 119.

On information of a mis-entry or omission of an entry in

the journal, a committee may be appointed to examine and rectify it, and report it to the House. 2 *Hats.*, 194, 5.

SEC. L.—ADJOURNMENT.

The two houses of Parliament have the sole, separate, and independent power of adjourning each their respective houses. The King has no authority to adjourn them; he can only signify his desire, and it is in the wisdom and prudence of either house to comply with his requisition, or not, as they see fitting. 2 *Hats.*, 332; 1 *Blackstone*, 186; 5 *Grey*, 122.

[By the Constitution of the United States a smaller number than a majority may adjourn from day to day. I 5. But "neither house, during the session of Congress, shall, without the consent of the other, adjourn for more than three days, nor to any other place than that in which the two houses shall be sitting." I, 5. And in case of disagreement between them, with respect to the time of adjournment, the President may adjourn them to such time as he shall think proper. *Const.* II, 3.]

A motion to adjourn, simply, cannot be amended, as by adding "to a particular day;" but must be put simply "that this House do now adjourn?" and if carried in the affirmative, it is adjourned to the next sitting day, unless it has come to a previous resolution, "that at its rising it will adjourn to a particular day," and then the House is adjourned to that day. 2 *Hats.*, 82.

Where it is convenient that the business of the House be suspended for a short time, as for a conference presently to be held, &c., it adjourns during pleasure; 2 *Hats.*, 305; or for a quarter of an hour. 5 *Grey*, 331.

If a question be put for adjournment, it is no adjournment till the Speaker pronounces it. 5 *Grey*, 137. And from courtesy and respect, no member leaves his place till the Speaker has passed on.

SEC. LI.—A SESSION.

Parliament have three modes of separation, to wit: By adjournment, by prorogation or dissolution by the King, or by the efflux of the term for which they were elected. Prorogation or dissolution constitutes there what is called a session, provided some act has passed. In this case all matters depending before them are discontinued, and at their next meeting are to be taken up de novo, if taken up at all. 1 *Blackst.*, 186. Adjournment, which is by themselves, is no more than a continuance of the session from one day to another, or for a fortnight, a month, &c., ad libitum. All matters depending remain in statu quo, and when they meet again, be the term ever so distant, are resumed, without any fresh commencement, at the point at which they were left. 1 *Lev.*, 165; *Lex. Parl.*, *c.* 2; 1 *Ro. Rep.*, 29; 4 *Inst.*, 7, 27, 28; *Hutt.*, 61; 1 *Mod.* 252; *Ruffh. Jac. L. Dict. Parliament;* 1 *Blackst.*, 186. Their whole session is considered in law but as one day, and has relation to the first day thereof. *Bro. Abr. Parliament*, 86.

Committees may be appointed to sit during a recess by adjournment, but not by prorogation. 5 *Grey*, 374; 9 *Grey*, 350; 1 *Chandler*, 50. Neither house can continue any portion of itself in any parliamentary function beyond the end of the session without the consent of the other two branches. When done, it is by a bill constituting them commissioners for the particular purpose.

[Congress separate in two ways only, to wit: by adjournment, or dissolution by the efflux of their time. What, then, constitutes a session with them? A dissolution closes one session, and the meeting of the new Congress begins another. The Constitution authorizes the President, "on extraordinary occasions to convene both houses, or either of them." I, 3. If convened by the President's proclamation, this must begin a new session, and of course determine the preceding one to have been a session. So if it meets under the clause of the Constitution, which says, "the Congress shall assemble at least once in every year, and such meeting shall be on the first Monday in December, unless they shall by law appoint a different day." I, 4. This must begin a new session; for even if the last adjournment was to this day, the act of adjournment is merged in the higher authority of the Constitution, and the meeting will be under that, and not under their adjournment. So far we have fixed landmarks for determining sessions. In other cases it is declared by the joint vote authorizing the President of the Senate and Speaker to close the session on a fixed day, which is usually in the following form: "Resolved by the Senate and House of Representatives, that the President of the Senate and Speaker of the House of Representatives be authorized to close the present session by adjourning their respective houses on the —— day of ——."]

When it was said above that all matters depending before Parliament were discontinued by the determination of the session, it was not meant for judiciary cases, depending before the House of Lords, such as impeachments, appeals, and writs of error. These stand continued, of course, to the next session. *Raym.*, 120, 381, *Ruffh. Jack. L. D.*, *Parliament.*

[Impeachments stand, in like manner, continued before the Senate of the United States.]

SECTION LII.—TREATIES.

[The President of the United States has power, by and with the advice and consent of the Senate, to make treaties, provided two-thirds of the Senators present concur. *Const. U. S.*, II, 2.]

[Resolved, that all confidential communications made by the President of the United States to the Senate shall be, by the members thereof, kept secret; and that all treaties which may hereafter be laid before the Senate shall also be kept secret, until the Senate shall, by their resolution, take off the injunction of secrecy. *Rule* 38.]

Treaties are legislative acts. A treaty is the law of the land. It differs from other laws only as it must have the consent of a foreign nation, being but a contract with respect to that nation. In all countries, I believe, except England, treaties are made by the legislative power; and there also, if they touch the laws of the land, they must be approved by Parliament. Ware *v.* Hayton, 3 *Dallas' Rep.*, 223. It is acknowledged, for instance, that the King of Great Britain cannot by a treaty make a citizen of an alien. *Vattel, b.* 1, *c.* 19, *sec.* 214. An act of Parliament was necessary to validate the American treaty of 1783. And abundant examples of such acts can be cited. In the case of the treaty of Utrecht, in 1712, the commercial articles required the concurrence of Parliament; but a bill brought in for that purpose was rejected. France, the other contracting party, suffered these articles, in practice, to be not insisted on, and adhered to the rest of the treaty. 4 *Russel's Hist. Mod. Europe*, 457; 2 *Smollet*, 242, 246.

[By the Constitution of the United States this department of legislation is confided to two branches only of the ordinary legislature; the President originating, and the Senate having a negative. To what subjects this power extends has not been defined in detail by the Constitution; nor are we entirely agreed among ourselves. 1. It is admitted that it must concern the foreign nation party to the contract, or it would be a mere nullity, res inter alios acta. 2. By the general power to make treaties, the Constitution must have intended to comprehend only those subjects which are usually regulated by treaty, and cannot be otherwise regulated. 3. It must have meant to except out of these the rights reserved to the States; for surely the President and Senate cannot do by treaty what the whole government is interdicted from doing in any way. 4. And also to except those subjects of legislation in which it gave a participation to the House of Representatives. This last exception is denied by some, on the ground that it would leave very little matter for the treaty power to work on. The less the better, say others. The Constitution thought it wise to restrain the Executive and Senate from entangling and embroiling our affairs with those of Europe. Besides, as the negotiations are carried on by the executive alone, the subjecting to the ratification of the representatives such articles as are within their participation, is no more inconvenient than to the Senate. But the ground of this exception is denied as unfounded. For examine, *e. g.* the treaty of commerce with France, and it will be found that, out of 31 articles, there are not more than small portions of two or three of them which would not still remain as subjects of treaties, untouched by these exceptions.]

[Treaties being declared, equally with the laws of the United States, to be the supreme law of the land, it is understood that an act of the legislature alone can declare them infringed and rescinded. This was accordingly the process adopted in the case of France in 1798.]

[It has been the usage for the Executive, when it communicates a treaty to the Senate for their ratification, to communicate also the correspondence of the negotiators. This having been omitted in case of the Prussian treaty, was asked by a vote of the House, of February 12, 1800, and was obtained. And in December, 1800, the convention of that year between the United States and France, with the report of the negotiations by the envoys, but not their instructions, being laid before the Senate, the instructions were asked for, and communicated by the President.]

[The mode of voting on questions of ratification is by nominal call.]

[Whenever a treaty shall be laid before the Senate for ratification, it shall be read a first time for information only; when no motion to reject, ratify, or modify the whole, or any part, shall be received. Its second reading shall be for consideration, and on a subsequent day, when it shall be taken up as in a committee of the whole, and every one shall be free to move a question on any particular article, in this form: "Will the Senate advise and consent to the ratification of this article?" or to propose amendments thereto, either by inserting or by leaving out words, in which last case the question shall be, "shall the words stand part of the article?" And in every of the said cases, the concurrence of two-thirds of the Senators present shall be requisite to decide affirmatively. And when, through the whole, the proceedings shall be stated to the house, and questions be again severally put thereon, for confirmation, or new ones proposed, requiring in like manner a concurrence of two-thirds for whatever is retained or inserted.]

[The votes so confirmed shall, by the house, or a committee thereof, be reduced into the form of a ratification, with or without modifications, as may have been decided, and shall be proposed on a subsequent day, when every one shall again be free to move amendments, either by inserting or leaving out words; in which last case the question shall be, "Shall the words stand part of the resolution?" And in both cases the concurrence of two-thirds shall be requisite to carry the affirmative; as well as on the final question to advise and consent to the ratification in the form agreed to. *Rule* 37.]

[When any question may have been decided by the Senate, in which two-thirds of the members present are necessary to carry the affirmative, any member who voted on that side which prevailed in the question may be at liberty to move for a reconsideration; and a motion for reconsideration shall be decided by a majority of votes. *Rule* 44.]

SEC. LIII.—IMPEACHMENT.

[The House of Representatives shall have the sole power of impeachment. *Const. U. S.*, I, 3.]

[The Senate shall have the sole power to try all impeachments. When sitting for that purpose, they shall be on oath or affirmation. When the President of the United States is tried, the chief justice shall preside; and no person shall be convicted without the concurrence of two-thirds of the members present. Judgment in cases of impeachment shall not extend further than to removal from office, and disqualification to hold and enjoy any office of honor, trust, or profit under the United States. But the party convicted shall nevertheless be liable and subject to indictment, trial, judgment and punishment according to law. *Const.*, I, 3.]

[The President, Vice President, and all civil officers of the United States, shall be removed from office on impeachment for, and conviction of, treason, bribery, or other high crimes and misdemeanors. *Const.*, II, 4.]

[The trial of crimes, except in cases of impeachment, shall be by jury. *Const.*, III, 2.]

These are the provisions of the Constitution of the United States on the subject of impeachments. The following is a sketch of some of the principles and practices of England on the same subject:

Jurisdiction. The lords cannot impeach any to themselves, nor join in the accusation, because they are the judges. *Seld. Judic. in Parl.*, 12, 63. Nor can they proceed against a commoner but on complaint of the commons. *Ib.*, 84. The lords may not, by the law, try a commoner for a capital offence, on the information of the King or a private person, because the accused is entitled to a trial by his peers generally; but on accusation by the House of Commons, they may proceed against the delinquent, of whatsoever degree, and whatsoever be the nature of the offence; for there they do not assume to themselves trial at common law. The commons are then instead of a jury, and the judgment is given on their demand, which is instead of a verdict. So the lords do only judge, but not try the delinquent. *Ib.*, 6, 7. But Wooddeson denies that a commoner can now be charged capitally before the lords, even by the commons; and cites Fitzharris's case, 1681, impeached for high treason, where the lords remitted the prosecution to the inferior court. 8 *Grey's Deb.*, 325–7; *Wooddeson*, 601, 576; 3 *Seld.*, 1610, 1619, 1641; 4 *Blackst.*, 25; 73 *Seld.*, 1604, 1618; 9, 1656.

Accusation. The commons, as the grand inquest of the nation, become suitors for penal justice. 2 *Woodd.*, 597; 6 *Grey*, 356. The general course is to pass a resolution containing a criminal charge against the supposed delinquent, and then to direct some member to impeach him by oral accusation, at the bar of the House of Lords, in the name of the commons. The person signifies that the articles will be exhibited, and desires that the delinquent may be sequestered from his seat, or be committed, or that the peers will take order from his appearance. *Sachev. Trial*, 325; 2 *Woodd.*, 602, 605; *Lords' Journ.*, 3 *June*, 1701, 101; 1 *Wms.*, 616; 6 *Grey*, 324.

Process. If the party do not appear, proclamations are to be issued, giving him a day to appear. On their return they are strictly examined. If any error be found in them, a new proclamation issues, giving a short day. If he appear not, his goods may be arrested, and they may proceed. *Seld. Jud.*, 98, 99.

Articles. The accusation (articles) of the commons is substituted in place of an indictment. Thus, by the usage of Parliament, in impeachment for writing or speaking, the particular words need not be specified. *Sach. Tr.*, 325; 2 *Woodd.*, 602, 605; *Lord's Journ.*, 3 *June*, 1701; 1 *Wms.*, 616.

Appearance. If he appears, and the case be capital, he answers in custody: though not if the accusations be general. He is not to be committed but on special accusations. If it be for a misdemeanor only, he answers, a lord in his place, a commoner at the bar, and not in custody, unless, on the answer, the lords find cause to commit him, till he finds sureties to attend, and lest he should fly. *Seld. Jud.*, 98, 99. A copy of the articles is given him, and a day fixed for his answer. *T. Ray*; 1 *Rushw.*. 268; *Fost.*, 232; 1 *Clar. Hist. of the Reb.*, 379. On a misdemeanor, his appearance may be in person, or he may answer in writing, or by attorney. *Seld. Jud.*, 100. The general rule on accusation for a misdemeanor is, that in such a state of liberty or restraint as the party is when the commons complain of him, in such he is to answer. *Ib.*, 101. If previously committed by the commons, he answers as a prisoner. But this may be called in some sort judicium parium suorum. *Ib.* In misdemeanors the party has a right to counsel by the common law, but not in capital cases. *Seld. Jud.*, 102–5.

Answer. The answer need not observe great strictness of form. He may plead guilty as to part, and defend as to the residue; or, saving all exceptions, deny the whole or give a particular answer to each article separately. 1 *Rush.*, 274; 2 *Rush.*, 1374; 12 *Parl. Hist.*, 442; 3 *Lords' Journ.*, 13 *Nov.*, 1643; 2 *Woodd.*, 607. But he cannot plead a pardon in bar to the impeachment. 2 *Woodd.*, 615; 2 *St. Tr.*, 735.

Replication, rejoinder, &c. There may be a replication, rejoinder, &c. *Sel. Jud.*, 114; 8 *Grey's Deb.*, 233; *Sach. Tr.*, 15; *Journ. H. of Commons*, 6 *March*, 1640, 1.

Witnesses. The practice is to swear the witnesses in open House, and then examine them there; or a committee may be named, who shall examine them in committee, either on interrogatories agreed on in the House, or such as the committee in their discretion shall demand. *Seld. Jud.*, 120, 123.

Jury. In the case of Alice Pierce, 1 *R.* 2, a jury was empannelled for her trial before a committee. *Seld. Jud.*, 123. But this was on a complaint, not on impeachment by the commons. *Seld. Jud.*, 163. It must also have been for a misdemeanor only, as the lords spiritual sat in the case, which they do on misdemeanors, but not in capital cases. *Id.*, 148. The judgment was a forfeiture of all her lands and goods. *Id.*, 188. This, Seldon says, is the only jury he finds recorded in Parliament for misdemeanor; but he makes no doubt, if the delinquent doth put himself on the trial of his country, a jury ought to be empannelled, and he adds that it is not so on impeachment by the commons; for they are in loco proprio, and there no jury ought to be empannelled. *Id.*, 124. The Ld. Berkely, 6 *E.* 3, was arraigned for the murder of L. 2, on an information on the part of the King, and not on impeachment of the commons; for then they had been patria sua. He waived his peerage, and was tried by a jury of Gloucestershire and Warwickshire. *Id.*, 125. In 1 *H.* 7, the commons protest that they are not to be considered as parties to any judgment given, or hereafter to be given, in Parliament. *Seld. Jud.*, 133. They have been generally and more justly considered, as is before stated, as the grand jury; for the conceit of Seldon is certainly not accurate, and they are the patria sua of the accused, and that the lords do only judge, but not try. It is undeniable that they do try; for they examine witnesses as to the facts, and acquit or condemn, according to their own belief of them. And Lord Hale says "the peers are judges of law as well as of fact;" 2 *Hale, P. C.*, 275; consequently of fact as well as of law.

Presence of commons. The commons are to be present at the examination of witnesses. *Seld. Jud.*, 124. Indeed, they are to attend throughout, either as a committee of the whole House, or otherwise, at discretion, appoint managers to conduct the proofs. *Rushw. Tr. of Straff.*, 37; *Com. Journ.*, 4 *Feb.*, 1709–10; 2 *Woodd.*, 614. And judgment is not to be given till they demand it. *Seld. Jud.*, 124. But they are not to be present on impeachment when the lords consider of the answer of proofs and determine of their judgment. Their presence, however, is necessary at the answer and judgment in cases capital (*Id.*, 58, 159) as well as not capital; 162. The lords debate the judgment among themselves. Then the vote is first taken on the question of guilty or not guilty; and if they convict, the question, or particular sentence, is out of that which seemeth to be most generally agreed on. *Seld. Jud.*, 167; 2 *Woodd.*, 612.

Judgment. Judgments in Parliament, for death, have been strictly guided per legem terræ, which they cannot alter; and not at all according to their discretion. They can neither omit any legal part of the judgment nor add to it. Their sentence must be secundum, non ultra legem. *Seld. Jud.*, 168–171. This trial, though it varies in external ceremony, yet differs not in essentials from criminal prosecutions before inferior courts. The same rules of evidence, the same legal notions of crimes and punishments, prevailed; for impeachments are not framed to alter the law, but to carry it into more effectual execution against too powerful delinquents. The judgment, therefore, is to be such as is warranted by legal principles or precedents. 6 *Sta. Tr.*, 14; 2 *Woodd.*, 611. The chancellor gives judgment in misdemeanors; the lord high steward formerly in cases of life and death. *Seld. Jud.*, 180. But now the steward is deemed not necessary. *Fost.*, 144; 2 *Woodd.*, 613. In misdemeanors the greatest corporal punishment hath been imprisonment. *Seld. Jud.*, 184. The King's assent is necessary in capital judgments. (2 *Woodd.*, 614, contra,) but not in misdemeanors. *Seld. Jud.*, 136.

Continuance. An impeachment is not discontinued by the dissolution of Parliament, but may be resumed by the new Parliament. *T. Ray.*, 383; 4 *Com. Journ.*, 23 *Dec.*, 1790; *Lord's Jour.*, *May*, 15, 1791; 2 *Woodd.*, 618.

INDEX TO THE MANUAL.

A

D.

E.

F.

G.

H.

I.

J.

K.

L.

M.

P.

W.

Y.

RULES AND ORDERS

OF

THE HOUSE OF REPRESENTATIVES.

STANDING RULES AND ORDERS

FOR CONDUCTING BUSINESS IN

THE HOUSE OF REPRESENTATIVES OF THE UNITED STATES.

TOUCHING THE DUTY OF THE SPEAKER.

1. He shall take the chair every day precisely at the hour to which the House shall have adjourned on the preceding day; shall immediately call the members to order; and, on the appearance of a quorum, shall cause the journal of the preceding day to be read.—*April* 7, 1789.

2. He shall preserve order* and decorum;† may speak to points of order in preference to other members, rising from his seat for that purpose; and shall decide questions of order, subject to an appeal to the House by any two members—*April* 7, 1789; on which appeal no member shall speak more than once, unless by leave of the House.‡—*December* 23, 1811.

* By rule 22 it is made the duty of the Sergeant-at-arms to aid in the enforcement of order, under the direction of the Speaker.

† See rules 57, 58, 61, 62, and 65, on the subject of "decorum."

‡ Difficulties have often arisen as to a supposed discrepancy between the appeal contemplated in this rule and that referred to in rule 61. There is no discrepancy. The question of order mentioned in the second rule relates to motions or propositions, the applicability or relevancy, or their admissibility on the score of time, or in the order of business, &c. The "call to order," mentioned in rule 61, on which, in case of an appeal, there can be no debate, has reference only to "transgressions of the rules in speaking," or to indecorum of any kind. See also rule 133, in which debate on an appeal, pending a call for the previous question, is prohibited.

3. He shall rise to put a question, but may state it sitting.—*April* 7, 1789.

4. Questions shall be distinctly put in this form, to wit: "As many as are of opinion that (as the question may be) say *Ay;*" and after the affirmative voice is expressed, "As many as are of the contrary opinion, say *No.*" If the Speaker doubt, or a division be called for, the House shall divide; those in the affirmative of the question shall first rise from their seats, and afterwards those in the negative.* If the Speaker still doubt, or a count be required, by at least one-fifth of a quorum of the members, the Speaker shall name two members, one from each side, to tell the members in the affirmative and negative ; which being reported, he shall rise and state the decision to the House.—*March* 16, 1860.

5. The Speaker shall examine and correct the journal before it is read. He shall have a general direction of the Hall, and the unappropriated rooms in that part of the Capitol assigned to the House shall be subject to his order and disposal until the further order of the House. He shall have a right to name any member to perform the duties of the Chair, but such substitution shall not extend beyond an adjournment.—*December* 23, 1811, and *May* 26, 1824.

6. No person shall be permitted to perform divine service in the chamber occupied by the House of Representatives, unless with the consent of the Speaker.—*May* 19, 1804.

7. In all cases of ballot† by the House, the Speaker shall

* The manner of dividing the House, as originally established by the rule of April 17, 1789, was, that the members who voted in the affirmative went to the right of the Chair, those in the negative to the left. This was, doubtless, taken from the old practice of the House of Commons of England. The passing of the members to and fro across the House was found so inconvenient, and took up so much time, that the mode of dividing the House was, on the 9th of June, 1789, changed to the present form: the members of each side of the question rising in their seats and being there counted.

† The word here used in the original formation of the rule was *election*. On the 14th January, 1840, it was changed to the word *ballot*. According to the practice, however, this rule is held to apply to all cases of *election*.

vote; in other cases he shall not be required to vote, unless the House be equally divided, or unless his vote, if given to the minority, will make the division equal; and in case of such equal division, the question shall be lost.*—*April* 7, 1789.

8. All acts, addresses, and joint resolutions, shall be signed by the Speaker; and all writs, warrants and subpœnas, issued by order of the House, shall be under his hand and seal, attested by the Clerk.—*November* 13, 1794.

9. In case of any disturbance or disorderly conduct in the galleries or lobby, the Speaker (or chairman of the Committee of the Whole House,) shall have power to order the same to be cleared.—*March* 14, 1794.

OF THE CLERK AND OTHER OFFICERS.

10. There shall be elected at the commencement of each Congress, to continue in office until their successors are appointed, a Clerk, Sergeant-at-arms, Doorkeeper, and Postmaster, each of whom shall take an oath for the true and faithful discharge of the duties of his office, to the best of his knowledge and abilities, and to keep the secrets of the House; and the appointees of the Doorkeeper and Postmaster shall be subject to the approval of the Speaker; and, in all cases of election by the House of its officers, the vote shall be taken *viva voce.*—*March* 16, 1860.†

* On a very important question, taken December 9, 1803, on an amendment to the Constitution, so as to change the form of voting for President and Vice-President, which required a vote of two-thirds, there appeared eighty-three in the affirmative, and forty-two in the negative; it wanted one vote in the affirmative to make the constitutional majority. The Speaker, (Macon,) notwithstanding a prohibition in the rule as it then existed, claimed and obtained his right to vote, and voted in the affirmative; and it was by that vote that the amendment to the Constitution was carried. The right of the Speaker, as a member of the House, to vote on all questions is secured by the Constitution. No act of the House can take it from him when he chooses to exercise it.

† Until the adoption of this rule there was no law, resolution, rule, or order directing the appointment of the Clerk of the House. On the 1st of April, 1789, being the first day that a quorum of the House assembed under the

11. In all cases where other than members of the House may be eligible to an office by the election of the House, there shall be a previous nomination.—*April* 7, 1789.

12. In all other cases of ballot than for committees, a majority of the votes given shall be necessary to an election; and where there shall not be such a majority on the first ballot, the ballots shall be repeated until a majority be obtained.—*April* 7, 1789. And in all ballotings blanks shall be rejected, and not taken into the count in enumeration of votes, or reported by the tellers.—*September* 15, 1837.

13. It shall be the duty of the Clerk to make, and cause to be printed, and delivered to each member, at the commencement of every session of Congress, a list of the reports which it is the duty of any officer or department of the government to make to Congress; referring to the act or resolution, and page of the volume of the laws or journal in which it may be contained; and placing under the name of each officer the list of reports required of him to be made, and the time when the report may be expected.—*March* 13, 1822.

14. It shall be the duty of the Clerk of the House, at the end of each session, to send a printed copy of the journals thereof to the Executive, and to each branch of the legislature of every State.—*November* 13, 1794.

new Constitution, the House immediately elected a Clerk by ballot, without a previous order having been passed for that purpose; although in the case of a Speaker who was chosen on the same day, an order was previously adopted. A Clerk has been regularly chosen at the commencement of every Congress since. By the rules adopted in 1789, provision was made for the appointment of a Sergeant-at-arms and Doorkeeper. Immediately after the organization of the government under the present Constitution, a room was set apart in the Capitol for the reception and distribution of letters and packets to and from members of the House, without an order for that purpose, and was called the post office; it was superintended by the *Doorkeeper* and his assistants. On the 9th of April, 1814, a special allowance was made to the *Doorkeeper* to meet the expenses of this office. and he was authorized to appoint a Postmaster. The office continued on this footing till April 4, 1838, when an order was passed for the appointment of a Postmaster by the House itself. The provision for the election of all the officers of the House by a *viva voce* vote was adopted *December* 10, 1839

15. All questions of order shall be noted by the Clerk, with the decision, and put together at the end of the journal of every session.—*December* 23, 1811.

16. The Clerk shall, within thirty days after the close of each session of Congress, cause to be completed the printing and primary distribution, to members and delegates, of the Journal of the House, together with an accurate index to the same.—*June* 18, 1832.

17. There shall be retained in the library of the Clerk's office, for the use of the members there, and not to be withdrawn therefrom, two copies of all the books and printed documents deposited in the library.—*December* 22, 1826.

18. The Clerk shall have preserved for each member of the House, an extra copy, in good binding, of all the documents printed by order of either house at each future session of Congress.—*February* 9, 1831.

19. The Clerk shall make a weekly statement of the resolutions and bills (Senate bills inclusive) upon the Speaker's table, accompanied with a brief reference to the orders and proceedings of the House upon each, and the date of such orders and proceedings; which statement shall be printed for the use of the members.—*April* 21, 1836.

20. The Clerk shall cause an index to be prepared to the acts passed at every session of Congress, and to be printed and bound with the acts.—*July* 4, 1832.*

21. All contracts, bargains, or agreements, relative to the furnishing any matter or thing, or for the performance of any labor, for the House of Representatives, shall be made with the Clerk, or approved by him, before any allowance shall be made therefor by the Committee of Accounts.—*January* 30, 1846.

22. It shall be the duty of the Sergeant-at-arms to attend

* The Clerk is relieved of this duty by the Joint Resolution of September 28, 1850, which authorizes Little & Brown to furnish their Annual Statutes at Large instead of the edition formerly issued by the order of the Secretary of State.

the House during its sittings; *to aid in the enforcement of order, under the direction of the Speaker;** to execute the commands of the House from time to time; together with all such process, issued by authority thereof, as shall be directed to him by the Speaker.—*April* 14, 1789.

23. The symbol of his office (the mace) shall be borne by the Sergeant-at-arms when in the execution of his office.—*April* 14, 1789.†

24. The fees of the Sergeant-at-arms shall be, for every arrest, the sum of two dollars; for each day's custody and releasement, one dollar; and for travelling expenses for himself or a special messenger, going and returning, one-tenth of a dollar for each mile—*April* 14, 1789—necessarily and actually travelled by such officer or other person in the execution of such precept or summons.—*March* 19, 1860.

25. It shall be the duty of the Sergeant-at-arms to keep the accounts for the pay and mileage of members, to prepare checks, and, if required to do so, to draw the money on such checks for the members, (the same being previously signed by the Speaker, and indorsed by the member,) and pay over the same to the member entitled thereto.—*April* 4, 1838.

* The words in italics were inserted March 16, 1860.

† At the time this rule was adopted, "a proper symbol of office" for the Sergeant-at-arms was directed to be provided, "of such form and device as the Speaker should direct." In pursuance of this order, a mace, or "symbol," was procured, which represented the Roman fasces, made of ebony sticks, bound transversely with a thin silver band, terminating in a double tie or beau-knot near the top; at each end a silver band an inch deep, and on the top of each of the rods a small silver spear. A stem of silver, three-fourths of an inch in diameter, and two inches long from the centre of the fasces, supported a globe of silver about two and a half inches in diameter, upon which was an eagle, his claws grasping the globe, and just in the act of flight, his wings somewhat more than half extended. The eagle was massive silver, richly carved. The design was fine, and its whole execution beautiful; the entire height about three feet. The mace was destroyed at the conflagration of the Capitol on the 24th August, 1814, and was not replaced until recently. A temporary one was hastily gotten up (of common pine and painted) for the then next session of Congress, and was tolerated till the session of 1841–'42, when the one now in use was procured.

26. The Sergeant-at-Arms shall give bond, with surety, to the United States, in a sum not less than five nor more than ten thousand dollars, at the discretion of the Speaker, and with such surety as the Speaker may approve, faithfully to account for the money coming into his hands for the pay of members.—*April* 4, 1838.

27. The Doorkeeper shall execute strictly the 134th and 135th rules, relative to the privilege of the hall.—*March* 1, 1838. And he shall be required at the commencement and close of each session of Congress to take an inventory of all the furniture, books, and other public property in the several committee and other rooms under his charge, and shall report the same to the House; which report shall be referred to the Committee on Accounts, who shall determine the amount for which he shall be held liable for missing articles.—*March* 2, 1865. It is the duty of the Doorkeeper ten minutes before the hour for the meeting of the House each day, to see that the floor is cleared of all persons except those privileged to remain during the sessions of the House.—*March* 31, 1869.

28. The Postmaster shall superintend the post office kept in the Capitol for the accommodation of the members.—*April* 4, 1838.

OF THE MEMBERS.

29. No member shall vote on any question in the event of which he is immediately and particularly interested,* or in any case where he was not within the bar of the House when the question was put.†—*April* 17, 1789. When the roll call is

* Of late differences of opinion have occasionally arisen as to the *kind* of interest alluded to in this rule. It has been contended to apply to members who were merchants or manufacturers, or engaged in other business to be affected by tariffs or other bills touching rates of duties, &c. This construction has never been sustained by the House. The original construction, and the only true one, is direct *personal* or *pecuniary* interest.

† As originally adopted, the word *present* was used in this rule where the words "*within the bar of the House*" now appear. The alteration was made on the 14th September, 1837. By a decision of the House, at the 1st session of the thirty-fifth Congress, (See Journal, p. 337,) soon after its occupancy of the present hall, the "bar of the House" was defined to be "upon the floor of the hall, and not outside of *any* of the doors leading into it." And when interrogated as to his presence every member must answer the question for himself.

completed, the Speaker shall state that any member offering to vote does so upon the assurance that he was within the bar before the last name on the roll was called.—*March*, 19, 1869. *Provided, however*, that any member who was absent by leave the House may vote at any time before the result is announced.—*March* 2, 1865. It is not in order for the Speaker to entertain any request for a member to change his vote on any question after the result shall have been declared, nor shall any member be allowed to record his vote on any question, if he was not present when such vote was taken.—*May* 27, 1870.

30. Upon a division and count of the House on any question, no member without the bar shall be counted.—*November* 13, 1794.

31. Every member who shall be in the House when the question is put shall give his vote, unless the House shall excuse him.*—*April* 7, 1789. All motions to excuse a member from voting shall be made before the House divides, or before the call of the yeas and nays is commenced; and the question shall then be taken without debate.—*September* 14, 1837.†

32. The name of a member who presents a petition or memorial, or who offers a resolution to the consideration of the House, shall be inserted on the journals.—*March* 22, 1806.

33. No member shall absent himself from the service of the House, unless he have leave, or be sick or unable to attend.—*April* 13, 1789.

OF CALLS OF THE HOUSE.

34. Any fifteen members (including the Speaker, if there be one) shall be authorized to compel the attendance of absent members.—*April* 17, 1789.

35. Upon calls of the House, or in taking the yeas and

* By rule 30, the date of which is subsequent in date to this, a member who may be "in the House" is not allowed to vote, unless he be "within the *bar*," upon a division or count of the House.

† That part of rule 31 which allowed a brief verbal statement of reasons to be given by any member for requesting to be excused from voting was rescinded *January* 2, 1847.

nays on any question, the names of the members shall be called alphabetically.—*April* 7, 1789.

36. Upon the call of the House, the names of the members shall be called over by the Clerk, and the absentees noted; after which the names of the absentees shall again be called over; the doors shall then be shut, and those for whom no excuse or insufficient excuses are made may, by order of those present, if fifteen in number, be taken into custody as they appear, or may be sent for and taken into custody, wherever to be found, by special messengers to be appointed for that purpose.*—*November* 13, 1789, *and December* 14, 1795.

37. When a member shall be discharged from custody, and admitted to his seat, the House shall determine whether such discharge shall be with or without paying fees; and in like manner, whether a delinquent member, taken into custody by a special messenger, shall or shall not be liable to defray the expenses of such special messenger.—*November* 13, 1794.

ON MOTIONS, THEIR PRECEDENCE, ETC.

38. When a motion is made and seconded, it shall be stated by the Speaker; or, being in writing, it shall be handed to the Chair and read aloud by the Clerk, before debated.—*April* 7, 1789.

39. Every motion shall be reduced to writing if the Speaker or any member desire it.—*April* 7, 1789. Every *written* motion made to the House shall be inserted on the journals, with the name of the member making it, unless it be with.

* The rule, as originally established in relation to a call of the House, which was on the 13th of November, 1789, differed from the present rule in this: there was one day's notice to be given, and it required a vote of the House, and not *fifteen* members, to order a member into custody. It was changed to its present form on the 14th December, 1795. On the 7th January, 1802, it was changed back to its original form, to require "an order of the House" to take absent members into custody, and so remained until the 23d December, 1811, when it was again changed to what it is now—*i. e.*, fifteen members.

drawn on the same day on which it was submitted.—*March* 26, 1806.

40. After a motion is stated by the Speaker, or read by the Clerk, it shall be deemed to be in the possession of the House; but may be withdrawn at any time before a decision or amendment.—*April* 7, 1789.

41. When any motion or proposition is made, the question, "Will the House now consider it?" shall not be put unless it is demanded by some member, or is deemed necessary by the Speaker.—*December* 12, 1817.

42. When a question is under debate, no motion shall be received but to adjourn, to lie on the table, for the previous question, to postpone to a day certain, to commit or amend, to postpone indefinitely; which several motions shall have precedence in the order in which they are arranged*—*March* 13, 1822—and no motion to postpone to a day certain, to commit, or to postpone indefinitely, being decided, shall be again allowed on the same day, and at the same stage of the bill or proposition.

43. When a resolution shall be offered, or a motion made, to refer any subject, and different committees shall be proposed, the question shall be taken in the following order:

The Committee of the Whole House on the state of the Union; the Committee of the Whole House; a Standing Committee; a Select Committee.—*March* 13, 1825.

*This rule, as originally established, April 7, 1789, read thus: "When a question is under debate, no motion shall be received unless to *amend* it, to *commit* it, for the *previous* question, or to *adjourn*." On the 13th November, 1794, the *motion to postpone to a day certain* was introduced next after the previous question. On the 17th December, 1805, the rule was changed as follows: 1st, the previous question; 2d, to postpone indefinitely; 3d, to postpone to a day certain; 4th, to lie; 5th, to commit; 6th, to amend; 7th, to adjourn. On the 23d December, 1811, the order was changed as follows: 1st, to adjourn; 2d, to lie; 3d, the previous question; 4th, to postpone indefinitely; 5th, to postpone to a day certain; 6th, to commit; 7th, to amend. On the 13th March, 1822, they were classed as above, and were declared, for the first time, to have precedence according to their arrangement; previous to which the notions of the Speaker often governed as to the precedence of these motions; and hence the direction of the rule.

44. A motion to adjourn, and a motion to fix the day to which the House shall adjourn, shall be always in order*—*April* 7, 1789, *and January* 14, 1840; these motions, and the motion to lie on the table, shall be decided without debate.†—*November* 13, 1794; *March* 13, 1822.

45. The hour at which every motion to adjourn is made shall be entered on the journal.—*October* 9, 1837.

46. Any member may call for the division of a question, *before or after the main question is ordered*,‡ which shall be divided if it comprehend propositions in substance so distinct that, one being taken away, a substantive proposition shall remain for the decision of the House.—*September* 15, 1837. A motion to strike out and insert shall be deemed indivisible—*December* 23, 1811; but a motion to strike out being lost, shall preclude neither amendment nor a motion to strike out and insert.—*March* 13, 1822.

47. Motions and reports may be committed at the pleasure of the House.—*April* 7, 1789.

48. No motion or proposition on a subject different from that under consideration shall be admitted under color of amendment.§—*March* 13, 1822. No bill or resolution shall,

* It has been decided and acted upon that, under this rule, "a motion to fix the day to which the House shall adjourn" takes precedence of a motion to adjourn. The reason of this decision is, that, before the House adjourned, it was proper to fix the time to which it should adjourn. To this decision, and upon this reasoning, no objection has been made.

† In the first rules established by the House, on the 7th April, 1789, it was directed that "when the House adjourns, the members shall keep their seats until the Speaker goes forth, and then the members shall follow." This rule was left out of the rules established 13th November, 1794. On the 13th March, 1822, a rule was adopted prohibiting a motion to adjourn before four o'clock if there was a pending question; it was rescinded on the 13th of March, 1824. On the 13th of March, 1822, a rule was also adopted against the rising of the Committee of the Whole before four o'clock, which was abrogated on the 25th of March, 1824.

‡ The words in italics were inserted in this rule *March* 16, 1860.

§ This rule was originally established on the 7th April, 1789, and was in these words: "*No new* motion or proposition shall be admitted under color of at any time, be amended by annexing thereto, or incorporating therewith, any other bill or resolution pending before the House.*—*September* 15, 1837.

49 When a motion has been once made, and carried in the affirmative or negative, it shall be in order for any member of the majority to move for the reconsideration thereof —*January* 7, 1802—on the same or succeeding day—*December* 23, 1811; and such motion shall take precedence of all other questions, except a motion to adjourn†—*May* 6, 1828—and shall not be withdrawn after the said succeeding

amendment, as a *substitute* for the motion or proposition under debate." On the 13th March, 1822, it was changed to its present form, in which the words *new* and *substitute* do not appear.

* The latter clause of this rule was adopted at the first session of the 25th Congress; and as originally reported by the committee, the following words were contained at the end of it: "Nor by any proposition containing *the substance*, in whole or in part, of any other bill or resolution pending before the House." These words were stricken out by the House before it would agree to the rule; by which it would seem to be decided that a bill or resolution might be amended by incorporating therein the *substance* of any other bill or resolution before the House. Such has been the general practice of the House.

† A difference of opinion and a discrepancy in action have sometimes occurred in administering this rule. Twenty years ago, and previously, a motion to reconsider could not be made after the subject was disposed of, if there was another subject before the House, until that subject had passed away; it was then often too late to make the motion. It was under this practice that Mr. Randolph was unable to move a reconsideration of the settlement of the celebrated Missouri question, (notice of which he gave out of time,) as, before he could do so, the bill had been taken to the Senate. The practice of late years has been changed, so as to allow the motion to reconsider to be made at any moment within the prescribed time. If the motion be made when a different subject is before the House, it is entered, and remains until that subject is disposed of, and then "takes precedence of all other business, except a motion to adjourn." When any final vote has been taken, and a motion made to reconsider, that motion may be laid on the table; in which case, according to the practice of several years past, the vote stands as though the motion to reconsider had not been made. This is correct; as, if the House wished to retain the matter, it would agree to the motion to reconsider, instead of laying it on the table. Motions to reconsider should be promptly acted on, otherwise it is in the power of a single member (voting on the strong side against his sentiments, solely for the purpose of placing himself in a situation to make the motion) to arrest business which a majority have determined to despatch.

day without the consent of the House; and thereafter any member may call it up for consideration.—*March* 2, 1848.

50. In filling up blanks, the largest sum and longest time shall be first put.—*April* 7, 1789.

ORDER OF BUSINESS OF THE DAY.

51. As soon as the journal is read, and the unfinished business in which the House was engaged at the last preceding adjournment has been disposed of, reports from committees shall be called for and disposed of; in doing which the Speaker shall call upon each standing committee in regular order, and then upon select committees; and if the Speaker shall not get through the call upon the committees before the House passes to other business, he shall resume the next call where he left off—*September* 15, 1837—giving preference to the report last under consideration: *Provided*, That whenever any committee shall have occupied the morning hour on two days, it shall not be in order for such committee to report further until the other committees shall have been called in their turn.*—*December* 7, 1857.†

52. Reports from committees having been presented and disposed of, the Speaker shall call for resolutions from the members of each State and delegate from each Territory, beginning with Maine and the Territory last organized, alternately; and they shall not be debated on the very day of their being presented, nor on any day assigned by the House for the receipt of resolutions, unless where the House shall direct otherwise, but shall lie on the table, to be taken up

* This proviso does not restrain the House from considering a report already made for a longer period than two days; simply prevents a committee from *reporting further* after occupying that period.

† This rule, as it originally stood, was amended in the revision of the rules at the 1st session of the 36th Congress, viz: so as to provide for the consideration of the unfinished business at the last adjournment immediately after the journal is read; to give preference to the report last under consideration, without the necessity for the pendency of a motion to commit; other amendments were made at the same time, which were rescinded January 11, 1867.

in the order in which they were presented; and if on any day the whole of the States and Territories shall not be called, the Speaker shall begin on the next day where he left off the previous day: *Provided*, That no member shall offer more than one resolution, or one series of resolutions, all relating to the same subject, until all the States and Territories shall have been called.—*January* 14, 1829.

53. A proposition requesting information from the President of the United States, or directing it to be furnished by the head of either of the executive departments, or by the Postmaster General, shall lie on the table one day for consideration, unless otherwise ordered by the unanimous consent of the House—*December* 13, 1820—and all such propositions shall be taken up for consideration in the order they were presented, immediately after reports are called for from select committees, and when adopted, the Clerk shall cause the same to be delivered.—*January* 22, 1822.

54. After one hour shall have been devoted to reports from committees and resolutions, it shall be in order, pending the consideration or discussion thereof, to entertain a motion that the House do now proceed to dispose of the business on the Speaker's table, and to the orders of the day—*January* 5, 1832; which being decided in the affirmative, the Speaker shall dispose of the business on his table in the following order, viz:

1st. Messages and other executive communications.

2d. Messages from the Senate, and amendments proposed by the Senate to bills of the House.

3d. Bills and resolutions from the Senate on their first and second reading, that they be referred to committees and put under way; but if, on being read a second time, no motion being made to commit, they are to be ordered to their third reading, unless objection be made; in which case, if not otherwise ordered by a majority of the House, they are to be laid on the table in the general file of bills on the Speaker's table, to be taken up in their turn.

4th. Engrossed bills and bills from the Senate on their third reading.

5th. Bills of the House and from the Senate, on the Speaker's table, on their engrossment, or on being ordered to a third reading, to be taken up and considered in the order of time in which they passed to a second reading.

The messages, communications, and bills on his table having been disposed of, the Speaker shall then proceed to call the orders of the day.—*September* 14, 1837.

55. The business specified in the 54th and 130th rules shall be done at no other part of the day, except by per mission of the House.—*December* 23, 1811.

56. The consideration of the unfinished business in which the House may be engaged at an adjournment shall be resumed as soon as the journal of the next day is read, and at the same time each day thereafter until disposed of; and if, from any cause, other business shall intervene, it shall be resumed as soon as such other business is disposed of. And the consideration of all other unfinished business shall be resumed whenever the class of business to which it belongs shall be in order under the rules.—*March* 18, 1860.*

OF DECORUM AND DEBATE.

57. When any member is about to speak in debate, or deliver any matter to the House, he shall rise from his seat and respectfully address himself to "Mr. Speaker"—*April* 7, 1789—and shall confine himself to the question under debate, and avoid personality.—*December* 23, 1811.

* The rule of November 13, 1794, for which this was substituted, provided that "the unfinished business in which the House was engaged at the last preceding adjournment shall have preference in the orders of the day; and no motion on any other business shall be received, without special leave of the House, until the former is disposed of." The object of the new rule was to give the unfinished business a more certain, as well as highly privileged, position. According to the construction given this rule, the unfinished business on *private bill days* is not resumed until the *next private bill day*, and the first hour after the reading of the journal on Monday is devoted to the objects contemplated by the 51st and 130th rules.

58. Members may address the House or committee from the Clerk's desk, or from a place near the Speaker's chair.

59. When two or more members happen to rise at once, the Speaker shall name the member who is first to speak.—*April* 7, 1789.

60. No member shall occupy more than one hour in debate on any question in the House, or in committee; but a member reporting the measure under consideration from a committee may open and close the debate: *Provided*, That where debate is closed by order of the House, any member shall be allowed, in committee, five minutes to explain any amendment he may offer—*December* 18, 1847—after which any member who shall first obtain the floor shall be allowed to speak five minutes in opposition to it, and there shall be no further debate on the amendment; but the same privilege of debate shall be allowed in favor of and against any amendment that may be offered to the amendment; and neither the amendment nor an amendment to the amendment shall be withdrawn by the mover thereof, unless by the unanimous consent of the committee.—*August* 14, 1850: *Provided, further*, That the House may, by the vote of a majority of the members present, at any time after the five minutes' debate has taken place upon proposed amendments to any section or paragraph of a bill, close all debate upon such section or paragraph, or at their election upon the pending amendments only.—*March* 19, 1860.*

61. If any member, in speaking or otherwise, transgress the rules of the House, the Speaker shall, or any member may, call to order; in which case, the member so called to order shall immediately sit down, unless permitted to explain; and the House shall, if appealed to, decide on the

* This proviso was adopted so as to enable a majority to get a bill out of Committee of the Whole after a reasonable time has been occupied in debating amendments, and was reported at the same time with an amendment to the 123d rule, the effect of which was to prevent a practice of doubtful propriety by which the friends of a bill were in the habit of taking it out of Committee of the Whole by adopting a recommendation to strike out the enacting clause.

case, but without debate;* if there be no appeal, the decision of the Chair shall be submitted to. If the decision be in favor of the member called to order, he shall be at liberty to proceed; *if otherwise, he shall not be permitted to proceed, in case any member object, without leave of the House*;† and if the case require it, he shall be liable to the censure of the House.—*April* 7, 1789, *and March* 13, 1822.

62. If a member be called to order for words spoken in debate, the person calling him to order shall repeat the words excepted to, and they shall be taken down in writing at the Clerk's table; and no member shall be held to answer, or be subject to the censure of the House, for words spoken in debate, if any other member has spoken, or other business has intervened, after the words spoken, and before exception to them shall have been taken.—*September* 14, 1837.

63. No member shall speak more than once to the same question without leave of the House—*April* 7, 1789—unless he be the mover, proposer, or introducer of the matter pending; in which case he shall be permitted to speak in reply, but not until every member choosing to speak shall have spoken.—*January* 14, 1840.

64. If a question depending be lost by adjournment of the House, and revived on the succeeding day, no member who shall have spoken on the preceding day shall be permitted again to speak without leave.‡—*April* 7, 1789.

65. While the Speaker is putting any question, or ad-

* See rule 2, with note appended to it.

† That part of this rule which is printed in *italics* was adopted on the 13th March, 1822, with the exception of the words "in case any member object," which were inserted on the 14th September, 1837.

‡ There is no proceeding in the House to which this rule can be applied. It was originally framed in reference to that law of Parliament which says that all pending questions are lost by adjournment, and to be again considered must be moved anew. In the rules as revised and established on the 7th January, 1802, the prohibition to speak on the next day was confined to those who had spoken *twice* on the preceding day. It so remained until the 14th January, 1840, when the word *twice* was left out.

dressing the House, none shall walk out of or across the House ; nor in such case, or when a member is speaking, shall entertain private discourse ; nor while a member is speaking, shall pass between him and the Chair.—*April* 7, 1789. Every member shall remain uncovered during the session of the House.—*September* 14, 1837. No member or other person shall visit or remain by the Clerk's table while the ayes and noes are calling, or ballots are counting.—*September* 14, 1837. Smoking is prohibited within the bar of the House or gallery.—*February* 28, 1871.

66. All questions relating to the priority of business to be acted on shall be decided without debate.—*February* 21, 1803.

OF COMMITTEES.

67. All committees shall be appointed by the Speaker, unless otherwise specially directed by the House, in which case they shall be appointed by ballot ;* and if upon such ballot the number required shall not be elected by a majority of the votes given, the House shall proceed to a second ballot, in which a plurality of votes shall prevail ; and in case a greater number than is required to compose or complete a committee shall have an equal number of votes, the House shall proceed to a further ballot or ballots.—*January* 13, 1790.

68. The first named member of any committee shall be the chairman ; and in his absence, or being excused by the House, the next named member, and so on, as often as the case shall happen, unless the committee, by a majority of their number, elect a chairman.†—*December* 28, 1805.

* The rule as originally adopted, April 17, 1789, directed that the Speaker should appoint all committees, unless the number was directed to consist of more than three members ; in which case, the ballot was to be resorted to.

† The occasion of this rule was this : Mr. John Cotton Smith, of Connecticut, had been chairman of the Committee of Claims for several years, and on the 5th November, 1804, was reappointed. On the succeeding day he was excused from service on the committee, and his colleague, Samuel W. Dana, was appointed "in his stead." The committee considered Mr. Dana its chairman ; he

69. Any member may excuse himself from serving on any committee at the time of his appointment, if he is then a member of two other committees.—*April* 13, 1789.

70. It shall be the duty of a committee to meet on the call of any two of its members, if the chairman be absent, or decline to appoint such meeting.—*December* 20, 1805.

71. The several standing committees of the House shall have leave to report by bill or otherwise.—*March* 13, 1822.

72. No committee shall sit during the sitting of the House without special leave.—*November* 13, 1794.

73. No committee shall be permitted to employ a clerk at the public expense, without first obtaining leave of the House for that purpose.—*December* 14, 1838.

74. Thirty-four standing committees shall be appointed at the commencement of each Congress,* viz:

declined to act, contending that he was the tail. Being unable to agree, the committee laid the case before the House on the 20th November. Up to this time there was no rule or regulation as to the head of a committee. The *usage* had been that the first named member acted; but it was *usage* only. The subject was referred to a committee. On the 22d November, 1804, the committee reported, and recommended that the first named member be the chairman; and in case of his absence, or of his being excused by the House, the committee should appoint a chairman by a majority of its votes. The House rejected this proposition. The Committee of Claims the next day notified the House that, unless some order was taken in the premises, no business could be done by the committee during the session; and thereupon, on the 20th December, 1805, the House adopted the above rule. In this case the Committee of Claims availed itself of the privilege contained in the last clause of the rule, and elected Mr. Dana chairman, much against his wishes.

* Prior to the revision of the rules, in March, 1860, it was provided that the standing committees should be appointed at the commencement of each *session*. At the said revision the Committee on Engraving was abolished, and its duties transferred to the House members of the Committee on Public Printing.—(See Rule 100.) Originally the Committee of Claims was charged with revolutionary and land claims, and all sorts of pensions. On the 22d December, 1813, the duties of that committee were divided, and a committee was appointed called the *Committee on Pensions and Revolutionary Claims*. On the 9th of December, 1825, a separate committee on *Revolutionary Pensions* was created, leaving the business of *Invalid* pensions to the committee created on the 22d December,

A Committee of Elections.—*Nov.* 13, 1789.
A Committee of Ways and Means.—*Jan.* 7, 1802.
A Committee on Appropriations.—*March* 2, 1865.
A Committee on Banking and Currency.—*March* 2, 1865.
A Committee on the Pacific Railroad.—*March* 2, 1865.
A Committee of Claims.—*Nov.* 13, 1794.*
A Committee on Commerce.—*Dec.* 14, 1795.†
A Committee on Public Lands.—*Dec.* 17, 1805.‡
A Committee on the Post Office and Post Roads.—*Nov.* 9, 1808.§
A Committee for the District of Columbia.—*Jan.* 27, 1808.**
A Committee on the Judiciary.—*June* 3, 1813.
A Committee on Revolutionary Claims.—*Dec.* 22, 1813.‖
A Committee on Public Expenditures.—*Feb.* 26, 1814.
A Committee on Private Land Claims.—*April* 29, 1816.¶

} To consist of eleven members each. (March 3, 1873.)

1813. On the 13th December, 1825, four days after its institution, the designation of the Committee on Revolutionary Pensions was changed to the Committee on *Military Pensions*, and it was charged with both revolutionary and invalid pensions. On the 10th January, 1831, the Committee on Military Pensions became the present Committee on *Revolutionary Pensions*, and an additional committee was created called the *Committee on Invalid Pensions;* and the pension business was apportioned to the two committees, as set out in the duties assigned to the committees.

* See note (*) page 175.

† This committee was originally a Committee on Commerce and *Manufactures*. On the 8th December, 1819, a Committee on *Manufactures* was constituted, but no duties have been assigned to that committee in the rules.

‡ The 3d of January, 1805, was the first time at which it was proposed to appoint a Committee on Public Lands. The proposition was then made by Mr. John Boyle, of Kentucky, and was *rejected.* On the 17th December, 1805, the committee was constituted for the first time. Previous to that day the business relating to the lands of the United States was either sent to the Committee of Claims or to a select committee, and frequently in parts to both.

§ From the earliest stages of the government a *select* committee was annually raised upon the subject of "the Post Office and Post Roads," and was always composed of a member from each State. A *standing* committee was instituted on the 9th November, 1808, and, like the select committees, was directed to be composed of a member from each State. On the 23d December, 1811, it was directed to be composed of the same number of members as the other standing committees.

‖ See note (*) page 175.

¶ When the Committee on Private Land Claims was first constituted, it was composed of five members—two less than the other committees. On the 19th December, 1817, it was directed to be composed of seven members.

** By Rule 162 the Speaker is directed to appoint the Delegate from the said District an additional member of the said committee.

A Committee on Manufactures.—*Dee.* 8, 1819.*
A Committee on Agriculture.—*May* 3, 1820.*
A Committee on Indian Affairs.—*Dec.* 18, 1821.*
A Committee on Military Affairs.—*March* 13, 1822.
A Committee on the Militia.—*Dec.* 10, 1835.
A Committee on Naval Affairs.—*March* 13, 1822.
A Committee on Foreign Affairs.—*March* 13, 1822.
A Committee on the Territories.—*Dec.* 13, 1825.§
A Committee on Revolutionary Pensions.—*Dec.* 9, 1825.†
A Committee on Invalid Pensions.—*Jan.* 10, 1831.
A Committee on Railways and Canals.—April 9, 1869.
A Committee on Mines and Mining.—*Dec.* 19, 1865.
A Committee on Freedmen's Affairs.—*Dec.* 4, 1866.
A Committee on Education and Labor.—*March* 21, 1867.
A Committee on the Revision of the Laws.—*July* 25, 1868.
A Committee on Public Buildings and Grounds.—*March* 10, 1871.

} To consist of eleven members each. (March 3, 1873.)

A Committee on Coinage, Weights, and Measures.—*Jan.* 21, 1864—*March* 2, 1867. } To consist of seven members.

A Committee on Patents.—*Sept.* 15, 1837.
A Committee of Accounts.—*Nov.* 7, 1804.‡
A Committee on Mileage.—*Sept.* 15, 1837.

} To consist of five member each.

75. It shall be the duty of the Committee of Elections to examine and report upon the certificates of election, or other credentials, of the members returned to serve in this House, and to take into their consideration all such petitions and other matters touching elections and returns as shall or may be presented or come into question, and be referred to them by the House.—*November* 13, 1789; *November* 13, 1794.

76. It shall be the duty of the Committee on Appropriations to take into consideration all executive communications and such other propositions in regard to carrying on the several departments of the government as may be presented and referred to them by the House.—*March* 2, 1865. In

* There are no duties assigned to the Committees on Manufactures, Agriculture, and Indian Affairs, in the Rules.

† See note (*), page 175.

‡ The Committee of Accounts was first constituted as a select committee on the 7th of November, 1804. It was made a standing committee December 17, 1805.

§ By Rule 162 the Speaker is directed to appoint one of the Delegates an additional member of the said committee.

preparing bills of appropriations for other objects, the Committee on Appropriations shall not include appropriations for carrying into effect treaties made by the United States; and where an appropriation bill shall be referred to them for their consideration, which contains appropriations for carrying a treaty into effect, and for other objects, they shall propose such amendments as shall prevent appropriations for carrying a treaty into effect being included in the same bill with appropriations for other objects.—*March* 2, 1865.

77. It shall also be the duty of the Committee on Appropriations, within thirty days after their appointment, at every session of Congress, commencing on the first Monday of December, to report the general appropriation bills—*September* 14, 1837—for legislative, executive, and judicial expenses; for sundry civil expenses; for consular and diplomatic expenses; for the army; for the navy; for the expenses of the Indian department; for the payment of invalid and other pensions; for the support of the Military Academy; for fortifications; for the service of the Post Office Department, and for mail transportation by ocean steamers; or, in failure thereof, the reasons of such failure. And said committee shall have leave to report said bills (for reference only) at any time.—*March* 2, 1865.* In all cases where appropriations cannot be made specific in amount, the maximum to be expended shall be stated, and each appropriation bill, when reported from the committee, shall, in the concluding clause, state the sum total of all the items contained in said bill.—*March* 15, 1867.

78. It shall be the duty of the Committee of Claims to take into consideration all such petitions and matters or things

* By the rule of *September* 14, 1837, the general appropriation bills were declared to be the "civil and diplomatic," "army," "navy," and "Indian." The present enumeration includes all that in the recent practice of the House have been treated as general appropriation bills. The authority to the Committee of Ways and Means to report said bills at *any time* (for reference) was first conferred on the 19th March, 1860, and when the duty of reporting the appropriation bills was imposed upon the Committee on Appropriations, like authority was conferred on the latter committee. By *rule* 119 these bills may, at any time, by a majority vote, be made special orders.

touching claims and demands on the United States as shall be presened, or shall or may come in question, and be referred to them by the House; and to report their opinion thereupon, together with such propositions for relief therein as to them shall seem expedient.—*November* 13, 1794.

79. It shall be the duty of the Committee on Commerce to take into consideration all such petitions and matters or things touching the commerce of the United States as shall be presented, or shall or may come into question, and be referred to them by the House; and to report from time to time their opinion thereon.*—*December* 14, 1795.

80. It shall be the duty of the Committee on the Public Lands to take into consideration all such petitions and matters or things respecting the lands of the United States as shall be presented, or shall or may come in question, and be referred to them by the House; and to report their opinion thereon, together with such propositions for relief therein as to them shall seem expedient.—*December* 17, 1805.

81. It shall be the duty of the Committee on the Post Office and Post Roads to take into consideration all such petitions and matters or things touching the post office and post roads as shall be presented, or shall come in question, and be referred to them by the House; and to report their opinion thereon, together with such propositions relative thereto as to them shall seem expedient.—*November* 9, 1808.

82. It shall be the duty of the Committee for the District of Columbia to take into consideration all such petitions and matters or things touching the said District as shall be presented, or shall come in question, and be referred to them by the House; and to report their opinion thereon, together with such propositions relative thereto as to them shall seem expe-

* This commmittee was originally a Committee on Commerce *and Manufactures*. On the 8th December, 1819, a separate Committee on Manufactures was constituted, and the duties of the original Committee on Commerce and Manufactures have been confirmed, as above, by leaving out the words "*and Manufactures.*" There are no duties assigned in these rules to the Committee on Manufactures.

dient.—*January* 27, 1808. The third Friday of each month, from the hour of 2 o'clock p. m. until the adjournment of that day, shall, when claimed by the Committee for the District of Columbia, devoted exclusively to business reported from said committee; and said committee shall henceforth be omitted by the Speaker in the regular call of committee.—*March* 9, 1870.

83. It shall be the duty of the Committee on the Judiciary to take into consideration such petitions and matters or things touching judicial proceedings as shall be presented, or may come in question, and be referred to them by the House; and to report their opinion thereon, together with such propositions relative thereto as to them shall seem expedient.—*June* 3, 1813.

84. It shall be the duty of the Committee on Revolutionary Claims to take into consideration all such petitions and matters or things touching claims and demands originating in the revolutionary war, or arising therefrom, as shall be presented, or shall or may come in question, and be referred to them by the House; and to report their opinion thereupon, together with such propositions for relief therein as to them shall seem expedient.—*December* 22, 1813.

85. It shall be the duty of the Committee on Public Expenditures to examine into the state of the several public departments, and particularly into laws making appropriations of money, and to report whether the moneys have been disbursed conformably with such laws; and also to report from time to time such provisions and arrangements as may be necessary to add to the economy of the departments, and the accountability of their officers.*—*February* 26, 1814.

86. It shall be the duty of the Committee on Private Land Claims to take into consideration all claims to land which

* See note to rule 76. And further: on the 30th March, 1816, six Committees on Expenditures in the several departments of the government were created and added to the list of standing committees. On the 16th March, 1860, a Com mittee on Expenditures in the Interior Department was created. The duties assigned to the several committees would seem entirely to cover the duties of the Committee on Expenditures. (See rules 102 and 103.)

may be referred to them, or shall or may come in question; and to report their opinion thereupon, together with such propositions for relief therein as to them shall seem expedient.—*April* 29, 1816.

87. It shall be the duty of the Committee on Military Affairs to take into consideration all subjects relating to the military establishment and public defence which may be referred to them by the House, and to report their opinion thereupon; and also to report, from time to time, such measures as may contribute to economy and accountability in the said establishment.—*March* 13, 1822.

88. It shall be the duty of the Committee on the Militia to take into consideration and report on all subjects connected with the organizing, arming, and disciplining the militia of the United States.—*December* 10, 1835.

89. It shall be the duty of the Committee on Naval Affairs to take into consideration all matters which concern the naval establishment, and which shall be referred to them by the House, and to report their opinion thereupon; and also to report, from time to time, such measures as may contribute to economy and accountability in the said establishment.—*March* 13, 1822.

90. It shall be the duty of the Committee on Foreign Affairs to take into consideration all matters which concern the relations of the United States with foreign nations, and which shall be referred to them by the House, and to report their opinion on the same.—*March* 13, 1822.

91. It shall be the duty of the Committee on the Territories to examine into the legislative, civil, and criminal proceedings of the Territories, and to devise and report to the House such means as, in their opinion, may be necessary to secure the rights and privileges of residents and non-residents.—*December* 13, 1825.

92. It shall be the duty of the Committee on Revolutionary Pensions to take into consideration all such matters respecting pensions for services in the revolutionary war,

other than invalid pensions, as shall be referred to them by the House.—*January* 10, 1831.

93. It shall be the duty of the Committee on Invalid Pensions to take into consideration all such matters respecting invalid pensions as shall be referred to them by the House.—*January* 10, 1831.

94. It shall be the duty of the Committee on Roads and Canals* to take into consideration all such petitions and matters or things relating to roads and canals, and the improvement of the navigation of rivers, as shall be presented, or may come in question, and be referred to them by the House; and to report thereupon, together with such propositions relative thereto as to them shall seem expedient.—*December* 15, 1831.

95. It shall be the duty of the Committee on Patents to consider all subjects relating to patents which may be referred to them; and report their opinion thereon, together with such propositions relative thereto as may seem to them expedient.—*September* 15, 1837.

96. It shall be the duty of the Committee on Public Buildings and Grounds to consider all subjects relating to the public edifices and grounds within the city of Washington, and all the public buildings constructed by the United States which may be referred to them; and report their opinion thereon, together with such propositions relating thereto as may seem to them expedient.—*September* 15, 1837.—*March* 10, 1871.

97. [This rule, which prescribed the duty of the Committee of Revisal and Unfinished Business, was virtually rescinded by the resolution of July 25, 1868, abolishing the said committee and creating a Committee on the Revision of the Laws.]

98. It shall be the duty of the Committee of Accounts to superintend and control the expenditures of the contingent fund of the House of Representatives.—*December* 17, 1805; also to audit and settle all accounts which may be charged thereon.—*December* 23, 1811.

* The name of this Committee changed to "Railroads and Canals."—*April* 9, 1869.

99. It shall be the duty of the Committee on Mileage to ascertain and report the distance to the Sergeant-at-Arms for which each member shall receive pay.—*September* 15, 1837.

100. There shall be *referred by the Clerk to the members of the Committee on Printing on the part of the House*,* all drawings, maps, charts, or other papers, which may at any time come before the House for engraving, lithographing, or publishing in any way; which committee shall report to the House whether the same ought, in their opinion, to be published; and if the House order the publication of the same, that said committee shall direct the size and manner of execution of all such maps, charts, drawings, or other papers, and contract by agreement, in writing, for all such engraving, lithographing, printing, drawing, and coloring, as may be ordered by the House; which agreement, in writing, shall be furnished by said committee to the Committee of Accounts, to govern said committee in all allowances for such works, and it shall be in order for said committee to report at all times.—*March* 16, 1844.

101. It shall be in order for the Committee on Enrolled Bills—*March* 13, 1822—and the Committee on Printing to report at any time.—*March* 16, 1860.

102. Seven additional standing committees shall be appointed at the commencement of the first session in each Congress, whose duty shall continue until the first session of the ensuing Congress.—*March* 30, 1816.

To consist of five members each.

1. A committee on so much of the public accounts and expenditures as relates to the Department of State;

2. A committee on so much of the public accounts and expenditures as relates to the Treasury Department;

*So much of this rule as is printed in *italics* was inserted on the 19th of *March* 1860, and so much of the rule of *March* 16, 1844, as imposed these duties upon the Committee on Engraving was stricken out, thereby abolishing the latter committee.

3. A committee on so much of the public accounts and expenditures as relates to the Department of War;

4. A committee on so much of the public accounts and expenditures as relates to the Department of the Navy;

5. A committee on so much of the public accounts and expenditures as relates to the Post Office;

6. A committee on so much of the public accounts and expenditures as relates to the Public Buildings; and

7. A committee on so much of the public accounts and expenditures as relates to the Interior Department.*

103. It shall be the duty of the said committees to examine into the state of the accounts and expenditures respectively submitted to them, and to inquire and report particularly—

Whether the expenditures of the respective departments are justified by law;

Whether the claims from time to time satisfied and discharged by the respective departments are supported by sufficient vouchers, establishing their justness both as to their character and amount;

Whether such claims have been discharged out of funds appropriated therefor, and whether all moneys have been disbursed in conformity with appropriation laws; and

Whether any, and what, provisions are necessary to be adopted, to provide more perfectly for the proper application of the public moneys, and to secure the government from demands unjust in their character or extravagant in their amount.

And it shall be, moreover, the duty of the said committees to report, from time to time, whether any, and what, retrenchment can be made in the expenditures of the several departments, without detriment to the public service; whether any, and what, abuses at any time exist in the failure to enforce the payment of moneys which may be due to the United States from public defaulters or others; and

* The last named committee was created *March* 16, 1860.

to report, from time to time, such provisions and arrangements as may be necessary to add to the economy of the several departments and the accountability of their officers.—*March* 30, 1816.

It shall be the duty of the several committees on public expenditures to inquire whether any offices belonging to the branches or departments, respectively, concerning whose expenditures it is their duty to inquire, have become useless or unnecessary; and to report, from time to time, on the expediency of modifying or abolishing the same; also, to examine into the pay and emoluments of all offices under the laws of the United States; and to report, from time to time, such a reduction or increase thereof as a just economy and the public service may require.—*February* 19, 1817.

OF COMMITTEES OF THE WHOLE.

104. The House may at any time, by a vote of a majority of the members present, suspend the rules and orders for the purpose of going into the Committee of the Whole House on the state of the Union; and also for providing for the discharge of the Committee of the Whole House, and the Committee of the Whole House on the state of the Union—*January* 25, 1848; from the further consideration of any bill referred to it, after acting without debate on all amendments pending and that may be offered.*—*March* 11, 1844.

105. In forming a Committee of the Whole House, the Speaker shall leave his chair, and a chairman, to preside in committee, shall be appointed by the Speaker.†—*April* 7, 1789.

*In the re-arrangement of the rules under the resolutions of the House of *March* 16, 1860, this rule was separated from the 145th rule, of which it had previously formed a part.

†Originally the rule was silent as to the mode of appointing a chairman of the Committee of the Whole. He was appointed by the House by *nomination* and vote thereon. That practice became very inconvenient; and on the 13th November, 1794, the rule was amended by adding "by the Speaker." By rule 9, the chairman has power, in case of any disturbance or disorderly conduct in the galleries or lobby, to order the same to be cleared.

106. Whenever the Committee of the Whole on the state of the Union, or the Committee of the Whole House, finds itself without a quorum, the chairman shall cause the roll of the House to be called, and thereupon the committee shall rise, and the chairman shall report the name of the absentees to the House, which shall be entered on the journal.—*December* 18, 1847.

107. Upon bills committed to a Committee of the Whole House, the bill shall be first read throughout by the Clerk, and then again read and debated by clauses, leaving the preamble to be last considered; the body of the bill shall not be defaced or interlined; but all amendments, noting the page and line, shall be duly entered by the Clerk on a separate paper, as the same shall be agreed to by the committee, and so reported to the House.* After report, the bill shall again be subject to be debated and amended by clauses, before a question to engross it be taken.—*April* 17, 1789.

108. All amendments made to an original motion in committee shall be incorporated with the motion, and so reported.—*April* 7, 1789.

109. All amendments made to a report committed to a Committee of the Whole House shall be noted, and reported, as in the case of bills.—*April* 7, 1789.

110. No motion or proposition for a tax or charge upon the people shall be discussed the day on which it is made or offered, and every such proposition shall receive its first discussion in a Committee of the Whole House.—*November* 13, 1794.

111. No sum or quantum of tax or duty, voted by a Committee of the Whole House, shall be increased in the House until the motion or proposition for such increase shall be first discussed and voted in a Committee of the Whole House; and so in respect to the time of its continuance.—*November* 13, 1794.

*This refers to bills in manuscript and bills from the Senate. It was long after the date of this rule that the practice of printing the bills obtained.

112. All proceedings touching appropriations of money shall be first discussed in a Committee of the Whole House.*—*November* 13, 1794.

113. The rules of proceedings in the House shall be observed in a Committee of the Whole House, so far as they may be applicable, except the rule limiting the times of speaking—*April* 7, 1789; but no member shall speak twice to any question until every member choosing to speak shall have spoken.—*December* 18, 1805.

114. In Committee of the Whole on the state of the Union, the bills shall be taken up and disposed of in their order on the calendar; but when objection is made to the consideration of a bill, a majority of the committee shall decide, without debate, whether it shall be taken up and disposed of, or laid aside: provided, that general appropriation bills, and, in time of war, bills for raising men or money, and bills concerning a treaty of peace, shall be preferred to all other bills, at the discretion of the committee; and when demanded by any member, the question shall first be put in regard to them—*July* 27, 1848; and all debate on special orders shall be confined strictly to the measure under consideration.—*March* 16, 1860.†

OF BILLS.

115. Every bill shall be introduced on the report of a committee, or by motion for leave. In the latter case, at least one day's notice shall be given of the motion‡ in the

* This rule, as first adopted, required all proceedings touching appropriations of money to be first *moved* in Committee of the Whole. The word "*moved*" was struck out on the 17th December, 1805, as it was found in practice greatly to retard public business.

† This amendment was adopted for the purpose of reforming to some extent the practice which had previously prevailed in Committee of the Whole on the state of the Union, of indulging in general debate without regard to the measure under consideration.

‡ In the early stages of the government, before the institution of standing committees, it was the common practice to introduce bills, on motion for leave.

House, or by filing a memorandum thereof with the Clerk, and having it entered on the journal; and the motion shall be made, and the bill introduced, if leave is given, when resolutions are called for;* such motion, or the bill when introduced, may be committed.—*April* 7, 1789; *September* 15, 1837; *and March* 2, 1838. But the Speaker shall not entertain a motion for leave to introduce a bill or joint resolution for the establishment or change of post routes, and all propositions relating thereto shall be referred, under the rule, like petitions and other papers, to the appropriate committee.—*May* 5, 1870.

116. Every bill shall receive three several readings in the House previous to its passage; and bills shall be despatched in order as they were introduced, unless where the House shall direct otherwise; but no bill shall be twice read on the same day, without special order of the House.—*April* 7, 1789.

117. The first reading of a bill shall be for information, and, if opposition be made to it, the question shall be, "Shall this bill be rejected?" If no opposition be made, or if the question to reject be negatived, the bill shall go to its second reading without a question.†—*April* 7, 1789.

118. Upon the second reading of a bill, the Speaker shall state it as ready for commitment or engrossment; and, if committed, then a question shall be, whether to a select or

by individual members; the bills were then referred to a select committee, to examine and report upon. The practice, however, of introducing bills by members on leave, gradually grew into disuse as standing committees were created, and, for nearly thirty years, no case occurs on the journals. Within a few years past the practice has been revived and has now become very common, but it is, nevertheless, a very inconvenient one, and does not facilitate business. Previous to the 13th March, 1822, so strict was the House upon the introduction of bills, that standing committees had to obtain leave, in every case, to report by bill. On that day the 71st rule was adopted.

* See rule 130.

† If no opposition be made to a bill, or if the question to reject be negatived, and the bill receives its second reading forthwith, (as is usual,) it is always *understood* that it is by "special order of the House." In the rapid and hurried manner in which bills are now reported and acted upon, the motion is seldom or never made, nor is the question put, "Shall the bill be *now* read a second time?" The Speaker takes it for granted that the motion has been made and allowed, and announces the second reading as soon as the first reading is completed.

standing committee, or to a Committee of the Whole House; if to a Committee of the Whole House, the House shall determine on what day—*November* 13, 1794; if no motion be made to commit, the question shall be stated on its engrossment; and if it be not ordered to be engrossed on the day of its being reported, it shall be placed on the general file on the Speaker's table, to be taken up in order.—*September* 14, 1837. But if the bill be ordered to be engrossed, the House shall appoint the day when it shall be read the third time.—*November* 13, 1794.

119. General appropriation bills shall be in order in preference to any other bills of a public nature unless otherwise ordered by a majority of the House.—*September* 14, 1837.

And the House may, at any time, by a vote of a majority of the members present, make any of the general appropriation bills a special order.—*March* 16, 1860.*

120. No appropriation shall be reported in such general appropriation bills, or be in order as an amendment thereto, for any expenditure not previously authorized by law—*September* 14, 1837—unless in continuation of appropriations for such public works and objects as are already in progress, and for the contingencies for carrying on the several departments of the government.—*March* 13, 1838.

121. Upon the engrossment of any bill making appropriations of money for works of internal improvement of any kind or description, it shall be in the power of any member to call for a division of the question, so as to take a separate vote of the House upon each item of improvement or appropriation contained in said bill, or upon such items separately, and others collectively, as the members making the call may specify; and if one-fifth of the members present second said call, it shall be the duty of the Speaker to make such divisions

* This latter provision was inserted in the 145th rule March 16, 1860, but in the re-arrangement under the resolution of that date it was deemed more appropriate to annex it to this rule. By rule 114 all debate on special orders is confined strictly to the measure under consideration.

of the question, and put them to vote accordingly.—*February* 26, 1846.

122. The bills from the Court of Claims shall, on being laid before the House, be read a first and second time, committed to a Committee of the Whole House, and, together with the accompanying reports, printed.—*March* 16, 1860.

123. A motion to strike out the enacting words of a bill shall have precedence of a motion to amend; and, if carried, shall be considered equivalent to its rejection.—*March* 13, 1822. Whenever a bill is reported from a Committee of the Whole, with a recommendation to strike out the enacting words, and such recommendation is disagreed to by the House, the bill shall stand recommitted to the said committee without further action by the House.—*March* 16, 1860.* But before the question of concurrence is submitted, it is in order to entertain a motion to refer the bill to any committee, with or without instructions, and when the same is again reported to the House, it shall be referred to the Committee of the Whole without debate, and resume its original place on the calendar.—*May* 26, 1870.

124. After commitment and report thereof to the House, or at any time before its passage, a bill may be recommitted—*April* 7, 1789; and should such recommitment take place after its engrossment, and an amendment be reported and agreed to by the House, the question shall be again put on the engrossment of the bill.—*March* 16, 1860.†

125. All bills ordered to be engrossed shall be executed in a fair round hand.—*April* 7, 1789.

* This latter clause was inserted for the purpose of correcting a practice which had begun to obtain, whereby the friends of a bill were enabled, by striking out the enacting clause, to cut off debate and amendment and take a bill back into the House and there pass it. At the same time, however, an amendment was made to the 60th rule, whereby a majority is enabled, "at any time after the five minutes' debate has taken place upon proposed amendments to any paragraph or section of a bill, to close all debate upon such section or paragraph, or, at their election, upon the pending amendments only."

† Of late years, according to the practice, if the previous question on its passage be pending or ordered, a motion to recommit is not in order. The latter clause of this rule was adopted, for the first time, March 16, 1860, previous to which there had been no fixed rule in regard to the case therein provided for.

126. No amendment by way of *rider* shall be received to any bill on its third reading.--*April* 8, 1814.

127. When a bill shall pass, it shall be certified by the Clerk, noting the day of its passage at the foot thereof.—*April* 7, 1789.

LOCAL OR PRIVATE BUSINESS.

128. Friday and Saturday in every week shall be set apart for the consideration of private bills and private business, in preference to any other, unless otherwise determined by a majority of the House.—*January* 22, 1810, and *January* 26, 1826.*

129. On the first and fourth Friday and Saturday of each month the calendar of private bills shall be called over, (the chairman of the Committee of the Whole House commencing the call where he left off the previous day,) and the bills to the passage of which no objection shall then be made shall be first considered and disposed of.—*January* 25, 1839. But when a bill is again reached, after having been once objected to, the committee shall consider and dispose of the same, unless it shall again be objected to by at least five members.—*March* 16, 1860.†

OF BILLS ON LEAVE AND RESOLUTIONS.

130. All the States and Territories shall be called for bills on leave and resolutions every Monday during each session of Congress; and, if necessary to secure the object on said

* Under the rule of 26th April, 1828, relative to a postponement or change of the order of business, it has been decided that it takes *two-thirds* to proceed to public business on Friday and Saturday. The reason of this decision is, that the rule of the 26th of April, 1828, made no exception in favor of the clause for a *majority*, contained in this rule; and that therefore that provision was annulled. There have been three appeals upon this point, but the House in all instances affirmed the decision in favor of two-thirds.

† The rule of January 25, 1839, simply provided for calling over the calendar on the first and fourth Friday; the words "*and Saturday*" were added on the 16th March, 1860. The latter branch of the rule, which provides that upon a second call at least five members shall object, was adopted at the same time.

days, all resolutions which shall give rise to debate shall lie over for discussion, under the rules of the House already established; and the whole of said days shall be appropriated to bills on leave and resolutions, until all the States and Territories are called through.—*February* 6, 1838. And the Speaker shall first call the States and Territories for bills on leave; and all bills so introduced during the first hour after the journal is read shall be referred, without debate, to their appropriate committees: *Provided, however,* That a bill so introduced and referred, and all bills at any time introduced by unanimous consent and referred, shall not be brought back into the House upon a motion to reconsider.—*March* 16, 1860,* *and January* 11, 1872. And on said call, joint resolutions of State and Territorial legislatures for printing and reference may be introduced.—*January* 11, 1867.

OF PETITIONS AND MEMORIALS.

131. Members having petitions and memorials to present may hand them to the Clerk, indorsing the same with their names, and the reference or disposition to be made thereof; and such petitions and memorials shall be entered on the journal, subject to the control and direction of the Speaker, and if any petition or memorial be so handed in which, in the judgment of the Speaker, is excluded by the rules, the same shall be returned to the member from whom it was received.—*March* 29, 1842.†

OF THE PREVIOUS QUESTION.

132. The previous question‡ shall be in this form : "Shall

* The words "bills on leave" where they occur were inserted in this rule on the 16th March, 1860. By rule 115 it is required that at least one day's notice shall be given of the motion to introduce a bill on leave.

† So much of the rules as authorized the presentation of petitions in the House was stricken out December 12, 1853. According to the practice under this rule it is competent for a member to withdraw from the files petitions and memorials presented at a former Congress, and re-refer them.

‡ The previous question was recognized in the rules established April 7, 1789, and could be demanded by five members, (the parliamentary law places it in

the main question be now put?"—*April* 7, 1789. It shall only be admitted when demanded by a majority of the members present—*February* 24, 1812; and its effects shall be to put an end to all debate, and to bring the House to a direct vote upon a motion to commit, if such motion shall have been made; and if this motion does not prevail, then upon amendments reported by a committee, if any; then—*August* 5, 1848—upon pending amendments, and then upon the main question.—*January* 14, 1840. But its only effect, if a motion to postpone is pending, shall be to bring the House to a vote upon such motion. Whenever the House shall refuse to order the main question, the consideration of the subject shall be resumed as though no motion for the previous question had been made. The House may also, at any time, on motion seconded by a majority of the members present, close all debate upon a pending amendment, or an amendment thereto, and cause the question to be put thereon; and this shall not preclude any further amendment or debate

the power of two members—one to move, the other to second.) On the 23d December, 1811, it was placed on a footing with the yeas and nays; that is, at the command of *one-fifth of the members* present. It remained so until the 24th February, 1812, when the rule was changed to its present form of a *majority*. According to former practice, the previous question brought the House to a direct vote on the *main* question; that is, to agree to the main *proposition*, to the exclusion of all amendments and incidental motions; but on the 14th January, 1840, it was changed to embrace, first, *pending* amendments, and then the main proposition.

The original intent of the previous question was, to ascertain the sense of the House, in the early stages of a subject, as to the propriety of entertaining the matter; and if decided affirmatively, the debate went on; if decided negatively, the debate ceased, and the subject passed from before the House without motion or further question. This was the practice in Congress under the confederation; and it is still the practice in the British Parliament. Now, by the practice of the House, as well as by the terms of the rule, it is reversed: if the motion for the previous question is decided in the affirmative, debate ceases, and the House proceeds to vote; if in the negative, the proceedings go on as if the motion for the previous question had not been made. Until the revision of the rules in *March*, 1860, whenever the previous question was seconded, and the main question ordered, pending a motion to postpone, the motion to postpone was cut off.

upon the bill. A call of the House* shall not be in order after the previous question is seconded, unless it shall appear, upon an actual count by the speaker, that no quorum is present.—*March* 16, 1860.

133. On a previous question there shall be no debate.—*December* 17, 1805. All incidental questions of order, arising after a motion is made for the previous question, and pending such motion, shall be decided, whether on appeal or otherwise, without debate.—*September* 15, 1837.

OF ADMISSION ON THE FLOOR.

134. No person except members of the Senate, their secretary, heads of departments, the President's private secretary, foreign ministers, the governor for the time being of any State, senators and representatives elect, judges of the Supreme Court of the United States and of the Court of Claims, and such persons as have by name received the thanks of Congress—*March* 15, 1867—shall be admitted within the hall of the House of Representatives—*March* 19, 1860†—or any of the rooms upon the same floor or

* For the mode of proceeding in the case of a call of the House, see rules 36 and 37.

† The first rule for the admission within the hall of other than members was adopted on the 7th January, 1802, and was confined to "*Senators*, officers of the general and State governments, foreign ministers, and such persons as members might introduce." On the 11th January, 1802, an attempt was made to amend so as to exclude persons "introduced by members," which failed. On the 8th November, 1804, a proposition was made to confine the privilege to *Senators*, which also failed. On the 17th December, 1805, *officers of State governments* were excluded. On the 1st February, 1808, a proposition was made to admit ex-members of Congress and the judges of the Supreme Court. After a good deal of debate it was rejected. On the 11th February, 1809, the rule was enlarged so as to admit judicial officers of the United States, as also ex-members of Congress. On the 25th February, 1814, those who had been heads of departments were admitted. On the 10th February, 1815, officers who had received the thanks of Congress were included. On the 12th January, 1816, the navy commissioners. On the 21st February, 1816, governors of States and Territories. March 13, 1822, the President's secretary. On the 26th January, 1833, the rule was further enlarged by admitting "*such persons as the*

leading into the same—*March* 2, 1865; provided that ex-members of Congress who are not interested in any claim pending before Congress, and shall so register themselves, may also be admitted within the hall of the House; and no persons except those herein specified shall at any time be admitted to the floor of the House.—*March* 15, 1867.

OF REPORTERS.

135. Stenographers and reporters, other than the official reporters of the House, wishing to take down the debates, may be admitted by the Speaker to the reporters' gallery over the Speaker's chair, but not on the floor of the House; but no person shall be allowed the privilege of said gallery under the character of stenographer or reporter without a written permission of the Speaker, specifying the part of said gallery assigned to him; nor shall said stenographer or reporter be admitted to said gallery unless he shall state in writing for what paper or papers he is employed to report; nor shall he be so admitted, or, if admitted, be suffered to retain his seat, if he shall be or become an agent to prosecute any claim pending before Congress; and the Speaker shall give his written permission with this condition.—*December* 23, 1857.

UNFINISHED BUSINESS OF THE SESSION.

136. After six days from the commencement of a second or subsequent session of any Congress, all bills, resolutions,*

Speaker or a member might introduce;" and on the 10th December, 1833, the House, by a vote almost unanimous, rescinded that amendment. On the 23d of December, 1857, soon after removing into the new hall in the south wing of the Capitol Extension, the privilege of admission was restricted to "members of the Senate, their secretary, heads of departments, President's private secretary, the governor for the time being of any State, and judges of the Supreme Court of the United States." On the 19th of March, 1860, it was adopted in its present form, excepting the last clause, a proposition to admit ex-members having been rejected. The last clause, adopted March 2, 1865, was intended to prevent persons not entitled to the privilege of the hall from occupying the cloak and other adjoining rooms.

* The word "resolutions," as here used, has been construed to apply to joint resolutions only.

and reports which originated in the House, and at the close of the next preceding session remained undetermined, shall be resumed and acted on in the same manner as if an adjournment had not taken place.—*March* 17, 1848. And all business before committees of the House at the end of one session shall be resumed at the commencement of the next session of the same Congress, as if no adjournment had taken place.—*March* 16, 1860.*

MISCELLANEOUS.

137. Whenever confidential communications are received from the President of the United States, the House shall be cleared of all persons, except the members, Clerk, Sergeant-at-arms, and Doorkeeper,† and so continue during the reading of such communications, and (unless otherwise directed by the House) during all debates and proceedings to be had thereon. And when the Speaker, or any other member, shall inform the House that he has communications to make which he conceives ought to be kept secret, the House shall, in like manner, be cleared till the communication be made; the House shall then determine whether the matter communicated requires secrecy or not, and take order accordingly.—*February* 17, 1792, *and December* 30, 1793.

138. The rule for paying witnesses summoned to appear before this House, or either of its committees, shall be as follows: For each day a witness shall attend, the sum of four

* Prior to this date it had been the practice for several years, near the close of the first session of a Congress, for the House to adopt a resolution making a similar provision. This amendment was adopted to save the necessity for the passage of a similar resolution at every Congress.

† In the rule as originally established, on the 17th of February, 1792, it is provided that the House be cleared of all persons, except "the members and the Clerk." In the rules of the 13th of November, 1794, the language used is "the members of the House and its *officers*." In the edition of 7th January, 1802, the terms "members and Clerk" are again used, and on the 23d December, 1811, it was changed to its present form, so as to include the Sergeant-at-arms and Doorkeeper. By rule 10 it is provided that the Clerk, Sergeant-at-arms, Doorkeeper, and Postmaster, shall be sworn "to keep the secrets of the House."

dollars; for each mile he shall travel in coming to or going from the place of examination, the sum of five cents each way; but nothing shall be paid for travelling when the witness has been summoned at the place of trial.—*May* 31, 1872.

139. Maps accompanying documents shall not be printed, under the general order to print, without the special direction of the House.—*March* 2, 1837; *September* 11, 1837.*

140. No extra compensation shall be allowed to any officer or messenger, page, laborer, or other person in the service of the House, or engaged in or about the public grounds or buildings; and no person shall be an officer of the House, or continue in its employment, who shall be an agent for the prosecution of any claim against the government, or be interested in such claim otherwise than as an original claimant; and it shall be the duty of the Committee of Accounts to inquire into and report to the House any violation of this rule.—*March* 8, 1842.

141. When the reading of a paper is called for, and the same is objected to by any member, it shall be determined by a vote of the House.†—*November* 13, 1794.

142. When a question is postponed indefinitely, the same shall not be acted upon again during the session.—*December* 17, 1805.

143. Every order, resolution, or vote, to which the concurrence of the Senate shall be necessary, shall be read to the House, and laid on the table, on a day preceding that in which the same shall be moved, unless the House shall otherwise expressly allow.—*April* 7, 1789.

144. The rules of parliamentary practice comprised in Jefferson's Manual shall govern the House in all cases to which they are applicable, and in which they are not incon-

* See rule 100.

† As originally adopted, this rule contained, after the word "for," the words 'which had before been read to the House." They were stricken out on the 14th December, 1795.

sistent with the standing rules and orders of the House, and joint rules of the Senate and House of Representatives.—*September* 15, 1837.

145. No standing rule or order of the House shall be rescinded or changed without one day's notice being given of the motion therefor—*November* 13, 1794; nor shall any rule be suspended, except by a vote of at least two-thirds of the members present*—*March* 13, 1822; nor shall the order of business, as established by the rules, be postponed or changed, except by a vote of at least two-thirds of the members present; nor shall the Speaker entertain a motion to suspend the rules, except during the last ten days of the session, and on Monday of every week at the expiration of one hour after the journal is read†—*April* 26, 1828—unless the call of States and Territories for bills on leave and resolutions has been earlier concluded, when the Speaker may entertain a motion to suspend the rules.—*June* 8, 1864.

146. All elections of officers of the House, including the Speaker, shall be conducted in accordance with these rules, so far as the same are applicable; and, pending the election of a Speaker, the Clerk shall preserve order and decorum, and shall decide all questions of order that may arise, subject to appeal to the House.—*March* 19, 1860.

147. These rules shall be the rules of the House of Representatives of the present and succeeding Congresses unless otherwise ordered.—*March* 19, 1860.

148. An additional standing committee shall be appointed at the commencement of each Congress, whose duties shall continue until the first session of the ensuing Congress, to

* By *rule* 104 a *majority* may, *at any time*, suspend the rules for the purpose of going into Committee of the Whole on the state of the Union, and also for closing debate therein; and by *rule* 119 to make any of the general appropriation bills a special order. These are exceptions to this rule.

†The words "at the expiration of one hour after the journal is read" were inserted March 16, 1860, so as to enable the House, on Mondays, to receive reports, bills on leave, and resolutions, as provided for in *rules* 51 and 130, without interruption

consist of seven members, to be entitled a "Committee on Coinage, Weights, and Measures;" and to this committee shall be referred all bills, resolutions, and communications to the House upon that subject.—*January* 21, 1864; *March* 2, 1867.

149. The names of members not voting on any call of the ayes and noes shall be recorded in the journal immediately after those voting in the affirmative and negative, and the same record shall be made in the Congressional Globe. —*June* 8, 1864.

150. It shall be the duty of the Committee on the Pacific Railroad to take into consideration all such petitions and matters or things relative to railroads or telegraph lines between the Mississippi valley and the Pacific coast as shall be presented or shall come in question, and be referred to them by the House, and to report their opinion thereon, together with such propositions relative thereto as to them shall seem expedient.—*March* 2, 1865.

151. It shall be the duty of the Committee of Ways and Means to take into consideration all reports of the Treasury Department, and such other propositions relative to raising revenue and providing ways and means for the support of the government as shall be presented or shall come in question, and be referred to them by the House, and to report their opinion thereon by bill or otherwise, as to them shall seem expedient; and said committee shall have leave to report for commitment at any time.—*March* 2, 1865.

152. It shall be the duty of the Committee on Banking and Currency to take into consideration all propositions relative to banking and the currency as shall be presented or shall come in question, and be referred to them by the House, and to report thereon by bill or otherwise.—*March* 2, 1865.

153. It shall be the duty of the Committee on Mines and Mining to consider all subjects relating to mines and mining that may be referred to them, and to report their opinion thereon, together with such propositions relative thereto as may seem to them expedient.—*December* 19, 1865.

154. The allowance of stationery to each member and delegate shall be of the value of seventy-five dollars for a long session, and forty-five dollars for a short session of Congress.—*December* 19, 1865. [By the act of March 3, 1873, it is provided that the increased compensation thereby allowed shall be in lieu of the foregoing and other allowances.—*Stat. at Large, Vol. XVII, p.* 486.

155. The hall of the House shall not be used for any other purpose than the legitimate business of the House, nor shall the Speaker entertain any proposition to use it for any other purpose, or for the suspension of this rule: *Provided*, That this shall not interfere with the performance of divine service therein, under the direction of the Speaker, or with the use of the same for caucus meetings of the members, or upon occasions where the House may, by resolution, agree to take part in any ceremonies to be observed therein.—*January* 31, 1866.

156. There shall be appointed at the commencement of each Congress a standing Committee on Freedmen's Affairs, to consist of nine members, whose duty it shall be to take charge of all matters concerning freedmen, which shall be referred to them by the House.—*December* 4, 1866.

157. When an act has been approved by the President, the usual number of copies shall be printed for the use of the House.—*March* 15, 1867.

158. Messages from the Senate and the President of the United States, giving notice of bills passed or approved, shall be reported forthwith from the Clerk's desk.—*March* 15, 1867.

159. Estimates of appropriations, and all other communications from the executive departments, intended for the consideration of any of the committees of the House, shall be addressed to the Speaker and by him submitted to the House for reference.—*March* 15, 1867.

160. There shall be appointed at each Congress a Committee on Education and Labor, to consist of nine members, to whom shall be referred all petitions, bills, reports, and

resolutions on those subjects, and who shall from time to time report thereon.—*March* 21, 1867.

161. Pending a motion to suspend the rules the Speaker may entertain one motion that the House do now adjourn; but after the result thereon is announced he shall not entertain any other dilatory motion till the vote is taken on suspension.—*Feb.* 25, 1868.

162. The Speaker shall appoint from among the Delegates from the Territories one additional member of the Committee on the Territories, and shall appoint the Delegate from the District of Columbia an additional member of the Committee for the District of Columbia; but the said Delegates, in their respective committees, shall have the same privileges only as in the House.—*December* 13, 1871.

163. Whenever the seats of members shall have been drawn, no proposition shall be in order for a second drawing during the same Congress.—*February* 8, 1872.

JOINT RULES AND ORDERS

OF

THE TWO HOUSES.

1. In every case of an amendment of a bill agreed to in one house and dissented to in the other, if either house shall request a conference, and appoint a committee for that purpose, and the other house shall also appoint a committee to confer, such committees shall, at a convenient hour, to be agreed upon by their chairman, meet in the conference chamber, and state to each other, verbally or in writing, as either shall choose, the reasons of their respective houses for and against the amendment, and confer freely thereon.—*November* 13, 1794.

2. When a message shall be sent from the Senate to the House of Representatives, it shall be announced at the door of the house by the Doorkeeper, and shall be respectfully communicated to the Chair by the person by whom it may be sent.—*November* 13, 1794.

3. The same ceremony shall be observed when a messenger shall be sent from the House of Representatives to the Senate.—*November* 13, 1794.

4. Messages shall be sent by such persons as a sense of propriety in each house may determine to be proper.—*November* 13, 1794.

5. While bills are on their passage between the two houses, they shall be on paper, and under the signature of the Secretary or Clerk of each house, respectively.—*November* 13, 1794.

6. After a bill shall have passed both houses, it shall be duly enrolled on parchment by the Clerk of the House of Representatives, or the Secretary of the Senate, as the bill may have originated in the one or the other house, before it shall be presented to the President of the United States.—*November* 13, 1794.

7. When bills are enrolled, they shall be examined by a joint committee of two from the Senate and two from the House of Representatives, appointed as a standing committee for that purpose, who shall carefully compare the enrolment with the engrossed bills as passed in the two houses, and correcting any errors that may be discovered in the enrolled bills, make their report forthwith to their respective houses.—*November* 13, 1794, and *February* 1, 1827.

8. After examination and report, each bill shall be signed in the respective houses, first by the Speaker of the House of Representatives, then by the President of the Senate.—*November* 13, 1794.

9. After a bill shall have been thus signed in each house, it shall be presented, by the said committee, to the President of the United States, for his approbation, (it being first indorsed on the back of the roll, certifying in which house the same originated; which indorsement shall be signed by the Secretary or Clerk, as the case may be, of the house in which the same did originate,) and shall be entered on the journal of each house. The said committee shall report the day of presentation to the President; which time shall also be carefully entered on the journal of each house.—*November* 13, 1794.

10. All orders, resolutions, and votes which are to be presented to the President of the United States for his approbation, shall also, in the same manner, be previously enrolled, examined, and signed; and shall be presented in

the same manner, and by the same committee, as provided in the cases of bills.--*November* 13, 1794.

11. When the Senate and House of Representatives shall judge it proper to make a joint address to the President, it shall be presented to him in his audience chamber by the President of the Senate, in the presence of the Speaker and both houses.--*November* 13, 1794.

12. When a bill or resolution which shall have passed in one house is rejected in the other, notice thereof shall be given to the house in which the same shall have passed.--*June* 10, 1790.

13. When a bill or resolution which has been passed in one house shall be rejected in the other, it shall not be brought in during the same session, without a notice of ten days and leave of two-thirds of that house in which it shall be renewed.—*June* 10, 1790.

14. Each house shall transmit to the other all papers on which any bill or resolution shall be founded.—*June* 10, 1790.

15. After each house shall have adhered to their disagreement, a bill or resolution shall be lost.—*June* 10, 1790.

16. No bill that shall have passed one house shall be sent for concurrence to the other on either of the three last days of the session.—*January* 30, 1822.

17. No bill or resolution that shall have passed the House of Representatives and the Senate shall be presented to the President of the United States, for his approbation, on the last day of the session.—*January* 30, 1822.

18. When bills which have passed one house are ordered to be printed in the other, a greater number of copies shall not be printed than may be necessary for the use of the house making the order.—*February* 9, 1829.

19. No spirituous or malt liquors, or wines, shall be offered for sale, exhibited, or kept within the Capitol, or in

any room or building connected therewith, or on the public grounds adjacent thereto. And it shall be the duty of the Sergeants-at-arms of the two houses, under the supervision of the presiding officers thereof, respectively, to enforce the foregoing provisions. And any officer or employé of either house who shall in any manner violate or connive at the violation of this rule shall be dismissed from office.—*March* 18, 1867.

20. There shall be a joint committee on the library, to consist of three members on the part of the Senate and three on the part of the House of Representatives, to superintend and direct the expenditure of all moneys appropriated for the library, and to perform such other duties as are or may be directed by law.—*December* 7, 1843.

21. After six days from the commencement of a second or subsequent session of Congress, all bills, resolutions, or reports which originated in either house, and at the close of the next preceding session remained undetermined in either house, *shall* be resumed and acted on in the same manner as if an adjournment had not taken place.—*August* 14, 1848.

22. The two houses shall assemble in the hall of the House of Representatives at the hour of 1 o'clock p. m. on the second Wednesday in February next succeeding the meeting of the electors of President and Vice-President of the United States, and the President of the Senate shall be their presiding officer; one teller shall be appointed on the part of the Senate, and two on the part of the House of Representatives, to whom shall be handed, as they are opened by the President of the Senate, the certificates of the electoral votes; and said tellers having read the same in the presence and hearing of the two houses thus assembled, shall make a list of the votes as they shall appear from the said certificates; and the votes having been counted,

the result of the same shall be delivered to the President of the Senate, who shall thereupon announce the state of the vote and the names of the persons, if any elected, which announcement shall be deemed a sufficient declaration of the persons elected President and Vice-President of the United States, and, together with a list of the votes, be entered on the journals of the two houses.

If, upon the reading of any such certificate by the tellers, any question shall arise in regard to counting the votes therein certified, the same having been stated by the presiding officer, the Senate shall thereupon withdraw, and said question shall be submitted to that body for its decision; and the Speaker of the House of Representatives shall, in like manner, submit said question to the House of Representatives for its decision. And no question shall be decided affirmatively, and no vote objected to shall be counted, except by the concurrent votes of the two houses; which being obtained, the two houses shall immediately reassemble, and the presiding officer shall then announce the decision of the question submitted; and upon any such question there shall be no debate in either house. And any other question pertinent to the object for which the two houses are assembled may be submitted and determined in like manner.

At such joint meeting of the two houses seats shall be provided as follows: for the President of the Senate, the "Speaker's chair;" for the Speaker, a chair immediately upon his left; for the senators, in the body of the hall upon the right of the presiding officer; for the representatives, in the body of the hall not occupied by the senators; for the tellers, Secretary of the Senate, and Clerk of the House of Representatives, at the Clerk's desk; for the other officers of the two houses, in front of the Clerk's desk and upon either side of the Speaker's platform.

Such joint meeting shall not be dissolved until the electoral votes are all counted and the result declared; and no recess shall be taken, unless a question shall have arisen in regard to counting any of such votes, in which case it shall be competent for either house, acting separately in the manner hereinbefore provided, to direct a recess not beyond the next day, at the hour of one o'clock p. m.—*February* 6. 1865.

INDEX

TO THE

RULES AND ORDERS OF THE HOUSE OF REPRESENTATIVES,

AND TO THE JOINT RULES.

A.

15

S.

T.

U.

V.

W.

Y.

STANDING RULES

FOR CONDUCTING BUSINESS IN

THE SENATE OF THE UNITED STATES.

STANDING RULES

FOR CONDUCTING BUSINESS

IN THE SENATE OF THE UNITED STATES.

COMMENCEMENT OF DAILY SESSIONS.

1.——The Presiding Officer having taken the chair, and a quorum being present, the journal of the preceding day shall be read, to the end that any mistake may be corrected that shall be made in the entries.

[16 April, 1789—March 25, 1868.

A quorum shall consist of a majority of the Senators duly chosen and sworn.

[4 May, 1864—March 25, 1868.

BUSINESS NOT TO BE INTERRUPTED.

2.——No Senator shall speak to another, or otherwise interrupt the business of the Senate, or read any newspaper, while the journals or public papers are reading, or when any Senator is speaking in any debate.

[16 April, 1789—14 Feb., 1828—March 25, 1868.

RULES IN SPEAKING OR DEBATE.

3.——Every Senator, when he speaks, shall address the Chair, standing in his place, and when he has finished shall sit down.

[16 April, 1789—March 25, 1868.

4.——No Senator shall speak more than twice, in any one debate, on the same day, without leave of the Senate, which question shall be decided without debate.

[16 April, 1789—March 25, 1868.

5.——When two Senators rise at the same time, the Presiding Officer shall name the person to speak; but in all cases the Senator who shall rise first and address the Chair shall speak first.

[16 April, 1789—14 Feb., 1828—March 25, 1868.

CALLS TO ORDER AND APPEALS.

6.——If any Senator, in speaking or otherwise, transgress the rules of the Senate, the Presiding Officer shall, or any Senator may, call to order; and when a Senator shall be called to order by the Presiding Officer, or a Senator, he shall sit down, and shall not proceed without leave of the Senate. And every question of order shall be decided by the Presiding Officer, without debate, subject to an appeal to the Senate; and the Presiding Officer may call for the sense of the Senate on any question of order. But when an appeal shall be taken from the decision of the Presiding Officer, any subsequent question of order, which may arise before the decision of such appeal by the Senate, shall be decided by the Presiding Officer without debate, and every appeal therefrom shall also be decided at once, and without debate.

[16 April, 1789—14 Feb., 1828—26 June, 1856—March 25, 1868.

EXCEPTIONABLE WORDS.

7.——If a Senator be called to order by another for words spoken, the exceptionable words shall immediately be taken down in writing, that the Presiding Officer may be better able to judge of the matter.

[16 April, 1789—March 25, 1868.

ABSENT SENATORS MAY BE SENT FOR.

8.——No Senator shall absent himself from the service of the Senate, without leave of the Senate first obtained. And in case a less number than a quorum of the Senate shall convene, they are hereby authorized to send the Sergeant-at-Arms, or any other person or persons by them authorized, for any or all absent Senators, as the majority of such Senators present shall agree, at the expense of such absent Senators, respectively, unless such excuse for non-attendance shall be made as the Senate, when a quorum is convened, shall judge sufficient, and in that case the expense shall be paid out of the contingent fund. And this rule shall apply as well to the first convention of the Senate, at the legal time of meeting, as to each day of the session, after the hour has arrived to which the Senate stood adjourned.

[16 April, 1789—25 June, 1798—4 Feb., 1828—March 25, 1868.

RULE FOR DEBATE.

9.——No motion shall be debated until the same shall be seconded.

[16 April, 1789—March 25, 1868.

RULE FOR MOTIONS, DEBATE, AND WITHDRAWAL.

10.——When a motion shall be made and seconded, it shall be reduced to writing, if desired by the Presiding Officer, or any Senator, delivered in at the table, and read, before the same shall be debated; and any motion may be withdrawn by the mover at any time before a decision, amendment, or ordering of the yeas and nays, except a motion to reconsider, which shall not be withdrawn without leave of the Senate.

[16 April, 1789—14 Feb., 1828—21 Jan., 1851—March 25, 1868.

PRECEDENCE OF MOTIONS WHEN A QUESTION IS UNDER DEBATE.

11.——When a question is under debate, no motion shall be received but—

to adjourn;
to proceed to the consideration of Executive business;
to lie on the table;
to postpone indefinitely:
to postpone to a day certain;
to commit; or
to amend;

which several motions shall have precedence in the order they stand arranged; and motions to adjourn, to proceed to the consideration of Executive business, and to lie on the table, shall be decided without debate, and motions to take up or proceed to the consideration of any question shall be determined without debate upon the merits of the question proposed to be considered.

[16 April, 1789—13 Jan., 1820—14 Feb., 1828—March 25, 1868.

DIVISION OF A QUESTION.

12.——If the question in debate contain several points, any Senator may have the same divided; but, on a motion to strike out and insert, it shall not be in order to move for a division of the question; but the rejection of a motion to strike out and insert one proposition, shall not prevent a motion to strike out and insert a different proposition; nor prevent a subsequent motion simply to strike out; nor shall the rejection of a motion simply to strike out, prevent a subsequent motion to strike out and insert.

[16 April, 1789—23 June, 1832—March 25, 1868.

FILLING BLANKS.

13.——In filling up blanks, the largest sum and longest time shall be first put.

[16 April, 1789—3 Jan., 1820—14 Feb., 1828—March 25, 1868.

OBJECTION TO READING A PAPER.

14.——When the reading of a paper is called for, and the same is objected to by any Senator, it shall be determined by a vote of the Senate, and without debate.

[3 Jan., 1820—14 Feb., 1828—March 25, 1868.

UNFINISHED BUSINESS—PRIOR SPECIAL ORDER.

15.——The unfinished business in which the Senate was engaged at the last preceding adjournment shall have the preference in the special orders of the day.

[3 Jan., 1820—14 Feb., 1828—March 25, 1868.

YEAS AND NAYS.

16.——When the yeas and nays shall be called for by one-fifth of the Senators present, each Senator called upon shall, unless for special reasons he be excused by the Senate, declare openly, and without debate, his assent or dissent to the question. In taking the yeas and nays, and upon a call of the Senate, the names of the Senators shall be called alphabetically.

[16 April, 1789—March 25, 1868.

17.——When the yeas and nays shall be taken upon any question, in pursuance of the above rule, no Senator shall be permitted, under any circumstances whatever, to vote after the decision is announced from the Chair.

[4 April, 1822—14 Feb., 1828—March 25, 1868.

CLOSING THE DOORS AND CLEARING THE GALLERY.

18.——On a motion made and seconded to shut the doors of the Senate, on the discussion of any business which may, in the opinion of a Senator, require secrecy, the Presiding Officer shall direct the gallery to be cleared; and during the discussion of such motion the doors shall remain shut.

[20 Feb., 1794—March 25, 1868.

NO PERSON ADMITTED TO PRESENT PETITION, ETC.

19.——No motion shall be deemed in order to admit any person whatsoever within the doors of the Senate Chamber to present any petition, memorial, or address, or to hear any such read.

[27 April, 1798—March 25, 1868.

RECONSIDERATION.

20.——When a question has been made and carried in the affirmative or negative, whether previously reconsidered or not, it shall be in order for any Senator of the majority to move for the reconsideration thereof; but no motion for the reconsideration of any vote shall be in order after the bill, resolution, message, report, amendment, or motion upon which the vote was taken shall have gone out of the possession of the Senate, announcing their decision, except a resolution confirming or rejecting a nomination by the President; nor shall any motion for reconsideration be in order, unless made on the same day on which the vote was taken, or within the two next days of actual session of the Senate thereafter; but a motion to reconsider a vote upon a nomination shall always, if the resolution announcing the decision of the Senate has been sent to the President, be accompanied by a motion requesting the President to return the same to the Senate. When any question may have been decided by the Senate, in which two-thirds of the Senators present are necessary to carry the affirmative, any Senator who votes on that side which prevailed in the question may be at liberty to move for a reconsideration; and a motion for reconsideration shall be decided by a majority of votes. But no motion to reconsider a vote upon a motion to reconsider shall be in order at any time.

[25 Feb., 1790—26 March, 1806—April 6, 1867—March 25, 1868.

CASTING VOTE OF THE VICE-PRESIDENT.

21.——When the Senate are equally divided, the President may announce his vote upon the question.

[18 July, 1789—March 25, 1868.

QUESTION PUT BY THE PRESIDING OFFICER.

22.——All questions shall be put by the Presiding Officer of the Senate, either in the presence or absence of the President of the United States, and the Senators shall signify their assent or dissent, by answering aye or no.

[21 Aug., 1789—March 25, 1868.

APPOINTMENT OF A SENATOR TO THE CHAIR.

23.——The Presiding Officer of the Senate shall have the right to name a Senator to perform the duties of the Chair; but such substitution shall not extend beyond an adjournment.

[3 Jan., 1820—March 25, 1868.

MORNING BUSINESS, PETITIONS, REPORTS, ETC.

24.——After the journal is read, the Presiding Officer shall lay before the Senate messages from the President, reports from the Executive Departments, and bills and joint resolutions, or other messages from the House of Representatives. He shall then call for—

Petitions and memorials;
Reports of committees;
The introduction of bills;
Joint resolutions;
Resolutions;

all which shall be received and disposed of in such order, unless unanimous consent shall be otherwise given; and every petition or memorial, or other paper, shall be referred, of course, without putting a question for that purpose, unless the reference is objected to by a Senator at the time such petition, memorial, or other paper is presented. And before any petition or memorial, addressed to the Senate, shall be received and read at the table, whether the same shall be introduced by the Presiding Officer, or a Senator, a brief statement of the contents of the petition or memorial shall verbally be made by the introducer.

[18 April, 1789—10 April, 1834—March 25, 1868.

NOTICE AND PRINTING OF BILLS, ETC.

25.——One day's notice, at least, shall be given of an intended motion for leave to bring in a bill or joint resolution; and all bills and joint resolutions reported by a committee shall, after the first reading, be printed for the use of the Senate, and also all reports of committees, unless otherwise ordered; but no other paper or document shall be printed for the use of the Senate without special order.

[16 April, 1789—3 Feb., 1801—3 Jan., 1820—8 April, 1822—14 Feb., 1828—March 25, 1868.

JOINT RESOLUTIONS.

26.——Every bill and joint resolution shall receive three readings previous to its being passed, and the Presiding Officer shall give notice at each whether it be the first, second, or third; which reading shall be on three different days, unless the Senate unanimously direct otherwise. And all resolutions proposing amendments to the Constitution, or to which the approbation and signature of the President may be requisite, or which may grant money out of the contingent or any other und, shall be treated, in all respects, in the introduction and form of proceeding on them, in the Senate, in a similar manner with bills; and all other resolutions shall lie on the table one day for consideration, and also reports of committees.

[March 25, 1868.

COMMITMENT OF BILLS.

27.——No bill or joint resolution shall be committed oı amended until it shall have been twice read, after which it may be referred to a committee.

[16 April, 1789—March 25, 1868.

IN COMMITTEE OF THE WHOLE.

28.——All bills and joint resolutions on a second reading shall first be considered by the Senate in the same manner as if the Senate were in committee of the whole, before they shall be taken up and proceeded on by the Senate agreeably to the standing rules, unless otherwise ordered.

[21 May, 1789—26 March, 1806—3 Jan., 1820—March 25, 1868.

FINAL QUESTIONS—REFERENCE TO COURT OF CLAIMS.

29.——The final question upon the second reading of every bill, resolution, or constitutional amendment, originating in the Senate, and requiring three readings previous to being passed, shall be, whether it shall be engrossed and read a third time; and no amendment shall be received for discussion at a third reading of any bill, resolution, or amendment, unless by unanimous consent of the Senators present; but it shall at all times be in order, before the final passage of any such bill, resolution, or constitutional amendment, to move its commitment; and should such commitment take place, and any amendment be reported by the committee, the said bill, resolution, or constitutional amendment shall be again read a second time, and considered as in Committee of the Whole, and then the aforesaid question shall be again put. Whenever a private bill is under consideration, it shall be in order to move, as a substitute for it, a resolution of the Senate referring the case to the Court of Claims.

[4 Feb., 1807—26 June, 1856—March 25, 1868.

AMENDMENTS TO APPROPRIATION BILLS.

30.——No amendment proposing additional appropriations shall be received to any general appropriation bill, unless it be made to carry out the provisions of some existing law, or some act or resolution previously passed by the Senate during that session, or moved by direction of a standing or select committee of the Senate, or in pursuance of an estimate from the head of some of the Departments; and no amendment shall be received whose object is to provide for a private claim, unless it be to carry out the provisions of an existing law or a treaty stipulation.

All amendments to general appropriation bills reported from committees of the Senate, proposing new items of appropriation, shall, one day before they are offered, be referred to the Committee on Appropriations, and all general appropriation bills shall be referred to the said committee. Any pending amendment to a general appropriation bill may be laid on the table without affecting the bill.

[19 Dec., 1850—7 May, 1852—13 Jan., 1854—3 May, 1854—7 March, 1867—March 25 1868—Feb. 22, 1871.

SPECIAL ORDERS.

31.——When the hour shall arrive for the consideration of a special order, it shall be the duty of the Presiding Officer to take it up, unless the unfinished business of the preceding day shall be under consideration.

[26 June, 1856—March 25, 1868.

PRECEDENCE IN SPECIAL ORDERS.

When two or more subjects shall have been specially assigned for consideration, they shall take precedence according to the order of time at which they were severally assigned, and such order shall at no time be lost or changed, except by the direction of the Senate.

[26 June, 1856—March 25, 1868.

PRECEDENCE IN SPECIAL ORDERS AND OVER GENERAL ORDERS.

When two or more subjects shall have been assigned for the same hour, the subject first assigned for that hour shall take precedence; but special orders shall always have precedence of general orders, unless such special orders shall be postponed by direction of the Senate.

[26 June, 1856—March 25, 1868.

TWO-THIRDS REQUIRED TO MAKE A SPECIAL ORDER.

No bill, joint resolution, or other subject shall be made a special order for a particular day and hour without the concurrence of two-thirds of the Senators present.

[13 January, 1862—March 25, 1868.

MAKING UP THE JOURNAL.

32.——The titles of bills and joint resolutions, and such parts thereof only as shall be affected by proposed amendments, shall be inserted on the journal.

[12 March, 1792—March 25, 1868.

33.——The proceedings of the Senate shall be entered on the journal as concisely as possible, care being taken to detail a true and accurate account of the proceedings; but every vote of the Senate shall be entered on the journal, and a brief statement of the contents of each petition, memorial, or paper, presented to the Senate, shall also be inserted on the journal.

[19 May, 1789—12 March, 1792—14 Feb., 1828—March 25, 1868.

STANDING COMMITTEES.

34.——The following standing committees shall be appointed at the commencement of each session, with leave to report by bill or otherwise:

[5 March, 1857—March 25, 1868.

A Committee on Privileges and Elections, to consist of seven Senators.

[March 10, 1871.

A Committee on Foreign Relations, to consist of seven Senators.

[16 Dec., 1816—5 March, 1857—March 25, 1868.

A Committee on Finance, to consist of seven Senators.

[10 Dec., 1816—5 March, 1857—March 25, 1868.

A Committee on Appropriations, to consist of seven Senators.

[6 March, 1867—March 25, 1868.

A Committee on Commerce, to consist of seven Senators.

[10 Dec., 1816—7 Dec., 1825—5 March, 1857—March 25, 1868.

A Committee on Manufactures, to consist of five Senators.

[10 Feb., 1864—March 25, 1868.

A Committee on Agriculture, to consist of five Senators.

[6 March, 1863—March 25, 1868.

A Committee on Military Affairs, to consist of seven Senators.

[10 Dec., 1816—5 March, 1857—March 25, 1868.

A Committee on Naval Affairs, to consist of seven Senators.

[10 Dec., 1816—5 March, 1857—March 25, 1868.

A Committee on the Judiciary, to consist of seven Senators.

[10 Dec., 1816—5 March, 1857—March 25, 1868.

A Committee on Post Offices and Post Roads, to consist of seven Senators.

[10 Dec., 1816—5 March, 1857—March 25, 1868.

A Committee on Public Lands, to consist of seven Senators.

[10 Dec., 1816—5 March, 1857—March 25, 1868.

A Committee on Private Land Claims, to consist of five Senators.

[27 Dec., 1826—5 March, 1857—March 25, 1868.

A Committee on Indian Affairs, to consist of seven Senators.

[3 Jan., 1820—5 March, 1857—March 25, 1868.

A Committee on Pensions, to consist of seven Senators.

[10 Dec., 1816—5 March, 1857—March 25, 1868.

A Committee on Revolutionary Claims, to consist of five Senators.

[28 Dec., 1832—5 March, 1857—March 25, 1868.

A Committee on Claims, to consist of seven Senators.

[10 Dec., 1816—5 March, 1857—26 Jan., 1860—March 25, 1868.

A Committee on the District of Columbia, to consist of seven Senators.

[18 Dec., 1816—5 March, 1857—March 25, 1868.

A Committee on Patents, to consist of five Senators.

[7 Sept., 1837—5 March, 1857—March 25, 1868.

A Committee on Public Buildings and Grounds, to consist of five Senators, who shall have power also to act jointly with the same committee of the House of Representatives.

[16 Dec., 1819—19 Dec., 1837—28 May, 1850—5 March, 1857—March 25, 1868.

A Committee on Territories, to consist of seven Senators.

[25 March, 1844—5 March, 1857—March 25, 1868.

A Committee on the Pacific Railroad, to consist of eleven Senators.

[22 December, 1863—March 25, 1868—Dec. 21, 1868.

A Committee on Mines and Mining, to consist of seven Senators.

[8 March, 1865—March 25, 1868.

A Committee on the Revision of the Laws of the United States, to consist of five Senators.

[Dec. 10, 1868.

A Committee on Education and Labor, to consist of five Senators.

[Jan. 28, 1869—Feb. 14, 1870..

A Committee to Audit and Control the Contingent Expenses of the Senate, to consist of three Senators, to which shall be referred all resolutions directing the payment of money out of the contingent fund of the Senate, or creating a charge on the same.

[4 Nov., 1807—7 April, 1853—5 March, 1857—March 25, 1868.

A Committee on Printing, to consist of three Senators, to whom shall be referred every question on the printing of documents, reports, or other matters transmitted by either of the executive Departments, and all memorials, petitions, accompanying documents, together with all other matter the printing of which shall be moved, excepting bills originating in Congress, resolutions offered by any Senator, communications from the Legislatures or Conventions lawfully called of the respective States, and motions to print by order of the standing committees of the Senate; motions to print additional numbers shall likewise be referred to said committee; and when the report shall be in favor of printing additional numbers, it shall be accompanied by an estimate of the probable cost; the said committee shall also supervise and direct the procuring of maps and drawings accompanying documents ordered to be printed.

[15 Dec., 1841—18 Dec., 1850—22 Jan., 1855—5 March, 1857—March 25, 1868.

A Committee on Engrossed Bills, to consist of three Senators, whose duty it shall be to examine all bills, amendments, and resolutions, before they go out of the possession of the Senate; and shall deliver the same to the Secretary of the Senate, who shall enter upon the journal that the same have been correctly engrossed.

[3 Jan., 1820—March 25, 1868.

A Committee on Enrolled Bills, to consist of three Senators, who, or some one of whom, shall forthwith present all enrolled Senate bills to the President in person, for his signature, and report the fact and date of such presentation to the Senate.

[6 Aug., 1789—5 March, 1857—March 25, 1868.

APPOINTMENT OF COMMITTEES.

35.——In the appointment of the standing committees, the Senate shall proceed, by ballot, to appoint severally the chairman of each committee, and then, by one ballot, the other members necessary to complete the same; and a majority of the whole number of votes given shall be necessary to the choice of a chairman of a standing committee, but a plurality of votes shall elect the other members thereof. All other committees shall be appointed by ballot, and a plurality of votes shall make a choice.

[3 Jan., 1820—8 Dec., 1826—14 Feb., 1828—March 25, 1868.

REFERENCE TO STANDING OR SELECT COMMITTEES.

36.——When motions are made for reference of the same subject to a select committee and to a standing committee, the question on reference to the standing committee shall be first put.

[14 Feb., 1828—March 25, 1868.

EXECUTIVE BUSINESS—PROCEEDINGS ON NOMINATIONS.

37.——When nominations shall be made by the President of the United States to the Senate, they shall, unless otherwise ordered by the Senate, be referrred to appropriate committees; and the final question on every nomination shall be, "Will the Senate advise and consent to this nomination?" which question shall not be put on the same day on which the nomination is received, nor on the day on which it may be reported by a committee, unless by the unanimous consent of the Senate. Nominations neither approved nor rejected during the session at which they are made shall not be acted upon at any succeeding session without being again made by the President; and if the Senate shall adjourn or take a recess for more than thirty days, all nominations pending and not finally acted upon at the time of taking such adjournment or recess shall be returned to the President, and shall not be afterwards acted upon, unless again submitted to the Senate by the President; and all motions pending to reconsider a vote upon a nomination shall fall on such adjournment or recess; and the Secretary of the Senate shall thereupon make out and furnish to the heads of Departments and other officers the list of nominations rejected or not confirmed, as required by law. When the President of the United States shall meet the Senate in the Senate Chamber for the consideration of executive business, the Presiding Officer of the Senate shall have a chair on the floor, be considered as the head of the Senate, and his chair shall be assigned to the President of the United States. When the Senate shall be convened by the President of the United States to any other place, the Presiding Officer of the Senate and the Senators shall attend at the place appointed, with the necessary officers of the Senate.

[21 Aug., 1789—18 Feb., 1843—March 25, 1868.

PROCEEDINGS ON TREATIES.

38.——When a treaty shall be laid before the Senate for ratification, it shall be read a first time, when no motion in respect to it shall be in order except to refer it to a committee or to print it in confidence for the use of the Senate. Its second reading shall be for consideration, and shall be on a subsequent day, when it shall be taken up as in Committee of the Whole and be considered by articles, when amendments may be proposed; but when amendments are reported by a committee they shall be first acted on, after which other amendments may be proposed; and when through, the whole proceeding had as in Committee of the Whole shall be reported to the Senate, when the question shall be, if the treaty be amended, "Will the Senate concur in the amendments made in Committee of the Whole?" and the amendments may be taken separately or in gross, as the Senate may elect, after which new amendments may be proposed. The decisions thus made shall be reduced to the form of a resolution of ratification, with or without amendments, as the case may be, which shall be proposed on a subsequent day, unless by unanimous consent the Senate determine otherwise, when every one shall again be free to move amendments, the question on which shall be proposed and taken as in the case of amendments to the article. And on the final question to advise and consent to the ratification in the form agreed to, the concurrence of two-thirds of the Senators present shall be requisite to determine it in the affirmative, but all other motions and questions thereon shall be decided by a majority vote.

[6 Jan., 1801—March 25, 1868.

MATTERS CONFIDENTIAL AND SECRET.

39.——All confidential communications made by the President of the United States to the Senate shall be by the Senators and the officers of the Senate kept secret, and all treaties which may be laid before the Senate, and all remarks and proceedings thereon, shall also be kept secret until the Senate shall, by their resolution, take off the injunction of secrecy; but this rule shall not apply to treaties with Indian tribes, which shall be considered and acted upon in open Senate, unless the same shall be transmitted by the President to the Senate in confidence.

[22 Dec., 1800—3 Jan., 1820—March 25, 1868—Feb. 8, 1870.

SECRECY OF REMARKS ON NOMINATIONS.

40.——All information or remarks concerning the character or qualifications of any person nominated by the President to office shall be kept a secret; but the fact that a nomination has been made shall not be regarded as a secret.

[3 Jan., 1820—March 25, 1868.

CLEARING OF THE SENATE.

41.——When acting on confidential or executive business, the Chamber shall be cleared of all persons except the Secretary of the Senate, the principal or executive clerk, the Sergeant-at-Arms and Doorkeeper, the assistant doorkeeper, and such other officers as the Presiding Officer shall think necessary; and all such officers shall be sworn to secrecy.

[3 Jan., 1820—March 25, 1868.

SEPARATE BOOKS TO BE KEPT.

42.——The legislative proceedings, the executive proceedings, and the confidential legislative proceedings of the Senate, shall be kept in separate books.

[19 May, 1789—15 April, 1828—March 25, 1868.

EXECUTIVE PROCEEDINGS FURNISHED TO THE PRESIDENT.

43.——Nominations approved or definitely acted on by the Senate shall not be returned by the Secretary of the Senate to the President until the expiration of the time limited for making a motion to reconsider the same, or while a motion to reconsider is pending, unless otherwise ordered by the Senate. The President of the United States shall, from time to time, be furnished with an authenticated transcript of the executive records of the Senate, but no further extract from the executive journal shall be furnished, except by special order; and no paper, except original treaties, transmitted to the Senate by the President of the United States, or any executive officer, shall be returned or delivered from the office of the Secretary of the Senate, without an order of the Senate for that purpose.

[27 Jan., 1792—27 March, 1818—5 Jan., 1829—6 April, 1867—March 25, 1868

PROCEEDINGS ON AMENDMENTS TO THE CONSTITUTION.

44.——When an amendment to be proposed to the Constitution is under consideration, the concurrence of two-thirds of the Senators present shall not be requisite to decide any question for amendments, or extending to the merits, being short of the final question.

[26 March, 1806—March 25, 1868.

MESSAGES TO THE HOUSE OF REPRESENTATIVES.

45.——Messages shall be sent to the House of Representatives by the Secretary, who shall previously indorse the final determination of the Senate upon bills and other papers communicated.

[26 March, 1806—March 25, 1868.

MESSENGERS INTRODUCED.

46.——Messengers may be introduced in any state of business, except while a question is putting, while the yeas and nays are calling, or while the ballots are counting.

[26 March, 1806—March 25, 1868.

PERSONS ADMITTED ON FLOOR.

47.——No person shall be admitted to the floor of the Senate, while in session, except as follows, viz: The officers of the Senate, members of the House of Representatives and their Clerk, the President of the United States and his private secretary, the heads of Departments, ministers of the United States and foreign ministers, ex-Presidents and ex-Vice-Presidents of the United States, ex-Senators, Senators elect, judges of the Supreme Court, and Governors of States and Territories.

[17 March, 1853—23 Jan., 1854—24 Jan., 1854—6 March, 1856—11 Jan., 1859—7 Feb., 1862—March 25, 1868.

REGULATION OF SENATE WING OF THE CAPITOL.

48.——The Presiding Officer of the Senate shall have the regulation and control of such parts of the Capitol, and of its passages, as are or may be set apart for the use of the Senate and its officers.

[22 Jan., 1824—14 Feb., 1828—March 25, 1868.

RESTRICTION OF PRESENTING REJECTED CLAIMS.

49.——Whenever a claim is presented to the Senate and referred to a committee, and the committee report that the claim ought not to be allowed, and the report be adopted by the Senate, it shall not be in order to move to take the papers from the files for the purpose of referring them at a subsequent session, unless the claimant shall present a memorial for that purpose, stating in what respect the committee have erred in their report, or that new evidence has been discovered since the report, and setting forth the new evidence in the memorial.

[25 Jan., 1842—21 Dec., 1842—March 25, 1868.

PENALTIES FOR VIOLATING CONFIDENCE OF SENATE.

50.——Any Senator or officer of the Senate who shall disclose the secret or confidential business or proceedings of the Senate shall be liable, if a Senator, to suffer expulsion from the body, and if an officer, to dismissal from the service of the Senate, and to punishment for contempt.

[10 May, 1844—March 25, 1868.

OATHS OF OFFICE.

51.——The oaths or affirmations prescribed by the Constitution and by the act of Congress of July 2, 1862, to be taken and subscribed before entering upon the duties of office, shall be taken and subscribed by every Senator in open Senate before entering upon his duties. They shall also be taken and subscribed in the same way by the Secretary of the Senate; but the other officers of the Senate may take and subscribe them in the office of the Secretary.

[25 Jan., 1864—March 25, 1868.

BUSINESS CONTINUED FROM SESSION TO SESSION.

52.——At the second or any subsequent session of a Congress, the legislative business of the Senate which remains undetermined at the close of the next preceding session of that Congress shall be resumed and proceeded with in the same manner as if no adjournment of the Senate had taken place; and all subjects referred to committees, and not reported upon at the close of a session of Congress, shall be returned to the office of the Secretary of the Senate, and be by him retained until the next succeeding session of that Congress, when they shall be returned to the several committees to which they had been previously referred.

[March 25, 1868.

SUSPENSION AND AMENDMENT OF RULES.

53.——No motion to suspend, modify, or amend the rules, or any thereof, shall be in order, except on one day's notice in writing, specifying the rule to be suspended, modified, or amended, and the purpose thereof. But any rule may be suspended by unanimous consent, except the seventeenth rule, which shall never be suspended.

A motion to suspend, or to concur in a resolution of the House of Representatives to suspend, the 16th and 17th joint rules, or either of them, shall always be in order, be immediately considered, and be decided without debate.

[16 April, 1789—26 March, 1806—3 Jan., 1820—24 Feb., 1828—7 May, 1852—March 25, 1868

ANALYTICAL INDEX

TO

THE STANDING RULES OF THE SENATE.

A.

16*

B.

C.

D.

N.

O.

R.

S.

W.

Y.

O

DIGEST OF THE RULES

OF THE

HOUSE OF REPRESENTATIVES U. S.,

THE

JOINT RULES OF THE TWO HOUSES,

AND OF

SO MUCH OF JEFFERSON'S MANUAL AS UNDER THE RULES GOVERNS THE HOUSE; OF PRECEDENTS OF ORDER AND USAGES OF THE HOUSE; TOGETHER WITH SUCH PORTIONS OF THE CONSTITUTION OF THE UNITED STATES, LAWS OF CONGRESS, AND RESOLUTIONS OF THE HOUSE AS RELATE TO THE PROCEEDINGS OF THE HOUSE, AND THE RIGHTS AND DUTIES OF ITS MEMBERS.

COMPILED BY

JOHN M. BARCLAY,

JOURNAL CLERK OF THE HOUSE OF REPRESENTATIVES U. S.

ARRANGED ALPHABETICALLY

WASHINGTON:
GOVERNMENT PRINTING OFFICE.
1ST SESS. 43D CONG.

BARCLAY'S DIGEST

OF THE

RULES AND PRACTICE

OF THE

HOUSE OF REPRESENTATIVES U. S.

ABSENCE FROM THE HOUSE.

"No member shall absent himself from the service of the House, unless he have leave, or be sick or unable to attend."—*Rule* 33.

Prohibited, unless by leave or from inability to attend.

"A smaller number than a quorum *may* be authorized to compel the attendance of absent members, in such manner and under such penalties as each House may provide."—*Const.*, 1, 5, 8.

Less than a quorum may be authorized to compel attendance.

"Any fifteen members (including the Speaker, if there be one) shall be authorized to compel the attendance of absent members."—*Rule* 34.

Fifteen members authorized to compel attendance.

For mode of proceeding in case of the absence of members, see CALLS OF THE HOUSE.

Proceedings in case of.

By the act of August 16, 1856, it is made the duty of the Sergeant-at-Arms to deduct from the monthly payment of each member the amount of his compensation for each day that such member shall be absent from the House, unless such member shall assign as the reason for such absence the sickness of himself or of some member of his family.—*Stat. at Large, Vol. XI, p.* 49.

Deduction from compensation for.

By the Joint Resolution of July 17, 1862, it is declared that when any Senator or Representative shall hereafter withdraw from his seat in anticipation of the adjournment of Congress and before the adjournment, and does not return, he shall, in addition to the sum now deducted

Further deduction from compensation for, without leave.

for each day, forfeit a further sum equal to the mileage now allowed by law for his return home, and it shall be deducted from his compensation, unless where said withdrawal is with the leave of the Senate or House of Representatives.—*Stat. at Large, Vol. XII, p.* 628.

ABSENCE FROM COMMITTEES OF THE WHOLE.

When no quorum by reason of, roll to be called.

"Whenever the Committee of the Whole on the state of the Union, or the Committee of the Whole House, finds itself without a quorum, the chairman shall cause the roll of the House to be called, and thereupon the committee shall rise and the chairman shall report the names of the absentees to the House, which shall be entered on the Journal."—*Rule* 106. [As soon as the roll-call is completed, the practice is for the chairman *immediately* to vacate the chair, and consequently to report as absentees all such as failed to answer to their names when called.]

ACCOUNTS, COMMITTEE OF.

Its number, and when appointed.

This committee, to consist of five members, is directed to be appointed at the commencement of each Congress.—*Rule* 74. Its duty is to superintend and control the expenditures of the contingent fund of the House; also to audit and settle all accounts which may be charged thereon.—*Rule* 98. And it is made its further duty by Rule 140 to inquire into and report to the House any violation of the said rule in regard to the allowance of extra compensation to employés of the House, or their being interested in claims against the Government. And by Rule 27 the said committee is directed to determine the amount for which the doorkeeper shall be liable for articles missing from the committee and other rooms under his charge.

Duties of.

ACCOUNTS FOR PAY AND MILEAGE.

(See COMPENSATION.)

ACTS AND ADDRESSES.

To be signed by the Speaker.

Acts and addresses shall be signed by the Speaker.—*Rule* 8.

ADDRESS TO THE PRESIDENT.

"Whenever the Senate and House of Representatives shall judge it proper to make a joint address to the President, it shall be presented to him in his audience chamber by the President of the Senate in the presence of the Speaker and both Houses."—*Joint Rule* 11.

Where to be presented, by whom, &c.

ADHERE, MOTION TO.

The questions respecting amendments from another House are: 1st, to agree; 2d, disagree; 3d, recede; 4th, insist; 5th, adhere—*Manual, p.* 114—and take precedence in that order.—*Journals*, 1, 23, *p.* 229; 1, 34, *p.* 1516 to 1518.

On questions on amendments between the two houses. Order in putting question on.

"In the ordinary parliamentary course, there are two free conferences, at least, before an adherence"—*Manual, p.* 126—and sometimes three or four.—*Journals* 1, 34, *p.* 943; 1, 35, *p.* 1136. Although "either House is free to pass over the term of insisting, and to adhere in the first instance; but it is not respectful to the other."—*Manual, p.* 226.

Usually at least two conferences before adherence.

A conference may take place after a vote of adherence by one House.—*Journals*, 1, 3, *pp.* 281, 283; 2, 3, *p.* 254; 1, 34, *pp.* 1600, 1602; 1, 35, *pp.* 604, 615, 620; *Senate Journal, Jan.* 20, 1834; *Manual, p.* 129.

Conference after one house adheres.

"After each House shall have adhered to their disagreement, a bill or resolution shall be lost."—*Joint Rule* 15.

After each house adheres, bill, &c., lost.

(See AMENDMENTS BETWEEN THE TWO HOUSES and CONFERENCE COMMITTEES.)

ADJOURN, MOTION TO.

"A motion to adjourn, and a motion to fix the day to which the House shall adjourn, shall be always in order, and these motions shall be decided without debate."—*Rule* 44. It has been decided and acted upon that the motion "to fix the *day* to which the House shall adjourn" takes precedence of a motion "to adjourn;" the reason being that, before the House adjourns, it is proper to fix the time to which it shall adjourn—*Note to same rule*—but when less than a quorum is present no motion can be

And to fix the day of next meeting always in order. Not debatable.

Motion to fix the day takes precedence of, unless no quorum present.

entertained, except to adjourn, or for a call of the House.—*Journal*, 1, 29, *p*. 356, and *Const.*, 1, 5, 8. [Consequently, at such a time, the motion to adjourn would take precedence.]

Only one can be entertained while motion to suspend rules pending.

Only one motion to adjourn can be entertained pending a motion to suspend the rules.—*Rule* 161.

For more than three days is privileged.

A resolution proposing, with the concurrence of the Senate, an adjournment for more than three days is held to be privileged.—*Journal* 2, 37, *pp*. 718 to 720.

Cannot be made while another member is speaking, unless he yields for.

"A motion for adjournment cannot be made while another is speaking."—*Manual*, *p*. 85.—[But according to the practice, a member speaking may yield for a motion to adjourn, or that the committee rise, without losing his right to the floor when the subject is resumed.]

Not in order while voting on another question.

"Nor can a motion to adjourn be received after another question is actually put, and while the House is actually engaged in voting."—*Manual*, *p*. 98.

Cannot be amended.

"A motion to adjourn simply cannot be amended, as by adding 'to a particular day,' but must be put simply 'that this House do now adjourn;' and if carried in the affirmative, it is adjourned to the next sitting day, unless it has come to a previous resolution, 'that at its rising it will adjourn to a particular day,' and then the House is adjourned to that day."—*Manual*, *p*. 135.

When may be repeated.

A motion to adjourn may be repeated, although no question has been put or decided since the former motion—*Journal*, 1, 23, *p*. 651—but there must have been some intervening business.—*Ibid.*, 1, 31, 1092. [Another motion submitted, progress in debate, or reading a paper by the Clerk, an order of the yeas and nays, &c., has been considered such "intervening business" as will authorize a repetition of the motion to adjourn.]

Hour of making to be entered on Journal.

"The hour *at which* every motion to adjourn is made shall be entered on the journal."—*Rule* 45.

Motion to fix the hour to which the House shall adjourn.

A motion to fix the hour *to which* the House shall adjourn does not take precedence of a motion to adjourn—*Journal*, 1, 29, *p*. 186—and can only be made when resolutions are in order—*Journal*, 1, 29, *p*. 933—[or under a suspension of the rules when in order.]

No adjournment till Speaker pronounces it.

"If a question be put for adjournment, it is no adjournment till the Speaker pronounces it."—*Manual*, *p*. 135.

There must be an adjournment before the legislative day will terminate—*Journal*, 1, 33, *p.* 804—and an adjournment does not take place by reason of the arrival of the time for the regular daily meeting of the House.—*Ibid.*, *pp.* 803, 811. And an adjournment does not necessarily take place at 12 o'clock a. m. on Sunday, nor is it against order for a majority to continue in session after the said hour, it being a question which must be left to be decided by the judgment and discretion of the House itself.—*Journal*, 1, 24, *pp.* 577, 582.

Legislative day does not end until an adjournment.

For the House to determine when it shall adjourn.

"Neither house during the session of Congress shall, without the consent of the other, adjourn for more than three days, nor to any other place than that in which the two houses shall be sitting."—*Const.*, 1, 5, 9.

House cannot adjourn of itself for more than three days.

Where the two houses adjourn for more than three days, and not to, or beyond, the period fixed by the Constitution or law for the next regular session, the session is not thereby terminated, but continues until an adjournment without day, or until the next regular session.—See *Journals*, 1, 39, *pp.* 107, 108; 2, 39, *p.* 106; 1, 40, *pp.* 157, 158, 184. And it is competent by concurrent resolution to provide for an adjournment to a particular day, and if upon that day a quorum is not present in each house, that the session shall terminate.—*Journal*, 1, 40, *pp.* 157, 158, 184.

For more than three days does not terminate session.

Session may be made to terminate by failure of a quorum in either house.

"In case of disagreement between them (the two houses) with respect to the time of adjournment, the President may adjourn the two houses to such time as he may think proper."—*Const.*, 2, 3, 18.

When President may adjourn two houses.

ADJOURNMENT, SINE DIE.

The adjournment of a session (other than that which terminates with the expiration of the term of service of the members) is provided for by the joint vote of the two houses, and usually in the following form: "Resolved by the Senate and House of Representatives, That the President of the Senate and the Speaker of the House of Representatives be authorized to close the present session by adjourning their respective houses on the —— day of ———, at — o'clock — m." And such resolutions are held to be privileged.

Form of resolution for.

A privileged motion.

When takes place. And upon the arrival of the day and hour thus fixed, or the hour of 12 o'clock m. of the 4th of March of each alternate year, when, by the usage, the last session of a Congress terminates, the Speaker (either on or without motion) pronounces the House adjourned *sine die.—Journals*, 1, 28, *p.* 1362; 1, 33, *p.* 1345; 1, 35, *p.* 1148; 2, 32, *p.* 431; 3, 34, *p.* 691; 2, 35, *p.* 625.

AGENTS FOR CLAIMS.

(See Claim Agents.)

AGRICULTURE, COMMITTEE ON.

When appointed, and its number. There shall be appointed at the commencement of each Congress a Committee on Agriculture, to consist of eleven members.—*Rule* 74.

Duties of. [No duties are assigned to the Committee on Agricul ture by the rules.]

AMENDMENT.

Precedence of motion to amend. When a question is under debate, no motion shall be received but to adjourn, to lie on the table, for the previous question, to postpone to a day certain, to commit or *amend*, to postpone indefinitely; which several motions shall have *precedence in the order in which they are arranged.—Rule* 42.

Motion to strike out enacting words. A motion to strike out the enacting words of a bill takes precedence of a motion to amend.—*Rule* 123.—(See Enacting words, Motion to strike out.)

When in order to a bill. A bill cannot be amended on the first reading.—*Manual*, *p.* 87. [Indeed, it has become the settled practice of the House not to receive an amendment to a House bill except when the question is on its engrossment, and to a Senate bill except when the question is on ordering it to a third reading.]

Not cut off by previous question. If the motion to amend is pending when a demand for the previous question is made, it is not cut off by the order of the previous question.—*Rule* 132.

An amendment to, only in order. An amendment may be moved to an amendment, but it is not admitted in another degree.—*Manual*, *p.* 104. [But it is the well-settled practice of the House that there may be pending, at the same time with such amendment to the amendment, an amendment in the nature of a substitute for part or the whole of the original text, and an amendment to that amendment.—(See *Journal*, 1, 31, *pp.* 1074, 1075.) It was decided many years ago that if the motion to amend the original matter was *first* submitted, it was not then in order to submit an amendment in the nature of a substitute—*Journal* 1, 19, *p.* 794; but it was subsequently decided otherwise—*Journal*, 1, 28, *p.* 807—and the practice ever since has been in accordance with the latter decision. So, now, notwithstanding the pendency of a motion to amend an amendment to the original matter, a motion to amend, in the nature of a substitute, and a motion to amend that amendment may be received, but cannot be voted upon until the original matter is perfected.]

But there may be also an amendment (in nature of substitute) and amendment to it.

An amendment of the House to a Senate amendment is only in the first degree; for, as to the Senate, the first amendment with which they passed the bill is a part of its text; it is the only text they have agreed to.—*Manual*, *p.* 127.—(See AMENDMENTS BETWEEN THE HOUSES.)

Amendment of Senate's amendment.

"When it is proposed to amend *by inserting a paragraph*, or part of one, the friends of the paragraph may make it as perfect as they can, by amendments, before the question is put for inserting it. If it be received, it cannot be amended afterwards in the same stage, because the House has, on a vote, agreed to it in that form."—*Manual*, *p.* 108. But an amendment which has been inserted may be added to.—*Journal*, 1, 19, *p.* 794.

Paragraph proposed to be inserted may be first amended.

But not afterwards, except by adding to.

Although it is not in order to strike out by itself what has been inserted, it may be moved to strike out a portion of the original paragraph, comprehending what has been inserted, provided the coherence to be struck out be so substantial as to make this effectively a different proposition.—*Manual*, *p.* 110.

Or striking out part of original paragraph including it.

If it is proposed to amend by striking out a paragraph, the friends of the paragraph are first to make it as perfect as they can, by amendments, before the question is put for striking it out.—*Manual*, *p.* 109. But (contrary to the parliamentary practice) if on the question it be

Paragraph proposed to be struck out may be first amended.

Motion to strike out failing.

retained, neither amendment nor a motion to strike out and insert shall be precluded thereby, and a motion to strike out and insert is indivisible.—*Rule* 46.—(See STRIKE OUT, MOTION TO.)

To strike out and insert indivisible.

No withdrawal after.

After a proposition is amended it cannot be withdrawn. —*Rule* 40. [Nor after the previous question is seconded.] It may, however, be withdrawn while the House is dividing on a demand for the previous question.—*Journal*, 2, 29, *p*. 241.

No modification of, after previous question seconded.

A motion to amend cannot be modified after the previous question is seconded—*Journal*, 1, 28, *p*. 811—[doubtless for the reason that the pendency of the particular amendment may be the inducement for seconding the previous question.]

Member yielding for, loses floor.

If a member yields the floor to another to offer an amendment, as he may do, the member yielding loses his right to reoccupy it.—*Journal*, 1, 26, *p*. 248.

Proposing a general provision of law to a private bill not in order.

An amendment proposing to ingraft a general provision of law upon a private bill is against order.—*Journal*, 1, 31, *p*. 784. It is also out of order to ingraft upon a bill for the relief of one individual a provision for the relief of another.—*Journal*, 2, 32, *p*. 414.

Must be germane, and not incorporate any other pending bill.

No motion or proposition on a subject different from that under consideration shall be admitted under color of amendment. And no bill or resolution shall, at any time, be amended by annexing thereto, or incorporating therewith, any other bill or resolution pending before the House.—*Rule* 48. The latter clause of the 48th rule, as originally reported to the House, contained at the end of it, "nor by any proposition containing the *substance*, in whole or in part, of any other bill or resolution pending before the House." These words were stricken out by the House before it would agree to the rule, by which it would seem to have been decided that an amendment containing the *substance* of another bill or resolution may be entertained.—*Note to Rule* 48. [Such, too, has been the practice ever since.] It has been decided that an amendment including the same provisions, to a very great extent, as other bills pending before the House, is in order.—*Journal*, 1, 31, *p*. 1333.

May contain substance of pending bill.

If an amendment be proposed inconsistent with one already agreed to, it is a fit ground for its rejection by the House, but not within the competence of the Speaker to suppress as if it were against order.—*Manual, p.* 108.

Where inconsistent not out of order.

On an amendment being moved, a member who has spoken to the main question may speak again to the amendment.—*Manual, p.* 108.

Presents new question, and a member who has spoken to main question may speak again.

A bill granting lands to a State for railroad purposes may be amended by adding thereto a similar provision for other States.—*Journal*, 1, 32, *pp.* 427, 967.

To bills granting lands for railroads.

A resolution of the House cannot be amended so as to be converted into a *Joint* Resolution.—*Journal*, 1, 32, *p.* 679.

Of resolutions.

No amendment by way of *rider* shall be received to any bill on its third reading.—*Rule* 126.

By way of rider to bill on third reading.

An amendment to the rules cannot be proposed without one day's notice—*Rule* 145—nor, without a similar notice, is it in order to offer an amendment, the effect of which is to change a standing rule.—*Journal*, 1, 17, *p.* 282. And it is virtually an amendment of the rules to impose other duties upon an officer of the House than those already prescribed.—*Journal*, 1, 31, *p.* 456.

To the rules.

An amendment reported from the Committee of the Whole as an entire amendment is not divisible.—*Journals*, 1, 28, *p.* 1061; 1, 29, *pp.* 366, 642; 1, 30, *p.* 1059; 2, 30, *p.* 574. Nor is an amendment of the Senate divisible. —*Journal*, 2, 32, *p.* 401.

From Committee of the Whole or Senate not divisible.

After a bill has been reported from the Committee of the Whole with amendments, it is in order to submit an additional amendment, but the first question put is upon the amendments reported.—*Journal*, 1, 29, *p.* 865. If, in Committee of the Whole, an amendment is adopted, and subsequently the paragraph as amended is struck out, the amendment striking out is the only one to be reported to the House. And if the latter is voted down in the House, the first amendment is not thereby revived. —*Journal*, 2, 31, *p.* 346.

Additional, after report from Committee of Whole.

Where, in Committee of the Whole, paragraph amended and then struck out.

No appropriations shall be reported in a general appropriation bill, or be in order as an amendment thereto, for any expenditure not previously authorized by law, unless

To general appropriation bills.

in continuation of appropriations for such public works and objects as are already in progress, and for the contingencies for carrying on the several Departments of the Government.—*Rule* 120. [This rule, so far as relates to amendments offered, is usually enforced with much strictness, but an instance is not known where the Committee of the Whole has ever ruled out any portion of a bill as reported from the Committee of Ways and Means, although containing provisions in violation of said rule where the bill was committed without any reservation of points of order.]

(See APPROPRIATION BILLS.)

Debate may be closed on, without precluding further.

"The House may at any time, on motion seconded by a majority of the members present, close all debate upon a pending amendment, or an amendment thereto, and cause the question to be put thereon; and this shall not preclude any further amendment or debate upon the bill." —*Rule* 132.

AMENDMENTS BETWEEN THE TWO HOUSES.

Regular progression from disagreement to adherence.

When either house, *e. g.*, the House of Representatives send a bill to the other, the other may pass it with amendments. The regular progression in this case is: that the House disagree to the amendment; the Senate insist on it; the House insist on their disagreement; the Senate adhere to their amendment; the House adhere to their disagreement.—(See *Manual*, *pp.* 125, 126.)

Effect of adherence by both houses.

"After each house shall have adhered to their disagreement, a bill or resolution shall be lost."—*Joint Rule* 15.

Either house may recede.

Motion to recede takes precedence of motion to insist.

House cannot recede from or insist on its amendment with amendment, but may amend other house's amendment.

"Either house may recede from its amendment and agree to the bill; or recede from their disagreement to the amendment, and agree to the same absolutely, or with an amendment."—*Manual*, *p.* 126. And a motion to recede takes precedence of a motion to insist.—*Journals*, 1, 23, *p.* 229; 1, 29, *p.* 696. "But the House cannot recede from or insist on its own amendment with an amendment. * * * They may modify an amendment from the other house by ingrafting an amendment on it."—*Manual*, *p.* 126.

Motion to amend an amendment of other house.

"A motion to amend an amendment from the other house takes precedence of a motion to agree or disagree.

A bill originating in one house is passed by the other with an amendment. The originating house agrees to their amendment with an amendment. The other may agree to their amendment, with an amendment, that being only in the second and not the third degree; for, as to the amending house, the first amendment with which they passed the bill is a part of its text; it is the only text they have agreed to."—*Ibid.*, *p.* 123.

One house may amend the other's amendment to its amendment.

"In the ordinary parliamentary course there are two free conferences, at least, before an adherence."—*Manual*, *p.* 126; *Journals*, 1, 34, *p.* 943; 1, 35, *p.* 1136. Although either house is free to pass over the term of insisting and to adhere in the first instance; but it is not respectful to the other.—*Manual*, *p.* 126. A motion to insist, however, takes precedence of a motion to adhere.—*Journal*, 1, 34, *pp.* 1518, 1526. (See CONFERENCE COMMITTEES.)

Two conferences at least before adherence.

But House may adhere in first instance, but motion to insist takes precedence.

After one House has adhered, the other may recede—*Journals*, 1, 1, *pp.* 113, 114; 1, 2, *p.* 152; 1, 8, *pp.* 671, 673—or ask a conference, which may be agreed to by the adhering house.—*Journals*, 1, 1, *pp.* 156, 157; 1, 3, *pp.* 281, 283; 1, 35, *pp.* 604, 615, 620.—(See ADHERE, MOTION TO.)

After adherence by one house.

APPEAL.

"A question of order arising out of any other question must be decided before that question."—*Manual*, *p.* 105.

Question of order arising out of another question to be decided first.

Questions of order decided by the Speaker shall be "subject to an appeal to the House by any two members; on which appeal no member shall speak more than once, unless by leave of the House."—*Rule* 2. [The questions of order herein referred to relate to motions or propositions, their applicability or relevancy, &c.—*Note to Rule.* 2.] But "all incidental questions of order arising after a motion is made for the previous question, and pending such motion, shall be decided, whether on appeal or otherwise, without debate."—*Rule* 133. [So, too, under the practice, all questions of order which may arise, pending a question which is not debatable, must be decided without debate.] And "all questions relating to the priority of business to be acted on shall be decided without debate."—*Rule* 66.

Questions of order relative to motions, their relevancy, &c., subject to. Debate on.

When not debatable.

In case of member transgressing rules in speaking or indecorum.

"If any member, in speaking or otherwise, transgress the rules of the House, the Speaker shall, or any member may, call to order; in which case the member so called to order shall immediately sit down, unless permitted to explain; and the House shall, if appealed to, decide on the case, but without debate."—*Rule* 61. [The call to order herein referred to has reference only to "transgressions of the rules in speaking," or to indecorum of any kind.]

Not debatable.

(See ORDER.)

No appeal on point of order during a division.

"If any difficulty arises in point of order during the division, the Speaker is to decide peremptorily, subject to the future censure of the House, if irregular."—*Manual, p.* 122.

May be laid on table, and its effect.

An appeal may be laid on the table—*Journal*, 1, 26, *p.* 529—and being laid on the table does not carry with it the whole subject.—*Ibid., p.* 530. [Of late years this motion is almost invariably made in case of an appeal; and if carried, its effect is considered equivalent to a vote sustaining the decision of the Chair.]

Where too late to raise the question of order.

It is too late to renew a question of order on the admissibility of a proposition which has been overruled on the preceding day, where debate has been allowed to progress on such proposition.—*Journal*, 1, 30, *p.* 989. And it is also too late to raise a question of order on a motion entertained without objection on a former day, and entered on the journal.—*Ibid.*, 2, 30, *p.* 382; 1, 38, *p.* 538.

Question just decided on, cannot be renewed.

A question of order just decided on appeal cannot be renewed, even upon the suggestion of additional reasons.—*Ibid.*, 1, 32, *p.* 935.

Where too late to reconsider vote on appeal.

Where an appeal has been decided, and by virtue of such decision a bill taken up and passed, it is too late to move a reconsideration of the vote on the appeal.—*Ibid.*, 1, 31, *pp.* 860, 861.

Pending the election of Speaker, Clerk to decide questions of order.

Pending the election of a Speaker, the Clerk shall decide all questions of order that may arise, subject to appeal to the House.—*Rule* 146.

Not in order while another is pending.

An appeal is not in order while another appeal is pending.—*Cong. Globe*, 1, 27, *p.* 154; 2, 29, *p.* 290.

How questions on, stated.

[The form of stating the question on an appeal is

"Shall the decision of the Chair stand as the judgment of the House?"]

"All questions of order shall be noted by the Clerk, with the decision, and put together at the end of the journal of every session."—*Rule* 15.

Questions of order to be noted and put at end of Journal.

APPROPRIATION BILLS.

"It shall be the duty of the Committee on Appropriations, within thirty days after their appointment, at every session of Congress, commencing on the first Monday of December, to report the general appropriation bills for legislative, executive, and judicial expenses; for sundry civil expenses; for consular and diplomatic expenses; for the Army; for the Navy; for the expenses of the Indian Department; for the payment of invalid and other pensions; for the support of the Military Academy; for fortifications; for the service of the Post Office Department, and for mail transportation by ocean steamers; or, in failure thereof, the reasons of such failure. And said committee shall have leave to report said bills (for reference only) at any time. In all cases where appropriations cannot be made specific in amount the maximum to be expended shall be stated, and each appropriation bill when reported from the committee shall, in the concluding clause, state the sum total of all the items contained in said bill."—*Rule* 77.

General, when to be reported.

General, may be reported at any time.

Amount of appropriations in, must be stated.

"In preparing bills of appropriation for other objects, the Committee on Appropriations shall not include appropriations for carrying into effect treaties made by the United States; and when an appropriation bill shall be referred to them for their consideration which contains appropriations for carrying a treaty into effect, and for other objects, they shall propose such amendments as shall prevent appropriations for carrying a treaty into effect being included in the same bill with appropriations for other objects."—*Rule* 76.

Appropriations for carrying out treaties not to be included in.

But where a general appropriation bill containing an item for carrying out a treaty has been committed by the House, it cannot be ruled out of order by the Committee of the Whole.—*Cong. Globe*, 2, 31, *pp.* 356, 357.

But where committed cannot be ruled out of order.

Amendment to general.

"No appropriation shall be reported in such general appropriation bills, or be in order as an amendment thereto, for any expenditure not previously authorized by law, unless in continuation of appropriations for such public works and objects as are already in progress, and for the contingencies for carrying on the several Departments of the Government."—*Rule* 120. [It has been decided that under this rule it is not in order to propose an amendment to a general appropriation bill, which changes an existing law.—*Journal*, 1, 38, *pp.* 598, 599. But it was also decided that the latter branch of the rule not only permitted amendments increasing salaries, but was framed for that very purpose.—See *Cong. Globe, vol.* 54, *pp.* 306, 325—also *Cong. Globe, vol.* 6, *p.* 224.]

[This rule is rigidly enforced, so far as relates to amendments offered in the House or in committee, but it not unfrequently happens that bills are reported which are in conflict with it; and as they are usually received by the House and committed without being read *in extenso*, the conflict is not discovered until they are considered in committee, when it is too late (unless it is reserved in the House) to make the point.]

All proceedings touching, to be first discussed in Committee of the Whole.

"All proceedings touching appropriations of money shall be first discussed in a Committee of the Whole House."—*Rule* 112. [The construction given to this rule is, that all bills, or amendments thereto, containing an appropriation of money, must be committed to a Committee of the Whole before being considered in the House; hence, if such a bill, on its engrossment, or third reading, or such an amendment, be pending before the House, and no motion is made to commit or postpone, the House must pass from its consideration, and the bill go to the Speaker's table. But House bills with Senate amendments reducing the amount of, or restricting appropriations, need not be committed.]

Bills which need not be committed as.

But a bill directing the disbursement of money *already appropriated*—*Journal*, 1, 24, *p.* 254—or directing payment of money hereafter to be appropriated—*Journal*, 1, 31, *p.* 1216; 1, 38, *p.* 538—need not be committed. Neither is it necessary that a bill containing an appropriation of *lands* should be committed.—*Journal*, 1, 30, *p.* 526. And when the rules have been suspended for the purpose of enabling the report of a measure to be made, and also for its consideration, a point of order that it contains an appropriation cannot be well taken.—*Journal*, 1, 34, *pp*. 1172, 1173.

When point of order on, cannot be well taken.

"General appropriation bills shall be in order in preference to any other bills of a public nature, unless otherwise ordered by a majority of the House. And the House may, at any time, by a vote of a majority of the members present, make any of the general appropriation bills a special order."—*Rule* 119.

Preference given to general, in the House.

General, may be made special order at any time.

"And in Committee of the Whole House on the state of the Union, general appropriation bills, and, in time of war, bills for raising men and money, and bills concerning a treaty of peace, shall be preferred to all other bills, at the discretion of the committee; and when demanded by any member, the question (of consideration) shall first be put in regard to them."—*Rule* 114. [Existing special orders, however, (being made under a suspension of the rules,) take precedence of all other business.]

Preference given to general, in Committee of the Whole.

[In the consideration of general appropriation bills, the *clauses* are invariably treated as *sections* in other bills.]

Clauses of, to be treated as sections.

"Upon the engrossment of any bill making appropriations of money for works of internal improvement of any kind or description, it shall be in the power of any member to call for a division of the question, so as to take a separate vote of the House upon each item of improvement or appropriation contained in said bill, or upon such items separately, and others collectively, as the members making the call may specify; and if one-fifth of the members present second said call, it shall be the duty of the Speaker to make such divisions of the question, and put them to vote accordingly."—*Rule* 121.

Division of the question on, for internal improvements.

APPROPRIATIONS, COMMITTEE ON.

This committee, to consist of eleven members, is directed to be appointed at the commencement of each Congress.—*Rule* 74. Its duty shall be to take into consideration all executive communications, and such other propositions in regard to carrying on the several departments of the

Its number, and when appointed.

Duties of.

Government, as may be presented and referred to them by the House. In preparing bills of appropriations for other objects, the said committee shall not include appropriations for carrying into effect treaties made by the United States; and where an appropriation bill shall be referred to them for their consideration, which contains appropriations for carrying a treaty into effect and for other objects, they shall propose such amendments as shall prevent appropriations for carrying a treaty into effect being included in the same bill with appropriations for other objects.—*Rule* 76.

It shall also be the duty of the said committee, within thirty days after their appointment, at every session of Congress commencing on the first Monday of December, to report the general appropriation bills for legislative, executive, and judicial expenses; for sundry civil expenses; for consular and diplomatic expenses; for the Army; for the Navy; for the expenses of the Indian department; for the payment of invalid and other pensions; for the support of the Military Academy; for fortifications; for the service of the Post Office Department and for mail transportation by ocean steamers; or in failure thereof, the reasons of such failure. And said committee shall have leave to report said bills (for reference only) at any time. In all cases where appropriations cannot be made specific in amount, the maximum to be expended shall be stated, and each appropriation bill, when reported from the committee, shall in the concluding clause state the sum total of all the items contained in said bill.—*Rule* 77.

Amount in appropriation bills to be stated.

In reporting the reasons above referred to, the report must be in writing.—*Congressional Globe*, 1, 31, *pp.* 1207,'8.

Reasons to be reported in writing.

AYES AND NOES.

(See YEAS AND NAYS.)

BALLOT.

When committees are to be appointed by.

"All committees shall be appointed by the Speaker, unless otherwise specially directed by the House, in which case they shall be appointed by ballot; and if, upon such ballot, the number required shall not be elected by a majority of the votes given, the House shall proceed to a second ballot, in which a plurality shall prevail; and in case a greater number than is required to compose or complete a committee shall have an equal number of votes, the House shall proceed to a further ballot or ballots."—*Rule* 67. "In all other cases of ballot than for committees, a majority of the votes given shall be necessary to an election; and where there shall not be such a majority on the first ballot, the ballots shall be repeated until a majority be obtained; and in all ballotings blanks shall be rejected, and not taken into the count in enumeration of votes, or reported by the tellers."—*Rule* 12.

"In all cases of ballot by the House, the Speaker shall vote."—*Rule* 7. Speaker shall vote in cases of.

"No member or other person shall visit or remain by the Clerk's table while ballots are counting."—*Rule* 65. No person to visit Clerk's desk while counting.

[There has been no instance for many years where a vote by ballot has been taken in the House, the Speaker and other officers having been elected by *viva voce* votes, and the committees appointed by the Speaker.] Vote of late years not taken by.

(See ELECTIONS and COMMITTEES.)

BANKING AND CURRENCY, COMMITTEE ON.

This committee, to consist of eleven members, is directed to be appointed at the commencement of each Congress.—*Rule* 74. Its number, and when appointed. Its duty shall be to take into consideration all propositions relative to banking and the currency as shall be presented or shall come in question and be referred to them by the House, and to report thereon by bill or otherwise. Its duty.

BAR OF THE HOUSE.

"No member shall vote in any case where he was not within the bar of the House when the question was put. In order to vote, members must be "within the bar." When the roll-call is completed, the Speaker shall state that any member offering to vote does so upon the assurance that he was within the bar before the last name on the roll was called: *Provided, however*, That any member who was absent by leave of the House may vote at any time before the result is announced."—*Rule* 29.

Smoking prohibited within the bar.

Smoking is prohibited within the bar of the House.—*Rule* 65.

What is meant by "within."

[At the 1st session 35th Congress, (see *Journal, p.* 337,) soon after the occupancy of the present hall, it was decided that, in order to be entitled to vote, a member must have been upon the floor of the hall, and not outside of *any* of the doors leading into it.]

No vote of a member without the bar counted.

"Upon a division and count of the House on any question, no member without the bar shall be counted."—*Rule* 30.

BILLS.

(See also PRIVATE BILLS AND PRIVATE BUSINESS.)

How bills are introduced.

Every bill shall be introduced on the report of a committee, or by motion for leave—*Rule* 115—or upon the report of the Court of Claims.—(*Stat. at Large, Vol. X, pp.* 613, 614.)

Revenue bills.

"All bills for raising revenue shall originate in the House of Representatives, but the Senate may propose or concur with amendments, as on other bills."—*Const.*, 1, 7, 10.

Bills on leave.

"In the case of a bill on leave, at least one day's notice shall be given of the motion in the House, or by filing a memorandum thereof with the Clerk, and having it entered on the Journal; and the motion shall be made and the bill introduced, if leave is given, when resolutions are called for; such motion, or the bill when introduced, may be committed. But the Speaker shall not entertain a motion for leave to introduce a bill or joint resolution for the establishment or change of post routes, and all propositions relating thereto shall be referred, under the rule, like petitions and other papers, to the appropriate committee."—*Rule* 115.

In relation to post routes.

Bills on leave, when and how introduced.

"All the States and Territories shall be called for bills on leave and resolutions every Monday during each session of Congress; and, if necessary to secure the object on said days, all resolutions which shall give rise to debate shall lie over for discussion, under the rules of the House already established; and the whole of said days shall be appropriated to bills on leave and resolutions, until all the States and Territories are called through. And the Speaker shall first call the States and Territories for bills on leave; and all bills so introduced during the first hour after the Journal is read shall be referred, without debate, to their appropriate committees: *Provided, however*, That a bill so introduced and referred, and all bills at any time introduced by unanimous consent and referred, shall not be brought back into the House upon a motion to reconsider."—*Rule* 130. (See MORNING HOUR ON MONDAYS.)

What bills not to be brought back by motion to reconsider.

[The notice above referred to is rarely given in the House, (it being in order to give it there only when resolutions are in order,) but is usually given to the Clerk by sending to him a written memorandum in this form: "Mr. —— gives notice that to-morrow, or on some subsequent day, he will ask leave to introduce a bill (here insert its title.") If the member desires his notice to appear in the newspaper report of the proceedings of the House, he should furnish the reporter of such paper with a copy of the memorandum furnished the Clerk. Having given his notice, it is then in order, on any subsequent day, when bills on leave and resolutions are being called for, and when his particular State is called, to move for leave to introduce his bill. The practice of introducing bills on leave, it may be remarked, however, does not facilitate business. If, instead of waiting for an opportunity to introduce his bill on leave, the member would file his petition, or whatever other matter he may have in favor of the proposed legislation, and have *it* referred to the appropriate committee, as he may do on *any day*, under *Rule* 131, (see PETITIONS,) he will thus have the subject before them, and will get a bill reported as speedily as if it had been originally referred. Besides, the bill thus reported comes before the House unencumbered with amendments, as is not likely to be the case with a bill previously referred. These suggestions, of course, do not apply to cases where the immediate passage of a bill, without the intervention of a committee, is sought for, or where it is desirable to refer it to a *select* committee.]

Form of notice

To have notice appear in newspaper.

When to move for leave.

Objections to the practice of introducing bills on leave.

For information in regard to bills reported from a committee, see COMMITTEES.

Bills reported from committees.

Bills reported from Court of Claims. So in regard to bills reported from and to be referred to the Court of Claims.—See CLAIMS, COURT OF.

Every bill shall have three readings. "Every bill shall receive three several readings in the House previous to its passage; and bills shall be dispatched in order as they were introduced, unless where the House shall direct otherwise; but no bill shall be twice read on the same day without special order of the House."—*Rule* 116. [The "special order" here referred to is generally assumed to have been given, for unless objection is made, immediately after the bill is read a first time, the Speaker announces "the second reading of the bill," and it thereupon receives its second reading.]

Objection after first reading. The first reading of a bill shall be for information, and if opposition be made to it, the question shall be: "Shall this bill be rejected?"—*Rule* 117. And this question is debatable.—*Journal*, 2, 32, *p.* 152. But "if no opposition be made, or if the question to reject be negatived, the bill shall go to its second reading without a question."—*Rule* 117.

Second reading.

Usually read by their title. [The three readings of a bill are usually by the title, the readings throughout usually taking place in Committee of the Whole; but where there is no commitment, it then takes place whenever it is proposed to put the bill on its passage. It is the undoubted right, however, of any member to have a bill read through at every stage of its progress through the House.—See READING OF PAPERS.]

Right of a members to have read through.

After second reading. "Upon the second reading of the bill, the Speaker shall state it as ready for commitment or engrossment; and, if committted, then a question shall be, whether to a select or standing committee, or to a Committee of the Whole House; if no motion be made to commit, the question shall be stated on its engrossment; and if it be not ordered to be engrossed on the day of its being reported, it shall be placed on the general file on the Speaker's table, to be taken up in order. But if the bill be ordered to be engrossed, the House shall appoint the day when it shall be read the third time."—*Rule* 118.

Open to debate, &c. [The settled practice of the House upon the second reading of a bill, unless it be an APPROPRIATION BILL, (which see,) is to consider it as open to debate,] when, under the 42d *Rule*, it is in a condition for a motion to lie on the table, for the previous question, to postpone to a day certain, to commit or amend, to postpone indefinitely, which several motions take precedence in the order in which they are arranged. "But a motion to strike out the enacting words of a bill shall have precedence of a motion to amend; and, if carried, shall be considered equivalent to its rejection."—*Rule* 123. (See all of said motions respectively.)

Commitment.

Amendment.

Enacting words may be stricken out.

[The question of engrossment is put in this form, viz: "Shall the bill be engrossed and read a third time?" If it be negatived, the bill is rejected; but if it be decided in the affirmative, and the bill is actually engrossed, or no question is made on its failure to be engrossed, the Speaker *immediately* directs "the third reading of the bill." But if the question is made, and it be not actually engrossed, the bill goes to the Speaker's table. In the case of a Senate bill, the engrossment having already been made before it came to the House, the question which arises is, "Shall the bill be read a third time?" which being decided negatively the bill is rejected, but being decided affirmatively the bill is immediately read a third time.]

Engrossment and third reading.

Third reading of Senate bills.

[Where the bill has a preamble, although there is no rule, and until lately no settled practice, defining the stage at which it is to be considered, it would seem to be most appropriate that its consideration should take place *after the bill has been ordered to be engrossed and read a third time, and before the third reading takes place.* By this course, the bill can be engrossed either with or without the preamble, as the House shall have determined.]

In case of a bill with a preamble.

[After the third reading of a bill, the question which next arises in course is, "Shall the bill pass?" At this stage the bill is again open to debate, but is not amendable; it may, however, under the 124th *Rule*, be recommitted at any time before passage.—(See RECOMMIT, MOTION TO.)]

After third reading.

Debate.

Recommitment.

[The bill having passed, and the title having been read, the Speaker states, "If there be no objection this

After passage.

Title. will remain the title of the bill." The title, however, is subject to amendment, and, unless the previous question is ordered on it, is also debatable.]

After title disposed of. [After the title is disposed of, it is usual for the member having charge of the bill to move "that the vote last taken be reconsidered, and that the motion to reconsider be laid on the table;" which latter motion having been decided in the affirmative, no reconsideration can take place, and the transmission of the bill to the Senate cannot be delayed. Indeed, it is not uncommon to make the motion "to reconsider and lie" at every stage of the bill.]

Motion to reconsider and lie.

Certified by Clerk and taken to the Senate. The bill is then, as required by *Rule* 127, "certified by the Clerk, notifying the day of its passage at the foot thereof," and conveyed by him to the Senate, "together with all the papers on which it is founded," as required by *Joint Rule* 14. But "no bill that shall have passed one house shall be sent for concurrence to the other on either of the last three days of the session."—*Joint Rule* 16. [This rule is almost invariably suspended by the two houses near the close of a session.]

Not to be taken to the Senate on last three days of session.

To be on paper, when on passage between the two houses. "While bills are on their passage between the two houses, they shall be on paper, and under the signature of the Secretary or Clerk of each house respectively."—*Joint Rule* 5.

After the return of, from Senate, with amendment. [After the bill has been acted on by the Senate, it is brought back to the House by the Secretary of the Senate, together with a report of their action thereon. If it has passed with amendment, it is placed on the Speaker's table, to be taken up in its order under the 54th *Rule.*

Action on Senate amendment to. When taken up, the amendment of the Senate may be either agreed to, disagreed to, or agreed to with amendment; in case of an appropriation of money being involved in the amendment, however, it must be first considered in a Committee of the Whole.

When the Senate amendment is agreed to. If the amendment of the Senate is agreed to, that body is notified of the fact by message through the Clerk, and the bill is enrolled.]

In case of disagreement by the House to, or amendment of, the Senate's amendment, see AMENDMENTS BETWEEN THE HOUSES and CONFERENCE COMMITTEES. Amendments between the houses.

"After a bill shall have passed both houses, it shall be duly enrolled on parchment by the Clerk of the House of Representatives or the Secretary of the Senate, as the bill may have originated in the one or the other house, before it shall be presented to the President of the United States."—*Joint Rule* 6. After passage by both houses, to be enrolled on parchment.

"When bills are enrolled, they shall be examined by a joint committee of two from the Senate and two from the House of Representatives, appointed as a standing committee for that purpose, who shall carefully compare the enrollment with the engrossed bills, as passed in the two houses, and, correcting any errors that may be discovered in the enrolled bills, make their report forthwith to their respective houses."—*Joint Rule* 7. When enrolled, to be examined.

(See ENROLLED BILLS, COMMITTEE ON.)

"After examination and report, each bill shall be signed in their respective houses, first by the Speaker of the House of Representatives, then by the President of the Senate."—*Joint Rule* 8. When examined, to be reported to House and signed by Speaker.

"After a bill shall have been thus signed in each house, it shall be presented by the said committee to the President of the United States for his approbation, it being first indorsed on the back of the roll, certifying in which house the same originated; which indorsement shall be signed by the Secretary or Clerk (as the case may be) of the house in which the same did originate, and shall be entered on the Journal of each house. The said committee shall report the day of presentation to the President, which time shall also be carefully entered on the Journal of each house."—*Joint Rule* 9. After being signed by presiding officers, to be presented to President. But "no bill or resolution that shall have passed the House of Representatives and the Senate shall be presented to the President of the United States for his approbation on the last day of the session."—*Joint Rule* 17. [This rule, like the 16th, is generally suspended near the close of the session.] But not on last day of session.

After being presented to President. After a bill is presented to the President, "if he approve he shall sign it; but if not, he shall return it, with his objections, to that house in which it shall have originated."—*Const.*, 1, 7, *p.* 10. [Where the President approves a bill, it is customary for him to notify the house where the bill originated of the fact, and the date of his approval, which is entered on the Journal.]

Where bill is approved.

When an act has been approved by the President the usual number of copies shall be printed for the use of the House.—*Rule* 157. And messages from the President giving notice of bills approved shall be repeated from the Clerk's desk forthwith.—*Rule* 158.

Where vetoed. In case of a bill returned with the objections of the President, see VETO.

Where not returned within ten days. "If any bill shall not be returned by the President within ten days (Sundays excepted) after it shall have been presented to him, the same shall be a law, in like manner as if he had signed it, unless the Congress, by their adjournment, prevent its return, in which case it shall not be a law."—*Const.*, 1, 7, *p.* 10. Where a bill is allowed to become a law by reason of the failure of the President to return the same, it is usual for him to notify the House of that fact, as in the case of approval.—*Journals*, 2, 36, *pp.* 424, 480; 2, 39, *p.* 479. And where he is prevented by an adjournment from returning a bill, it is usual for him to communicate his reasons at the next session for not approving it.—*Journals*, 2, 12, *p.* 544; 1, 30, *p.* 82; 2, 35, *p.* 151.

Where President is prevented from returning by reason of adjournment.

Where bill of one house is rejected in the other. "When a bill or resolution which shall have passed in one house is rejected in the other, notice thereof shall be given to the house in which the same shall have passed."—*Joint Rule* 12. And when so rejected, "it shall not be brought in during the same session, without a notice of ten days and leave of two-thirds of that house in which it shall be renewed."—*Joint Rule* 13.

Not to be brought in again without leave of two-thirds.

Bills undisposed of at end of session. In regard to bills left undisposed of at the end of a session, see UNFINISHED BUSINESS.

Printing of. In regard to the printing of bills, see PRINTING, PUBLIC.

BINDING.

Extra copies of documents, the size of which shall not be less than 250 pages, shall be bound under the direction of the Committee on Printing on the part of the House, at a cost not exceeding 12½ cents per volume."—Act of March 3, 1853.—*Stat. at Large, Vol. X, p.* 190. Of extra copies of documents.

"The Clerk shall have preserved for each member of the House an extra copy, in good binding, of all the documents printed by order of either house at each future session of Congress."—*Rule* 18. Of session documents.

By the joint resolution of June 23, 1860, the Superintendent of Public Printing is directed to have the binding of each house executed.—*Stat. at Large, Vol. XII, p.* 117 to 120. Superintendent of Public Printing to have executed.

(See PRINTING, PUBLIC.)

BLANK BOOKS.

All the blank books ordered by Congress, or by either House of Congress, shall be done and executed under the Superintendent of Public Printing.—*Stat. at Large, Vol. XII, p.* 118. To be furnished by Superintendent of Public Printing.

BLANKS.

"In filling up blanks, the largest sum and longest time shall be first put."—*Rule* 50. [But where a specific time or sum stands part of a motion, it is not until it is struck out, and a blank thereby produced, that this rule can begin to operate.] How filled.

"A bill passed by the one House with blanks. These may be filled up by the other by way of amendments, returned to the first as such, and passed."—*Manual, p.* 111. Left by one house, may be filled by the other.

"In all ballotings blanks shall be rejected, and not taken into the count in enumeration of votes, or reported by the tellers."—*Rule* 12. Not to be counted in ballotings.

BOND.

The Sergeant-at-Arms shall give bond, with surety, to the United States, in a sum not less than five nor Of Sergeant-at-Arms.

more than ten thousand dollars, at the discretion of the Speaker, and with such surety as the Speaker may approve, faithfully to account for the money coming into his hands for the pay of members."—*Rule* 26.

Of Clerk.

The Clerk shall, within thirty days after he enters upon the duties of his office, give bond to the United States, with one or more sureties, to be approved by the Comptroller of the Treasury, in the penal sum of twenty thousand dollars, with condition for the faithful application and disbursement of the contingent fund of the House."—*Stat. at Large, Vol. III, p.* 212.

BOOKS.

Price of, received by members, to be deducted from compensation.

"If any books shall hereafter be ordered to and received by members of Congress by a resolution of either or both houses of Congress, the price paid for the same shall be deducted from the compensation provided for such member or members: *Provided, however*, That this shall not extend to books ordered to be printed by the Public Printer during the Congress for which the said member shall have been elected."—*Stat. at Large, Vol. XI, p.* 49.

BRIBERY.

Attempted, of member, breach of privilege.

An offer to bribe a member is held to be a breach of the privileges of the House.—*Journals* 1, 4, *p.* 389; 1, 15, *pp.* 117, 154; *Manual, p.* 59.

Of members of Congress.

By the act of February 26, 1853, it is provided "that if any person or persons shall, directly or indirectly, promise, offer, or give, or cause or procure to be promised, offered, or given, any money, goods, right in action, bribe, present, or reward, or any promise, contract, undertaking, obligation, or security for the payment or delivery of any money, goods, right in action, bribe, present, or reward, or any other valuable thing whatever, to any member of the Senate or House of Representatives, after his election as such member, and either before or after he shall have qualified and taken his seat, or to any officer of the United States, or person holding any place of profit or trust, or discharging any official functions under or in connection with any department of the Government of the United States, or under the Senate or House of Representatives of the United States, with intent to influence his vote or decision on any question, matter, cause, or proceeding which may then be pending, or may by law, or under the Constitution of the United States, be brought before him in his official capacity, or in his place of trust or profit, and shall be convicted thereof, such person or persons so offering, promising, or giving, or causing or procuring to be promised, offered, or given, any such money, goods, right in action, bribe, present, or reward or any promise, contract, undertaking, obligation, or security for the payment or delivery of any money, goods, right in action, bribe, present, or reward, or other valuable thing whatever; and the member, officer, or person who shall in any wise accept or receive the same, or any part thereof, shall be liable to indictment, as for a high crime and misdemeanor, in any court of the United States having jurisdiction for the trial of crimes and misdemeanors, and shall, upon conviction thereof, be fined not exceeding three times the amount so offered, promised, or given, and imprisoned in a penitentiary not exceeding three years; and the person convicted of so accepting or receiving the same, or any part thereof, if an officer or person holding any such place of trust or profit as aforesaid, shall forfeit his office or place; and any person so convicted under this section shall forever be disqualified to hold any office of honor, trust, or profit under the United States."—*Stat. at Large, Vol. X, p.* 171.

Of employés of the House.

Acceptance of bribes.

Penalty for.

BUSINESS—DAILY ORDER OF.

"The Speaker shall take the chair every day precisely at the hour to which the House shall have adjourned on the preceding day; shall immediately call the members to order; and, on the appearance of a quorum, shall cause the Journal of the preceding day to be read."—*Rule* 1.

Reading of the Journal.

"The consideration of the unfinished business in which the House may be engaged at an adjournment shall be resumed as soon as the Journal of the next day is read,

Unfinished business of preceding day considered.

and at the same time each day thereafter until disposed of."—*Rule* 56.

Reports of committees called for.

"As soon as the Journal is read, and the unfinished business in which the House was engaged at the last preceding adjournment has been disposed of, reports from committees shall be called for and disposed of; in doing which the Speaker shall call upon each standing committee in regular order, and then upon select committees; and if the Speaker shall not get through the call upon the committees before the House passes to other business, he shall resume the next call where he left off—giving preference to the report last under consideration: *Provided*, That whenever any committee shall have occupied the morning hour on two days, it shall not be in order for such committee to report further until the other committees shall have been called in their turn. [But this proviso does not prevent the House from occupying the morning hour on more than two days in the consideration of a report previously made.]—*Rule* 51.—(See MORNING HOURS ON MONDAYS.)

Call of States and Territories for resolutions and bills on leave.

"Reports from committees having been presented and disposed of, the Speaker shall call for resolutions from the members of each State and delegate from each Territory, beginning with Maine and the Territory last organized, alternately; and they shall not be debated on the very day of their being presented, nor on any day assigned by the House for the receipt of resolutions, unless where the House shall direct otherwise, but shall lie on the table to be taken up in the order in which they were presented; and if on any day the whole of the States and Territories shall not be called, the Speaker shall begin on the next day where he left off the previous day: *Provided*, That no member shall offer more than one resolution, or one series of resolutions, all relating to the same subject, until all the States and Territories shall have been called."—*Rule* 52. And at this time bills on leave may be introduced.—*Rule* 115.

Business on the Speaker's table.

"After one hour shall have been devoted to reports from committees, and resolutions, it shall be in order, pending the consideration or discussion thereof, to entertain a motion that the House do now proceed to dispose of the business on the Speaker's table, and to the orders of the day, which being decided in the affirmative, the Speaker shall dispose of the business on his table in the following order, viz:

"1st. Messages and other Executive communications.

"2d. Messages from the Senate, and amendments proposed by the Senate to bills of the House.

"3d. Bills and resolutions from the Senate on their first and second reading, that they be referred to committees and put under way; but if, on being read a second time, no motion being made to commit, they are to be ordered to their third reading, unless objections be made; in which case, if not otherwise ordered by a majority of the House, they are to be laid on the table in the general file of bills on the Speaker's table, to be taken up in their turn.

"4th. Engrossed bills and bills from the Senate on their third reading.

"5th. Bills of the House and from the Senate, on the Speaker's table, on their engrossment, or on being ordered to a third reading, to be taken up and considered in the order of time in which they passed to a second reading.

"The messages, communications, and bills on his table having been disposed of, the Speaker shall then proceed to call the orders of the day."—*Rule* 54.

May be interfered with.

[The foregoing is the order of business which may be pursued, under the rules, each day, except Fridays, Saturdays, and Mondays; but it is often interfered with by questions of privilege, special orders, privileged questions, &c.]

On Friday and Saturday, and mode of proceeding on those days.

"Friday and Saturday in every week shall be set apart for the consideration of private bills and private business, in preference to any other, unless otherwise determined by a majority of the House."—*Rule* 128. [On those days, as soon as the Journal is read, and the unfinished business of the last private-bill day is disposed of, the Speaker proceeds to call the committees for reports of a private nature, which being disposed of, it is his practice, without motion, to lay before the House such private business as may be upon his table. It is then usual for some member (commonly the chairman of the Committee of Claims) to move that the House resolve itself into a Committee of the Whole on the private calendar. This motion may be, and often is, made as soon as the Journal is read. Although it takes precedence of the motion to go into Committee of the Whole on the state of the Union, (unless there be a special order pending therein,) and, if made, must be first voted on, the latter motion is often made and carried, and thus private bills fail to receive consideration.]

First and fourth Fridays and Saturdays of the month.

"On the first and fourth Friday and Saturday of each month the calendar of private bills shall be called over, (the chairman of the Committee of the Whole House commencing the call where he left off the previous day,) and the bills to the passage of which no objection shall then be made shall be first considered and disposed of. But when a bill is again reached, after having been once objected to, the committee shall consider and dispose of the same, unless it shall again be objected to by at least five members."—*Rule* 129. It has been decided that this rule, so far as relates to the consideration of bills only which are not objected to, applies as well to private bills in the House as in committee.—*Journal*, 1, 31, *p.* 697.

On Monday, call for resolutions and bills on leave.

"All the States and Territories shall be called for bills on leave and resolutions every Monday during each session of Congress; and, if necessary to secure the object on said days, all resolutions which shall give rise to debate shall lie over for discussion, under the rules of the House already established; and the whole of said days shall be appropriated to bills on leave and resolutions, until all the States and Territories are called through. And the Speaker shall first call the States and Territories for bills on leave; and all bills so introduced during the first hour after the Journal is read shall be referred, without debate, to their appropriate committees: *Provided, however*, That a bill so introduced and referred shall not be brought back into the House upon a motion to reconsider. And on said call joint resolutions of State and Territorial legislatures for printing and reference may be introduced."—*Rule* 130.—(See MORNING HOUR ON MONDAYS.)

Resolutions of State legislatures.

On Monday of every week, at the expiration of one hour after the Journal is read, or earlier if the call of States and Territories for bills and resolutions is concluded, the Speaker may entertain a motion to suspend the rules.—*Rule* 125.

On every Monday, after one hour has expired.

"The order of business, as established by the rules, shall not be changed, except by a vote of at least two-thirds of the members present."—*Rule* 145.

Order of business only changed by two-thirds vote.

BUSINESS—ON THE SPEAKER'S TABLE.

"After one hour shall have been devoted to reports from committees and resolutions, it shall be in order, pending the consideration or discussion thereof, to entertain a motion that the House do now proceed to dispose of the business on the Speaker's table."—*Rule* 54. [The "hour"—known as the "morning hour"—is construed to begin from the announcement by the Speaker to the House that reports of committees are in order, and it is not necessary that resolutions shall have been called for. It is an invariable practice, too, to permit a member, upon the expiration of the morning hour, to take the floor, even though another may be occupying it, to make the motion to proceed to business on the Speaker's table.]

When motion may be made to go to.

When morning hour begins.

Floor may be taken from member to make motion.

"The motion to go to business on the Speaker's table being decided in the affirmative, the Speaker shall dispose of it in the following order, viz:

Order of disposing of.

"1st. Messages and other Executive communications.

"2d. Messages from the Senate, and amendments proposed by the Senate to bills of the House.

"3d. Bills and resolutions from the Senate on their first and second reading, that they be referred to committees and put under way; but if, on being read a second time, no motion being made to commit, they are to be ordered to their third reading, unless objection be made; in which case, if not otherwise ordered by a majority of the House, they are to be laid on the table in the general file of bills on the Speaker's table, to be taken up in their turn.

"4th. Engrossed bills and bills from the Senate on their third reading.

"5th. Bills of the House and from the Senate on the Speaker's table, on their engrossment, or on being ordered to a third reading, to be taken up and considered in the order of time in which they passed to a second reading.

"The messages, communications, and bills on his table having been disposed of, the Speaker shall then proceed to call the orders of the day."—*Rule* 54.

Weekly statement of, on table.

"The Clerk shall make a weekly statement of the resolutions and bills upon the Speaker's table."—*Rule* 19. [A printed copy of this statement is laid upon each member's table every Monday morning.]

BUSINESS—UNFINISHED AT END OF A FIRST SESSION.

Bills, resolutions, and reports to be resumed after six days.

"After six days from the commencement of a second or subsequent session of any Congress, all bills, resolutions, and reports, which originated in the House, and at the close of the next preceding session remained undetermined, shall be resumed and acted on in the same manner as if an adjournment had not taken place. And all business before Committees of the House at the end of one session shall be resumed at the commencement of the next session of the same Congress, as if no adjournment had taken place."—*Rule* 136.

Before committees, to be resumed as though no adjournment.

[And by the 21st *Joint Rule* the resumption of all undisposed-of bills, resolutions, and reports, which originated in either house, is in like manner provided for. The word "resolutions" in the foregoing rule has been invariably held to apply to "Joint Resolutions" only.]

CALLS ON THE PRESIDENT AND DEPARTMENTS.

(See PRESIDENT and EXECUTIVE DEPARTMENTS.)

CALL OF THE HOUSE.

Less than a quorum may be authorized to compel attendance.

By the Constitution of the United States a smaller number than a quorum of each house "may be authorized to compel the attendance of absent members in such manner and under such penalties as each house may provide."—*Const.*, 1, 5, *p.* 8.

"Any fifteen members (including the Speaker, if there be one) shall be authorized to compel the attendance of absent members."—*Rule* 34. But where less than that number are present a motion for a call cannot be entertained.—*Journal* 1, 28, *p.* 885.

Fifteen members authorized to compel attendance, but not less.

"A call of the House shall not be in order after the previous question is seconded, unless it shall appear, upon an actual count by the Speaker, that no quorum is present."—*Rule* 132.

Unless no quorum, not in order after previous question is seconded.

A call of the House may be moved before the Journal is read, if no quorum is present.—*Journal*, 1, 34, *p.* 1253.

In order before the Journal is read, if no quorum present.

"Upon calls of the House, the names of the members shall be called over (alphabetically—*Rule* 35) by the Clerk, and the absentees noted. After which the names of the absentees shall again be called over. The doors shall then be shut, and those for whom no excuse or insufficient excuses are made, may, by order of those present, if fifteen in number, be taken into custody as they appear, or may be sent for and taken into custody wherever to be found, by special messengers to be appointed for that purpose."—*Rule* 36.

Proceedings in case of.
Roll to be called twice.
Doors shut.
Excuses received.
Order for arrest of absentees, &c.

[The order of arrest is not usually made by the House unless a quorum cannot otherwise be obtained; and upon the appearance of a quorum, a motion is usually made and carried that "all further proceedings in the call be dispensed with;" and this motion is held to be in order at any period of the proceedings. The order for arrest is usually in this form, viz: "That the Sergeant-at-Arms take into custody and bring to the bar of the House, such of its members as are now absent without the leave of the House;" and, upon its adoption, a warrant, under the hand and seal of the Speaker, and attested by the Clerk, with a list of the absentees thereto attached, is immediately placed in the hands of the Sergeant-at-Arms. Upon his appearance with members under arrest, he is announced at the bar of the House by the Doorkeeper,

Order of arrest, when usually made.
Call may be dispensed with at any time.
Form of order of arrest.
Issue of warrant.
Return of warrant.

whereupon he makes his return. The members brought in by him are then severally arraigned by the Speaker and interrogated by him as to what excuses they may have to offer for being absent from the sitting of the House without its leave.]

Arraignment of absent members.

"When a member shall be discharged from custody and admitted to his seat, the House shall determine whether such discharge shall be with or without paying fees; and in like manner, whether a delinquent member, taken into custody by a special messenger, shall or shall not be liable to defray the expense of such special messenger."—*Rule* 37. In regard to the fees of Sergeant-at-Arms and special messenger, see SERGEANT-AT-ARMS.

House to determine as to payment of fees.

Fees against delinquent members.

Until a member has paid the fees assessed against him, he is not at liberty to address the Chair or make a question of order.—*Journal*, 1, 36, *p*. 1025.

Member must pay fees before he can be recognized.

It is not in order for the House to take a recess during a call of the House.—*Journal*, 1, 26, *p*. 843. [Indeed, no motion, except to adjourn or with reference to the call, is ever entertained during a call.]

Recess not in order during.

Only to adjourn or with reference to call.

[By an adjournment pending a call all proceedings in the call are terminated; but where the House has previously passed an order specially directing otherwise, such special direction should doubtless be executed.—See *Journal*, 2, 27, *p*. 672.]

By an adjournment proceedings in, ordinarily fall.

CAPITOL.

"The unappropriated rooms in that part of the Capitol assigned to the House shall be subject to the order and disposal of the Speaker until the further order of the House."—*Rule* 5. The Speaker shall also "have a general direction of the hall."—*Rule* 5. And "no person shall be permitted to perform divine service in the chamber occupied by the House of Representatives unless with the consent of the Speaker."—*Rule* 6. The hall of the House shall not be used for any other purpose than the legitimate business of the House, nor shall the Speaker entertain any proposition to use it for any other purpose or for the suspension of this rule: *Provided*, That this shall not interfere with the performance of divine ser-

Speaker has control over hall and other rooms.

Hall not to be used except for legitimate business.

vice therein under the direction of the Speaker, or with the use of the same for caucus meetings of the members, or upon occasions when the House may, by resolution, agree to take part in any ceremonies to be observed therein.—*Rule* 155.

Spirituous liquors prohibited in, or grounds.

No spirituous or malt liquors or wines shall be offered for sale, exhibited, or kept within the Capitol, or in any room or building connected therewith, or on the public grounds adjacent thereto. And it shall be the duty of the Sergeants-at-Arms of the two houses, under the supervision of the presiding officers thereof, respectively, to enforce the foregoing provisions. And any officer or employé of either house who shall in any manner violate or connive at the violation of this rule shall be dismissed from office.—*Joint Rule* 19.

The Vice-President and the Speaker to prescribe rules for keeping, and grounds not in exclusive occupancy of either house.

By the act of Congress of May 2, 1828, *Stat. at Large, Vol. IV, page* 266, the Commissioner of Public Buildings is directed to take charge of and superintend the public buildings: "And it shall be the duty of the Commissioner of Public Buildings to obey such rules and regulations as may, from time to time, be prescribed, jointly, by the presiding officers of the two houses of Congress, for the care, preservation, orderly keeping, and police of all such portions of the Capitol, its appurtenances, and the inclosures about it, and the public buildings and property in its immediate vicinity, as are not in the exclusive use and occupation of either house of Congress; that it shall also be his duty to obey such rules and regulations as may be, from time to time, prescribed by the presiding officer of either house of Congress for the care, preservation, orderly keeping, and police of those portions of the Capitol and its appurtenances which are in the exclusive use and occupation of either house of Congress, respectively."—(See SPEAKER.)

Speaker to control the keeping of that part of, in the use of the House.

Chief engineer to have charge of.

By the act of March 2, 1867, the office of Commissioner of Public Buildings is abolished, and the Chief Engineer of the Army is directed to perform the duties required of said Commissioner; and the appointment of the police of the Capitol is conferred upon the Ser-

Police of, to be appointed by Sergeants-at-Arms

geants-at-Arms of the two houses.—*Stat. at Large, Vol. XIV., p.* 466.

Also, certain watchmen.

By the act approved March 30, 1867, the Sergeants-at-Arms of the two houses are authorized to appoint the eight watchmen on the dome, at the stables, the gate-keeper, and watchmen of the grounds surrounding the Capitol, also three additional watchmen. And said Sergeants-at-Arms are also authorized to uniform and arm the Capitol police and watchmen, and to make such rules and regulations as they may deem necessary to preserve the peace and secure the Capitol from defacement, and for the protection of the public property therein; and shall have power to arrest and detain any person violating said rules until such person can be brought before the proper authorities for trial, without further order of Congress.—*Stat. at Large, Vol. XV., pp.* 11 *&* 12.

Rules and regulations in regard to.

Police, by whom to be appointed and by whom suspended.

By the act of March 3, 1873, it is provided that the appointment of the Capitol police shall hereafter be made by the Sergeants-at-Arms of the two houses, and the architect of the Capitol extension; and the captain of the Capitol force may suspend any member of said force, subject to the action of the officers above referred to.—*Stat. at Large, Vol. XVII, p.* 488.

No statuary, paintings, &c., belonging to private individuals, to be exhibited in.

By the act of July 20, 1868, it is provided that no statuary, paintings, or other articles, the property of private individuals, shall thereafter be allowed to be exhibited in the rotunda, or any other portion of the Capitol building.—*Ibid, p.* 110.

Improvements, repairs, &c., of, can only be made by direction of architect.

By act of the same date, it is provided that no improvements, alterations, or repairs of the Capitol building shall be made, except by direction and under the supervision of the architect of the Capitol extension.—*Ibid, p.* 115.

Telegraph from, to public offices.

By the act of March 3, 1873, an appropriation is made for connecting the Capitol by telegraph, to be used solely for public business with all the Departments of Government, and the Government Printing Office in the city of Washington: *Provided*, That the immediate connection of the wires with any of the public buildings shall be made under ground, or in such manner as not to injure the appearance of the Capitol or other public buildings.—*Stat. at Large, Vol. XVII, p.* 519.

CHAIR.

"The Speaker shall have a right to name any member to perform the duties of the Chair, but such substitution shall not extend beyond an adjournment."—*Rule* 5.

Speaker may name person to fill for the day.

(See SPEAKER PRO TEMPORE.)

CHAIRMAN OF A STANDING COMMITTEE.

(See COMMITTEES.)

CHAIRMAN OF COMMITTEE OF THE WHOLE.

A chairman to preside in Committee of the Whole shall be appointed by the Speaker.—*Rule* 105.

Appointed by the Speaker.

The chairman of the Committee of the Whole shall have power to order the galleries or lobby to be cleared in case of any disturbance or disorderly conduct therein.—*Rule* 9.

May cause galleries to be cleared.

He is also authorized to administer oaths or affirmations to witnesses.—*Stat. at Large, Vol. I, p.* 554.

May administer oaths.

(See also COMMITTEES OF THE WHOLE.)

CHARGE UPON THE PEOPLE.

"No motion or proposition for a tax or charge upon the people shall be discussed the day on which it is made or offered, and every such proposition shall receive its first discussion in a Committee of the Whole."—*Rule* 110.

No proposition for, to be discussed on the day made, and must be committed.

CHAPLAINS.

The practice, which had prevailed for several years, of the election by each House of a chaplain, who should open their daily sessions with prayer, alternating weekly between the House and Senate, was suspended during the 35th Congress. At the first session of that Congress, a resolution was adopted by the House, which directed "that the daily sessions of that body be opened with prayer, and requesting the ministers of the gospel in this city to attend and alternately perform this solemn duty."—*Journal*, 1, 35, *p.* 58. The clergymen of Washington generally responded to this request, and for the remainder of the Congress performed the duty of chaplains. At the first session of the 36th Congress, the old practice of the election of a chaplain by each House was revived, and it was at that time decided that a proposition to proceed to such election presented a question of privilege.—*Journal*, 1, 36, *pp.* 442, 443.

Election of chaplains dispensed with.

Clergymen generally invited to act.

Election of, revived.

CLAIM AGENTS.

House employés shall not be.

"No person shall be an officer of the House, or continue in its employment, who shall be an agent for the prosecution of any claim against the Government, or be interested in such claim otherwise than as an original claimant."—*Rule* 140.

Stenographers and reporters also prohibited from being.

"No stenographer or reporter shall be admitted to the reporters' gallery, or if admitted, be suffered to retain his seat, if he shall be or become an agent to prosecute any claim pending before Congress."—*Rule* 135.

Members and employés prohibited by law from acting as.

Members of Congress are prohibited from acting as claim agents for compensation paid or to be paid; and officers and employés of the House are prohibited from acting as claim agents, either with or without compensation, under the penalty, in either case, of a fine not exceeding five thousand dollars, or imprisonment in the penitentiary not exceeding one year, or both, in the discretion of the court.—*Stat. at Large, Vol. X, p.* 170.

CLAIMS, COMMITTEE OF.

When to be appointed, and of what number.

A Committee of Claims, to consist of eleven members, shall be appointed at the commencement of each Congress.—*Rule* 74.

Duties of.

"It shall be the duty of the Committee of Claims to take into consideration all such petitions and matters or things touching claims and demands on the United States as shall be presented, or shall or may come in question, and be referred to them by the House, and to report their opinion thereupon, together with such propositions for relief therein as to them shall seem expedient."—*Rule* 78.

Authorized to employ a clerk.

The Committee of Claims is authorized by resolution of February 18, 1843, to employ a clerk.—*Journal*, 3, 27, *p.* 399.

CLAIMS, COURT OF.

When report to be made.

By the act of 24th February, 1855, it was provided that "the Court of Claims shall keep a record of their proceedings, and shall, at the commencement of each session of Congres, and at the commencement of each month during the session of Congress, report to Congress the cases upon which they shall have finally acted, stating in each the material facts which they find established by the evidence, with their opinion in the case, and the reasons upon which such opinion is founded. Any judge who may dissent from the opinion of the majority shall append his reasons for such dissent to the report; and such report, together with the briefs of the solicitor and of the claimant, which shall accompany the report, upon being made to either house of Congress, shall be printed in the same manner as other public documents. And said court shall prepare a bill or bills in those cases which have received the favorable decision thereof, in such form as, if enacted, will carry the same into effect. And two or more cases may be embraced in the same bill, where the separate amount proposed to be allowed in each case shall be less than one thousand dollars. And the said court shall transmit with the said reports the testimony in each case, whether the same shall receive the favorable or adverse action of said court.

Dissenting opinions.

Court to prepare their bills.

Testimony to be reported.

"The said reports, and the bills reported as aforesaid, shall, if not finally acted upon during the session of Congress to which the said reports are made, be continued from session to session, and from Congress to Congress, until they shall be finally acted upon; and the consideration of said reports and bills shall, at the subsequent session of Congress, be resumed and the said reports and bills be proceeded with in the same manner as though finally acted upon at the session when presented.

Reports and bills to be continued from session to session and Congress to Congress.

"The claims reported upon adversely shall be placed upon the calendar when reported, and if the decision of said court shall be confirmed by Congress, said decision shall be conclusive, and the said court shall not at any subsequent period consider said claims, unless such reasons shall be presented to said court as, by the rules of common law or chancery in suits between individuals, would furnish sufficient ground for granting a new trial."—*Stat. at Large, Vol. X, pp.* 613, 614.

Adverse reports.

It shall be the duty of the Speaker of the House, within a reasonable time after the passage of this act, to appropriate such rooms in the Capitol at Washington, for the use of said court, as may be necessary for their accommodation, unless it shall appear to the Speaker that such rooms cannot be appropriated without interfering with

Court rooms to be provided.

the business of Congress; and in that event the said court shall procure at the city of Washington such rooms as may be necessary for the convenient transaction of their business.—*Ibid., p.* 614.

Removal of clerks to be reported.

The said court is required to make report in case of the removal of its clerks, with the cause of such removal, to Congress, if in session, or at the next session of Congress.—*Ibid., p.* 614.

Judgments of, final, subject to appeal to Supreme Court.

By the act of March 3, 1863, it is provided that the judgment of said court shall be final, with the right of appeal to the Supreme Court of the United States, and that in all cases of final judgments by said court, or on appeal by the Supreme Court where the same shall be affirmed in favor of the claimant, the sum due thereby shall be paid out of any general appropriation made by law for the payment and satisfaction of private claims.—*Stat. at Large, Vol. XII, p.* 766. [Since the passage of this act the monthly reports of cases, required by the act of February 24, 1855, have not been made to Congress.]

Petitions and bills to be transmitted to.

By the same act it is provided "that all petitions and bills praying or providing for the satisfaction of private claims against the Government, founded upon any law of Congress, or upon any regulation of an Executive Department, or upon any contract, express or implied, with the Government of the United States, shall, unless otherwise ordered by resolution of the House in which the same are presented or introduced, be transmitted by the Secretary of the Senate, or the Clerk of the House of Representatives, with all the accompanying documents, to the Court of Claims."—*Stat. at Large, Vol. XII, p.* 765.

[Where it is proposed to refer a case, of which the court has no jurisdiction under existing laws, the usual mode is by joint resolution.]

Members of Congress not to practice before.

By the same act members of Congress are prohibited from practicing in said court.—*Ibid., p.* 766.

Transmission of papers to.

The Clerk of the House is directed "to transmit to said court, on the application of the clerk of said court, the papers in his office in any case that is now or may be hereafter pending in said court, taking a receipt therefor."—*Journal* 1, 34, *p.* 583.

"The papers in all cases heretofore referred by this House to the Court of Claims, arising under contract or departmental decision, may be withdrawn from said court upon the order of the Clerk of the House, to be given upon the application therefor of any member to him, with the assent of the claimant; and when said papers are received by the Clerk, they shall be held by the Clerk the same as if never referred."—*Journal*, 1, 34, *p*. 614.

Withdrawal of papers from.

"All petitions for pensions heretofore referred to the Court of Claims, may be withdrawn and referred to their appropriate committees in the House."—*Journal*, 1, 34, *p*. 631.

Pension papers may be withdrawn.

[Ordinarily, except in the foregoing cases, papers are referred to or withdrawn from the Court of Claims on motion in the House; and, except in the case of the reference of a matter then before the House, the motion can only be made by unanimous consent, or at such time as resolutions are in order under the rules.]

How papers are ordinarily withdrawn from and referred to.

"The bills from the Court of Claims shall, on being laid before the House, be read a first and second time, committed to the Committee of the Whole House, and, together with the accompanying reports, printed."—*Rule* 122.

Bills from, to be placed on private calendar and reports printed.

When bills and reports from said court, reported to the House, are left undisposed of at the end of a Congress, at the beginning of the next Congress the bills shall be again read twice and referred, and the adverse reports restored to the private calendar.—*Journals*, 1, 35, *pp*. 134, 135; 1, 36, *p*. 247. [And when bills from said court shall have passed the Senate and remain undisposed of in the House at the end of a Congress, they shall be returned to the Senate.]

Bills and reports undisposed of at the end of a Congress.

Judges of the Court of Claims are admitted within the hall of the House.—*Rule* 134.

Judges of, admitted within the hall.

CLERK OF THE HOUSE.

A Clerk shall be elected at the commencement of each Congress.—*Rule* 10. The act of June 1, 1789, provides that at the first session of Congress after every general election of Representatives, the oath or affirmation therein prescribed "shall be administered by any one member of the House of Representatives to the Speaker; and

Shall be elected at the commencement of Congress.

Speaker shall administer oath to.

by him to all the members present, and to the *Clerk*, previous to entering on any other business." And in the case of a vacancy which occurred in the office of Clerk during the 31st Congress, (see *Journal*, 1, 31, *p.* 789,) it was decided that the House could take no action upon, nor transact, any other business until a Clerk was elected.

The following is the oath of office prescribed for the Clerk by the 10th *Rule* and the act of *June* 1, 1789, viz:

Oath of office.

"I do solemnly swear (or affirm) that I will support the Constitution of the United States, and that I will truly and faithfully discharge the duties of Clerk of the House of Representatives, to the best of my knowledge and abilities, and keep the secrets of the House."

Additional oath of.

He is also required by the act of July 2, 1862, to take an additional oath.—(See OATH.)

Mode of election.

In the election of a Clerk there shall be a previous nomination—*Rule* 11; and the vote shall be taken *viva voce.*—*Rule* 10. A majority of the votes given shall be necessary to an election; and where there shall not be such a majority on the first ballot the ballot shall be repeated until a majority be obtained. And in all ballotings blanks shall be rejected, and not taken into the count in enumeration of votes, or reported by the tellers.—*Rule* 12.

Tellers appointed by the Speaker.

Before proceeding to the election of a Clerk, the Speaker appoints four tellers to keep and make report of the vote.—(See ELECTIONS BY THE HOUSE.)

Enters upon his duties as soon as he takes oath.

[As soon as the Speaker has declared a person elected Clerk, the oath of office is administered to him, and he enters upon the duties of the same.] By the act of February 23, 1815, (*Stat. at Large, Vol. III, p.* 212,) it is made the duty of the Clerk, within thirty days after he enters

Gives bond.

upon the duties of his office, to give bond to the United States, with one or more sureties, to be approved by the Comptroller of the Treasury, in the penal sum of twenty thousand dollars, with condition for the faithful application and disbursement of the contingent fund of the House.

Continues in office until his successor is appointed.

The Clerk shall continue in office until his successor is appointed.—*Rule* 10.

Duty of, in preparation of roll of members elect.

By the act of February 21, 1867, *Stat. at Large, Vol. XIV, p.* 397, it is provided:

"That before the first meeting of the next Congress,

and of every subsequent Congress, the Clerk of the next preceding House of Representatives shall make a roll of the Representatives elect, and place thereon the names of all persons claiming seats as Representatives elect from States which were represented in the next preceding Congress, and of such persons only, and whose credentials show that they were regularly elected in accordance with the laws of their States respectively, or the laws of the United States." And—

"That in case of a vacancy in the office of Clerk of the House of Representatives, or of absence or inability of said Clerk to discharge the duties imposed on him by law or custom relative to the preparation of the roll of Representatives or the organization of the House, the said duties shall devolve on the Sergeant-at-Arms of the next preceding House of Representatives; and in case of vacancies in both of the before-mentioned offices, or of the absence or inability of both the Clerk and Sergeant-at-Arms to act, then the said duties shall be performed by the Doorkeeper of the next preceding House of Representatives."

Shall certify monthly pay of members from beginning of their term until first session of each Congress.

By the act of March 3, 1873, it is provided that hereafter Representatives and Delegates elect to Congress whose credentials in due form of law have been duly filed with the Clerk of the House of Representatives in accordance with the provisions of the act of Congress approved March third, eighteen hundred and sixty-three, may receive their compensation monthly, from the beginning of their term until the begining of the first session of each Congress, upon a certificate in the form now in use, to be signed by the Clerk of the House, which certificate shall have the like force and effect as is given to the certificate of the Speaker under existing laws: *Provided*, That in case the Clerk of the House of Representatives shall be notified that the election of any such holder of a certificate of election will be contested, his name shall not be placed upon the roll of members elect so as to entitle him to be paid, until he shall have been sworn in as a member, or until such contest shall be determined.—*Stat. at Large, Vol. XVII, pp.* 488–'9. (See ELECTIONS, CONTESTED.)

Preserves order,

"Pending the election of a Speaker, the Clerk shall

&c., pending election of Speaker.

preserve order and decorum, and shall decide all questions of order that may arise, subject to appeal to the House."—*Rule* 146. [This rule, together with Rule 147, which provides that the existing rules shall govern future Congresses, *unless otherwise ordered*, was adopted at the 1st session of the 36th Congress, and was intended to facilitate the organization of the House. Previously, under the authority contained in the *Manual, p.* 68, and the usage of the House, the Clerk had presided over its deliberations while there was no Speaker, but simply put questions, and (where specially authorized) preserved order, not, however, undertaking to decide questions of order.]—(See MEETING OF CONGRESS.)

Contracts, &c., to be approved by him.

All contracts, bargains, or agreements, relative to the furnishing any matter or thing, or for the performance of any labor for the House of Representatives, must be made with the Clerk, or approved by him, before any allowance shall be made therefor by the Committee of Accounts.—*Rule* 21. And in making purchases for the House he is required to confine his purchases exclusively to articles of the growth and manufacture of the United States, provided the same can be procured on as good terms and of as suitable quality as foreign articles.—*Stat. at Large, Vol. V, p.* 681.

Purchases to be of home production.

He shall furnish a statement of contingent expenses.

The Clerk is required by law (*Stat. at Large, Vol. V, pp.* 25, 527) to lay before the House, at the commencement of each session, a full and detailed statement of the expenditure of the contingent fund of the House; also (*Stat. at Large, Vol. V, p.* 525) a statement of the clerks and other persons employed in the service of the House during the preceding year. He is also required by a resolution of the House (*Journal*, 1, 27, *p.* 495) to report, at the commencement of each session, the quantity and cost of all the stationery used by the House and the Clerk's office. He, in conjunction with the Secretary of the Senate, shall also, as soon as may be after the close of each session of Congress, prepare and publish a statement of all appropriations made during the session; and also a statement of the new offices created and the salaries of each, and also a statement of the offices the salaries of which are increased, and the amount of such in-

Also, statement of persons employed in service of House.

Also, statement of stationery.

Also, statement of appropriations new offices, &c.

crease.—*Stat. at Large, Vol. V, p.* 117. And it shall be the duty of the Secretary of the Senate and the Clerk of the House of Representatives of the United States severally to report to Congress on the first day of each regular session, and at the expiration of their terms of service, a full and complete statement of all their receipts and expenditures as such officers, showing in detail the items of expense and classifying them under the proper appropriations, showing the aggregate thereof, and exhibiting in a clear and concise manner the exact condition of all public moneys by them received, paid out, and in their possession as such officers.

Secretary of Senate and Clerk of the House of Representatives to report to Congress their receipts and expenditures in detail, &c.

And it shall also be the duty of the officers hereinbefore named, and of the Sergeant-at-Arms, Postmasters of the Senate and House of Representatives, and the Doorkeeper of the House of Representatives, to make out a full and complete account of all the property belonging to the United States in their possession, at such dates and at the expiration of their terms of service, as provided in section one of this act.—*Stat. at Large, Vol. XVI, p.* 365.

They and the Sergeant-at-Arms, Postmasters, and Doorkeeper to make full account of the property of the United States in their possession.

He shall, on application, certify extracts from the Journal of the House of Representatives, and for such copies shall receive the same fees as are allowed by law to the Secretary of State for similar services.—*Stat. at Large, Vol. IX, p.* 80.

Shall certify extracts from Journal.

Fees.

He may, with permission of the President of the Senate and Speaker of the House, have the use of the books in the Congressional Library upon the same conditions as members of Congress.—*Stat. at Large, Vol. IV, p.* 429.

May use books in Congressional Library.

He shall advertise for proposals for furnishing stationery for the use of the House of Representatives.—*Stat. at Large, Vol. V, pp.* 526, 527.—(See STATIONERY.)

Shall advertise for proposals for stationery.

By the act of March 3, 1863, he is required to transmit to the Court of Claims all petitions and bills praying or providing for the satisfaction of all private claims against the Government, founded upon any law of Congress, or upon any regulation of an Executive Department, or upon any contract, express or implied, with the Government, unless otherwise ordered by resolution of the House.—*Stat. at Large, Vol. XII, p.* 765.

Shall transmit certain petitions and bills to Court of Claims.

By the act of March 2, 1867, *Stat. at Large, Vol. XIV, p.*

To select newspapers in States

lately in rebellion for publication of laws, &c.

466, it is provided that it shall be the duty of the Clerk of the House of Representatives to select in Virginia, South Carolina, North Carolina, Georgia, Florida, Alabama, Mississippi, Louisiana, Texas, and Arkansas, one or more newspapers, not exceeding the number now allowed by law, in which such treaties and laws of the United States as may be ordered for publication in newspapers according to law shall be published, and in some one or more of which so selected all such advertisements as may be ordered for publication in said districts, by any United States court or judge thereof, or by any officer of such courts, or by any executive officer of the United States, shall be published, the compensation for which, and other terms of publication, shall be fixed by said Clerk at a rate not exceeding two dollars per page for the publication of treaties and laws, and not exceeding one dollar per square of eight lines of space for the publication of advertisements, the accounts of which shall be adjusted by the proper accounting officers and paid in the manner now authorized by law in the like cases; and said Clerk shall, as soon as practicable after the passage of this act, notify each head of the several Executive Departments, and each judge of the United States courts therein, of the papers selected by him in accordance with the foregoing provisions; and thereupon and thereafter it shall be the duty of the several executive officers charged therewith to furnish to such selected papers only an authentic copy of the publications to be made as aforesaid; and no money hereby or otherwise appropriated shall be paid for any publications or advertisements hereafter to be made in said districts; nor shall any such publication or advertisement be ordered by any Department or public officer otherwise than as herein provided: *Provided*, That the rates fixed in this section to be paid for the publication of the treaties and laws of the United States in the States therein designated shall also be paid for the same publications in all the States not designated in this section; and that all printing of any kind ordered by the Executive Departments shall be executed by the Government Printer, when practicable; and, if not, at such office as may be designated by the Clerk of the

To designate where executive printing shall be executed in certain cases.

House of Representatives, at rates not exceeding the current rates for such printing.

To select newspapers in the other States and Territories for publication of laws and treaties.

By the act of March 29, 1867, (*Stat. at Large, Vol. XV, pp.* 7, 8,) it is provided that so much of section seven of of an act entitled "An act making appropriations for sundry civil expenses of the Government for the year ending June thirty, eighteen hundred and sixty-eight, and for other purposes," approved March second, eighteen hundred and sixty-seven, as relates to the publication of the treaties and laws of the United States, be, and the same is hereby, extended to the States not therein designated, and to the Territories; and that it shall be the duty of the Secretary of State, upon receiving notice of the designation of newspapers under the act aforesaid and this section, promptly to furnish to such newspapers authentic copies of the treaties and laws of the United States, to be published as aforesaid: *Provided*, That it shall be lawful to print the laws and treaties of the United States as aforesaid in three newspapers in Louisiana: *And provided further*, That the rates fixed by previous laws shall not be hereby increased.

List of members, &c., to be furnished to the publishers of the Globe.

By resolution of February 16, 1867, he is directed to furnish the "Globe," at each session, a list of the members, with their post-office address, and the number of their seats.—*Journal*, 2, 39, *p*. 405.

The following duties are imposed upon the Clerk by the *Rules* of the House, viz:

Attest writs.

He shall attest all writs, warrants, and subpœnas issued by the House.—*Rule* 8.

Enter petitions.

He shall enter upon the Journal, subject to the control and direction of the Speaker, such petitions and memorials as may be handed to him by members for reference.—*Rule* 131.

Delivers calls upon the President and heads of Departments.

He shall cause to be delivered all propositions adopted by the House, requesting information from the President, or directing it to be furnished by the heads of Departments.—*Rule* 53. [His practice is to deliver in person all calls upon the President, and to transmit calls upon the Departments by a messenger or through the mail.]

Shall refer maps, &c., to the House members of the

He shall refer all drawings, maps, charts, or other papers, which may at any time come before the House

Committee on Printing.

for engraving, lithographing, or publishing in any way, to the members of the Committee on Printing on the part of the House.—*Rule* 100.

Shall prepare list of reports to be made by officers of Government.

He shall prepare and cause to be delivered to each member, at the commencement of every session of Congress, a list of the reports which it is the duty of any officer or Department of the Government to make to Congress.—*Rule* 13.

Shall send copies of the Journal to States.

He shall, at the end of each session, send a printed copy of the Journal of the House to the executive, and to each branch of the legislature, of every State.—*Rule* 14.

In regard to advertisements in the District of Columbia and other places.

By the act of July 20, 1868, it is provided that the provisions of section ten of an act "making appropriations for sundry civil expenses of the Government for the year ending June thirteenth, eighteen hundred and sixty-eight, and for other purposes," approved March two, eighteen hundred and sixty-seven, be, and they are hereby, extended to one additional newspaper in the District of Columbia from the date of the approval of said act, the same to be selected by the Clerk of the House of Representatives.

And also, that all advertisements, notices, proposals for contracts, executive proclamations, treaties, and laws to be published in the District of Columbia, Maryland, and Virginia, shall be published in the papers now selected under the provisions of section ten of an act approved March second, eighteen hundred and sixty-seven, entitled "An act making appropriations for sundry civil expenses of the Government for the year ending June thirtieth, eighteen hundred and sixty-eight, and for other purposes," and shall also be published in the paper selected under the provisions of the second section of this act: *Provided*, That no advertisement to any State, District, or Territory other than the District of Columbia, Maryland, or Virginia, shall be published in the papers designated, unless at the direction first made of the proper head of a Department.—*Stat. at Large, Vol. XV, p.* 110.

Shall put decisions of questions of order at end of Journal.

He shall note all questions of order, with the decision, and put them together at the end of the Journal of every session.—*Rule* 15.

He shall enter upon the Journal notices of bills which may be handed in by members.—*Rule* 15.

Shall enter notices of bills.

He shall certify a bill that has passed, noting the day of its passage at the foot thereof.—*Rule* 127.

Shall certify bills which pass.

He shall sign all House bills which have passed the House.—*Joint Rule* 5.

Shall sign all House bills which pass.

He shall enroll on parchment all House bills which shall have passed both houses.—*Joint Rule* 6. And shall certify on the back of the roll that the bill originated in the House of Representatives.—*Joint Rule* 9. And all orders, resolutions, and votes which are to be presented to the President for his approbation, shall also, in the same manner, be previously enrolled, examined, and signed.—*Joint Rule* 10.

Shall enroll and certify House bills, &c., which pass both houses.

He shall enter on a separate paper all amendments adopted in Committee of the Whole to a bill or report.—*Rules* 107, 109. [The 107*th Rule* refers to manuscript bills, having been adopted prior to the practice of printing bills.]

Entry of amendments in committee.

He shall, within thirty days after the close of each session of Congress, cause to be completed the printing and primary distribution, to members and delegates, of the Journal of the House, together with an accurate index to the same.—*Rule* 16.

Shall distribute Journal and index to members within thirty days after adjournment.

He shall retain in the library of his office, for the use of the members there, two copies of all the books and printed documents deposited in the library.—*Rule* 17.

Shall retain in library two copies of all public documents.

He shall have preserved for each member of the House an extra copy, in good binding, of all the documents printed by order of either house at each session.—*Rule* 18.

Shall preserve one bound copy of all documents for each member.

He shall make a weekly statement of the resolutions and bills upon the Speaker's table.—*Rule* 19. [This statement is printed and placed upon each member's table every Monday morning. There is, in like manner, placed upon their tables, every Friday morning, a statement of all the bills and resolutions upon the calendar, designating whether in Committee of the Whole House or of the Whole House on the state of the Union.]

Shall make weekly statement of business on Speaker's table.

Weekly statement of bills, &c., on calendar also prepared.

The number prefixed to the section of a bill, being merely a marginal indication, and no part of the text of

He numbers the sections of bills.

the bill, the Clerk regulates that.—*Manual, p.* 111. [He also gives numbers to the bills and joint resolutions as they are introduced or reported.]

And also bills and joint resolutions.

Messages (between the two houses) shall be sent by such persons as a sense of propriety in each house may determine to be proper.—*Joint Rule* 4. [All messages from the House to the Senate are conveyed by the Clerk or one of his assistants.]

He conveys messages to the Senate.

Other duties of Clerk.

In addition to the foregoing, there are various other duties appertaining to the office of Clerk, under the usage and practice of the House, which are discharged by himself and his appointees.

Prepares estimates and disburses contingent fund.

He prepares estimates of the expenses of the House of Representatives, and disburses the contingent fund of the House, keeping accounts with the Treasury of the United States of the various items of appropriation for that object. He also disburses the salary fund of the various officers and employés of the House.

Pays salaries.

Keeps Journal.

He keeps the minutes of proceedings in the House, and makes out, subject to the control of the Speaker, the Journal of said proceedings, in readiness for the same to be read at the next meeting of the House. He also prepares the index to the Journal at the end of each session.

Keeps minutes of Committees of the Whole.

He keeps the minutes of proceedings in Committees of the Whole; records all votes taken by yeas and nays, and prepares copies of the same for the printer of the Journal.

Reads.

He reads all messages, bills, and other papers required by the House to be read, and calls the roll of members.

Keeps the files.

He keeps the files of the House, preserving all petitions and other papers belonging to its archives, arranged alphabetically, and under the head of the Congress at which they were last acted upon.

Keeps bill-book.

He keeps a book in which are entered, numerically, the titles of all bills and joint resolutions; opposite which are noted, as they occur, all proceedings of the House thereon; also all proceedings of the Senate as they are reported to the House.

Papers ordered to be printed, &c., indorsed, &c.

He places appropriate indorsements upon all papers

presented in the House, and, after entering the same in books kept for the purpose, sends to the Government Printing Office all such as are ordered to be printed, and to the appropriate committee such as are referred without printing.

He engrosses upon paper all bills, joint resolutions, and resolutions of the House, and amendments of the House to Senate bills and joint resolutions which pass the House of Representatives, certifying the date of the passage of the same at the foot thereof. Engrosses bills and resolutions.

He enrolls upon parchment all House bills and joint resolutions which have passed both houses, certifying upon the back that the same originated in the House, and then delivers them to the Committee on Enrolled Bills. Enrolls bills and resolutions.

He journalizes all petitions and other papers handed to him under the 131st *rule*, and having indorsed them appropriately, takes them to the rooms of the proper committees, and there enters them in the committee books. He also keeps what is called the "Petition Book," in which is entered, alphabetically, each petition as presented, and the further action of the House thereon as it occurs. Petitions referred under rule.

He keeps what is called the "Newspaper Book," in which are entered the accounts of members under the newspaper resolution, and orders from the publishers such newspapers and periodicals as may be directed. Newspapers.

He contracts for and furnishes to members all books voted to them by the House, and keeps the accounts of the members for the same. Books.

He distributes to members, governors, State legislatures, &c., all public documents (other than extra numbers) required by law, rule, or resolution to be distributed. Public documents.

He purchases, keeps, and distributes the stationery required for the use of the House. (See STATIONERY.) Stationery.

He keeps the library of the House, in which are kept copies of all documents printed by order of either house. Library.

CLERKS OF COMMITTEES.

Not to be employed without leave.

"No committee shall be permitted to employ a clerk at the public expense without first obtaining leave of the House for that purpose."—*Rule* 73. [Such leave is usually granted to a portion of the committees, for a part or the whole of the session, as they may deem the service necessary; and four of the committees have permanent clerks, viz: of Claims, by resolution of February 18, 1843; of Ways and Means, by resolution of February 18, 1856; on Public Lands, by resolution of May 27, 1862; and on Appropriations, by resolution of December 12, 1865.]

Committees which have leave to employ.

COINAGE, WEIGHTS, AND MEASURES, COMMITTEE ON.

When appointed, and of what number.

There shall be appointed, at the commencement of each Congress, a Committee on Coinage, Weights, and Measures, to consist of seven members, and to this committee shall be referred all bills, resolutions, and communications to the House upon that subject.—*Rule* 148.

Duties of.

COMMERCE, COMMITTEE ON.

When appointed, and of what number.

There shall be appointed, at the commencement of each Congress, a Committee on Commerce, to consist of eleven members.—*Rule* 74.

Duties of.

"It shall be the duty of the Committee on Commerce to take into consideration all such petitions and matters or things touching the commerce of the United States as shall be presented, or shall or may come into question, and be referred to them by the House, and to report, from time to time, their opinion thereon."—*Rule* 79.

[This committee was originally a Committee on Commerce *and Manufactures*. On the 8th December, 1819, a separate Committee on Manufactures was constituted, and the duties of the original Committee on Commerce and Manufactures have been confirmed, as above, by leaving out the words "*and Manufactures*." There are no duties assigned in the Rules to the Committee on Manufactures.]

COMMIT, MOTION TO.

When it may be received.

"When a question is under debate, no motion shall be received but to adjourn, to lie on the table, for the previous question, to postpone to a day certain, to *commit* or amend, to postpone indefinitely; which several motions shall have precedence in the order in which they are arranged; and no motion to commit, or to postpone indefinitely, being decided, shall be again allowed on the same day, and at the same stage of the bill or proposition."—*Rule* 42. [When any one of the foregoing motions is received, the practice is not to receive one of lower dignity until the former is disposed of.]

Precedence with reference to other motions.

Not to be repeated same day and stage of bill.

"When a resolution shall be offered, or a motion made to refer any subject, and different committees shall be proposed, the question shall be taken in the following order: the Committee of the Whole House on the state of the Union; the Committee of the Whole House; a standing committee; a select committee."—*Rule* 43.

Where different committees are proposed.

A motion to commit may be amended by the addition of instructions. Also by striking out one committee and inserting another.—*Journals, passim.*

May be amended.

A division of the question is not in order on a motion to commit with instructions, or on the different branches of instructions.—*Journals*, 1, 17, *p.* 507; 1, 31, *pp.* 1395, 1397; 1, 32, *p.* 611.

With instructions, not divisible.

"Upon the second reading of a bill, the Speaker shall state it as ready for commitment."—*Rule* 118.

A bill, when ready for commitment.

[On a motion to commit, the whole question is open to debate.]

Debate on.

After the previous question is ordered, if no motion to postpone is pending, the House is brought *first* "to a direct vote on the motion to commit, if such motion shall have been made."—*Rule* 132.

Effect of previous question upon motion to commit.

"Motions and reports may be committed at the pleasure of the House."—*Rule* 47.

Motions and reports may be committed.

COMMITTEES.

Thirty-four standing committees shall be appointed at the commencement of each Congress, viz: Of Elections, of Ways and Means, on Appropriations, on Banking and Currency, on the Pacific Railroad, of Claims, on Commerce, on the Public Lands, on the Post Office and Post Roads, for the District of Columbia, on the Judiciary, on Revolutionary Claims, on Public Expenditures, on Private Land Claims, on Manufactures, on Agriculture,

Standing committees to be appointed at the commencement of each Congress.

on Indian Affairs, on Military Affairs, on the Militia, on Naval Affairs, on Foreign Affairs, on the Territories, on Revolutionary Pensions, on Invalid Pensions, on Railways and Canals, on Mines and Mining, on Freedmen's Affairs, on Education and Labor, on the Revision of the Laws, on Public Buildings and Grounds—*to consist of eleven members each;* on Coinage, Weights, and Measures —*to consist of seven members;* on Patents, of Accounts, and on Mileage—*to consist of five members each.*—*Rule* 74.

Territories and the District of Columbia.

By Rule 162 the Speaker is directed to appoint one of the Delegates an additional member of the Committee on the Territories, and the Delegate from the District of Columbia an additional member of the Committee for the District of Columbia.

Joint committees to be appointed at the commencement of each Congress.

There shall be a joint committee *on Enrolled Bills*, to consist of *two members* of each house, (*Joint Rule* 7;) there shall be a joint committee *on the Library of Congress*, to consist of *three members* of each house, (*Joint Rule* 20;) there shall be a joint committee *on Public Printing*, to consist of *three members* of each house. (*Stat. at Large, Vol. X, p.* 34.) [The rules do not designate for what period these joint committees shall be appointed; but the practice is for the Speaker to appoint them at the commencement of each Congress.]

Standing committees to be appointed at the commencement of each Congress.

There shall be appointed at the commencement of the first session in each Congress seven additional standing committees, whose duties shall continue until the first session of the ensuing Congress, viz: *On Expenditures in the Department of State, on Expenditures in the Treasury Department, on Expenditures in the War Department, on Expenditures in the Post Office Department, on Expenditures in the Navy Department, on Expenditures in the Interior Department, on Expenditures on the Public Buildings*, to consist of *five members* each.—*Rule* 102.

Duties of the committees.

For duties of the several committees, *see under their respective names.*

Committees, how appointed.

"All committees shall be appointed by the Speaker, unless otherwise specially directed by the House, in which case they shall be appointed by ballot; and if upon such ballot the number required shall not be elected by a majority of the votes given, the House shall proceed to a second ballot, in which a plurality of votes shall prevail; and in case a greater number than is required to compose or complete a committee shall have an equal number of votes, the House shall proceed to a further ballot or ballots."—*Rule* 67. [The latter mode of appointing committees is, of late years, never resorted to; but the practice has been for the House to adopt an order "that the Speaker be authorized to appoint the regular standing committees." And after adopting such order, it is usual for the House to adjourn over for two or three days to enable him to make the appointments.]

Member may be appointed on, before he is sworn.

Before a return be made a member elected may be named of a committee, and is to every extent a member, except that he cannot vote until he is sworn.—*Manual*, *p.* 61. [While this is the law, it has not been a common practice in the House to appoint a member on a committee until he has been sworn.]

Who shall be chairman of a committee.

"The first-named member of any committee shall be the chairman; and in his absence, or being excused by the House, the next named member, and so on, as often as the case shall happen, unless the committee, by a majority of their number, elect a chairman."—*Rule* 68.

Who may be excused from serving on a committee.

"Any member may excuse himself from serving on any committee at the time of his appointment, if he is then a member of two other committees."—*Rule* 69. [And under the practice, it is sufficient for him to offer such an excuse at any subsequent period of the session.]

Who shall call a meeting of a committee.

"It shall be the duty of a committee to meet on the call of any two of its members, if the chairman be absent, or decline to appoint such meeting."—*Rule* 70.

Committees shall not sit while House is sitting without leave.

"No committee shall sit during the sitting of the House without special leave."—*Rule* 72. And "so soon as the House sits, and a committee is notified of it, the chairman is in duty bound to rise instantly, and the members to attend the service of the House."—*Manual*, *p.* 70. [But upon the suggestion to the House by a member of a committee that it is important to the dispatch of public business that they should have such leave, it is usually granted, especially near the close of the session.]

Committees sitting during recess.

"Committees may be appointed to sit during the recess by adjournment, but not by prorogation. Neither house can continue any portion of itself in any parliamentary function beyond the end of the session without the consent of the other two branches. When done, it is by a bill constituting them commissioners for the particular purpose."—*Manual, p.* 136. [This has been construed (and, in view of the distinction which exists between a "session" of Parliament and of Congress, very properly so) not to restrain a committee of the House, with the leave of the House, from sitting during the recess between a first and second session of Congress.]—(See *Journal*, 1, 32, *p.* 1119.)

Clerks of committees.

"No committee shall be permitted to employ a clerk at the public expense without first obtaining leave of the House for that purpose."—*Rule* 73. [Such leave is usually granted to a portion of the committees for a part or the whole of the session, as they may deem the service necessary; and four of the committees have permadent clerks, viz: of Claims, by resolution of February 18, 1843; of Ways and Means, by resolution of February 18, 1856; and on Public Lands, by resolution of May 27, 1862; and on Appropriations, by resolution of December 12, 1865.]

Precedence of different motions to refer.

"When a resolution shall be offered or a motion made to refer any subject, and different committees shall be proposed, the question shall be taken in the following order: the Committee of the Whole House on the state of the Union; the Committee of the Whole House; a standing committee; a select committee."—*Rule* 43. [But where more than one standing committee is proposed, the last one proposed is first voted upon, as an amendment to strike out and insert.]

Precedence of motion to commit over other motions, and of others over it.

"When a question is under debate, no motion shall be received but to adjourn, to lie on the table, for the previous question, to postpone to a day certain, to *commit* or amend, to postpone indefinitely; which several motions shall have precedence in the order in which they are arranged; and no motion to postpone to a day certain, to *commit*, or to postpone indefinitely, being decided, shall be again allowed on the same day, and at the same stage of the bill or proposition."—*Rule* 42.

Motion to commit not to be repeated at same stage on same day.

"Upon the second reading of a bill, the Speaker shall state it as ready for commitment."—*Rule* 118.

A bill, when ready for commitment.

"After the previous question is ordered, if no motion to postpone is pending, the House is first brought to a direct vote on the motion to *commit*, if such motion shall have been made."—*Rule* 132.

Previous question brings the House to vote first on motion to commit.

"A committee meet when and where they please, if the House has not ordered time and place for them; but they can only act when together, and not by separate consultation and consent, nothing being the report of a committee but what has been agreed to in committee actually assembled."—*Manual, p.* 89.

Committee can only act when met together.

"A majority of the committee constitutes a quorum for business."—*Manual, p.* 89. But it is not necessary that the committee shall be full when a paper is acted upon.—*Journal*, 1, 34, *p.* 1143. Nor is it even necessary that every member shall have been notified of an adjourned meeting, if it shall appear that at such meeting a quorum was present, and that a majority of such quorum authorized a report to be made.—*Same Journal, pp.* 1433, 1434.

A quorum of a committee.

Not necessary that committee be full.

Nor that every member was notified of an adjourned meeting.

[Committees very frequently appoint sub-committees to make investigations,] and in such case no member of the committee, as a matter of right, can take for examination papers referred to a sub-committee.—*Cong. Globe*, 1, 39, *p.* 4019.

Sub-committees.

"A committee cannot receive a petition but through the House."—*Manual, p.* 70. "Members having petitions and memorials to present may hand them to the Clerk, indorsing the same with their names, and the reference or disposition to be made thereof; and such petitions and memorials shall be entered on the Journal, subject to the control and direction of the Speaker."—*Rule* 131. [This is the only mode of presenting a petition for reference now recognized by the rules. The rule, however, is construed to authorize the withdrawal of old papers from the files, for the purpose of reference to the appropriate

Petitions, how to be referred to committees.

committee. And, in this connection, it may not be improper to call attention to that portion of this rule which requires that the *name of the member* and *that of the committee* shall be indorsed upon the paper to be referred. In order to secure its appearance *in the daily newspapers*, members should furnish a memorandum of the contents and reference of the same to the reporters.]

Members should indorse the papers referred by them.

Newspapers to be furnished with a memorandum.

Matters referred, how delivered to the committee.

"The Clerk may deliver the bill to any member of the committee, but it is usual to deliver it to him who is first named."—*Manual*, *p.* 89. [In the House of Representatives the long-settled practice has been, where the committee have a regular place of meeting, as is the case with all the standing committees, for the Clerk to take down to the committee-room and deposit there all matters referred to said committee, and make an entry of the same in the docket of the committee; and when they have no committee-room, as is the case with some of the select committees, to deliver the matter referred to the chairman.]

Not competent to instruct committee to do what House itself cannot do.

It is not competent for the House to instruct a committee to amend a bill in a manner that the House itself cannot amend it.—*Journal*, 2, 35, *p.* 389. [Indeed, it is the well-settled practice that the House cannot instruct a committee to do what the House itself cannot do.]

To commit with instructions not divisible.

A division of the question is not in order on a motion to commit or recommit with instructions, or on the different branches of instructions.—*Journals*, 1, 17, *p.* 507; 1, 31, *pp.* 1395, 1397; and, 1, 32, *p.* 611.

How amendments are to be noted by a committee.

"The committee may not erase, interline, or blot the bill itself, but must, in a paper by itself, set down the amendments, stating the words which are to be inserted or omitted, and where, by reference to the page, line, and word of the bill."—*Manual*, *p.* 91.

No reconsideration of a vote in committee.

"When a vote is once passed in a committee it cannot be altered but by the House, their votes being binding on themselves."—*Manual*, *p.* 91.

Committee cannot reject a paper.

"If the committee are opposed to the whole paper, and think it cannot be made good by amendments, they cannot reject it, but must report it back to the House without amendments, and there make their opposition."—*Manual*, *p.* 99.

The committee have full power over the bill or other paper, except that they cannot change the title or subject."—*Manual, p.* 89.

Committee cannot change title or subject.

As soon as the Journal is read, and the unfinished business in which the House was engaged at the last preceding adjournment has been disposed of, reports from committees shall be called for and disposed of; in doing which the Speaker shall call upon each standing committee in the following order, viz:

When and in what order committees are to report.

Committee of Elections.
Committee of Ways and Means.
Committee on Appropriations.
Committee on Banking and Currency.
Committee on the Pacific Railroad.
Committee of Claims.
Committee on Commerce.
Committee on the Public Lands.
Committee on the Post Office and Post Roads.
Committee on the District of Columbia.
Committee on the Judiciary.
Committee on Revolutionary Claims.
Committee on Public Expenditures.
Committee on Private Land Claims.
Committee on Manufactures.
Committee on Agriculture.
Committee on Indian Affairs.
Committee on Military Affairs.
Committee on the Militia.
Committee on Naval Affairs.
Committee on Foreign Affairs.
Committee on the Territories.
Committee on Revolutionary Pensions.
Committee on Invalid Pensions.
Committee on Railways and Canals.
Committee on Mines and Mining.
Committee on Freedmen's Affairs.
Committee on Education and Labor.
Committee on the Revision of the Laws.
Committee on Coinage, Weights, and Measures.
Committee on Patents.

Committee on Public Buildings and Grounds.
Committee of Accounts.
Committee on Mileage.
Committee on Printing.
Committee on Enrolled Bills.
Committee on the Library of Congress.
Committee on Expenditures in the State Department.
Committee on Expenditures in the Treasury Department.
Committee on Expenditures in the War Department.
Committee on Expenditures in the Navy Department.
Committee on Expenditures in the Post Office Department.
Committee on Expenditures in the Interior Department.
Committee on Expenditures on the Public Buildings.

Call of to be resumed where left off.

And when all the standing committees shall have been called, then it shall be the duty of the Speaker to call for reports from *select* committees. If the Speaker shall not get through the call upon the committees before the House passes to other business, he shall resume the call where he left off, giving preference to the report last under consideration: *Provided*, That whenever any committee shall have occupied the morning hour on two days, it shall not be in order for such committee *to report further* until the other committees shall have been called in their turn. [But this proviso does not restrain the House from occupying the morning hour on more than two days in the *consideration of a report.*]—*Rule* 51.

After occupying morning hour on two days, not to report further.

Call of committees for reports, how interfered with.

[The regular daily call for reports, as provided for by this rule, is liable to be interfered with by "special orders," "questions of privilege," and "privileged questions," also by the "call of States for bills on leave and resolutions," which, by *Rule* 130, is in order every Monday, and "motions to suspend the rules," which, by *Rule* 145, may be submitted every Monday, at the expiration of one hour after the Journal is read. So, too, by *Rule* 128, the call of committees is limited on *Fridays and Saturdays* to "business of a private nature."]

What committees report at any time.

"It shall be in order for the Committee on Enrolled

Bills and the Committee on Printing to report at any time—*Rules* 100 and 101—and also for the Committee on Appropriations to report (for the purpose of reference) the general appropriation bills at any time"—*Rule* 77—and the Committee of Ways and Means have leave to report, for commitment, at any time.—*Rule* 151.

"A committee having leave to report at all times may report in part at different times."—*Journal*, 1, 27, *p*. 104.

The right to report at any time carries with it the right to consider the matter when reported.—*Journal*, 1, 32, *p*. 195. And where authority is given to a committee to make a report at a particular time, the right follows to consider the report when made.—*Journal*, 1, 22, *p*. 1409.

Right to report carries right to consider.

"The several standing committees of the House shall have leave to report by bill or otherwise."—*Rule* 71.

Have leave to report by bill or otherwise.

It is not competent for a committee to report a bill where the subject-matter has not been referred to them by the House, by the rules, or otherwise.—*Journal*, 1, 31, *p*. 590.

Committee cannot report on a subject not referred by the rules, or otherwise.

A bill may be reported with a recommendation that it do *not* pass, if based upon a paper regularly referred.—*Journal*, 1, 32, *p*. 785.

Bill may be reported with a recommendation that it do not pass.

"The report being made, the committee is dissolved, and can act no more without a new power. But it may be revived by a vote, and the same matter recommitted to them."—*Manual*, *p*. 92. [This evidently refers to a *select committee*, and, under the practice of the House, a motion to recommit decided affirmatively has the effect of reviving the committee.—See *Journal*, 2, 37, *p*. 874; 3, 37, *pp*. 487 to 489.]

Select committee, how dissolved and revived.

If it is disputed that a report has been ordered to be made by a committee, the question of reception must be put to the House.—*Journal*, 2, 27, *p*. 1410.

Dispute as to whether committee have ordered report.

A minority of a committee cannot make a report, a minority not being the committee.—*Journal*, 1, 24, *p*. 562. [The common practice, however, is to permit the minority to submit their *views in writing*, which are usually printed and considered with the majority report.] And when such views are accompanied by a resolution or bill, such resolution or bill is not thereby brought before the House for its action, but must be submitted by some member.—*Congressional Globe*, 1, 31, *p*. 1345.

Minority cannot make a report.

Chairman may read report.

The chairman of a committee submitting a report has a right to read it.—*Journal*, 2, 27, *p.* 409.

Right of member reporting to debate.

"A member reporting the measure under consideration from a committee may open and close the debate"—*Rule* 60—and, under the invariable practice, he is entitled to be recognized, notwithstanding another member may have risen first and addressed the Chair— *Journal*, 3, 17, *p.* 211—and his right to close the debate is never denied him, even after the previous question is ordered, or debate has been closed.—*Journal*, 1, 31, *p.* 1056.

Proceedings of committee not to be published.

"The proceedings of a committee are not to be published, as they are of no force till confirmed by the House."—*Manual*, *p.* 70. And it is not in order, under the regular call for resolutions, to submit a resolution instructing a committee to continue its investigations without secrecy either as to their past or future proceedings.—*Journal*, 3, 42, *pp.* 121–2.

Reference to proceedings in committee not in order.

It is not in order to allude on the floor to anything that has taken place in committee, unless by a written report sanctioned by a majority of the committee.—*Journals*, 1, 26, *p.* 418; 1, 31, *p.* 393.

Recommitment.

"After commitment and report thereof to the House, or at any time before its passage, a bill may be recommitted; and should such recommitment take place after its engrossment, and an amendment be reported and agreed to by the House, the question shall be again put on the engrossment of the bill."—*Rule* 124. But recommitment cannot be moved after the previous question is ordered.—*Journal*, 1, 29, *p.* 643.

Effect of recommitment.

"If a report be recommitted before agreed to in the House, what has passed in committee is of no validity; the whole question is again before the committee, and a new resolution must be again moved, as if nothing had passed."—*Manual*, *p.* 92.

Repetition of motion to recommit.

"Two motions to recommit are not in order at the same stage of the bill."—*Journal*, 1, 20, *April* 11.

Select committee, how created and filled.

[A select committee is created either by resolution, when resolutions are in order, or upon motion to refer, when the subject to be referred is before the House; the number of which it is to consist being designated in the resolution or motion.] Under the parliamentary law—

Manual, pp. 87, 88—"none who speak directly against the body of the bill" are to be of the committee to which it is referred. The spirit of this law has prevailed in the House so far as that, in the formation of a select committee, in the case of the reference of a bill, a *majority* of the friends of the measure referred, and in the case of an investigation a majority of those favorable to the proposed investigation, are usually appointed thereon; and the member proposing the select committee is usually appointed the chairman.]

Select committees do not hold over to a second or subsequent session after their appointment—*Journal*, 2, 32, *p.* 207—unless specially authorized to do so.—*Ibid.*, 1, 35, *p.* 1020.

Select committees do not hold over.

A chairman of a select committee (*Stat. at Large, Vol. I, p.* 554) and a chairman of any standing committee (*Stat. at Large, Vol. III, p.* 345) shall be empowered to administer oaths or affirmations to witnesses in any case under their examination.

Administering of oaths by chairmen of committees.

Any person summoned as a witness by authority of the House to give testimony or to produce papers upon any matter before the House or any committee thereof, who shall willfully make default, or who, appearing, shall refuse to answer any question pertinent to the matter of inquiry in consideration before the House or committee by which he shall be examined, shall, in addition to the pains and penalties now existing, be liable to indictment as for a misdemeanor. And when a witness shall fail to testify, as above, and the facts shall be reported to the House, it shall be the duty of the Speaker to certify the fact, under the seal of the House, to the district attorney for the District of Columbia.—*Stat. at Large, Vol. XI, p.* 155.—(See also WITNESS.)

Failure of witness to appear or testify.

Duty of Speaker on failure of witness to testify.

COMMITTEES OF THE WHOLE.

[The rules and practice of the House recognize two Committees of the Whole, viz, the Committee of the Whole House on the state of the Union, to which are referred public bills and public business, and the Committee of the Whole House, to which are referred private bills and private business.]

Two Committees of the Whole.

Order of taking questions of commitment.

"When a resolution shall be offered, or a motion made to refer any subject, and different committees shall be proposed, the question shall be taken in the following order: The Committee of the Whole House on the state of the Union; the Committee of the Whole House; a standing committee; a select committee."—*Rule* 43.

Motion to go into, in order at any time.

"The House may at any time, by a vote of a majority of the members present, suspend the rules and orders for the purpose of going into the Committee of the Whole House on the state of the Union."—*Rule* 104. [On Fridays and Saturdays, which, under *Rule* 128, are set apart for the consideration of private business, the motion to go into Committee of the Whole House on the private calendar takes precedence of the motion to go into Committee of the Whole House on the state of the Union, but upon a failure of the former motion the latter motion may be entertained on those days. If the previous question shall have been seconded upon any pending proposition, under the practice it is not in order to entertain the motion to go into Committee of the Whole until it is disposed of.]

Fridays and Saturdays.

Seconding of previous question prevents motion to go into.

Motion to go into, takes precedence of motion to go to business on Speaker's table.

It is in order, pending a motion to go to business on the Speaker's table, to move that the House resolve itself into the Committee of the Whole House on the state of the Union.—*Journal*, 2, 32, *pp*. 155, 228.

How formed.

"In forming a Committee of the Whole House the Speaker shall leave his chair, and a chairman to preside in committee shall be appointed by the Speaker."—*Rule* 105.

Disturbance in.

"In case of any disturbance or disorderly conduct in the galleries or lobby, the Speaker (or chairman of the Committee of the Whole House) shall have power to order the same to be cleared."—*Rule* 9. And "in case of great heat and confusion arising in committee, the Speaker may take the chair and bring the House to order."—*Manual*, *p*. 72; *Journal*, 1, 26, *p*. 814.

Chairman of, may administer oaths.

The chairman of the Committee of the Whole has power to administer oaths or affirmations to witnesses in any case under its examination.—*Stat. at Large, Vols. I*, *p*. 554; *III*, *p*. 345.

"The quorum of a Committee of the Whole is the same as that of the House."—*Manual, p.* 71. Quorum of.

"If a message is announced during a committee, the Speaker takes the chair and receives it, because the committee cannot."—*Manual, p.* 72. [So, too, during a committee, the Speaker often takes the chair to receive the report of the Committee on Enrolled Bills, which having been announced, the chairman resumes the chair, and the House is again in committee.] Speaker takes chair to receive messages and report of Committee on Enrolled Bills.

"Whenever the Committee of the Whole House on the state of the Union, or the Committee of the Whole House, finds itself without a quorum, the chairman shall cause the roll of the House to be called, and thereupon the committee shall rise, and the chairman shall report the names of the absentees to the House, which shall be entered on the Journal."—*Rule* 106. [And all members are reported as absentees who fail to answer when their names are called, for, upon the completion of the roll, the chairman *immediately* vacates the chair. Whenever, upon such roll-call, a quorum answer to their names, and that fact is reported to the House, the Speaker declines to receive any motion whatever, and the committee resumes its session without further order. But if no quorum answer, a motion to adjourn, or for a call of the House, is in order; and if upon either of said motions a quorum shall vote, and the House refuse to adjourn or to order a call, the session of the committee is immediately resumed.—*Journals*, 2, 27, *p.* 592; 1, 29, *p.* 356; 2, 29, *p.* 343; 2, 32, *p.* 388.] Want of quorum. Roll to be called and absentees reported.

"The rules of proceedings in the House shall be observed in a Committee of the Whole House, *so far as they may be applicable*, except the rule limiting the times of speaking; but no member shall speak twice to any question until every member choosing to speak shall have spoken."—*Rule* 113. Rules of House to govern, except as to speaking.

"No previous question can be put in committee, nor can this committee adjourn as others may—*Manual, p.* 72—nor can the yeas and nays be taken—*Cong. Globe*, 1, 28, *p.* 618; 1, 26, *p.* 285—nor can a motion to lie on the table be entertained—*Cong. Globe*, 2, 31, *p.* 645—nor motions to reconsider."—*Cong. Globe*, 1, 27, *p.* 305. No motion for previous question or to adjourn, nor for yeas and nays, nor to lie on table, &c., &c., in.

Debate in, on the state of the Union.

In Committee of the Whole on the state of the Union, all debate on special orders shall be confined strictly to the measure under consideration.—*Rule* 114. [But it is otherwise where the measure has not been made a special order.—*Cong. Globe*, 2, 30, *p.* 587; 1, 31, *p.* 1475; 2, 31, *pp.* 630, 631; 1, 32, *p.* 1856.]

Debate one hour.

"No member shall occupy more than one hour in debate on any question in the House or in committee, but a member reporting the measure under consideration from a committee may open and close the debate: *Provided*, That when debate is closed by order of the House, any member shall be allowed, in committee, five minutes to explain any amendment he may offer, after which any member who shall first obtain the floor shall be allowed to speak five minutes in opposition to it; and there shall be no further debate on the amendment; but the same privilege of debate shall be allowed in favor of and against any amendment that may be offered to the amendment; and neither the amendment nor an amendment to the amendment shall be withdrawn by the mover thereof, unless by the unanimous consent of the committee: *Provided further*, That the House may, by the vote of a majority of the members present, at any time after the five minutes' debate has taken place upon proposed amendments to any section or paragraph of a bill, close all debate upon such section or paragraph, or at their election upon the pending amendments only."—*Rule* 60.

Five minutes' debate.

Amendment not to be withdrawn without unanimous consent.

All debate may be closed.

Hour debate may be closed.

"The House may at any time, by a vote of a majority of the members present, provide for the discharge of the Committee of the Whole House, and the Committee of the Whole House on the state of the Union, from the further consideration of any bill referred to it, after acting without debate on all amendments pending and that may be offered."—*Rule* 104. [The closing of debate herein referred to has reference only to the hour debate; the five minutes' debate contemplated by the 1st proviso of the 60th *Rule* (recited in the foregoing paragraph) commences upon the adoption of the order under this rule.

Form of resolution for closing debate.

The following is the form of resolution (sanctioned by long practice) for closing the hour debate, viz: "*Resolved*,

That all debate in the Committee of the Whole House (or Committee of the Whole House on the state of the Union, as the case may be) on (here insert title of bill of subject upon which it is proposed to close debate) shall cease (here insert time at which it is proposed to close debate) if the committee shall not sooner come to a conclusion upon the same; and the committee shall then proceed to vote on such amendments as may be pending or offered to the same, and shall then report it to the House with such amendments as may have been adopted by the committee."] The proposition to close debate may be made at any time, taking precedence even of a motion to go into Committee of the Whole; but to be in order at all, the subject upon which it is proposed to close debate must have been previously taken up and considered by the committee.—*Journal*, 1, 32, *p*. 147. This rule is construed to apply as well to messages as bills; indeed, to all subjects committed.—*Journal*, 1, 32, *p*. 146. And debate may be closed upon any one of the subjects referred to in a message.—*Journal*, 1, 32, *p*. 147. The right of the member who reports the measure under consideration to close debate is held not to be affected by this rule; but he may make his closing speech after the arrival of the time at which the House has directed that debate shall cease.—*Journal*, 1, 31, *p*. 1056; and such has been the invariable practice ever since.

Subject must have been previously considered.

Rule applies to messages as well as bills.

Member reporting measure still has right to close debate.

Where general debate has been closed, a member is not at liberty to speak in opposition to his own amendment.—*Cong. Globe*, 1, 31, *p*. 1408. Nor can he debate the main proposition.—*Ibid*., 2, 32, *p*. 1723.

Member offering amendment cannot speak against it, or to main question.

Debate having been closed at a particular hour by order of the House, it is not competent for the committee, even by unanimous consent, to extend the time.—*Cong. Globe*, 2, 32, *pp*. 784, 785.

Where debate closed, time cannot be extended by.

It is in order for the committee to lay aside a bill after having gone through with it, and, before rising, to proceed to other business on the calendar, notwithstanding the House may have adopted a resolution closing debate thereon.—*Cong. Globe*, 1, 33, *pp*. 1130, 1131.

May take up other business after getting through with a bill on which debate closed.

"All amendments made to an original motion in com-

Amendments to an original motion.

mittee shall be incorporated with the motion and so reported."—*Rule* 108. [Bills and resolutions are sometimes originally moved in Committees of the Whole, having for their bases messages or reports previously referred and then up for consideration.]

Bills and resolutions originating in Committees of the Whole.

Amendments to a report.

"All amendments made to a report committed to a Committee of the Whole House shall be noted and reported as in the case of bills."—*Rule* 109.

An amended clause subsequently stricken out.

Bill amended and substitute afterward adopted.

If the committee shall amend a clause, and subsequently strike out the clause as amended, the first amendment thereby falls, and cannot be reported to the House and voted on.—*Journal*, 2, 31, *p.* 346. [So, too, if the committee shall amend a bill ever so much, and subsequently adopt a substitute therefor, the bill is to be reported to the House with but a single amendment, viz, the substitute; and the House has only to choose between the original bill and the substitute.]

Motion to rise.

Member does not lose his right to floor by rising of, and may yield for that purpose.

Motion to rise may be withdrawn before vote announced.

In Committee of the Whole a motion to rise, like the motion to adjourn in the House, may be made at any time; and when at the rising a member is entitled to the floor, he is entitled to occupy it in preference to any other member at the next sitting of the committee.—*Cong. Globe*, 1, 31, *pp.* 358, 388. And a member occupying the floor may yield it to another member to move that the committee rise, without losing his right to reoccupy it at the next sitting.—*Ibid.*, 2, 31, *p.* 645. The motion to rise may be withdrawn at any time before the vote thereon is announced.—*Ibid.*, 1, 31, *p.* 318.

Motion for tax or charge upon people.

Increase of tax or duty.

"No motion or proposition for a tax or charge upon the people shall be discussed the day on which it is made or offered, and every such proposition shall receive its first discussion in a Committee of the Whole House."—*Rule* 110. And "no sum or quantum of tax or duty voted by a Committee of the Whole House shall be increased in the House, until the motion or proposition for such increase shall be first discussed and voted in a Committee of the Whole House, and so in respect to the time of its continuance."—*Rule* 111.

Appropriations of money to be first discussed.

"All proceedings touching appropriations of money shall be first discussed in a Committee of the Whole House."—*Rule* 112. (See APPROPRIATION BILLS.)

[The construction given to this rule is, that all bills, or amendments thereto, containing an appropriation of money must be committed to a Committee of the Whole before being considered in the House; hence, if such a bill, on its engrossment or third reading, or such an amendment, be pending before the House, and no motion is made to commit or postpone, the House must pass from its consideration and the bill go to the Speaker's table; but House bills with Senate amendments reducing the amount of or restricting appropriations need not be committed.]

Bills which need not be committed.

A bill directing the disbursement of money *already appropriated—Journal*, 1, 24, *p*. 254—or directing payment of money hereafter to be appropriated—*Journal*, 1, 31, *p*. 1216—need not be committed. Neither is it necessary that a bill containing an appropriation of *lands* should be committed.—*Journal*, 1, 30, *p*. 526. And when the rules have been suspended for the purpose of enabling the report of a measure to be made, and also for its consideration, a point of order that it contains an appropriation cannot be well taken.—*Journal*, 1, 34, *pp*. 1172, 1173.

Amendments to appropriation bills.

"No appropriation shall be reported in the general appropriation bills, or be in order as an amendment thereto, for any expenditure not previously authorized by law, unless in continuation of appropriations for such public works and objects as are already in progress, and for the contingencies for carrying on the several departments of the Government."—*Rule* 120.

An amendment in the nature of a private claim on the Government is not in order to a general appropriation bill.—*Cong. Globe*, 1, 31, *pp*. 1617, 1651; 2, 32, *p*. 736; 1, 33, *pp*. 385, 1483.

Cannot rule out of order any part of the bill committed.

[In the case of an appropriation reported by the Committee on Appropriations in conflict with the 120th *Rule*, and committed with the bill, it is not competent for the Committee of the Whole to rule it out of order, because the House having committed the bill (of course it is otherwise where the point was reserved before commitment) are presumed to have received, as in order, the report in its entirety. So far as proposed amendments

Practice in regard to amendments in. are concerned, the current of decisions in Committees of the Whole has been to exclude not only all appropriations not previously authorized by law, (with the exceptions contained in the rule,) but also all independent legislation; tolerating, however, limitations and provisos as to appropriations which are themselves in order.]

How bills are to be considered in. "Upon bills committed to a Committee of the Whole House, the bill shall be first read throughout by the Clerk, and then again read and debated by clauses, leaving the Preamble. preamble to be last considered; the body of the bill shall How amendments are to be noted in. not be defaced or interlined; but all amendments, noting the page and line, shall be duly entered by the Clerk on a separate paper, as the same shall be agreed to by After bill is reported from. the committee, and so reported to the House. After report, the bill shall again be subject to be debated and amended by clauses before a question to engross it be taken."—*Rule* 107. [The first reading herein required is usually dispensed with, but of course only by unanimous consent. Since the practice has obtained of printing all bills upon the order for their commitment, the amendments are usually noted upon a copy of the bill. The debate and amendment after report of a bill is usually precluded by an order for the previous question.]

What bills are considered by clauses and what by sections. [General appropriation, tariff, and tax bills are con sidered by *clauses;* other bills by *sections.*]

A clause or section cannot be recurred to when passed over. Where a bill is being considered by clauses or sections, and the committee has passed from the consideration of a particular clause or section, it is not in order to recur thereto.—*Cong. Globe*, 2, 32, *p.* 730; 2, 35, *p.* 1422.

How bills are taken up in Union. "In Committee of the Whole on the state of the Union, the bills shall be taken up and disposed of in their order on the calendar; but when objection is made to the consideration of a bill, a majority of the committee shall decide, without debate, whether it shall be taken up and Preferred bills in. disposed of or laid aside: *Provided*, That general appropriation bills, and, in time of war, bills for raising men or money, and bills concerning a treaty of peace, shall be preferred to all other bills at the discretion of the committee; and when demanded by any member, the question shall first be put in regard to them."—*Rule* 114.

[Where a bill has been taken up and is left undisposed of at the rising of the committee, it is the business first in order when the House shall again resolve itself into committee.]

A motion to strike out the enacting words of a bill shall have precedence of a motion to amend; and, if carried, shall be considered equivalent to its rejection. Whenever a bill is reported from a Committee of the Whole, with a recommendation to strike out the enacting words, and such recommendation is disagreed to by the House, the bill shall stand recommitted to the said committee without further action by the House.—*Rule* 123.

Report of, to strike out enacting words.

Where an amendment is reported from the Committee of the Whole as an entire and distinct proposition, it cannot be divided, but must be voted upon as a whole.—*Journals*, 1, 28, *p*. 1061; 1, 29, *pp*. 366, 642; 1, 30, *p*. 1059; 2, 30, *pp*. 574, 575.

Amendments from, not divisible.

[The following are the usual forms of report by the chairman of the Committee of the Whole, viz:

Forms of report to the House.

"The Committee of the Whole House on the state of the Union, having, according to order, had the state of the Union generally under consideration, and particularly (here insert title of bill or other matter,) have directed me to report the same with (or without, as the case may be) amendments."

In case of report with or without amendment.

Where the committee have failed to get through with the matter before them, instead of saying, "have directed me to report," &c., say, "have come to no resolution thereon."

In case of failure to get through.

Where the committee have risen for want of a quorum, instead of saying, "have directed me to report," &c., say, "having found itself without a quorum, I caused the roll to be called, and herewith report the names of the absentees to the House."

In case of want of quorum.

In case of reports from a Committee of the Whole House, omit the words "on the state of the Union," where they first occur, and strike out the words "state of the Union" where they next occur, and insert "*private calendar*."

Reports from a Committee of the Whole House.

[The report of the chairman of the Committee of the Whole is invariably received immediately upon the rising

Report of, when received and considered.

of the committee, and, under the uniform practice, the bill or other proposition reported is the business then in order for the consideration of the House. It might be otherwise in case it was made to appear that a quorum was not present when it was proposed to make the report.] But a mere assertion of the fact, without evidence, that a quorum is not present, will not prevent the reception of the report.—*Journal*, 1, 35, *pp*. 814, 822.

COMPENSATION.

Members shall receive.

"Representatives shall receive a compensation for their services, to be ascertained by law and paid out of the Treasury of the United States."—*Const.*, 1, 6, 9.

Of the Speaker.

By the act of March 3, 1873, it is provided that the Speaker of the House of Representatives shall, after the present Congress, receive in full, for all his services, compensation at the rate of ten thousand dollars per annum; and Senators, Representatives, and Delegates in Congress, including Senators, Representatives, and Delegates in the Forty-second Congress, holding such office at the passage of this act, and whose claim to a seat has not been adversely decided, shall receive seven thousand five hundred dollars per annum each, and this shall be in lieu of all pay and allowance, except actual individual traveling expenses from their homes to the seat of Government and return, by the most direct route of usual travel, once for each session, of the House to which such Senator, Member, or Delegate belongs, to be certified to under his hand to the disbursing officer, and filed as a voucher.—*Stat. at Large*, *Vol. XVII*, *p*. 486.

Of members and Delegates.

In lieu of all allowances except actual traveling expenses.

By the act of March 3, 1873, it is provided that hereafter Representatives and Delegates elect to Congress whose credentials in due form of law have been duly filed with the Clerk of the House of Representatives in accordance with the provisions of the act of Congress approved March third, eighteen hundred and sixty-three, may receive their compensation monthly from the beginning of their term until the begining of the first session of each Congress, upon a certificate in the form now in use, to be signed by the Clerk of the House, which certificate shall have the like force and effect as is given to the certificate

May be paid monthly from the beginning of their term until, &c.

of the Speaker under existing laws: *Provided*, That in case the Clerk of the House of Representatives shall be notified that the election of any such holder of a certificate of election will be contested his name shall not be placed upon the roll of members-elect so as to entitle him to be paid, until he shall have been sworn in as a member, or until such contest shall be determined.—*Stat. at Large, Vol. XVII, p.* 488, 489.

Members whose seats are contested, not to receive pay until they are sworn in.

By the act of August 16, 1856, it is provided that if any books shall hereafter be ordered to and received by members by resolution of either or both Houses of Congress, the price paid for the same shall be deducted from the compensation provided for such member or members; but this does not extend to books ordered to be printed by the Public Printer during the Congress for which the said member shall have been elected. It is also the duty of the Sergeant-at-Arms of the House, and the Secretary of the Senate, respectively, to deduct from the monthly payment of any member the amount of his compensation for each day that such member shall be absent from the House or Senate, respectively, unless such Representative, Senator, or Delegate shall assign as the reason for such absence the sickness of himself or of some member of his family.—*Stat. at Large, Vol. XI, p.* 48.

Price of books to be deducted from.

Deduction from, in case of absence.

By the joint resolution of July 17, 1862, it is declared that withdrawal from his seat by a member without leave, in anticipation of, and before, the adjournment of Congress, and a failure to return, shall, in addition to the deduction provided by the foregoing act, work a forfeiture of his mileage for returning home, the amount of which shall be deducted from his compensation.—*Stat. at Large, Vol. XIII, p.* 628.

Further deduction from, in case of absence.

By a resolution of the House of March 4, 1842, the Sergeant-at-Arms is required to deduct the amount of the excess of stationery to which he is entitled, received by a member, from the pay and mileage of such member.—*Journal*, 2, 27, *p.* 495. (See STATIONERY.)

Excess of stationery to be deducted from.

The compensation which shall be due the members of each House shall be certified to by the presiding officers thereof, respectively; and the same shall be passed as public accounts, and paid out of the public Treasury.—

Amount of, to be certified by the Speaker.

Certificates of the Speaker for, to be conclusive.

Stat. at Large, Vol. III, p. 404. And all certificates which may have been or may be granted by the presiding officers of the Senate and House of Representatives, respectively, of the amount of compensation due to the members of their several Houses, are, and ought to be, deemed, held, and taken, and are hereby declared to be, conclusive upon all the Departments and officers of the Government of the United States.—*Stat. at Large, Vol. IX, p.* 523.

Of member who shall die after the commencement of Congress.

By the joint resolution of March 3, 1859, it is provided that whenever, hereafter, any member of the House of Representatives shall die after the commencement of the Congress to which he shall have been elected, compensation shall be computed and paid his widow, or, if no widow survive him, to his heirs-at-law, for the period that shall have elapsed from the commencement of such Congress as aforesaid: *Provided*, That compensation shall be computed and paid in all cases for a period of not less than three months; and in no case shall constructive mileage be computed or paid. The compensation of each person elected or appointed afterward to supply the vacancy so occasioned shall hereafter be computed and paid from the time the compensation of his predecessor is hereby directed to be computed and paid for, and not otherwise.—*Stat. at Large, Vol. XI, pp.* 442, 443.

Of member elected to fill vacancy.

Of member elected to fill vacancy.

By the joint resolution of July 12, 1862, it is provided that in all cases of vacancy in either House of Congress, by death or otherwise, of any member elected or appointed thereto, after the commencement of the Congress to which he shall have been elected, each person afterward elected or appointed to fill such vacancy shall be compensated and paid from the time that the compensation of his predecessor ceased: *Provided*, That no member shall receive for his compensation more than three thousand dollars for any one year.—*Stat. at Large, Vol. XII, p.* 624. The present compensation is $7,500 per annum. (See *ante, p.* 74.)

(See SERGEANT-AT-ARMS and MILEAGE.)

CONCURRENCE.

Question on, is

[The question which first arises on a resolution, amendment, or conference report, is on concurrence. And as the negative of concurrence amounts to the affirmative of non-concurrence, no question is afterward put on the latter motion.]

the first which arises.

CONFERENCE COMMITTEES.

"It is on the occasion of amendments between the Houses that conferences are usually asked; but they may be asked in all cases of difference of opinion between the two Houses on matters depending between them."—*Manual*, *p.* 128. [A conference committee, under the usage, consists of three members of the Senate and three members of the House. The report of a conference committee must be signed by a majority of the members of each House composing the said committee.]

When conferences are asked.

Of what number to consist.

Report of, by whom to be signed.

"In every case of an amendment of a bill agreed to in one House and dissented to in the other, if either House shall request a conferrence and appoint a committee to confer, and the other House shall also appoint a committee to confer, such committee shall, at a convenient hour, to be agreed upon by their chairman, meet in the conference chamber, and state to each other, verbally or in writing, as either shall choose, the reasons of their respective Houses for and against the amendment, and confer freely thereon."—*Joint Rule* 1.

In case of disagreement as to amendments.

[Usually, and especially toward the close of a session, the request of the Senate for a conference is reciprocated immediately upon its being communicated to the House; but such request can only be considered in order at the time that messages from the Senate on the Speaker's table are in order.]

Request of Senate for, when considered.

The usual course of proceeding previous to a conference is for one House to disagree to the other's amendment, and for the amending House to insist upon its amendment and ask a conference.—*Journal*, 1, 35, *pp.* 711, 933, 1062. But it sometimes happens, near the close of a session, that one House disagrees to the other's amendments and thereupon asks a conference.—*Journal*, 1, 3, *pp.* 221, 222; 2, 35, *p.* 564. A conference sometimes takes place after one House has adhered.—*Journal*, 1, 3, *pp.* 281, 283; 2, 3, *p.* 254; 1, 34, *pp.* 1600, 1602; 1, 35, *pp.*

Usual proceeding previous to.

Conference after adherence.

604, 615, 620; *Senate Journal, January* 20, 1834; *Manual, p.* 129.

At least two conferences before adherence. "In the ordinary parliamentary course there are two free conferences at least before an adherence."—*Manual, p.* 126. There are sometimes three and even four conferences before a matter of difference is disposed of.—*Journal*, 1, 34, *pp.* 943, 1600; 1, 35, *p.* 1136.

To recede, to insist, to adhere. In the case of disagreeing votes between the two houses, the House may either *recede, insist and ask a conference*, or *adhere*, and motions for such purposes take precedence in that order. (See *Manual, pp.* 114, 115; *Journal*, 1, 23, *p.* 229; 1, 34, *pp.* 1516 to 1518.)

[Even though the previous question may be pending on a motion to *insist* or to *adhere*, a motion to *recede*, which removes the disagreement between the Houses and passes the bill, may be made, but of course is not debatable.]

Report may be made at any time. The report of a committee of conference is, under the practice of the House, so highly privileged that it has been held to be in order even pending a motion for a call of the House.—*Journal*, 1, 31, *p.* 1590.

[Indeed, under the practice, reports of conference committees are received at any time, (except when the rules are suspended,) even during the pendency of a motion to adjourn or to adjourn over, and, like the motion to go to the Speaker's table, may interrupt a member who is on the floor speaking.]

Member of, absent. [A member of a conference committee who may be absent on the business of the committee is, according to the practice, understood to be absent by leave of the House.]

Where unable to agree. Where a conference committee is unable to agree, that fact is reported, and another committee is usually asked for and appointed.—*Journals*, 1, 31, *p.* 1681; 1, 34, *pp.* 919, 938, 1516, 1518; 3, 34, *p.* 663; 1, 35, *p.* 1118.

Where report is disagreed to. So, too, when a report is disagreed to, another conference usually takes place.—*Journals*, 2, 27, *p.* 1248; 3, 34, *pp.* 653, 655; 1, 35, *pp.* 1105, 1106.

May be instructed. [A committee of conference may be instructed like any other committee, but the instructions cannot be moved when the papers are not before the House.]

The report of a committee of conference cannot be amended or altered as that of another committee may be.—*Manual, p.* 128. *Journal Senate, May* 24, 1796. Cannot be amended.

The report may be laid on the table.—*Journal*, 1, 31, *p.* 1590. [And its effect will be to lay the bill also on the table.] Report may be laid on the table.

The committee may report agreement as to some of the matters of difference, but unable to agree as to others.—*Journal*, 1, 29, *p.* 1302. May report agreement as to part and disagreement as to the rest.

"The request of a conference must always be by the House which is possessed of the papers."—*Manual, p.* 128. Must be asked by House which has the papers.

"In all cases of conference asked after a vote of disagreement, &c., the conferees of the House asking it are to leave the papers with the conferees of the other."—*Manual, p.* 129. [And of course the report must be first made to the House agreeing to the conference.] Papers to be left with conferees of House agreeing to conference. Where report to be first made.

CONFIDENTIAL COMMUNICATIONS.

(See SECRET SESSION.)

CONGRESS.

(See MEETING OF CONGRESS.)

CONGRESSIONAL DIRECTORY.

By the joint resolution of February 14, 1865, it is provided that the Congressional Directory shall be compiled under the direction of the Joint Committee on Public Printing, and published by the Superintendent of Public Printing; the first edition of each session to be ready for distribution within one week after the commencement thereof.—*Stat. at Large, Vol. XIII, p.* 568. By whom compiled. When to be ready for distribution.

CONGRESSIONAL GLOBE.

For many years prior to the close of the last session the daily proceedings of the House, including the debates, were published in the Congressional Globe. And, in order to facilitate the reporting of the same, the Doorkeeper was directed, by a resolution of the House, (*Journal*, 1, 32, *p.* 70,) to provide chairs for its reporters, to be placed in front of the Clerk's desk. Reported proceedings. Seats for reporters of.

It is not a privileged question to correct a report in the Globe.—*Cong. Globe*, 1, 31, *p.* 1148. Not privileged to correct a report in.

An appropriation is annually made to furnish each member and Delegate with twenty-four copies of the Congressional Globe and Appendix.

Names of members not voting to be recorded in.

A record is required to be made in the Congressional Globe, immediately after the names of those voting in the affirmative and negative, of those not voting, on any call of the yeas and nays.—*Rule*, 149.

Contract with publishers of, authorized.

By the act of April 2, 1872, (*Stat. at Large, Vol. XVII, p.* 47,) the Congressional Printer is directed to contract with Franklin Rives, Jefferson Rives, and George A. Bailey for reporting and printing the debates in Congress for two years from March 4, 1871, in accordance with a proposed form of contract from the said Rives & Bailey, submitted to and approved by the Joint Committee on Printing on the part of the Senate.

Reporters for, to be approved by Speaker.

In regard to future reporting.

And it is provided further "that no person shall be employed as a reporter for the House without the approval of the Speaker of the House: *Provided*, That it shall be the duty of the Joint Committee on Public Printing to publish an advertisement once a week, for four weeks, in one newspaper in each of the cities of Washington, Philadelphia, New York, Boston, Chicago, Cincinnati, Louisville, Saint Louis, and San Francisco, inviting proposals in detail for reporting and for printing, together and separately, the debates of the Forty-third, the Forty-fourth, and the Forty-fifth Congresses, together or separately, and to report all proposals which may be received before the designated day to Congress, at the earliest practicable date, with estimates, hereby directed to be made by the Congressional Printer, of the cost of reporting the debates and of printing them at the Government Printing Office, accompanied by the recommendations of the Joint Committee on Public Printing on all proposals and estimates so submitted; and that the bills for such advertising be paid in equal parts from the contingent funds of the Senate and of the House of Representatives: *And provided further*, That no debates shall be reported or published at public expense, after the close of the present Congress, except upon written contracts entered into therefor under the authority of Congress."

By the act of March 3, 1873, the last proviso to the act providing for printing and reporting the debates in Congress, approved April second, eighteen hundred and seventy-two, is repealed: *Provided*, That until a contract is made, the debates shall be printed by the Congressional Printer, under the direction of the Joint Committee on Public Printing on the part of the Senate.—*Stat. at Large, Vol. XVII, p.* 510.

Repeal of foregoing proviso - debates by whom to be printed.

On the 3d March, 1873, the following preamble and resolution were agreed to, viz:

Proceedings, &c., to be furnished by present corps of reporters of.

Whereas the present contract for publication of the debates expires with this session:

And whereas the sundry civil appropriation bill, about to become a law, provides that until a new contract be made, the debates shall be printed by the Congressional Printer, but makes no provision for reporting, leaving each House to adopt such arrangements on that subject as it may deem best: Therefore,

Resolved, That the reports of the House proceedings and debates, shall be furnished to the Congressional Printer by the present corps of Globe reporters, who shall hereafter, until otherwise ordered, be officers of the House under direction of the Speaker, and shall receive the same compensation now allowed to the official reporters of committees.—*Journal*, 3, 42, *pp.* 582, 583.

Reporters of, to be officers of the House.

By the act of March 2, 1865, it is provided that the proceedings of Congress shall be published in the Daily Globe of the day subsequent to the day such proceedings were had, and delivered to both Houses at their time of meeting; but the daily publication of not more than forty columns of such proceedings is required, and speeches not actually delivered shall be postponed until the same can be published without increasing the extent of proceedings beyond forty columns.—*Stat. at Large, Vol. XIII, p.* 460.

Proceedings shall appear in next daily paper &c.

By resolution of the House of May 7, 1866, it is directed that the reporters of the Congressional Globe be furnished with three copies each of all bills and resolutions printed by order of the House.—*Journal*, 1, 39, *p.* 675.

Copies of bills, &c., to be furnished to reporters of.

By resolution of the House of February 16, 1867, the Clerk is directed to furnish the publishers of the Globe,

List of members to be furnished to the publishers of.

at each session of Congress, a list of the members of the House, with their post office address and the number of their seats.—*Journal*, 2, 39, *p.* 405.

CONSIDERATION.

When question of, to be put.

"When any motion or proposition is made, the question 'Will the House now consider it?' shall not be put, unless it is demanded by some member, or is deemed necessary by the Speaker.—*Rule* 41. And it is competent for a member to raise the question of consideration upon a report, even though a question of privilege is involved in the report.—*Journal*, 1, 35, *pp.* 1083, 1085.

When too late.

But after a question has been stated, and its discussion commenced, it is too late to raise the question of consideration.—*Journal*, 1, 17, *pp.* 296, 297.

CONTESTED ELECTIONS.

(See Elections Contested.)

CONVERSATION.

When not to be indulged in.

"While the Speaker is putting any question or addressing the House, or when a member is speaking, none shall entertain private discourse."—*Rule* 65.

COURT OF CLAIMS.

(See Claims, Court of.)

DAILY GLOBE.

(See Congressional Globe.)

DEBATE.

Motion to be stated or read before.

"When a motion is made and seconded, it shall be stated by the Speaker; or being in writing, it shall be handed to the Chair and read aloud by the Clerk before debated."—*Rule* 38.

Member must rise and address "Mr. Speaker."

When any member is about to speak in debate, or deliver any matter to the House, he shall rise from his seat and respectfully address himself to "Mr. Speaker."—*Rule* 57. [According to the usage, he may rise from any seat he may happen to occupy.]

"When two or more members happen to rise at once, the Speaker shall name the member who is first to speak."—*Rule* 59. And it is the right of the Speaker generally to name the member entitled to the floor.—*Journal*, 2, 32, *p*. 405. (See also *Manual*, *p*. 78, where it is held, in reference to similar language in a rule of the Senate, that no appeal lies from the presiding officer's decision.)

When more than one member rises at same time.

By parliamentary courtesy, the member upon whose motion a subject is brought before the House is first entitled to the floor.—*Journal*, 2, 30, *p*. 247. [So, too, it is an invariable practice for the Speaker, at every new stage of a bill or proposition, to recognize first the member who has had charge of it, even if another member addressed him first: *Provided*, He is a competitor for the floor.]

Who entitled to floor by courtesy.

"No member shall speak more than once to the same question without leave of the House, unless he be the mover, proposer, or introducer of the matter pending; in which case, he shall be permitted to speak in reply, but not until every member choosing to speak shall have spoken."—*Rule* 63. But it is too late to make the question of order that a member has already spoken, if no one claims the floor until he has made some progress in his speech.—*Journal*, 1, 29, *p*. 934. "Members may address the House or committee from the Clerk's desk, or from a place near the Speaker's chair."—*Rule* 58. [Members very seldom speak from the place here indicated, but usually from some central position in the hall.]

No member shall speak but once, except the mover.

Where members may speak from.

Where an amendment is offered after a member has occupied the floor, he may again occupy the floor, the question being changed.—*Journal*, 1, 28, *p*. 532.

Members may speak again after amendment offered.

A member who has once spoken may be recognized to move the previous question.—*Journal*, 1, 24, *p*. 83.

Member may move previous question after having once spoken.

The right of the "member reporting the measure" to open and close debate is not affected by an order either for the previous question or that debate shall cease in committee.—*Journal*, 1, 31, *p*. 1056. *Cong. Globe*, 1, 31, *pp*. 1308 to 1310. [But he has only an hour allowed by the rules to close the debate; and if, after having occupied part of the hour in closing, he moves the previous

Right to open and close, not affected by previous question or close of debate.

question and it is seconded, he is then only entitled to so much of the hour as he has not already occupied.]

Where member moves previous question within his hour.

Where a member has spoken part of his hour, and moved the previous question, he may withdraw the motion and speak for the remainder of his time.—*Journal*, 1, 31, *pp.* 1367, 1368.

Member may yield for explanation, &c

While a member is occupying the floor, he may yield it to another for explanation of the pending measure as well as for personal explanation.—*Journal*, 1, 32, *p.* 524. [So, too, he may yield it for a motion to adjourn, or that the committee rise, without losing his right to reoccupy it for the remainder of his time whenever the pending question shall be resumed; but it is otherwise when he yields to enable another to offer or withdraw an amendment.]

Must be confined to the question and personality avoided. In Committee of the Whole.

"A member shall confine himself to the question under debate, and avoid personality"—*Rule* 57—but in committee of the Whole on the state of the Union he is not bound to confine himself to the question under debate—*Cong. Globe*, 2, 30, *p.* 587; 1, 31, *p.* 1475; 1, 32, *p.* 1856—except where a special order is pending, when the debate must be confined strictly to the measure under consideration.—*Rule* 114.

Contestant in debate to be subject to rules.

A contestant for a seat or other person occupying the floor by leave of the House, is subject alike with members to the rules regulating debate.—*Journal*, 1, 28, *p.* 1011.

Question of rejection of bill debatable.

The question of the rejection of a bill, arising upon its first reading, is debatable.—*Journal*, 2, 32, *p.* 152.

No member to speak more than once on appeals.

On an appeal growing out of questions as to the applicability or relevancy of propositions, &c., "no member shall speak more than once without the leave of the House."—*Rule* 2.

Where member transgresses the rules in speaking.

"If any member, in speaking or otherwise, trangress the rules of the House, the Speaker shall, or any member may, call to order; in which case, the member so called to order shall immediately sit down, unless permitted to explain; and the House shall, if appealed to, decide on the case, but without debate; if there be no appeal, the decision of the Chair shall be submitted to. If the decision be in favor of the member called to order he shall be at liberty to proceed; *if otherwise, he shall not be permitted to proceed, in case any member object, without leave of the House;* and if the case require it, he shall be liable to the censure of the House."—*Rule* 61.

He may proceed in order, if no member objects, or with leave.

"If a member be called to order for words spoken in debate, the person calling him to order shall repeat the words excepted to, and they shall be taken down in writing at the Clerk's table; and no member shall be held to answer, or be subject to the censure of the House, for words spoken in debate, if any other member has spoken, or other business has intervened, after the words spoken, and before exception to them shall have been taken."—*Rule* 62.

Words excepted to, to be reduced to writing.

When not censurable for words spoken.

It is a breach of order in debate to notice what has been said on the same subject in the other house, or the particular votes or majority on it there; because the opinion of each house should be left to its own independency, not to be influenced by the proceedings of the other; and the quoting them might beget reflections leading to a misunderstanding between the two houses.—*Manual, p.* 81.

Proceedings of other house not to be noticed in.

"For any speech or debate in either house, members shall not be questioned in any other place."—*Const.*, 1, 6, *p.* 9.

Not to be questioned out of House for debate.

While a member is speaking, none shall entertain private discourse, nor pass between him and the Chair.—*Rule* 65.

No conversation or passing between member and Chair.

"No member shall occupy more than one hour in debate on any question in the House or in committee; but a member reporting the measure under consideration from a committee may open and close the debate: *Provided*, That where debate is closed by order of the House, any member shall be allowed, in committee, five minutes to explain any amendment he may offer—after which any member who shall first obtain the floor shall be allowed to speak five minutes in opposition to it, and there shall be no further debate on the amendment; but the same privilege of debate shall be allowed in favor of and against any amendment that may be offered to the amendment; and neither the amendment nor

Hour rule.

Five minutes' debate.

an amendment to the amendment shall be withdrawn by the mover thereof, unless by the unanimous consent of the committee: *Provided further*, That the House may, by the vote of a majority of the members present, at any time after the five minutes' debate has taken place upon proposed amendments to any section or paragraph of a bill, close all debate upon such section or paragraph, or at their election upon the pending amendments only."—*Rule* 60.

Closing of all debate.

Debate may be closed in Committee of the Whole.

"The House may at any time discharge the Committee of the Whole House and the Committee of the Whole House on the state of the Union from the further consideration of any bill referred to it, after acting, without debate, on all amendments pending that may be offered."—*Rule* 104.

But subject must have been considered in committee.

But the subject must have been considered in Committee of the Whole; and this rule applies as well to messages as bills.—*Journal*, 1, 32, *pp*. 146, 147.

Not allowed on resolutions or bills on leave on day of presentation.

By *Rule* 52 debate on the day of their presentation is prohibited upon resolutions submitted on the call of the States and Territories after the reports of committees; and by *Rule* 130 all resolutions submitted on Mondays which shall give rise to debate shall lie over for discussion at least until all the States and Territories are called. And it has been decided (*Journal*, 1, 26, *pp*. 557, 763) that bills introduced on leave upon the call for resolutions, and which give rise to debate, must also lie over. It is a very common practice, however, when a resolution is submitted under these rules, for the mover to immediately demand the previous question, which, if ordered, prevents debate and brings the House to a direct vote on the resolution—thus avoiding the necessity for its lying over.—*Journal*, 1, 26, *pp*. 1064, 1067; 2, 27, *p*. 429; 1, 28, *p*. 558; 1, 29, *p*. 1235; 1, 30, *p*. 326.

Prohibited on bills introduced on Mondays.

By *Rule* 130 all bills introduced on leave during the first hour after the Journal is read on Mondays must be referred without debate.

Not allowed on private bills on 1st and 4th Fridays and Saturdays.

"On the first and fourth Friday and Saturday of each month the calendar of private bills shall be called over, and the bills to the passage of which no objection shall then be made shall be first considered and disposed of. But when a bill is again reached, after having been once objected to, the committee shall consider and dispose of the same, unless it shall again be objected to by at least five members."—*Rule* 129. [The universal practice under this rule is not to tolerate discussion in committee on any private bill on the days named; and it has been decided (*Journal* 1, 31, *p.* 697) that the rule applies equally to bills in the House.]

"A motion to adjourn, and a motion to fix the day to which the House shall adjourn, shall be always in order; these motions, and the motion to lie on the table, shall be decided without debate."—*Rule* 44.

Not allowed on motions to adjourn, to fix day, and to lie on table.

"On a motion to excuse a member from voting, the question shall be taken without debate."—*Rule* 31.

Not allowed on motion to be excused from voting.

"On a previous question there shall be no debate. All incidental questions of order arising after a motion is made for the previous question, and pending such motion, shall be decided, whether on appeal or otherwise, without debate." And under *Rule* 132, after the main question is ordered, its effect shall be "to put an end to all debate." And "the House may also, at any time, on motion, seconded by a majority of the members present, close all debate upon a pending amendment, or an amendment thereto, and cause the question to be put thereon; and this shall not preclude any further amendment or debate upon the bill."

Nor on previous question or incidental questions pending it.

Pending the demand for the previous question on the passage of a bill, it is not in order to debate a motion to reconsider the vote on its third reading; but the vote must be taken without debate.—*Journal*, 1, 34, *p.* 1009. Nor pending such demand is it in order even to ask a question of the mover of the proposition.—*Journal*, 1, 28, *p.* 1003.

Nor on motion to reconsider third reading while previous question is pending on passage.

"All questions relating to the priority of business to be acted on shall be decided without debate."—*Rule* 66.

Nor on questions of priority of business.

[It has been invariably held, too, that a motion to suspend the rules is not debatable; nor motions to reconsider votes on questions which were not themselves debatable, except where the original question was not

Nor on motions to suspend rules, or to reconsider votes on questions not debatable.

debatable by reason of the order for the previous question.]

Not after a member has answered to his name.

Where a question has been ordered to be taken by yeas and nays, and has been put by the Speaker, and upon the roll-call a vote has been given by a member, further debate is procluded.—*Journal*, 2, 10, *p*. 446. Such continues to be the practice; but if a member rises *before a response is given*, and is recognized by the Chair, he may proceed to debate the question.—*Journal*, 1, 17, *pp*. 216, 217.

On motion to postpone and commit.

[On a motion to *postpone*, the debate allowable is very limited; but on a motion to *commit* the whole question is open.]

DEBATES, REPORTING AND PUBLICATION OF.

(See CONGRESSIONAL GLOBE.)

DELEGATES.

Provision for election of.

By the act of March 3, 1817, it is provided, "that in every Territory of the United States in which a temporary government has been or hereafter shall be established, and which, by virtue of the ordinance of Congress of the 13th of July, 1787, or of any subsequent act of Congress passed or to be passed, now hath or hereafter shall have the right to send a Delegate to Congress, such delegate shall be elected every second year, for the same term of two years for which members of the House of Representatives of the United States are elected; and in that House each of the said Delegates shall have a seat, with a right of debating, but not of voting."

Shall have right to debate, but not to vote.

Compensation and franking privilege of.

The compensation and franking privilege of Delegates are the same as of members.—(See COMPENSATION and FRANKING PRIVILEGE.)

May make motions.

The right of a Delegate to submit a resolution is recognized by the 52d and 130th *Rules*, and it is also competent for him to submit any motion which a member may make, except the motion to reconsider, which is dependent upon the right to vote.—*Journals*, 2, 30, *p*. 503; 1, 31, *p*. 1280.

The Speaker shall appoint from among the Delegates from the Territories an additional member of the committee on the Territories; and he shall also appoint the Delegate from the District of Columbia an additional member of the Committee for the District of Columbia; but the said Delegates in their respective committees shall have the same privileges only as in the House.—*Rule* 162. To be appointed on certain committees.

[In the organization of the House, the names of Delegates are called over after those of members, and before taking their seats the same oath or affirmation is administered as in the case of members.] Names of, called in organization of the House.

By the act of January 16, 1873, the provisions of the act of June 11, 1864, prohibiting members from receiving pay for services where the United States is interested, are extended so as to apply to Delegates.—*Stat. at Large, Vol. XVII, p.* 411. Not to receive pay for services where the U. S. is interested.

DEPARTMENTS.

(See EXECUTIVE DEPARTMENTS.)

DISORDER.

"In case of any disturbance or disorderly conduct in the galleries or lobby, the Speaker (or chairman of the Committee of the Whole House) shall have power to order the same to be cleared."—*Rule* 9. In the galleries or lobby.

"Each house may punish its members for disorderly behavior."—*Const. U. S.*, 1, 5, 8. House may punish members for.

"The Speaker shall preserve order and decorum."—*Rule* 2. And the Sergeant-at-Arms shall aid in the enforcement of order under the direction of the Speaker.—*Rule* 22. Speaker shall preserve order.

"If any member, in speaking or otherwise, transgress the rules of the House, the Speaker shall, or any member may, call to order; in which case the member so called to order shall immediately sit down, unless permitted to explain; and the House shall, if appealed to, decide on the case, but without debate. If there be no appeal, the decision of the Chair shall be submitted to. If the decision be in favor of the member called to order he shall be at liberty to proceed; *if otherwise, he shall* In case of member called to order.

not be permitted to proceed, in case any member object, without leave of the House; and if the case require it, he shall be liable to the censure of the House."—*Rule* 61.

Member may be censured.

"If a member be called to order for words spoken in debate, the person calling him to order shall repeat the words excepted to, and they shall be taken down in writing at the Clerk's table; and no member shall be held to answer, or be subject to the censure of the House, for words spoken in debate, if any other member has spoken, or other business has intervened, after the words spoken, and before exception to them shall have been taken."—*Rule* 62. (See decision under latter clause of this rule, *Journal*, 2, 37, *p*. 610.)

Specific violations of order.

"While the Speaker is putting any question, or addressing the House, none shall walk out of or across the House; nor in such case, or when a member is speaking, shall entertain private discourse; nor while a member is speaking shall pass between him and the Chair. Every member shall remain uncovered during the session of the House. No member or other person shall visit or remain by the Clerk's table while the yeas and nays are calling or ballots are counting. Smoking is prohibited within the bar of the House or gallery."—*Rule* 65.

Member not to be named in debate.

"No person in speaking is to mention a member then present by his name."—*Manual*, *p*. 79.

Disorderly words in committee.

"Disorderly words spoken in a committee must be written down as in the House, but the committee can only report them to the House for animadversion."—*Manual*, *p*. 81.

Committee cannot punish for.

"A committee cannot punish a breach of order in the House. It can only rise and report it to the House, who may proceed to punish."—*Manual*, *p*. 94; *Journal*, 1, 28, *p*. 846.

Speaker may call member by name.

"If repeated calls do not produce order, the Speaker may call by his name any member obstinately persisting in irregularity."—*Manual*, *p*. 80.

Clerk shall preserve order and decorum before Speaker is elected.

"Pending the election of a Speaker, the Clerk shall preserve order and decorum, and shall decide all questions of order that may arise, subject to appeal to the House."—*Rule* 146.

DISTRICT OF COLUMBIA, COMMITTEE FOR.

"There shall be appointed at the commencement of each Congress a Committee for the District of Columbia, to consist of eleven members."—*Rule* 74. When appointed, and of what number.

"The Speaker shall appoint the Delegate from the District of Columbia an additional member of the said committee; but the said Delegate shall have the same privileges only as in the House."—*Rule* 162. Delegate to be added to the committee.

"It shall be the duty of the committee for the District of Columbia to take into consideration all such petitions and matters or things touching the said District as shall be presented, or shall come in question, and be referred to them by the House, and to report their opinion thereon, together with such propositions relative thereto as to them shall seem expedient. The third Friday of each month, from the hour of 2 o'clock p. m. until the adjournment of that day, shall, when claimed by the Committee for the District of Columbia, be devoted exclusively to business reported from said committee; and said committee shall henceforth be omitted by the Speaker in the regular calls of committees."—*Rule* 82. Its duties. To be only called on third Friday of each month.

DIVISION OF THE HOUSE.

(See VOTING.)

DIVISION OF QUESTIONS.

"Any member may call for the division of a question, before or after the main question is ordered, which shall be divided if it comprehend propositions in substance so distinct that one being taken away a substantive proposition shall remain for the decision of the House. A motion to strike out and insert shall be deemed indivisible."—*Rule* 46. But it has been decided on appeals that on motions to commit with instructions, or on the different branches of instructions—*Journals*, 1, 17, *p*. 507; 1, 31, *pp*. 1395–'97; 1, 32, *p*, 611—on a Senate amendment—*Journals*, 2, 32, *p*. 401—on an amendment reported as a single amendment from a Committee of the Whole—*Journals*, 1, 28, *p*. 1061; 1, 29, pp. 366, 642; 1, 30, *p*. 1059; 2, 37, *p*. 170, &c.—on a series of resolutions proposed to be inserted in lieu of other matter—*Congres-* How made. Motion to strike out and insert not divisible. Other questions not divisible.

sional Globe, 1, 31, *p.* 1301—a division of the question cannot be had.

Upon engrossment of internal improvement bills.

"Upon the engrossment of any bill making appropriations of money for works of internal improvement of any kind or description, it shall be in the power of any member to call for a division of the question, so as to take a separate vote of the House upon each item of improvement or appropriation contained in said bill, or upon such items separately, and others collectively, as the members making the call may specify; and if one-fifth of the members present second said call, it shall be the duty of the Speaker to make such divisions of the question, and put them to vote accordingly."—*Rule* 121.

Not allowed upon other bills.

[But it has been invariably held, and never appealed from, that the rules in regard to a division of the question apply to no other description of *bills* than such as make "appropriations of money for works of internal improvement."]

DIVINE SERVICE.

Not to be performed in the hall without the consent of the Speaker.

"No person shall be permitted to perform divine service in the chamber occupied by the House of Representatives unless with the consent of the Speaker."—*Rule* 6.

DOCUMENTS.

(See PUBLIC DOCUMENTS.)

DOORKEEPER.

To be elected at the commencement of each Congress. Oath of office.

A Doorkeeper shall be elected at the commencement of each Congress, to continue in office until his successor is appointed, who shall take an oath for the true and faithful discharge of the duties of his office, to the best of his knowledge and abilities, and to keep the secrets of the House; and his appointees shall be subject to the approval of the Speaker; and in his election the vote shall be taken *viva voce*.—*Rule* 10.

His appointees subject to the approval of the Speaker. *Viva voce* vote for.

Additional oath of.

He is also required, by the act of July 2, 1862, to take an additional oath.—(See OATH.)

Shall strictly execute the rules in regard to admission on the floor and in gallery.

"The Doorkeeper shall execute strictly the 134th and 135th *Rules*, relative to the privilege of the hall; and he shall be required, at the commencement and close of each session of Congress, to take an inventory of all the furniture, books, and other public property in the several committee and other rooms under his charge, and shall report the same to the House; which report shall be referred to the Committee on Accounts, who shall determine the amount for which he shall be held liable for missing articles. It is the duty of the Doorkeeper, ten minutes before the meeting of the House each day, to see that the floor is cleared of all persons except those privileged to remain during the sessions of the House."—*Rule* 27.

Shall take inventory of property in committee and other rooms.

Shall clear the floor of persons not privileged ten minutes before House meets.

By the act of second session Forty-first Congress, p. 365, it is made his duty to make out a full and complete account of all the property belonging to the United States in his possession, on the first day of each regular session, and at the expiration of his term of service.

Shall make full account of Government property in his possession.

"When a message shall be sent from the Senate to the House of Representatives, it shall be announced at the door of the House by the Doorkeeper."—*Joint Rule* 2.

Shall announce messages from the Senate.

[The Doorkeeper (with the aid of his appointees, viz: the superintendents of the "folding-room" and "document-room," messengers, pages, folders, and laborers) discharges various duties which are not enumerated in the rules, viz: he announces at the door of the House all messages from the President, &c.; keeps the doors of the House; folds and distributes extra documents; furnishes members with printed copies of bills, reports, and other documents; conveys messages from members; keeps the hall, galleries, and committee-rooms in order, &c., &c.]

Duties not enumerated in rules.

By a resolution of the House of June 4, 1872, (*Journal*, 2, 42, *p*. 1056,) it is provided that the Speaker order the Doorkeeper of the House to prevent strictly the occupation of any of the offices and rooms assigned by the Speaker and by orders of the House to the use of the several officers and committees of the House, by any person whatsoever, during any recess of the House, without the written consent of the officer having such office in charge, or of the chairman or chairmen of the committee or committees to whom such room has been assigned.

To prevent the occupation of rooms during the recess by unauthorized persons.

When to discharge certain duties of the Clerk.

By the act of February 21, 1867—*Stat. at Large, Vol. XIV, p.* 397—it is provided that in case of vacancies in the offices of Clerk and Sergeant-at-Arms, or of their absence or inability to act, the duties imposed on the Clerk by law or custom relative to the preparation of the roll of Representatives or the organization of the House, shall be performed by the Doorkeeper of the next preceding House of Representatives.

DUTIES OR TAXES.

Motion for, to be first discussed in Committee of the Whole.

"No motion or proposition for a tax or charge upon the people shall be discussed the day on which it is made or offered; and every such proposition shall receive its first discussion in a Committee of the Whole House."—*Rule* 110.

So also for increase of.

"No sum or quantum of tax or duty, voted by a Committee of the Whole House, shall be increased in the House until the motion or proposition for such increase shall be first discussed and voted in a Committee of the Whole House, and so in respect to the time of its continuance."—*Rule* 111.

(See also COMMITTEES OF THE WHOLE.)

It has been decided that the foregoing rules do not cover the case of a special duty or tax upon national banks to meet certain expenses to be incurred by the General Government on account of said banks.—*Journal*, 1, 38, *p.* 537 ; *Cong. Globe, vol.* 51, *p* 1680.

EDUCATION AND LABOR, COMMITTEE ON.

When appointed, number and duties of.

"There shall be appointed, at each Congress, a Committee on Education and Labor, to consist of eleven members, to whom shall be referred all petitions, bills, reports, and resolutions on those subjects, and who shall from time to time report thereon."—*Rule* 160.

ELECTIONS BY THE HOUSE.

House shall choose its officers.

"The House of Representatives shall choose their Speaker and other officers."—*Const.*, 1, 2, 6.

Majority necessary—blanks not counted.

"In all other cases of ballot than for committees a majority of the votes given shall be necessary to an election; and where there shall not be such a majority on the first ballot, the ballots shall be repeated until a majority be obtained. And in all ballotings blanks shall be rejected and not taken into the count in enumeration of votes or reported by the tellers."—*Rule* 12.

"In all cases of ballot by the House the Speaker shall vote."—*Rule* 7. Speaker shall vote.

"In all cases where others than members of the House may be eligible to an office by the election of the House there shall be a previous nomination."—*Rule* 11. Previous nomination.

"In all cases of election by the House of its officers the vote shall be taken *viva voce*."—*Rule* 10. Vote to be taken *viva voce*.

"No member or other person shall visit or remain by the Clerk's table while the ayes and noes are calling or ballots are counting."—*Rule* 65. No person to visit Clerk's table during.

After the election of a particular officer is postponed, it is not in order to move to proceed to the election of such officer before the arrival of the period to which the postponement was made.—*Journal*, 1, 31, *p*. 405. But if the House should fail to go into an election on the day specified in the order of postponement, the matter does not thereby drop, but the election may be proceeded with subsequently.—*Journal*, 1, 26, *p*. 253. After postponement, not in order to go into election. On failure to go into at a specified time, may be proceeded with subsequently.

[Ordinarily it has been held that the election by the House of any of its officers is a question of privilege.] Ordinarily held to be question of privilege.

(See also PRESIDENT, SPEAKER, CLERK, SERGEANT-AT-ARMS, DOORKEEPER, POSTMASTER, and PRINTER, PUBLIC.)

ELECTIONS, COMMITTEE OF.

The Committee of Elections is of the number of the committees which, under the 74th *Rule*, are to be appointed at the commencement of each Congress, and to consist of eleven members each. When to be appointed, and number.

"It shall be the duty of the Committee of Elections to examine and report upon the certificates of election, or other credentials, of the members returned to serve in this House, and to take into their consideration all such petitions and other matters touching elections and returns as shall or may be presented or come into ques- Its duties.

tion and be referred to them by the House."—*Rule* 75.

ELECTORAL VOTES.

(See PRESIDENT OF THE UNITED STATES.)

ELECTIONS, CONTESTED.

House may decide.

"Each House shall be the judge of the elections, returns, and qualifications of its own members."—*Const.*, 1, 5, 8.

Notice of contest.

By the act of February 19, 1851, (*Stat. at Large, Vol. IX, p.* 568,) it is provided that notice of intention to contest shall be given by contestant to returned member within thirty days after the result of the election shall be determined by the canvassers, specifying particularly the grounds upon which he relies in the contest.

Answer to notice.

Within thirty days after service of said notice the returned member shall answer the same, admitting or denying the alleged facts, and setting forth specifically any other grounds upon which he rests the validity of his election; and he shall serve a copy of his answer upon the contestant.

Before whom testimony may be taken.

Where either party desire to take testimony, application may be made to any judge of any court of the United States, or to any chancellor, judge, or justice of a court of record of any State, or to any mayor, recorder, or intendant of any town or city, said officer to reside within the congressional district in which said election was held, who shall issue subpœnas to the witnesses named.

Notice to be given to opposite party.

Notice of intention to examine witnesses shall be given to the opposite party at least ten days before their examination; but neither party shall give notice of taking testimony at different places at the same time, or within less than five days between the close of taking it in one place and its commencement in the other.

Testimony to be closed within sixty days.

No testimony shall be taken, unless with the consent of the House, (which may allow supplementary evidence to be taken,) after the expiration of sixty days from the service of the answer of the returned member;

And, together with notice and answer, to be sent to Clerk of House of Representatives.

and a copy of the notice of contest and of the answer of the returned member shall be prefixed to the depositions, and transmitted with them to the Clerk of the House of Representatives.

Testimony to be taken within ninety days, and in what order.

By the act of January 10, 1873, supplemental to and amendatory of the foregoing, it is provided that in all contested-election cases the time allowed for taking testimony shall be ninety days, and the testimony shall be taken in the following order: The contestant shall take testimony during the first forty days; the returned member during the succeeding forty days; and the contestant may take testimony in rebuttal only during the remaining ten days of said period. Such testimony in rebuttal may be taken on five days' notice. Testimony may be taken at two or more places at the same time.

Notice, and places.

Depositions of witnesses residing outside of the district and beyond the reach of a subpœna, may be taken before any officer authorized by law to take testimony in contested election cases in the district in which the witness to be examined may reside.

Depositions may be taken, before whom.

That the party desiring to take a deposition or depositions under the provisions of this act or of the act to which this is an amendment, shall give the opposite party notice, in writing, of the time and place, when and where, the same will be taken, as well as of the name of the witness or witnesses to be examined, and of the name of an officer before whom the same will be taken. The notice shall be personally served upon the opposite party, or upon any agent or attorney of his authorized by him to take testimony or cross-examine witnesses in the matter of such contest, if, by the use of reasonable diligence, such personal service can be made; but if, by the use of such diligence, personal service cannot be made, the service may be made by leaving a duplicate of the notice at the usual place of abode of the opposite party. The notice shall be served so as to allow the opposite party sufficient time by the usual route of travel to attend, and one day for preparation, exclusive of Sundays and the day of service. And the taking of the testimony may, if so stated in the notice, be adjourned from day to day. The notice, with the proof or acknowledgment of the service thereof, shall be attached to the depositions when completed. The party notified as aforesaid, his agent or attorney, may, if he see fit, select an officer (having authority to take depositions in such cases) to officiate, with the officer named in the notice,

Notice to the opposite party to state what and how to be served.

Adjournments of taking testimony.

Notice, &c., to be attached to deposition.

Party notified may select an officer to officiate with the one named in the notice.

in the taking of the depositions; and if both such officers attend, the depositions shall be taken before them both, sitting together, and be certified by them both.

Proceedings in such cases.

But if only one of such officers attend, the depositions may be taken before and certified by him alone. It shall be competent for the parties, their agents or attorneys

Parties may consent in writing to take depositions without notice, or before certain officers.

authorized to act in the premises, by consent in writing, to take depositions without notice; and it shall also be competent for them, by such written consent, to take depositions (whether upon or without notice) before any officer or officers authorized to take depositions in common law, or civil actions, or in chancery, by either the laws of the United States or of the State in which the same may be taken, and to waive proof of the official

The written consent to be returned with the deposition.

character of such officer or officers. Any written consent given as aforesaid shall be returned with the depositions; and every such officer so chosen by the parties, their agents or attorneys, and officiating, shall have all the powers in the premises that are conferred by the act to which this is an amendment upon the officers named therein. At the taking of any deposition under this act,

Parties may appear personally or by attorney.

or the act to which this is an amendment, either party may appear and act in person, or by agent or attorney.

Officers taking testimony to send the same when completed, by mail, under seal, to the Clerk of the House of Representatives, with indorsement.

All officers taking testimony to be used in a contested election case, whether by deposition or otherwise, shall, when the taking of the same is completed, and without unnecessary delay, certify the same, and carefully seal and immediately forward the same by mail, addressed to the Clerk of the House of Representatives of the United States, Washington, D. C.; and shall also endorse upon the envelope containing such deposition or testimony the name of the case in which it is taken, together with the name of the party in whose behalf it is taken, and

Depositions, how to be opened, &c.

shall subscribe such endorsement. Upon the written request of either party the Clerk of the House of Representatives shall open any deposition at any time after he shall have received the same, and he may furnish

Copies.

either party with a copy thereof.—*Stat. at Large, Vol. XVII, p.* 408–9.

No payment out of contingent

By the act of March 3, 1873, it is provided that after the expiration of the Forty-second Congress no payment shall be made by the House of Representatives, out of its contingent fund or otherwise, to either party to a contested-election case for expenses incurred in prosecuting or defending the same.—*Stat. at large, Vol. XVII, p.* 490.

fund to be made to contestants.

Upon the hearing of a case of contested election by the House, the *courtesy* of occupying a seat upon the floor, and of being heard in his own behalf, is usually extended by the House to the contestant—*Journals*, 1, 29, *p.* 278; 1, 34, *p.* 1258, &c.—and he is subject to all the rules of debate which are applicable to *members*.—*Journals*, 1, 28, *p.* 1012.

Contestant allowed to debate.

But subject to the rules.

[All questions relating to the right of a member to his seat are held to be questions of privilege, and hence take precedence of other business.]

Contested-election cases take precedence over other business.

ENACTING WORDS.

By the act approved February 25, 1871, Sess. Laws, p. 43, it is enacted, "That the enacting clause of all acts of Congress hereafter enacted shall be in the following form: 'Be it enacted by the Senate and House of Representatives of the United States of America in Congress assembled;' and the resolving clause of all joint resolutions shall be in the following form: 'Resolved by the Senate and House of Representatives of the United States of America in Congress assembled,' and no further enacting or resolving words shall be used in any subsequent section or resolution after the first; and each section shall be numbered and contain as nearly as may be a single proposition of enactment." [Prior to the passage of the foregoing act the style of enactment had rested entirely upon usage.]

Style of.

ENACTING WORDS—MOTION TO STRIKE OUT.

"A motion to strike out the enacting words of a bill shall have precedence of a motion to amend; and if carried, shall be considered equivalent to its rejection. Whenever a bill is reported from a Committee of the Whole, with a recommendation to strike out the enacting words, and such recommendation is disagreed to by the House, the bill shall stand recommitted to the said committee without further action by the House. But before

Takes precedence of a motion to amend.

Its effect if carried.

Effect of disagreement to recommendation of committee.

Effect of reporting from the Committee of the Whole.

the question of concurrence is submitted, it is in order to entertain a motion to refer the bill to any committee of the House, with, or without, instructions, and when the same is again reported to the House, it shall be referred to the Committee of the Whole without debate, and resume its original place on the calendar."—*Rule* 123.

Where reported with such recommendation, question that arises, &c.

The question which arises (under the recent practice) upon a report from the Committee of the Whole that the enacting words be stricken out is, "Shall the enacting words be stricken out?" and the previous question is exhausted upon the taking of such vote.—*Journals*, 1, 33, *p*. 872; 3, 34, *p*. 479; 1, 35, *p*. 107.

ENGRAVING.

Maps not to be printed without special order.

"Maps accompanying documents shall not be printed under the general order to print without the special direction of the House."—*Rule* 139.

To be procured by Superintendent of Public Printing, under direction of committee.

By the joint resolution of June 23, 1860, (*Stat. at Large Vol. XII, p*. 119,) it is provided that "when any charts, maps, diagrams, views, or other engravings shall be required to illustrate any document ordered to be printed by either House of Congress, such engravings shall be procured by the Superintendent of the Public Printing, under the direction and supervision of the Committee on Printing of the house ordering the printing of the same."—(See PRINTING, PUBLIC.)

To be referred to the House members of the Committee on Printing.

"There shall be *referred by the Clerk to the members of the Committee on Printing on the part of the House* all drawings, maps, charts, or other papers which may at any time come before the House for engraving, lithographing, or publishing in any way; which committee shall report to the House whether the same ought, in their opinion, to be published; and if the House order the publication of the same, that said committee shall direct the size and manner of execution of all such maps, charts, drawings, or other papers, and contract, by agreement in writing, for all such engraving, lithographing, printing, drawing, and coloring, as may be ordered by the House; which agreement, in writing, shall be furnished by said committee to the Committee of Accounts, to govern said committee in all allowances for such works; and it shall be in order for said committee to report at all times."—*Rule* 100.

By the joint resolution of March 3, 1863, it is directed that "all lithographing and engraving, where the probable cost exceeds two hundred and fifty dollars, shall be awarded to the lowest and best bidder for the interest of the Government, after due advertisement by the Superintendent of Public Printing, under the direction of the Committee on Printing."—*Stat. at Large*, *Vol. XII*, *p.* 826. "*Provided*, That the Joint Committee on Public Printing be authorized to empower the Superintendent of Public Printing to make immediate contracts for engraving, whenever, in their opinion, the exigencies of the public service will not justify waiting for advertisement and award."—*Ibid.*, *Vol. XIII*, *p.* 185.

Over two hundred and fifty dollars to be awarded to the lowest and best bidder.

(See also PRINTING, PUBLIC.)

ENGROSSED BILLS.

"All bills ordered to be engrossed shall be executed in a fair round hand."—*Rule* 125.

Engrossment, how executed.

"While bills are on their passage between the two houses they shall be on paper, and under the signature of the Secretary or Clerk of each house respectively."—*Joint Rule* 5.

To be on paper and signed by Clerk.

ENROLLED BILLS.

"After a bill shall have passed both houses, it shall be duly enrolled on parchment by the Clerk of the House of Representatives, or the Secretary of the Senate, as the bill may have originated in the one or the other house, before it shall be presented to the President of the United States."—*Joint Rule* 6.

To be on parchment.

(See also ENROLLED BILLS, COMMITTEE ON.)

ENROLLED BILLS, COMMITTEE ON.

"When bills are enrolled, they shall be examined by a joint committee of two from the Senate and two from the House of Representatives, appointed as a standing committee for that purpose, who shall carefully compare the enrollment with the engrossed bills as passed in the two houses, and, correcting any errors that may be dis-

Shall examine and report enrolled bills.

covered in the enrolled bills, make their report forthwith to their respective houses."—*Joint Rule* 7.

May report at any time.

"It shall be in order for the Committee on Enrolled Bills to report at any time."—*Rule* 101. [And it is a very common practice, when the House is in committee, for the Speaker to take the chair and receive a report of bills examined, and having signed the same, and the Clerk having read their titles, the committee resumes its session.]

[And said committee may report at any time *upon any subject* regularly referred to them.]

After report, bill to be signed by Speaker.

"After examination and report, each bill shall be signed in the respective houses, first by the Speaker of the House of Representatives, then by the President of the Senate."—*Joint Rule* 8.

Shall present bill to President.

"After a bill shall have been thus signed in each house, it shall be presented by the said committee to the President of the United States for his approbation, (it being first indorsed on the back of the roll, certifying in which house the same originated, which indorsement shall be signed by the Secretary or Clerk, as the case may be, of the house in which the same did originate,) and shall be entered on the Journal of each house. The said committee shall report the day of presentation to the President, which time shall also be carefully entered on the Journal of each house."—*Joint Rule* 9.

Shall notify House of day of presentation.

Other matters to be enrolled, examined, &c.

"All orders, resolutions, and votes which are to be presented to the President of the United States for his approbation shall also, in the same manner, be previously enrolled, examined, and signed; and shall be presented in the same manner, and by the same committee, as provided in the case of bills."—*Joint Rule* 10.

Not to present a bill to President on last day of session.

"No bill or resolution that shall have passed the House of Representatives and the Senate shall be presented to the President of the United States for his approbation on the last day of the session."—*Joint Rule* 17. [This rule is usually suspended on the last day of the session.]

ESTIMATES OF APPROPRIATIONS.

Shall be addressed to the Speaker.

Estimates of appropriations, and all other communications from the executive Departments, intended for the consideration of any of the committees of the House, shall be addressed to the Speaker, and by him submitted to the House for reference.—*Rule* 159.

EXECUTIVE DEPARTMENTS.

Calls on.

"A proposition requesting information from the President of the United States, or directing it to be furnished by the head of either of the executive Departments, shall lie on the table one day for consideration, unless otherwise ordered by the unanimous consent of the House; and all such propositions shall be taken up for consideration in the order they were presented, immediately after reports are called for from select committees, and, when adopted, the Clerk shall cause the same to be delivered."—*Rule* 53. [It is usual for the Clerk to deliver in person all calls upon the President, and to transmit by a messenger, or through the mail, calls upon the heads of Departments.]

Shall lie over one day.

When adopted Clerk to deliver.

"It shall be the duty of the Clerk to make and cause to be printed, and deliver to each member at the commencement of every session of Congress, a list of the reports which it is the duty of any officer or Department of the Government to make to Congress, referring to the act or resolution, and page of the volume of the laws or Journal in which it may be contained; and placing under the name of each officer the list of reports required of him to be made, and the time when the report may be expected."—*Rule* 13.

List of reports called for to be made out by Clerk.

Messages and other executive communications are the business first in order whenever the House proceeds to the consideration of the business on the Speaker's table.—*Rule* 54. [It is the practice, however, of the Speaker, with the unanimous consent of the House, (which is rarely refused,) to lay such communications as shall not give rise to debate before the House immediately after the expiration of the morning hour, in order that they may be printed and referred.]

Communications from, when considered.

EXCUSED FROM SERVING ON COMMITTEE.

(See COMMITTEES.)

EXCUSED FROM VOTING.

(See VOTING.)

EXPENDITURES IN THE STATE DEPARTMENT,
EXPENDITURES IN THE TREASURY DEPARTMENT,
EXPENDITURES IN THE WAR DEPARTMENT,
EXPENDITURES IN THE NAVY DEPARTMENT,
EXPENDITURES IN THE POST OFFICE DEPARTMENT,
EXPENDITURES ON THE PUBLIC BUILDINGS, AND
EXPENDITURES IN THE INTERIOR DEPARTMENT,

COMMITTEES ON EXPENDITURES.

When appointed and number of.

"Seven additional standing committees shall be appointed at the commencement of the first session in each Congress, whose duties shall continue until the first session of the ensuing Congress:

1. A committee on so much of the public accounts and expenditures as relate to the Department of State;
2. A committee on so much of the public accounts and expenditures as relate to the Treasury Department;
3. A committee on so much of the public accounts and expenditures as relate to the Department of War;
4. A committee on so much of the public accounts and expenditures as relate to the Department of the Navy;
5. A committee on so much of the public accounts and expenditures as relate to the Post Office;
6. A committee on so much of the public accounts and expenditures as relate to the Public Buildings; and
7. A committee on so much of the public accounts as relate to the Interior Department.

}To consist of five members each.

—*Rule* 102.

Duties of.

"It shall be the duty of the said committees to examine into the state of the accounts and expenditures respectively submitted to them, and to inquire and report particularly—

"Whether the expenditures of the respective Departments are justified by law;

"Whether the claims from time to time satisfied and discharged by the respective Departments are supported by sufficient vouchers, establishing their justness both as to their character and amount;

"Whether such claims have been discharged out of funds appropriated therefor, and whether all moneys have been disbursed in conformity with appropriation laws; and

"Whether any, and what, provisions are necessary to be adopted to provide more perfectly for the proper application of the public moneys, and to secure the Government from demands unjust in their character or extravagant in their amount.

"And it shall be, moreover, the duty of said committees to report from time to time whether any, and what, retrenchment can be made in the expenditures of the several Departments without detriment to the public service; whether any, and what, abuses at any time exist in the failure to enforce the payment of moneys which may be due to the United States from public defaulters or others; and to report, from time to time, such provisions and arrangements as may be necessary to add to the economy of the several Departments and the accountability of their several officers.

"It shall be the duty of the several committees on public expenditures to inquire whether any offices belonging to the branches or Departments, respectively, concerning whose expenditures it is their duty to inquire, have become useless or unnecessary; and to report, from time to time, on the expediency of modifying or abolishing the same; also, to examine into the pay and emoluments of all officers under the laws of the United States; and to report, from time to time, such a reduction or increase thereof as a just economy and the public service may require."—*Rule* 103.

FEES.

Against members.

"When a member shall be discharged from custody, and admitted to his seat, the House shall determine whether such discharge shall be with or without paying fees; and, in like manner, whether a delinquent member, taken into custody by a special messenger, shall or shall not be liable to defray the expense of such special messenger."—*Rule* 37.

Of Sergeant-at-arms for arrest, traveling, &c.

"The fees of the Sergeant-at-arms shall be, for every arrest, the sum of two dollars; for each day's custody and releasement, one dollar; and for traveling expenses for himself or a special messenger, going and returning, one-tenth of a dollar per mile."—*Rule* 24. And it is pro-

Constructive mileage prohibited.

vided by act of February 5, 1859, (*Stat. at Large, Vol. XI, p.* 379, "that hereafter the mileage or traveling allowance to the officer or other person executing precepts or summons of either house of Congress shall not exceed ten cents for each mile necessarily and actually traveled by such officer or other person in the execution of any such precept or summons."

Sergeant-at-arms to receive no fees.

But by the act of July 14, 1870, (*Stat. at large, Vol. XVI, p.* 231,) it is provided that in addition to his regular salary he shall receive, directly or indirectly, no fees, other compensation or emolument whatever, for performing the duties of his office, or in connection therewith.

Of witnesses summoned by authority of House.

"The rule for paying witnesses summoned to appear before this House or either of its committees shall be as follows: For each day a witness shall attend, the sum of four dollars; for each mile he shall travel in coming to or going from the place of examination, the sum of five cents each way; but nothing shall be paid for traveling when the witness has been summoned at the place of trial."—*Rule* 138.

Of Clerk for extracts from Journal.

The Clerk shall certify extracts from the Journals of the House of Representatives, and for such copies shall receive the same fees as are allowed by law to the Secretary of State for similar services.—*Stat. at Large, Vol. IX, p.* 80.

FIVE-MINUTES DEBATE.

House may at any time close debate in Committee of the Whole.

The House may at any time, by the vote of a majority of the members present, discharge the Committee of the Whole House and the Committee of the Whole House on the state of the Union from the further consideration of any bill referred to it, after acting without debate on all amendments pending and that may be offered—*Rule* 104—but the bill must have been first considered in Committee of the Whole; and this rule applies to messages, &c., as well as bills.—*Journal* 1, 32, *pp.* 146, 147.

Allowed on amendments, and on amendments to amendments.

"Where debate is closed by order of the House, any member shall be allowed, in committee, five minutes to explain any amendment he may offer, after which any member who shall first obtain the floor shall be allowed to speak five minutes in opposition to it, and there shall be no further debate on the amendment; but the same privilege of debate shall be allowed in favor of and against any amendment that may be offered to the amendment; and neither the amendment nor an amendment to the amendment shall be withdrawn by the mover thereof, unless by the unanimous consent of the committee: *Provided*, That the House may, by the vote of a majority of the members present, at any time after the five-minutes debate has taken place upon proposed amendments to any section or paragraph of a bill, close all debate upon such section or paragraph, or, at their election, upon the pending amendments only."—*Rule* 60.

May be closed on an amendment or paragraph.

(See also COMMITTEES OF THE WHOLE.)

FLOOR, PRIVILEGE OF ADMISSION ON.

Who shall have.

"No person, except members of the Senate, their Secretary, heads of Departments, the President's private secretary, foreign ministers, the governor for the time being of any State, Senators and Representatives elect, judges of the Supreme Court of the United States and of the Court of Claims, and such persons as have by name received the thanks of Congress, shall be admitted within the hall of the House of Representatives or any of the rooms upon the same floor or opening into the same: *Provided*, That ex-members of Congress who are not interested in any claim pending before Congress, and shall so register themselves, may also be admitted within the hall of the House; and no person except those herein specified shall at any time be admitted to the floor of the House."—*Rule* 134.

Doorkeeper to execute strictly rule relative to.

The Doorkeeper shall execute strictly the foregoing rule.—*Rule* 27.

FOREIGN AFFAIRS, COMMITTEE ON.

When appointed and number of.

There shall be appointed, at the commencement of each Congress, a Committee on Foreign Affairs, to consist of eleven members.—*Rule* 74.

Its duties.

"It shall be the duty of the Committee on Foreign Affairs to take into consideration all matters which concern the relations of the United States with foreign nations, and which shall be referred to them by the

House, and to report their opinion on the same."—*Rule* 90.

FOREIGN MINISTERS.

May be admitted within the hall.

Foreign ministers may be admitted within the hall of the House.—*Rule* 134.

FRANKING PRIVILEGE.

Abolished.

By the act of January 31, 1873, it is provided that the franking privilege be abolished from and after the first day of July, anno Domini eighteen hundred and seventy-three, and that thenceforth all official correspondence, of whatever nature, and other mailable matter sent from or addressed to any officer of the Government or person now authorized to frank such matter, shall be chargeable with the same rates of postage as may be lawfully imposed upon like matter sent by or addressed to other persons: *Provided*, That no compensation or allowance shall now or hereafter be made to Senators, Members, and Delegates of the House of Representatives on account of postage.—*Stat. at Large, Vol. XVII, p.* 421.

No allowance to be made for postage to members.

FREEDMEN'S AFFAIRS, COMMITTEE ON.

When appointed, number and duties of.

There shall be appointed at the commencement of each Congress a standing committee on Freedmen's Affairs, to consist of eleven members, whose duty it shall be to take charge of all matters concerning freedmen, which shall be referred to them by the House.—*Rule* 156.

FRIDAYS.

Set apart for private business.

Fridays and Saturdays are set apart for the consideration of private bills and private business.—*Rule* 128. And on the first and fourth Friday and Saturday of each month, bills to the passage of which no objection is made are first considered and disposed of; but when a bill is again reached, after having been once objected to, the committee shall consider and dispose of the same,

Bills not objected to, to be considered on first and fourth.

unless it shall again be objected to by at least five members.—*Rule* 129.

(See PRIVATE BILLS AND PRIVATE BUSINESS.)

FURNITURE.

By the resolution of the House of March 3, 1869, it is directed that the Committee on Public Buildings and Grounds shall determine the necessity of furnishing or refurnishing the rooms, &c., and that no such furnishing or refurnishing, exceeding $100 for any one room in a single year, shall be done by the Clerk without the resolution of said committee.—*Journal* 3, 40, *p.* 518.

For any one room, exceeding $100 in any one year, must be by resolution of the Committee on Public Buildings and Grounds.

GALLERIES.

"Stenographers and reporters, other than the official reporters to the House, wishing to take down the debates, may be admitted by the Speaker to the reporters' gallery over the Speaker's chair, but not on the floor of the House; but no person shall be allowed the privilege of said gallery under the character of stenographer or reporter without a written permission of the Speaker, specifying the part of said gallery assigned to him; nor shall said stenographer or reporter be admitted to said gallery unless he shall state in writing for what paper or papers he is employed to report; nor shall he be so admitted, or, if admitted, be suffered to retain his seat, if he shall be or become an agent to prosecute any claim pending before Congress; and the Speaker shall give his written permission with this condition."—*Rule* 135.

Certain portion for reporters.

[Other portions of the galleries are set apart for visitors.]

Visitors.

"In case of any disturbance or disorderly conduct in the galleries or lobby, the Speaker (or chairman of the Committee of the Whole House) shall have power to order the same to be cleared."—*Rule* 9. Or the House may order it cleared.—*Journal*, 1, 24, *p.* 331.

Speaker or Chairman may order cleared.

GLOBE.

(See CONGRESSIONAL GLOBE.)

GOVERNORS OF STATES.

Admitted on floor.

The governor for the time being of any State may be admitted within the hall of the House of Representatives.—*Rule* 134.

Copy of Journal to be sent to.

It shall be the duty of the Clerk, at the end of each session, to send a printed copy of the Journal to the executive of every State.—*Rule* 14.

HALL OF THE HOUSE.

Speaker to have direction of.

Not to be used except for legitimate business.

The Speaker shall have a general direction of the hall.—*Rule* 5. And no person shall be permitted to perform divine service therein unless with his consent.—*Rule* 6. The hall of the House shall not be used for any other purpose than the legitimate business of the House, nor shall the Speaker entertain any proposition to use it for any other purpose, or for the suspension of this rule: *Provided*, That this shall not interfere with the performance of divine service therein under the direction of the Speaker, or with the use of the same for caucus meetings of the members, or upon occasions where the House may, by resolution, agree to take part in any ceremonies to be observed therein.—*Rule* 155.

Who may be admitted within.

"No person except members of the Senate, their Secretary, heads of Departments, the President's private secretary, foreign ministers, the governor for the time being of any State, Senators and Representatives elect, judges of the Supreme Court of the United States and of the Court of Claims, and such persons as have by name received the thanks of Congress, shall be admitted within the hall of the House of Representatives or any of the rooms on the same floor or opening into the same: *Provided*, That ex-members of Congress who are not interested in any claim pending before Congress, and shall so register themselves, may also be admitted within the hall of the House; and no persons except those herein specified shall at any time be admitted to the floor of the House."—*Rule* 134. And by *Rule* 27 the Doorkeeper is required to execute this rule strictly.

HEADS OF DEPARTMENTS.

Heads of Departments may be admitted within the hall of the House.—*Rule* 134. May be admitted within the hall.

HOUR RULE.

"No member shall occupy more than one hour in debate on any question in the House or in committee; but a member reporting the measure under consideration from a committee may open and close the debate."—*Rule* 70. No member shall debate more than one hour.

(See DEBATE.)

HOUR AT WHICH ADJOURNMENT IS MOVED.

The hour at which every motion to adjourn is made shall be entered on the Journal.—*Rule* 45. To be entered on the Journal.

HOUR OF DAILY MEETING.

[The hour of daily meeting is fixed by an order of the House—usually on the first day of the session—and continues "until otherwise ordered."] How fixed.

A motion to fix the hour of meeting can only be made when resolutions (or motions to suspend the rules) are in order.—*Journal*, 1, 29, *p.* 933. When in order to fix.

IMPEACHMENT.

"The House of Representatives shall have the sole power of impeachment."—*Const.*, 1, 2, 6. House has sole power of.

[The proceedings in the case of the impeachment of Judge Peck, in the 21st Congress, were as follows:

The House having resolved that he be impeached of "high misdemeanors in office," (*Journal*, 1, 21, *pp.* 565, 566,) it was ordered "that Mr. ——— and Mr. ——— be appointed a committee to go to the Senate, and at the bar thereof, in the name of the House of Representatives, and of all the people of the United States, to impeach James H. Peck, judge of the district court of the United States, for the district of Missouri, of high misdemeanors Committee appointed to go to Senate.

in office, and acquaint the Senate that the House of Representatives will, in due time, exhibit particular articles of impeachment against him and make good the same; and that said committee do demand that the Senate take order for the appearance of the said James H. Peck, to answer to said impeachment."

Committee to prepare articles.

The House, then, on motion, appointed a committee of five "to prepare and report to the House articles of impeachment against James H. Peck, district judge of the United States for the district of Missouri, for misdemeanors in his said office."—(*p.* 567.)

Message from the Senate.

A message was received from the Senate notifying the House "that the Senate will take proper order therein, of which due notice shall be given to the House of Representatives."—(*p.* 574.)

Articles reported and adopted by House.

The committee appointed to prepare articles of impeachment made their report, (*p.* 584,) which was committed to the Committee of the Whole House on the state of the Union, (*p.* 588;) and having been considered therein, was reported with amendments, and so agreed to by the House.—(*pp.* 591 to 595.)

Managers appointed on the part of the House.

It was then ordered "that five managers be appointed by ballot to conduct the impeachment against James H. Peck, judge of the district court of the United States for the district of Missouri, on the part of the House," who were thereupon appointed.—(*p.* 595.)

Managers to carry articles to Senate.

Clerk to notify Senate of appointment of managers, &c.

It was then ordered "that the articles agreed to by the House, to be exhibited in the name of themselves and of all the people of the United States, against James H. Peck, in maintenance of their impeachment against him for high misdemeanors in office, be carried to the Senate by the managers appointed to conduct said impeachment." And the Clerk was directed to inform the Senate of the appointment of said managers, and of the last-mentioned order of the House.—(*p.* 596.)

Message from Senate, when to receive managers.

A message was received from the Senate informing the House of the time at which it would resolve itself into a court of impeachment, when it would receive the managers appointed to exhibit the articles of impeachment.—(*p.* 603.)

The managers having carried said articles to the Senate, made report of the fact to the House.—(*p.* 605.) Report of managers.

The Senate notified the House of its issue of summons to Judge Peck, (*p.* 606,) and of its order that he file his answer and plea with its Secretary by a certain day.—(*p.* 625.) Senate notifies House of its proceedings.

The House resolved that it would, on the day above named, "and at such hour as the Senate shall appoint, resolve itself into a Committee of the Whole House, and attend in the Senate" on the trial of the said impeachment—(*p.* 714.) House determined to go into Committee of the Whole and attend in Senate at trial.

The Senate on same day notified the House "that it was ready to proceed upon the impeachment of James H. Peck, judge, &c., in the Senate Chamber, which chamber was prepared with accommodations for the reception of the House of Representatives."—(*p.* 717.) Senate ready to proceed upon trial, and to receive the House.

Thereupon the House resolved itself into a Committee of the Whole House, and proceeded to the Senate in that capacity. Having spent some time therein, they returned into the chamber of the House, and the Speaker having resumed the chair, the chairman of the Committee of the Whole reported the proceedings which had taken place, and that the Senate, sitting as a high court of impeachment, had adjourned to meet at the next session.—(*p.* 717.) House attend in Senate.

At the next session (2, 21) Mr. Buchanan, from the managers, reported to the House a replication to the answer and plea of Judge Peck, which was agreed to by the House; and the said managers were instructed to maintain the same at the bar of the Senate, and the Senate were informed thereof.—(*pp.* 47, 48.) Replication adopted by House.

The Senate notified the House of their readiness to proceed to the trial, (*p.* 52,) and the House resolved that from day to day it would resolve itself into a Committee of the Whole, and attend the same.—(*p.* 97.) Senate notify the House of their readiness to proceed to trial. House resolve to attend trial.

Subsequently the House resolved that the managers be instructed to attend the trial, and that the attendance of the House be dispensed with until otherwise ordered.—(*p.* 141.) House ceases to attend trial.

The managers having announced that the testimony House attends during the argument.

had closed, (*p.* 175,) the House resolved that during the argument of counsel it would from day to day attend in the Senate.—(*p.* 186.)

Report of final action. The report of the final action of the Senate in the case, made to the House by the chairman of the Committee of the Whole.—(*p.* 236.)

Rules of Senate in impeachment cases. [The rules of proceedings of the Senate in cases of impeachment will be found in "*Trial of Judge Peck*," *pp.* 56 to 59.]

For further information on the subject of impeachment, see "*Chase's Trial*," and "*Trial of Judge Peck.*" Also proceedings in the case of Judge Humphreys.—*Journal*, 2, 37, *pp.* 646, 665, 684, 709, to 712, 717, 723, 726, 731, 821, 832, 940, 943. Also proceedings in the case of A. Johnson, President of the United States.—*Journal*, 2, 40.

INDEFINITE POSTPONEMENT.

(See POSTPONE, MOTION TO.)

INDEXES.

To the Journal. "The Clerk shall, within thirty days after the close of each session of Congress, cause to be completed the printing and primary distribution, to members and delegates, of the Journal of the House, together with an accurate index to the same."—*Rule* 16.

To the laws "The Clerk shall cause an index to be prepared to the acts passed at every session of Congress, and to be printed and bound with the acts."—*Rule* 20. [The Clerk has been relieved of the duty required by this rule by the joint resolution of September 26, 1850, which directs that the annual Statutes at Large, published by Little & Brown, (and indexed by them,) be contracted for instead of the edition previously issued by order of the Secretary of State.—*Stat. at Large, Vol. IX, p.* 564.]

To other documents. It also devolves upon the Clerk's office, under the usage, to prepare indexes to "Executive Documents," "Miscellaneous Documents," "Reports of Committees," "Reports of Court of Claims," "Bills and Joint Resolutions," &c.

INDIAN AFFAIRS, COMMITTEE ON.

There shall be appointed at the commencement of each Congress a Committee on Indian Affairs, to consist of eleven members.—*Rule* 74. When appointed, and number of.

[There are no duties assigned to this committee by the rules.] Duties of.

INTERESTED.

"No member shall vote on any question in the event of which he is immediately interested."—*Rule* 29. [As to the *kind* of interest here alluded to, the true construction doubtless is, that it shall be a direct *personal* or *pecuniary one*.—See *note to said rule.*] Member not to vote, where.

INTERNAL IMPROVEMENT BILLS.

"Upon the engrossment of any bill making appropriations of money for works of internal improvement of any kind or description, it shall be in the power of any member to call for a division of the question, so as to take a separate vote of the House upon each item of improvement or appropriation contained in said bill, or upon such items separately, and others collectively, as the members making the call may specify; and if one-fifth of the members present second said call, it shall be the duty of the Speaker to make such divisions of the question, and put them to vote accordingly."—*Rule* 121. Division of question on items of.

INVALID PENSIONS, COMMITTEE ON.

There shall be appointed, at the commencement of each Congress, a Committee on Invalid Pensions, to consist of eleven members.—*Rule* 74. When appointed, and number of.

"It shall be the duty of the Committee on Invalid Pensions to take into consideration all such matters respecting invalid pensions as shall be referred to them by the House."—*Rule* 93. Its duties.

By an order of the House of March 26, 1867, all matters relating to pensions to the soldiers of the war of 1812 are to be referred to the Committee on Revolutionary Pensions.—*Journal*, 1, 40, *p*. 117.

JEFFERSON'S MANUAL.

To govern where applicable, and not inconsistent with rules.

"The rules of parliamentary practice comprised in Jefferson's Manual shall govern the House in all cases to which they are applicable, and in which they are not inconsistent with the Standing Rules and Orders of the House and Joint Rules of the Senate and House of Representatives.—*Rule* 144.

JOINT RESOLUTIONS.

Resolving clause.

[The resolving clause of a joint resolution is, "Be it resolved by the Senate and House of Representatives of the United States of America in Congress assembled;"]

Governed by same rules as bills.

and, in all respects, joint resolutions are governed by the same rules as bills, the word "bill," where it occurs in the rules, being held to apply equally to a "joint resolution."—*Cong. Globe*, 3, 27, *p.* 384.

Cannot be converted into bill or simple resolutions by amendment.

[But joint resolutions cannot be *amended* so as to convert them into bills or simple resolutions, nor can bills or resolutions be so amended as to convert them into joint resolutions.]

Of State legislatures.

[Joint resolutions of State or territorial legislatures may be presented like *petitions* by handing to the Clerk, with the subject-matter, reference, and member's name indorsed thereon.] But where it is desired to have them printed, they may be presented when the States and Territories are called for bills on leave.—*Rule* 130.

As to the distinction between bills and.

[By the Constitution of the United States and the rules of the two houses, no absolute distinction is made between bills and joint resolutions, either in regard to the mode of proceeding with them before they become laws, or their force and effect afterwards. For more than fifty years, however, a very marked distinction seems to have been recognized in the legislation of Congress, and the form of joint resolution was resorted to chiefly, and almost entirely, for such purposes as the following, viz: "To express the sense of Congress;" "to construe provisions in former laws;" "to admit new States;" "to direct or regulate the printing of documents;" and until the 2d session of the 27th Congress no instance is to be found of an appropriation elsewhere than in a bill.

During the first fifty years of the Government, the whole number of joint resolutions passed scarcely amounted to two hundred, while since that period the number has been quadrupled, and at the 41st Congress alone amounted to more than five hundred The increase within the latter period in the number of joint resolutions containing appropriations has been in a still greater proportion. The early and long-continued practice of Congress indicates that the framers of the Constitution who sat in the first and succeeding Congresses, and those who followed them for many years, construed the constitutional provision that "no money shall be withdrawn from the Treasury but in consequence of appropriations made by law," as requiring the highest character of laws—namely, bills, not joint resolutions.]

JOURNAL.

"Each house shall keep a Journal of its proceedings, and from time to time publish the same, excepting such parts as may in their judgment require secrecy; and the yeas and nays of the members of either house on any question shall, at the desire of one-fifth of the members present, be entered on the Journal."—*Const.*, 1, 5, *p*. 9.

House shall keep.

And publish.

Yeas and nays when to be entered on.

The Constitution of the United States requires that "objections" returned to the House by the President with a bill shall be entered "at large on their Journal;" and in all cases the votes of both houses on the passage of a bill so returned shall be determined by yeas and nays, and the names of the persons voting for and against the bill shall be entered on the Journal of each house, respectively.—*Const.*, 1, 7, *p*. 10.

Veto message and yeas and nays on vetoed bill to be entered on.

The House may judge what are and what are not "proceedings."—*Journal*, 1, 29, *p*. 1047.

House may judge what are proceedings.

It is not in order to place on the Journal indirectly what the House has refused to place there directly.—*Journal*, 3, 37, *pp*. 122, 123.

What not to be placed on.

All proceedings of the House subsequent to the erroneous announcement of a vote, which would have been irregular if such vote had been correctly announced, are to be treated as a nullity, and are not to be entered on the Journal.—*Journals*, 1, 29, *p*. 1032; 1, 31, *p*. 1436.

Effect of erroneous announcement of a vote upon subsequent record.

Speaker shall examine. When to be read. "The Speaker shall examine and correct the Journal before it is read."—*Rule* 5. And every day after taking the chair, "on the appearance of a quorum, shall cause the Journal of the preceding day to be read."—*Rule* 1. [Since the rule authorizing the presentation of petitions *in the House* has been rescinded, that portion of the Journal which contains the record of petitions handed to the Clerk is never read, but is published.]

What portion not read.

Written motions to be inserted on. "Every *written* motion made to the House shall be inserted on the Journals, with the name of the member making it, unless it be withdrawn on the same day on which it was submitted."—*Rule* 39. [And such motions are often inserted even where subsequently withdrawn, especially where a vote is taken intermediately between its being submitted and withdrawal. All motions, however, to be entered on the Journal must be first *entertained* by the Speaker.]

To be entered on, must be entertained by Speaker.

Name of member offering petition to be entered on. The name of the member who presents a petition or memorial, or who offers a resolution to the consideration of the House, shall be inserted on the Journal.—*Rule* 32. [Indeed, the practice is to insert the name of the member who may submit any proposition which is entertained by the Speaker.]

Hour of motion to adjourn to be entered on. "The hour at which every motion to adjourn is made shall be entered on the Journal."—*Rule* 45.

Petitions to be entered on, subject to control of the Speaker. "Members having petitions and memorials to present may hand them to the Clerk, indorsing the same with their names, and the reference or disposition to be made thereof; and such petitions and memorials shall be entered on the Journal, subject to the control and direction of the Speaker; and if any petition or memorial be so handed in which, in the judgment of the Speaker, is excluded by the rules, the same shall be returned to the member from whom it was received."—*Rule* 131. [The entry of petitions, &c., above directed, is construed to require simply the entry of a brief statement of their contents, their reference, &c.]

Absentees in Committee of the Whole to be entered on. The names of the absentees reported upon a roll-call in Committee of the Whole "shall be entered on the Journal."—*Rule* 106.

The names also of members not voting on any call of the yeas and nays shall be recorded in the Journal immediately after those voting in the affirmative and negative.—*Rule* 149.

Names of members not voting to be entered on.

The day of presentation of a bill to the President shall be carefully entered on the Journal.—*Joint Rule* 9.

Date of presentation of bill to President to be entered on.

A demand to enter a protest upon the Journal does not present a question of privilege.—*Journal*, 2, 33, *p*. 451.

Demand to enter protest on, not a question of privilege.

A motion being made to amend the Journal while it is passing under judgment of the House for approval, should said motion to amend be laid on the table, the Journal does not accompany it.—*Journal*, 1, 26, *p*. 28.

Motion to amend being laid on table, Journal does not accompany it.

When a member's vote is *incorrectly* recorded, it is his right, on the next day, while the Journal is before the House for its approval, to have the Journal corrected accordingly.—*Journal*, 2, 30, *p*. 211. But it is not in order to change a *correct record* of a vote given under a *misapprehension*.—*Journal*, 1, 31, *p*. 1266.

Correction of recorded vote.

"All questions of order shall be noted by the Clerk, with the decision, and put together at the end of the Journal of every session."—*Rule* 15.

Questions of order to be put at end of.

"The Clerk shall, within thirty days after the close of each session of Congress, cause to be completed the printing, and primary distribution to members and delegates, of the Journal of the House, together with an accurate index to the same."—*Rule* 16.

Primary distribution of, to be made in thirty days after close of session.

"It shall be the duty of the Clerk of the House, at the end of each session, to send a printed copy of the Journal thereof to the executive and to each branch of the legislature of every State."—*Rule* 14.

Printed copy of, to be sent to governors, &c.

"Extracts from the Journal, duly certified by the Clerk, shall be admitted as evidence in the several courts of the United States, and shall have the same force and effect as the original thereof would have if produced in court and proved."—*Stat. at Large*, *Vol. IX*, *p*. 80.

Extracts from, admitted as evidence in courts.

JUDICIARY, COMMITTEE ON THE.

There shall be appointed, at the commencement of each Congress, a Committee on the Judiciary, to consist of eleven members.—*Rule* 74.

When appointed, and of what number.

Its duties.

"It shall be the duty of the Committee on the Judiciary to take into consideration such petitions and matters or things touching judicial proceedings as shall be presented, or may come in question, and be referred to them by the House; and to report their opinion thereon, together with such propositions relative thereto as to them shall seem expedient."—*Rule* 83.

LAWS OF THE UNITED STATES.

Little & Brown's edition of session laws to be furnished.

By the joint resolution of September 26, 1850, it is provided "that the Secretary of State be authorized and directed to contract with Little & Brown to furnish their annual Statutes at Large, printed in conformity with the plan adopted by Congress in 1845, instead of the edition usually issued by his order under the act of Congress of April 20, 1818, and which conforms to an edition of the laws now in use."—*Stat. at Large, Vol. IX, p.* 564.

Whole number contracted for.

One copy for each member.

Fifty copies to the Clerk for the use of members and committees.

By the act of April 20, 1818, above referred to, of the 11,000 copies of the session laws directed to be published and distributed under the direction of the Secretary of State, there shall be distributed "to each member of the House of Representatives and delegates in Congress from any Territory, one copy each," and "fifty copies to the Clerk of the House of Representatives for the general use of the committees and members of the House."

Three hundred copies to Library for use of members.

And it is further provided, "that 300 of the said copies shall be annually placed in the Library of Congress; and every member of Congress and every delegate shall be entitled to the use of a copy during the session, to be returned and accounted for," &c.

One thousand copies of Statutes at Large.

By the act of March 3, 1845, the Attorney General is authorized to contract with Messrs. Little & Brown for one thousand copies of their proposed edition of the laws and treaties of the United States, according to the plan in said law set forth.—*Stat. at Large, Vol. V, p.* 798. Of which number, by the act of August 8, 1846, there are to be distributed, under the direction of the Secretary of State, "two hundred and eighty copies to the Librarian of Congress for the use of the members of the Senate and House during the sessions of Congress," and "fifty

Two hundred and eighty copies for Library for use of members.

copies to the Clerk of the House of Representatives for the chambers and committee-rooms of the House."—*Stat. at Large, Vol. IX, p.* 75.

Fifty copies to Clerk for use of committees, &c.

By the act of February 5, 1859, the distribution provided for in the foregoing acts is directed to be made by the Secretary of the Interior; and of the number of Statutes at Large heretofore deposited in the Library of Congress for the use of members, it was directed that, after retaining ten copies, two-thirds of those remaining should be transferred to the Library of the House.—*Stat. at Large, Vol. XI, p.* 379.

Secretary of Interior to distribute.

Copies to be transferred to House Library.

By the act of June 25, 1864, it is made the duty of the Secretary of the Senate to furnish the Superintendent of Public Printing with correct copies of all laws and joint resolutions as soon as possible after their approval by the President; and the Superintendent shall immediately cause to be printed, separately, the usual number for the use of the two houses; and in addition thereto, he shall cause to be printed and bound, at the close of each session, three thousand for the use of the Senate and ten thousand copies for the use of the House, with a complete alphabetical index, prepared under the direction of the Joint Committee on Printing.—*Stat. at Large, Vol. XIII, p.* 185.

Copies of, to be furnished by Secretary of Senate and printed.

Extra copies of.

By the joint resolution approved March 31, 1866, the Secretary of State is directed to renew the contract with Little, Brown & Co., for the annual publication of the Statutes at Large until otherwise ordered by Congress, and the time for their delivery is extended to seventy days after the adjournment of each session of Congress.—*Stat. at Large, Vol. XIV, p.* 352.

Contract for, renewed and time for delivery extended.

When an act has been approved by the President, the usual number of copies shall be printed for the use of the House.—*Rule* 157.

To be printed for the use of the House.

LIBRARY OF CONGRESS.

By the act of April 24, 1800, the first appropriation for the purchase of books for the use of Congress, and for the fitting up in the Capitol an apartment therefor, was made; and said purchase was directed to be made

First appropriation for.

by the Secretary of the Senate and Clerk of the House, "pursuant to such directions as shall be given, and such catalogue as shall be furnished by a joint committee of both houses of Congress, to be appointed for that purpose;" and the regulations of said library were to be such "as the committee aforesaid shall devise and establish."—*Stat. at Large, Vol. II, p.* 56.

President of Senate and Speaker to make regulations for.

By the act of January 26, 1802, the President of the Senate and the Speaker of the House for the time being are "empowered to establish such regulations and instructions in relation to the said library as to them shall seem proper, and from time to time to alter or amend the same: *Provided,* That no regulation shall be made repugnant to any provision contained in this act." It confers the appointment of the librarian upon "the President of the United States solely," and provides further, "that no map shall be permitted to be taken out of said library by any person; nor any book, except by the President and Vice-President of the United States and members of the Senate and House of Representatives for the time being;" and "that the unexpended balance of the sum of $5,000 appropriated by the act of Congress aforesaid for the purchase of books and maps for the use of the two houses of Congress, together with such sums *as may hereafter be appropriated* to the same purpose, shall be laid out under the direction of a joint committee, to consist of three members of the Senate and three members of the House of Representatives."—*Stat. at Large, Vol. II, p.* 129.

President of U. S. to appoint librarian.

Who may take books from.

Joint Committee on.

By the acts of May 1, 1810, (*Stat. at Large, Vol. II, p.* 612;) March 2, 1812, (*Ibid., p.* 786;) April 16, 1816, (*Stat. at Large, Vol. III, p.* 284;) January 13, 1830, (*Stat. at Large, Vol. IV, p.* 429;) March 3, 1863, (*Stat. at Large, Vol. XII, p.* 765,) the privilege of using books in said library, with the consent of the President of the Senate and Speaker of the House, was extended to the agent of the Library Committee, judges of the Supreme Court, Attorney General, members of the diplomatic corps, heads of Departments, Secretary of the Senate, Clerk of the House, chaplains of Congress, and, while in the District of

Privilege of using books in, extended.

Columbia, ex-Presidents of the United States; also the judges, solicitors, and clerks of the Court of Claims.

By the act of July 14, 1832, the Librarian was directed to remove the law-books into a separate apartment, to be prepared for the purpose of a law library, and the justices of the Supreme Court were "authorized to make rules and regulations for the use of the same by themselves and the attorneys and counsellors, during the sittings of the said court, as they shall deem proper: *Provided*, Such rules and regulations shall not restrict the President of the United States, the Vice-President, or any member of the Senate or House of Representatives, from having access to the said library, or using the books therein, in the same manner that he now has, or may have, to use the books of the Library of Congress."—*Stat. at Large, Vol. IV, p.* 579.

Law library established.

Supreme judges to make regulations for.

LIBRARY OF CONGRESS, JOINT COMMITTEE ON.

"There shall be a Joint Committee on the Library, to consist of three members on the part of the Senate and three on the part of the House of Representatives, to superintend and direct the expenditure of all moneys appropriated for the library, and to perform such other duties as are or may be directed by law."—*Joint Rule* 20.

To be appointed and of what number.

Duties of.

[This committee is usually appointed at the commencement of each Congress.]

When appointed.

(See also LIBRARY OF CONGRESS.)

LIBRARY OF THE HOUSE.

"There shall be retained in the library of the Clerk's office for the use of the members there, and not to be withdrawn therefrom, two copies of all the books and printed documents deposited in the library."—*Rule* 17.

Two copies of all public documents to be retained in.

LIE ON THE TABLE, MOTION TO.

Under the parliamentary law, this motion is only made "when the House has something else which claims its

For what purpose usually made.

present attention, but would be willing to reserve in their power to take up a proposition whenever it shall suit them."—*Manual, p.* 96. [But in the House of Representatives it is usually made for the purpose of giving a proposition or bill its "death-blow;" and when it prevails, the measure is rarely ever taken up again during the session.]

Takes precedence of all other motions, except to adjourn.

By the 42d *Rule*, it is provided that when a question is under debate the motion to lie on the table takes precedence of every other motion except the motion to adjourn.

Not debatable.

"The motion to lie on the table shall be decided without debate."—*Rule* 44.

In general, carries to the table whatever is connected with subject of it.

"In general, whatever adheres to the subject of this motion goes on the table with it; as, for example, where a motion to amend is ordered to lie on the table, the subject which it is proposed to amend goes there with it."—*Cushing, p.* 565. But it is not so with the Journal, where it is voted to lay upon the table a proposed amendment thereto—*Journal*, 1, 26, *p.* 28; nor with the subject out of which a question of order may arise, where the appeal is laid on the table, the decision of the Chair being thereby virtually sustained—*Journal*, 1, 26, *p.* 529; nor with the bill or other proposition, where the motion to reconsider a vote thereon is laid on the table.—*Journals, passim.*

Exceptions.

Not precluded by order of main question.

An order for the main question to be put does not preclude the motion to lie on the table, but it may be made at any stage of the proceedings between the demand for the previous question and the final action by the House under it.—*Journals*, 1, 28, *p.* 490; 1, 30, *p.* 175.

Where motion cannot be repeated.

Where a motion has already been made and negatived to lay a bill on the table, and no change or alteration has been made in the bill, or no proceeding directly touching its merits has since taken place, the motion to lie on the table cannot be repeated.—*Journal*, 2, 27, *p.* 890. [But under the invariable practice, the motion may be entertained at every new stage of the bill or proposition, and upon any proceeding having been had touching its merits.]

In order at every new stage, &c.

Where a bill is laid on the table pending the motions to refer and print, the motion to print, as well as all other motions connected with it, accompanies it.—*Journal*, 2, 32, *p*. 195. But where, as in case of a message, report, &c., it is moved to lie on the table and print, the said motion may be voted on as an entirety, or, under the 46th *Rule*, it may be divided, and a separate vote taken on each branch of the motion.—*Journal*, 1, 32, *p*. 337.

Carries with it motion to print.

Where motion to lie and print is made.

A negative vote on a motion to lie on the table may be reconsidered.—*Journal*, 2, 32, *p*. 234.

Negative vote on, may be reconsidered.

If a motion to reconsider be laid on the table, the latter vote cannot be reconsidered.—*Journals*, 3, 27, *p*. 334; 1, 33, *p*. 357.

Where a motion to reconsider is laid on the table, it cannot be reconsidered.

The motion to lie on the table is in order, pending the consideration of Senate amendments to a bill.—*Journal*, 1, 33, *p*. 1250.

Bill may be laid on table pending consideration of Senate amendments threto.

The following propositions are required by the rules to lie on the table one day, viz:

Propositions which lie on table one day.

Every order, resolution, or vote to which the concurrence of the Senate shall be necessary, unless the House shall otherwise expressly allow—*Rule* 143; calls on the President or Departments for information—unless otherwise ordered by unanimous consent—and to be taken up in the order of presentation after reports from select committees are received—*Rule* 53; notices of motions to rescind or change a standing rule or order—*Rule* 145; and notices of motions for leave to introduce bills.—*Rule* 115.

Orders, &c., requiring concurrence of Senate.

Calls on Departments and to print extra copies.

Motion to change rules.

Notices of bills.

LITHOGRAPHING.

(See ENGRAVING.)

LOBBY.

"In case of any disturbance or disorderly conduct in the galleries or lobby, the Speaker (or chairman of the Committee of the Whole House) shall have power to order the same to be cleared."—*Rule* 9.

May be cleared.

MACE.

Directed to be provided.

By a resolution of the House of April 14, 1789, (*Journal* 1*st Cong.*, *p.* 14,) it was directed that a proper symbol of office should be provided for the Sergeant-at-arms, of such form and device as the Speaker should direct; and by *Rule* 23 it is directed that "the symbol of his office (the mace) shall be borne by the Sergeant-at-arms when in the execution of his office."

To be borne by Sergeant-at-arms when in execution of his office.

MAPS.

Not to be printed without special direction.

"Maps accompanying documents shall not be printed under the general order to print, without the special direction of the House."—*Rule* 139.

(See ENGRAVING.)

MANUFACTURES, COMMITTEE ON.

When appointed, and number of.

"There shall be appointed at the commencement of each Congress a Committee on Manufactures, to consist of eleven members.—*Rule* 74.

Duties of.

[There are no duties assigned to this committee by the rules.]

MEETING OF CONGRESS.

Shall be on first Monday in December.

"The Congress shall assemble at least once in every year, and such meeting shall be on the first Monday in December, unless they shall by law appoint a different day."—*Const.*, 1, 4, 8.

President may call.

"The President may, on extraordinary occasion, convene both houses, or either of them."—*Ibid.*, 2, 3, 18.

At the first session. When members assemble. Called to order by Clerk.

[On the day fixed for the first meeting of a Congress, the members elect assemble in the hall of the House of Representatives, and at the hour of 12 o'clock m. are called to order by the Clerk of the last House, standing at his desk. Having requested the members elect to respond to their names as called, he proceeds to call the roll by States, beginning with the State of Maine. In making up said roll, he is directed

Roll called.

to place thereon the names of all persons claiming seats as representatives elect from States which were represented in the next preceding Congress, and of such persons only, and whose credentials show that they were regularly elected in accordance with the laws of their States respectively, or the laws of the United States.—*Stat. at Large. Vol. XIV, p.* 397. Having ascertained whether or not a quorum is present, he announces the fact to the House. If a quorum shall have answered, it is then usual for some member to move "that the House do now proceed to the election of a Speaker *viva voce*." The question on this motion having been put by the Clerk, and decided affirmatively, he then designates four members who shall act as tellers of the vote about to be taken, usually making his selection from members of different parties. The tellers having taken their seats at the Clerk's desk, and nominations having been made and recorded, the Clerk then proceeds to call the roll of members alphabetically, each member, as his name is called, pronouncing audibly the name of the person voted for, and the Clerk (through one of his assistants) recording the name of the member voting in a column under that of the member voted for. After the roll-call is completed, and every member present (and desiring it) has voted, the lists of voters for each candidate are read over by the Clerk, when one of the tellers rises and announces to the House what number of votes each candidate has received. If no person shall have received a majority of all the votes given, the House then proceeds (if no other order be taken) to a *second* vote, and so on until an election is effected. But if any person shall have received a majority of all the votes given, and a quorum has voted, the Clerk declares such person "duly elected Speaker of the House of Representatives for the —— Congress." The Clerk then designates two members (usually of different politics, and from the number of those voted for as Speaker) "to conduct the Speaker elect to the chair;" and also one member (usually that one who has been longest a member of the House) "to administer to him the oath required

Who shall be placed on the roll.

Quorum present.

Election of Speaker.

Tellers.

Nominations.

Voting for Speaker.

Announcement of vote.

When no one elected.

Where Speaker elected.

Conducted to chair and sworn.

by the Constitution and laws of the United States." In case of a vacancy in the office of Clerk, or of his absence or inability, the duties imposed on him by law or custom relative to the preparation of the roll or the organization of the House shall devolve on the Sergeant-at-Arms; and in case of vacancies in both of said offices, or of their absence or inability to act, the said duties shall be performed by the Doorkeeper. Having been conducted to the chair, it is usual for the Speaker to deliver to the House a brief address, which being concluded, the oath is administered to him, and he then takes his seat as the presiding officer of the House. (See OATH.) He then directs the Clerk to call the roll of members by States, requesting each member, as his name is called, to approach the Chair, when he administers to them the oath to support the Constitution of the United States. The delegates from the Territories are then called and sworn.

In case of vacancy in office of Clerk.

Members and delegates sworn.

Senate notified of presence of a quorum and election of Speaker.

At this stage it is usual for the House to adopt an order "that a message be sent to the Senate to inform that body that a quorum of the House of Representatives has assembled, and that —— ——, one of the Representatives from the State of ——, has been chosen Speaker, and that the House is now ready to proceed to business."

Committee to wait on President.

And then, or upon the receipt of a message from the Senate informing the House of the presence of a quorum in that body, it is usual for the House to adopt the following order: "That a committee of three members be appointed on the part of the House, to join such committee as may be appointed on the part of the Senate, to wait on the President of the United States, and inform him that a quorum of the two houses has assembled, and that Congress is ready to receive any communication he may be pleased to make."

Rules of last House adopted.

It has been usual to adopt a resolution, providing "that the rules and orders of the last House of Representatives be adopted for the government of this House until otherwise ordered." But the adoption of the following rule during the 36th Congress would seem to render such a resolution unnecessary now, viz: "These rules shall be the rules of the House of Representatives of the present and succeeding Congresses, unless otherwise ordered."—*Rule* 147.

Election of officers.

The election of officers is next proceeded with, which, being completed, the House may be considered as fully organized.

Hour of daily meeting; order for newspapers.

Orders providing for the hour of the daily meeting of the House, and for furnishing members with newspapers, are amongst the earliest that are thereafter adopted.

[The foregoing are the proceedings which *usually* take place upon the assembling of a new House of Representatives, and which generally occur on the *first day* of the meeting of Congress.]

Delay in the organization.

There have been occasions, however, where the proceedings were very different, and where the organization of the House was much longer delayed.

Contested seats.

Chairman appointed.

In the 26th Congress, where the Clerk, upon the call of the roll by States for the ascertainment of the presence of a quorum, proposed to omit the call of either of the claimants for each of several contested seats, on the fifth day of the session, a chairman was appointed "to serve until the organization of the House by the election of a Speaker;" and such election did not take place until eleven days thereafter.—*Journal*, 1, 26, *pp.* 6, 79.

Failure of majority to vote for Speaker.

In the 31st Congress, by reason of a failure of a majority to vote for any candidate, there was no election of Speaker for nearly a month after the meeting.—*Journal*, 1, 31, *p.* 3 to 164.

And in the 34th Congress, for the same cause, an election of Speaker did not take place for two months after the meeting.—*Journal*, 1, 34, *p.* 3 to 446.

And also in the 36th Congress, for the same cause, the election of a Speaker was delayed for two months.—*Journal*, 1, 36, *p.* 8 to 162.

Clerk presides.

During the three last-named periods, while the House was without a Speaker, the Clerk presided over its deliberations; not, however, exercising the functions of Speaker to the extent of deciding questions of order, but, as in the case of other questions, putting them to the House for its decision. To relieve future Houses of some of the difficulties which grew out of the very limited power of the Clerk as a presiding officer, the House of the 36th Congress adopted the present 146th and 147th *rules*, which provide, that "pending the election of a Speaker, the Clerk shall preserve order and decorum, and shall decide all questions of order that may arise, subject to appeal to the House," and also for the permanency of the present rules, "unless otherwise ordered."

Speaker elected by plurality vote.

In the 31st and 34th Congresses a Speaker was finally elected by a *plurality* vote; such mode of election, however, was previously authorized by a resolution of the House, and subsequently confirmed by a resolution declaring him "duly elected."—*Journals*, 1, 31, *pp.* 156, 163, 164; 1, 34, *pp.* 429, 430, 444.

At a second or subsequent session.

Notify Senate of quorum.

Committee to wait on President.

The hour of daily meeting fixed.

[At a second or subsequent session of Congress the members are called to order by the Speaker, when he causes the clerk to call the roll of members by States for the purpose of ascertaining whether or not a quorum is present. As soon as a quorum has answered, it is usual for the House to pass an order "that the Clerk inform the Senate that a quorum of the House of Representatives has assembled, and is ready to proceed to business;" and subsequently, as at the first session, to pass an order for the appointment of a committee to wait on the President. An order is also passed fixing, until otherwise ordered, the hour of daily meeting.]

MEMBERS.

Qualifications of.

"No person shall be a Representative who shall not have attained the age of twenty-five years, and have been seven years a citizen of the United States, and who shall not, when elected, be an inhabitant of that State in which he shall be chosen."—*Const.*, 1, 2, *p.* 5.

Who shall not be.

"No person shall be a Representative in Congress who having previously taken an oath, as a member of Congress, or as an officer of the United States, or as a member of any State legislature, or as an executive or judicial officer of any State, to support the Constitution of the United States, shall have engaged in insurrection or rebellion against the same, or given aid or comfort to the enemies thereof. But Congress may by a vote of two-thirds of each house remove such disability."—*Ibid.*, *XIV Amendment*, *p.* 33.

By the act of May 22, 1872, (*Stat. at Large*, *Vol. XVII*, *p.* 142, the disabilities imposed by the foregoing article are removed from all persons whomsoever, except Senators and Representatives of the Thirty-sixth and Thirty-seventh Congresses, officers in the judicial, military, and naval service of the United States, heads of Departments, and foreign ministers of the United States.

House shall judge of election, &c., of.

"Each house shall be the judge of the elections, returns, and qualifications of its own members."—*Ibid.*, 1, 5, *p.* 8.

(See ELECTIONS, CONTESTED.)

Elections for, when and how held.

The times, places, and manner of holding elections for Senators and Representatives shall be prescribed in each State by the legislature thereof; but the Congress may at any time by law make or alter such regulations, except as to the places of choosing Senators.—*Const.*, 1, 4, 8.

Provisions of law for apportionment and election of.

By the acts of February 2 and May 30, 1872, it is provided that the House shall consist of two hundred and ninety-two members, to be elected by districts composed of contiguous territory and containing as near as practicable an equal number of inhabitants, and equal to the number of members to which said State may be entitled, and no one district to elect more than one Representative. The Tuesday after the first Monday in November, 1876, and in every second year thereafter, is fixed for the election in each of the States and Territories of Representatives and Delegates to the Congress commencing on the 4th of March thereafter. In case of a failure to elect or a vacancy, an election to fill such vacancy shall be held at such time as may be provided for by law in the State or Territory where the same may occur. The number of Representatives shall be reduced in the proportion which the number of male citizens being twenty-one years of age denied the right to vote therein shall bear to the whole number of male citizens twenty-one years of age in such State. In the election to the Forty-third Congress only is the additional Representative allowed to any State to be elected by the State at large.—*Stat. at Large, Vol. XVII, pp.* 28, 192.

Election of, in California for 44th Congress. By the act of March 3, 1873, it is provided that on the 1st Wednesday in September, 1874, there shall be elected in each congressional district in the State of California, one Representative to represent said State in the 44th Congress.—*Stat. at Large, Vol. XVII, p.* 578.

Right of, to resign recognized. A communication from a member informing the House that he had transmitted to the governor of his State his resignation of his seat in Congress, held to be sufficient evidence that he is no longer a member of the House.—*Journal*, 2, 41, *p.* 373.

(See RESIGNATION BY A MEMBER.)

Vacancies, how filled. "When vacancies happen in the representation from any State, the executive authority thereof shall issue writs of election to fill such vacancies."—*Const.* 1, 2, *p.* 6.

Roll of, at meeting of Congress. In making out the roll of members elect at the first meeting of a Congress, the Clerk of the next preceding House shall place thereon the names of all persons claiming seats as Representatives elect from States which were represented in the next preceding Congress, and of such persons only, whose credentials show that they were regularly elected in accordance with the laws of their States respectively, or the laws of the United States.—*Laws 2d Sess. 39th Cong., p.* 28.

Shall receive compensation. "Representatives shall receive a compensation for their services, to be ascertained by law, and paid out of the Treasury of the United States."—*Const.*, 1, 6, *p.* 9.

(See COMPENSATION and MILEAGE.)

Oath to be administered to. "The oath or affirmation required by the sixth article of the Constitution of the United States, to wit: '*I, A. B., do solemnly swear (or affirm, as the case may be) that I will support the Constitution of the United States,*' shall be administered at the first session of Congress after every general election of Representatives, first by any one of the members to the Speaker, and by him to all the members present, and to the Clerk previous to entering on any business, and to the members who shall afterward appear previous to taking their seats."—*Stat. at Large, Vol. I, p.* 23. An additional oath is prescribed by the act of July 2, 1862; and also (where legal disabilities have been removed) by the act of July 11, 1868.

(See OATH.)

Members not to be appointed to office.

"No Representative shall, during the time for which he was elected, be appointed to any civil office under the authority of the United States which shall have been created, or the emoluments whereof shall have been increased, during such time; and no person holding any office under the United States shall be a member of either house during his continuance in office."—*Const.*, 1, 6, 9.

Government officers not to be members.

No member to be an elector.

"No Representative shall be appointed an elector."—*Const.*, 2, 1, *p.* 15.

Privileges of.

"The Senators and Representatives shall, in all cases except treason, felony, and breach of the peace, be privileged from arrest during their attendance at the session of their respective houses, and in going to and returning from the same; and for any speech or debate in either house they shall not be questioned in any other place."—*Const.*, 1, 6, *p.* 9.

(See PRIVILEGE.)

May be punished or expelled.

"Each house may determine the rules of its proceedings, punish its members for disorderly behavior, and, with the concurrence of two-thirds, expel a member."—*Const.*, 1, 5, *p.* 8.

Compensation of, in case of vacancy.

In all cases of a vacancy in either house of Congress, by death or otherwise, of any member elected or appointed thereto, after the commencement of the Congress to which he shall have been elected, each person afterwards elected or appointed to fill such vacancy shall be compensated and paid from the time that the compensation of his predecessor ceased: *Provided*, That no member shall receive more than three thousand dollars for any one year.—*Stat. at Large, Vol. XII, p.* 624.

Bribery of.

By the act of February 26, 1853, it is provided that if any person shall bribe, or offer to bribe, a member of Congress, or officer or person holding any place of trust or profit, or discharging any official function under the

House of Representatives, he shall, on conviction thereof, be fined not exceeding three times the amount so offered or given, and imprisoned in a penitentiary not exceeding three years; and the person convicted of in anywise accepting or receiving the same, or any part thereof, shall be subject to the same penalty, and, if an officer or person holding any such place of trust or profit as aforesaid, shall forfeit his office or place; and any person so convicted shall forever be disqualified to hold any office of honor, trust, or profit under the United States.—*Stat. at Large, Vol. X, p.* 171.

Accepting bribes.

(See BRIBERY.)

Forbidden to act for claimants for compensation paid or to be paid.

By the same act it is provided that if any member of Congress shall, for compensation paid or to be paid, act as agent or attorney for, or aid in the prosecution or support of, any claim or claims against the United States, he shall, on conviction, pay a fine not exceeding five thousand dollars, or suffer imprisonment in the penitentiary not exceeding one year, or both, at the discretion of the court.—*Ibid., p.* 170.

Not to be interested in public contracts.

By the act of April 21, 1808, it is provided that no member of Congress shall be interested in any public contract, under a penalty of three thousand dollars fine; and if any officer of the United States, on behalf of the United States, shall make such a contract with a member of Congress, he shall be liable to the same penalty.—*Stat. at Large, Vol. II, p.* 404.

Not to practice in Court of Claims.

No member shall practice in the Court of Claims.—*Stat. at Large, Vol. XII, p.* 766.

Not to receive compensation for any services wherein the U. S. is a party.

By the act of June 11, 1864, it is provided that no member of the Senate or House of Representative shall, after his election and during his continuance in office, nor shall any head of a Department, head of a Bureau, clerk, or any other officer of the Government, receive, or agree to receive, any compensation whatsoever, directly or indirectly, for any services rendered, or to be rendered, after the passage of this act, to any person, either by himself or another, in relation to any proceeding, contract, claim, controversy, charge, accusation, arrest, or other matter or thing in which the United States is a party, or directly or indirectly interested, before any

Department, court-martial, bureau, officer, or any civil, military, or naval commission whatever. And any person offending against any provision of this act shall, on conviction thereof, be deemed guilty of a misdemeanor, and be punished by a fine not exceeding ten thousand dollars, and by imprisonment for a term not exceeding two years, at the discretion of the court trying the same, and shall be forever thereafter incapable of holding any office of honor, trust, or profit under the Government of the United States.—*Stat. at Large, Vol. XIII, p.* 123.

Provisions of foregoing act extended to Delegates.

By the act of January 16, 1873, the provisions of the last foregoing act are so extended as to apply to Delegates from the Territories and the District of Columbia.—*Stat. at Large, Vol. XVII, p.* 411.

Shall not absent themselves.

"No member shall absent himself from the service of the House, unless he have leave, or be sick, or unable to attend."—*Rule* 33.

(See Compensation.)

Less than a quorum may be authorized to compel attendance of absent.

"A smaller number than a quorum may be authorized to compel the attendance of absent members in such manner and under such penalties as each house may provide."—*Const.*, 1, 5, *p.* 8.

Attendance of, may be compelled by fifteen members.

"Any fifteen members (including the Speaker, if there be one) shall be authorized to compel the attendance of absent members."—*Rule* 34.

(See Calls of the House.)

Deportment of, in the House.

"While the Speaker is putting any question, or addressing the House, none shall walk out of or across the House; nor in such case, or when a member is speaking, shall entertain private discourse; nor, while a member is speaking, shall pass between him and the Chair. Every member shall remain uncovered during the session of the House. No member or other persons shall visit or remain by the Clerk's table while the ayes and noes are calling or ballots are counting."—*Rule* 65.

When not to visit Clerk's desk.

Shall not vote where interested or not within bar.

"No member shall vote on any question in the event of which he is immediately and particularly interested, or in any case where he was not within the bar of the House when the question was put. When the roll-call is completed, the Speaker shall state that any member offering to vote does so upon the assurance that he was within the bar before the last name on the roll was called: *Provided, however*, That any member who was absent by leave of the House may vote at any time before the result is announced. It is not in order for the Speaker to entertain any request for a member to change his vote on any question after the result shall have been declared, nor shall any member be allowed to record his vote on any question, if he was not present when such vote was taken."—*Rule* 29. And "upon a division and count of the House on any question, no member without the bar shall be counted."—*Rule* 36. (See BAR OF THE HOUSE.)

Shall vote if in House, unless excused.

"Every member who shall be in the House when the question is put shall give his vote, unless the House shall excuse him. All motions to excuse a member from voting shall be made before the House divides, or before the call of the yeas and nays is commenced, and the question shall then be taken without debate."—*Rule* 31.

Names to be called alphabetically.

"Upon calls of the House, or on taking the yeas and nays on any question, the names of the members shall be called alphabetically."—*Rule* 35.

Need not serve on more than two committees.

"Any member may excuse himself from serving on any committee at the time of his appointment, if he is then a member of two other committees."—*Rule* 69.

MEMORIALS.

(See PETITIONS.)

MESSAGES FROM THE PRESIDENT.

Shall from time to time give information and recommend measures.

"The President shall, from time to time, give to the Congress information of the state of the Union, and recommend to their consideration such measures as he shall judge necessary and expedient."—*Const.*, 2, 3, *p.* 18.

Annual message.

The annual message of the President, with the accompanying documents, is usually communicated to the House at the commencement of each session, but usually not until after he has been notified through a joint committee of the two houses that a quorum of each body has assembled, and is ready to receive any communication he may be pleased to make; although it was otherwise in the Thirty-fourth and Thirty-sixth Congresses, the message having been communicated on the first occasion on the 31st December, and on the latter not only before the appointment of such committee, but before the election of the Speaker, which latter did not take place until the month of February.—(See *Journals*, 1, 34, *pp*. 221 to 228, 231, 233, 444, 511; 1, 36.)

How announced.

All messages from the President are in writing, and are sent to the House by his private secretary, or such other person as he may delegate, and, as in the case of messages from the Senate, are announced at the door by the Doorkeeper and handed to the Speaker, who places them upon his table, to be taken up whenever the House, under the 54th *Rule*, shall go to the business thereon. In the case of the annual message, however, it is usually taken up, by unanimous consent, as soon as received. Whenever taken up, messages from the President are always read *in extenso*, the House never, as in the case of other communications, dispensing with the reading of the same.

When taken up.

Always read.

Printing of.

In regard to printing the messages and other documents, see PRINTING, PUBLIC.

To be sent to both houses on same day, except in certain cases.

"Where the subject of a message is of a nature that it can properly be communicated to both houses of Parliament, it is expected that this communication should be made to both on the same day. But where a message was accompanied with an original declaration, signed by the party to which the message referred, its being sent to one house was not noticed by the other, because the declaration, being original, could not possibly be sent to both houses at the same time."—*Manual*, *p*. 131. [So, too, in Congress, where they can be properly made, communications are expected to be made to both houses on the same day, except where the communication may be in response to a call from one branch only. The parliamentary practice prevails, too, in regard to the communication of an original paper.—*See Journal*, 1, 35, *p*. 270.]

Notifying the House of his approval of, or failure to return bills.

[Where the President approves a bill, it is customary for him to notify the house where it originated of the fact, and the date of approval, which is entered on the Journal. A similar notification is also given in case a bill is allowed to become a law by his failure to return the same with objections.—See PRESIDENT OF THE U. S.]

Of approvals to be read at Clerk's desk.

Messages from the President giving notice of bills approved shall be reported forthwith from the Clerk's desk.—*Rule* 158.

Veto.

Messages returning a bill with his objections. (See VETO.)

MESSAGES FROM THE SENATE.

Doorkeeper shall announce.

"When a message shall be sent from the Senate to the House of Representatives, it shall be announced at the door of the House by the Doorkeeper, and shall be respectfully communicated to the Chair by the person by whom it may be sent."—*Joint Rule* 2.

By whom to be sent.

"Messages shall be sent by such persons as a sense of propriety in each house may determine to be proper."—*Joint Rule* 4. [In the House they are commonly sent by its Clerk; in the Senate, by its Secretary.]

If in Committee of the Whole Speaker takes chair to receive.

Received promptly.

"If the House be in committee when a messenger attends, the Speaker takes the chair to receive the message, and then quits it to return into committee, without any question or interruption."—*Manual, p.* 130. [It is the practice of the House to receive messages promptly upon the appearance of the messenger, and without regard to the business in hand; in case a member is occupying the floor in debate, he suspends his remarks until the announcement is made and the message received, and a call of the yeas and nays is not unfrequently suspended for the same purpose; but when received it is placed upon the Speaker's table, to be taken up at the time indicated in the 54th *Rule*, viz, after messages and other executive communications.]

If error committed in message.

"If messengers commit an error in delivering their message, they may be admitted or called in to correct their message."—*Manual, p.* 130; *Journal,* 1, 2, *pp.* 171 172.

To be reported forthwith, from Clerk's desk.

Messages from the Senate, giving notice of bills passed or approved, shall be reported forthwith from the Clerk's desk.—*Rule* 158.

MILEAGE.

By the act of March 3, 1873, it is provided that the compensation of $7,500 thereby allowed to each Senator, Representative, and Delegate shall be in lieu of all pay and allowance, except actual individual traveling expenses from their homes to the seat of Government and return, by the most direct route of usual travel, once for each session, of the House to which such Senator, Representative, or Delegate belongs, to be certified to under his hand to the disbursing officer, and filed as a voucher.—*Stat. at Large, Vol. XVII, p.* 486.

Actual traveling expenses only allowed.

"It shall be the duty of the Sergeant-at-Arms to keep the accounts for pay and mileage of members; to prepare checks, and, if required to do so, to draw the money on such checks for the members, (the same being previously signed by the Speaker, and indorsed by the member,) and pay over the same to the member entitled thereto."—*Rule* 25.

Accounts for, to be kept by Sergeant-at-arms.

MILEAGE, COMMITTEE ON.

There shall be appointed at the commencement of each Congress a Committee on Mileage, to consist of five members.—*Rule* 74.

When appointed and number of.

"It shall be the duty of the Committee on Mileage to ascertain and report the distance, to the Sergeant-at-Arms, for which each member shall receive pay."—*Rule* 99.

Shall ascertain and report mileage of each member.

MILITARY ACADEMY.

Three members of the House shall be designated by the Speaker, at the session next preceding the time of the annual examination of cadets, to attend the said examination; and they shall report thereon within twenty days after the next meeting of Congress.—*Stat. at Large, Vol. XVI, p.* 67.

Three members to be appointed visitors to.

MILITARY AFFAIRS, COMMITTEE ON.

There shall be appointed at the commencement of each Congress a Committee on Military Affairs, to consist of eleven members.—*Rule* 74.

When appointed and number of.

Its duties. "It shall be the duty of the Committee on Military Affairs to take into consideration all subjects relating to the military establishment and public defense which may be referred to them by the House, and to report their opinion thereupon; and also to report, from time to time, such measures as may contribute to economy and accountability in the said establishment."—*Rule* 87.

MILITIA, COMMITTEE ON THE.

When appointed and number of. There shall be appointed at the commencement of each Congress a Committee on the Militia, to consist of eleven members.—*Rule* 74.

Its duties. "It shall be the duty of the Committee on the Militia to take into consideration and report on all subjects connected with the organizing, arming, and disciplining the militia of the United States."—*Rule* 88.

MINES AND MINING, COMMITTEE ON.

When appointed, number, and duties of. A Committee on Mines and Mining, to consist of eleven members, shall be appointed at the commencement of each Congress.—*Rule* 74.

"It shall be the duty of said committee to consider all subjects relating to mines and mining that may be referred to them, and to report their opinion thereon, together with such propositions relative thereto as may seem to them expedient."—*Rule* 153.

MODIFICATION.

When may be made. [Motions may be modified before the previous question is seconded, and before a decision or amendment,] but not after the previous question is seconded.—*Journals*, 1, 28, *p.* 811; 1, 31, *p.* 1397.

MORNING HOUR.

What is the "morning hour." The "morning hour," as it is called, is the hour after the reading of the Journal, which, under the 51st and 52d *Rules*, has been "devoted to reports from committees and resolutions," and after the expiration of which it is in order, under the 54th *Rule*, to entertain a motion "that the House do now proceed to dispose of the business on the Speaker's table," &c. And under the general practice it is held that this hour begins to run from the announcement by the Speaker that reports from committees are in order. When it commences to run.

MORNING HOUR ON MONDAYS.

On every Monday it is made the duty of the Speaker to call the States and Territories—*first* for bills on leave for reference only, and without debate, and not to be brought back by motions to reconsider, at which time joint resolutions of State and Territorial legislatures may be introduced for reference and printing; *then* for resolutions, at which time bills on leave may be introduced, and all resolutions which shall give rise to debate shall lie over for discussion.—*Rule* 130. [And so also in regard to bills introduced at this time and giving rise to debate. Ever since the foregoing rule has been in its present form the Speaker has declined to entertain even a request for unanimous consent to transact any other business within the time prescribed for calls for bills on leave for reference.] Call for bills on leave and resolutions during. Devoted strictly to the prescribed business.

MOTIONS.

For fullest information in regard to a particular motion, see under its name, as ADJOURNED, LIE ON THE TABLE, &c., &c.

"When any motion or proposition is made, the question, 'Will the House now consider it?' shall not be put unless it is demanded by some member or is deemed necessary by the Speaker."—*Rule* 41. Question of consideration not to be put in all cases.

"When a motion is made and seconded, it shall be stated by the Speaker, or, being in writing, it shall be handed to the Chair, and read aloud by the Clerk before debated."—*Rule* 38. When made and seconded.

"Every motion shall be reduced to writing, if the Speaker or any member desire it. Every *written* motion made to the House shall be inserted on the Journals, with the name of the member making it, unless it be withdrawn on the same day on which it was submitted."— Shall be reduced to writing, if required.

Rule 39. [And such motions are often inserted even where subsequently withdrawn. But to be entered on the Journal every motion must have been *entertained* by the Speaker.]

May be withdrawn before decision or amendment.

"After a motion is stated by the Speaker or read by the Clerk, it shall be deemed to be in the possession of the House, but may be withdrawn at any time before a decision or amendment."—*Rule* 40. [But not after the previous question is seconded.] It may, however, be withdrawn while the House is dividing on a demand for the previous question—*Journal*, 2, 29, *p*. 241; and all incidental questions fall with such withdrawal.—*Journal*, 1, 26, *p*. 57.

Precedence of various motions.

"When a question is under debate, no motion shall be received but to adjourn, to lie on the table, for the previous question, to postpone to a day certain, to commit or amend, to postpone indefinitely; which several motions shall have precedence in the order in which they are arranged."—*Rule* 42.

"The motion to reconsider shall take precedence of all other questions, except the motion to adjourn."—*Rule* 49.

Member may submit more than one.

"A member may submit more than one motion in connection with a pending proposition, if the latter motion is of higher dignity than the former."—*Journals*, 2, 33, *pp*. 483, 486; 2, 35, *p*. 477.

Such as are not to be repeated at same stage, &c.

"No motion to postpone to a day certain, to commit, or to postpone indefinitely, being decided, shall be again allowed on the same day and at the same stage of the bill or proposition."—*Rule* 42.

May be committed.

"Motions and reports may be committed at the pleasure of the House."—*Rule* 47.

To commit, order in which question to be taken.

"When a resolution shall be offered or a motion made to refer any subject, and different committees shall be proposed, the question shall be taken in the following order:

"The Committee of the Whole House on the state of the Union, the Committee of the Whole House, a standing committee, a select committee."—*Rule* 43.

"A motion to adjourn, and a motion to fix the day to which the House shall adjourn, shall be always in order. These motions and the motion to lie on the table shall be decided without debate."—*Rule* 44. Always in order.

"The hour at which every motion to adjourn is made shall be entered on the Journal."—*Rule* 45. Hour of, to adjourn.

"A motion to strike out and insert shall be deemed indivisible; but a motion to strike out being lost, shall preclude neither amendment nor a motion to strike out and insert."—*Rule* 46. To strike out and insert.

"A motion to strike out the enacting words of a bill shall have precedence of a motion to amend; and if carried, shall be considered equivalent to its rejection. Whenever a bill is reported from a Committee of the Whole, with a recommendation to strike out the enacting words, and such recommendation is disagreed to by the House, the bill shall stand recommitted to the said committee, without further action by the House. But before the question of concurrence is submitted, it is in order to entertain a motion to refer the bill to any committee of the House, with or without instructions, and when the same is again reported to the House, it shall be referred to the Committee of the Whole, without debate, and resume its original place on the calendar."—*Rule* 123. (See ENACTING WORDS, MOTION TO STRIKE OUT. To strike out enacting words.

"All amendments made to an original motion in committee shall be incorporated with the motion, and so reported."—*Rule* 108. Original, in committee.

NAVAL AFFAIRS, COMMITTEE ON.

"There shall be appointed at the commencement of each Congress a Committee on Naval Affairs, to consist of nine members."—*Rule* 74. When appointed and number of.

"It shall be the duty of the Committee on Naval Affairs to take into consideration all matters which concern the naval establishment, and which shall be referred to them by the House, and to report their opinion thereupon; and also to report from time to time such measures as may contribute to economy and accountability in the said establishment."—*Rule* 89. Its duties.

NEWSPAPERS.

Reporters for, admitted to gallery on certain conditions.

"Stenographers and reporters, other than the official reporters of the House, wishing to take down the debates, may be admitted by the Speaker to the reporters' gallery over the Speaker's chair, but not on the floor of the House; but no person shall be allowed the privilege of said gallery under the character of stenographer or reporter without a written permission of the Speaker, specifying the part of said gallery assigned to him; nor shall said stenographer or reporter be admitted to said gallery unless he shall state in writing for what paper or papers he is employed to report; nor shall he be so admitted, or, if admitted, be suffered to retain his seat, if he shall be or become an agent to prosecute any claim pending before Congress; and the Speaker shall give his written permission with this condition."—*Rule* 135.

NOMINATIONS.

Where necessary.

"In all cases where other than members of the House may be eligible to an office by the election of the House, there shall be a previous nomination."—*Rule* 11.

NOTICES.

Of bills.

In the case of a bill introduced by a motion for leave, "at least one day's notice shall be given of the motion in the House, or by filing a memorandum thereof with the Clerk, and having it entered on the Journal, and the motion shall be made and the bill introduced, if leave is given, when resolutions are called for; such motion, or the bill when introduced, may be committed."—*Rule* 115.

(See also BILLS, *p.* 21, *ante.*)

Of amendment of the rules.

"No standing rule or order of the House shall be rescinded or changed without one day's notice being given of the motion therefor."—*Rule* 145. [There is no authority given, as in the case of notices of bills, to file this notice with the Clerk. Consequently it can only be given in open House, and only at such time as any other independent motion can be made.]—*Journal*, 2, 25, *p.* 536.

OATH.

Members shall be bound by oath or affirmation to support the Constitution of the United States.—*Const.*, 6, 1, *p.* 23. The act of June 1, 1789, provides that the oath required above shall be administered in the form following, to wit: "I, ———, do solemnly swear (or affirm, as the case may be) that I will support the Constitution of the United States." It shall be administered to the Speaker by any one member of the House of Representatives; and by him to all the members present, and to the Clerk, previous to entering on any other business, and to the members who shall afterwards appear, previous to taking their seats.—*Stat. at Large, Vol. I, p.* 23.

Of members.

Form of.

The act of July 2, 1862, requires that every person elected or appointed to any office of honor or profit under the Government of the United States, either in the civil, military, or naval Departments of the public service, excepting the President of the United States, shall, before entering upon the duties of such office, and before being entitled to any of the salary or other emoluments thereof, take and subscribe the following oath or affirmation: "I, A. B., do solemnly swear (or affirm) that I have never voluntarily borne arms against the United States since I have been a citizen thereof; that I have voluntarily given no aid, countenance, counsel, or encouragement to persons engaged in armed hostility thereto; that I have neither sought nor accepted nor attempted to exercise the functions of any office whatever under any authority or pretended authority in hostility to the United States; that I have not yielded a voluntary support to any pretended government, authority, power, or constitution within the United States hostile or inimical thereto. And I do further swear (or affirm) that, to the best of my knowledge and ability, I will support and defend the Constitution of the United States against all enemies, foreign and domestic; that I will bear true faith and allegiance to the same; that I take this obligation freely, without any mental reserva-

To be taken by all persons in the public service.

tion or purpose of evasion; and that I will well and faithfully discharge the duties of the office on which I am about to enter: so help me God;" which said oath so taken and signed shall be preserved among the files of the court, House of Congress, or Department to which the said office may appertain. And any person who shall falsely take the said oath shall be guilty of perjury, and on conviction, in addition to the penalties now prescribed for that offense, shall be deprived of his office, and rendered incapable forever after of holding any office or place under the United States.—*Stat. at Large, Vol. XII, p.* 502.

To be preserved in the files.

Penalty for false swearing.

To be taken where legal disabilities have been removed.

By the act of July 11, 1868, it is provided that whenever any person who has participated in the late rebellion, and from whom all legal disabilities arising therefrom have been removed by act of Congress by a vote of two-thirds of each House, has been or shall be elected or appointed to any office or place of trust in or under the Government of the United States, he shall, before entering upon the duties thereof, instead of the oath prescribed by the act of July 2, 1862, take and subscribe the following oath or affirmation: "I, A. B., do solemnly swear (or affirm) that I will support and defend the Constitution of the United States against all enemies, foreign and domestic; that I will bear true faith and allegiance to the same; that I take this obligation freely, without any mental reservation or purpose of evasion; and that I will well and faithfully discharge the duties of the office on which I am about to enter: so help me God."—*Stat. at Large, Vol. XV, p.* 85.

Of officers of the House.

The Clerk, Sergeant-at-Arms, Doorkeeper, and Postmaster, shall each take an oath for the true and faithful discharge of the duties of his office, to the best of his knowledge and abilities, and to keep the secrets of the House.—*Rule* 10.

Who may administer.

The Speaker of the House, a chairman of a Committee of the Whole, or a chairman of a select committee—*Stat. at Large, Vol. I, p.* 554—and the chairman of any standing committee, shall be empowered to administer oaths or affirmations to witnesses in any case under their examination.—*Ibid., Vol. III, p.* 345.

OBJECTION DAYS.

"On the first and fourth Friday and Saturday of each month the calendar of private bills shall be called over, (the chairman of the Committee of the Whole House commencing the call where he left off the previous day,) and the bills to the passage of which no objection shall then be made shall be first considered and disposed of. But when a bill is again reached, after having been once objected to, the committee shall consider and dispose of the same, unless it shall again be objected to by at least five members."—*Rule* 129. [Sometimes the House, under a suspension of the rules, directs that other days than the above be treated as objection days.]

What are.

(See PRIVATE BILLS and PRIVATE BUSINESS.)

OFFICERS OF THE HOUSE.

(See ELECTIONS BY THE HOUSE; also, SPEAKER, CLERK, SERGEANT-AT-ARMS, DOORKEEPER, POSTMASTER.)

ORDER.

"The Speaker shall preserve order and decorum; may speak to points of order in preference to other members, rising from his seat for that purpose; and shall decide questions of order, subject to an appeal to the House by any two members; on which appeal no member shall speak more than once, unless by leave of the House."—*Rule* 2. [The "questions of order" here mentioned relate to motions or propositions, their application or relevancy, &c.]

Speaker shall preserve.

Appeal on questions of.

"If any member, in speaking or otherwise, transgress the rules of the House, the Speaker shall, or any member may, call to order, in which case the member so called to order shall immediately sit down, unless permitted to explain, and the House shall, if appealed to, decide on the case, but without debate. If there be no appeal, the decision of the Chair shall be submitted to. If the decision be in favor of the member called to order, he shall be at liberty to proceed; *if otherwise, he shall not be permitted to proceed, in case any member object,*

Where member called to, for transgressing rules in debate, or for indecorum.

without leave of the House ; and, if the case require it, he shall be liable to the censure of the House."—*Rule* 61.

Words to be taken down, and must be excepted to before other business occurs.

"If a member be called to order for words spoken in debate, the person calling him to order shall repeat the words excepted to, and they shall be taken down in writing at the Clerk's table ; and no member shall be held to answer, or be subject to the censure of the House, for words spoken in debate, if any other member has spoken, or other business has intervened, after the words spoken and before exception to them shall have been taken."—*Rule* 62.

Committee cannot punish breach of.

"A committee cannot punish a breach of order in the House. It can only rise and report it to the House, who may proceed to punish."—*Manual, p.* 94 ; *Journal*, 1, 28, *p.* 846.

During a division Speaker to decide question of, peremptorily.

"If any difficulty arises in point of order during the division, the Speaker is to decide peremptorily, subject to the future censure of the House if irregular."—*Manual, p.* 122.

Speaker may call member by name.

"If repeated calls do not produce order, the Speaker may call by his name any member obstinately persisting in irregularity."—*Manual, p.* 82.

Sergeant-at-Arms shall aid in the enforcement of.

It shall be the duty of the Sergeant-at-Arms to attend the House during its sittings, *to aid in the enforcement of order under the direction of the Speaker.*

Pending election of Speaker, the Clerk shall preserve.

"Pending the election of a Speaker, the Clerk shall preserve order and decorum, and shall decide all questions of order that may arise, subject to appeal to the House."—*Rule* 146.

(See BUSINESS, DAILY ORDER OF.)
(See APPEAL.)
(See SPECIAL ORDERS.)

PACIFIC RAILROAD, COMMITTEE ON THE

When appointed and number of.

Duties of.

There shall be appointed at the commencement of each Congress a Committee on the Pacific Railroad, to consist of eleven members.—*Rule* 74. It shall be the duty of the said committee to take into consideration all such petitions and matters and things relative to railroads or telegraph lines between the Mississippi Valley and the

Pacific Coast as shall be presented or shall come in question and be referred to them by the House, and to report their opinion thereon, together with such proposition relative thereto as to them shall seem expedient.—*Rule* 150.

PAPERS.

"The request of a conference must always be by the house which is possessed of the papers."—*Manual, p.* 124. Conference must be asked by house possessed of.

"In all cases of conference asked after a vote of disagreement, &c., the conferees of the house asking it are to leave the papers with the conferees of the other."—*Manual, p.* 129. With whom to be left in case of conference.

[Papers heretofore referred may be withdrawn from the files for the purpose of reference, but not for any other purpose without the consent of the House. (See PETITIONS.) Withdrawal of.

All papers accompanying Senate bills are restored to that body as soon as the bill passes the House, and should the bill fail to pass the House, then at the close of the Congress.] Accompanying Senate bills.

PARLIAMENTARY PRACTICE.

"The rules of parliamentary practice comprised in Jefferson's Manual shall govern the House in all cases to which they are applicable, and in which they are not inconsistent with the Standing Rules and Orders of the House and Joint Rules of the Senate and House of Representatives."—*Rule* 144. Jefferson's Manual to govern where applicable and not inconsistent with rules.

PATENTS, COMMITTEE ON.

There shall be appointed, at the commencement of each Congress, a Committee on Patents, to consist of five members.—*Rule* 74. When appointed and number of.

"It shall be the duty of the Committee on Patents to consider all subjects relating to patents which may be referred to them, and report their opinion thereon, together with such propositions relative thereto as may seem to them expedient."—*Rule* 95. Its duties.

PAY OF MEMBERS.

(See COMPENSATION.)

PERSONAL EXPLANATION.

Member may yield floor for.

While a member is occupying the floor he may yield it to another for explanation of the pending measure, as well as for personal explanation.—*Journal*, 1, 32, *p.* 524.

PERSONALITY.

Shall be avoided.

Every member "shall confine himself to the question under debate, and avoid personality."—*Rule* 57.

(See also DEBATE and DISORDER.)

PETITIONS.

Shall pass free in the mails.

Petitions to either branch of Congress shall pass free in the mails.—*Stat. at Large, Vol. XII, p.* 708.

How presented and referred.

"Members having petitions and memorials to present may hand them to the Clerk, indorsing the same with their names, and the reference or disposition to be made thereof; and such petitions and memorials shall be entered on the Journal, subject to the control and direction of the Speaker; and if any petition or memorial be so handed in, which, in the judgment of the Speaker, is excluded by the rules, the same shall be returned to the member from whom it was received."—*Rule* 131.

Only regular mode of presenting.

How ordered to be printed.

[There is now no other mode of presenting petitions prescribed by the rules, the old rule for presentation in the House having been rescinded December 12, 1853; and when a member desires to have a petition printed, it can only be done by unanimous consent, by a suspension of the rules, or by submitting a resolution to that effect when resolutions are in order.]

What to be referred to Court of Claims.

By the act of March 3, 1863, it is provided that all petitions and bills praying or providing for the satisfaction of private claims against the Government, founded upon any law of Congress, or upon any regulation of an executive Department, or upon any contract, express or implied, with the Government, shall, unless otherwise ordered by resolution of the House, be transmitted by the Clerk, with all the accompanying documents, to the Court of Claims.—*Stat. at Large, Vol. XII, p.* 765.

[Memorials and resolutions from State legislatures can be presented in order in the manner above described for "petitions and memorials;" and when it is desired to have them printed, they may be presented when bills on leave and resolutions are called for under *Rule* 130.]

Memorials, &c., from State legislatures.

It is the practice under this rule to allow members to withdraw from the files of the House petitions and other papers presented at former sessions, and refer them, as in the case of new petitions; and, in order to have it done, it is only necessary for the member to notify the Clerk of his desire by written memorandum.

Withdrawal of old papers for reference to a committee.

Where a member desires to withdraw papers from the files for the purpose of reference in the Senate, or to one of the executive Departments, it is usual for the House to give its unanimous consent whenever asked. But where the withdrawal is desired for the purpose of returning to the petitioner, the consent of the House is usually given, with a proviso that copies be left on file. And in all cases of withdrawal, except for reference to one of its committees, the consent of the House must first be had.

Withdrawal for reference to Senate or a Department.

Withdrawal to return to petitioner.

Withdrawals generally.

Where a member desires the fact of the presentation of a petition by him under the 131st *Rule* to appear in the newspapers of the day, he should furnish the reporters of such newspapers with a memorandum of the same; otherwise, as the proceeding does not occur in open house, no note will be taken of it.

Where member desires that presentation of, appear in newspapers.

[Petitions, &c., thus presented, are, as required by the rule, entered on the Journal, but that portion of the Journal is never read in the House.]

Petition part of Journal not read in House.

"The name of the member who presents a petition or memorial shall be inserted on the Journal."—*Rule* 32.

Name of member presenting entered on Journal.

"All business before committees of the House at the end of one session shall be resumed at the commence-

Undisposed of at end of one session

to be resumed the next. ment of the next session of the same Congress, as if no adjournment had taken place."—*Rule* 136.

PLURALITY.

Shall prevail on second ballot for members of a committee. "All committees shall be appointed by the Speaker unless otherwise specially directed by the House, in which case they shall be appointed by ballot; and if upon such ballot the number required shall not be elected by a majority of the votes given, the House shall proceed to a second ballot, in which a plurality of votes shall prevail," &c.—*Rule* 67.

Election of Speaker by. [This is the only case, under the rules, where a plurality of votes may prevail; and as the appointment of committees by the Speaker is almost universally conceded, it can very rarely occur. There have been two occasions, however, where, prior to the adoption of the rules, the election of Speaker has been effected by a plurality vote. But in both instances a resolution providing for such election by a plurality was first adopted by a majority of votes, and afterwards it was declared by a majority vote that the person who received such plurality was duly elected.—*Journals*, 1, 31, *pp.* 156, 163; 1, 34, *pp.* 429, 430, 444.]

POINTS OF ORDER.

(See APPEAL and ORDER.)

POSTAGE.

No allowance to members on account of. By the act of January 31, 1873, it is provided that no compensation or allowance shall now or hereafter be made to Senators, Members, and Delegates of the House of Representatives on account of postage.—*Stat. at Large, Vol. XVII, p.* 421.

POSTMASTER.

Election of, term of office, official oath. There shall be elected at the commencement of each Congress, to continue in office until his successor is appointed, a postmaster, who shall take an oath "for the true and faithful discharge of the duties of his office, to the best of his knowledge and abilities, and to keep the secrets of the House;" his appointees shall be subject to the approval of the Speaker.—*Rule* 10. Appointees of.

He is also required, by the act of July 2, 1862, to take an additional oath.—(See OATH.) Additional oath.

The Postmaster shall superintend the post office kept in the Capitol for the accommodation of the members.—*Rule* 28. Duty of.

By the act of July 15, 1870, (*Stat. at Large, Vol. XVI, p.* 365,) it is made his duty to make out a full and complete account of all the property belonging to the Government in his possession on the first day of each regular session, and at the expiration of his term of service. Shall make return of Government property in his possession.

[The Postmaster, with the aid of his assistants, messengers, &c., delivers promptly, upon the arrival of the mails, all mail matter received for members, either at his office or at their lodgings; also delivers at the city post office all mail matter deposited in his office by members; he also delivers at their lodgings all books ordered from the library by members, &c., &c.] Other duties of.

POST OFFICE AND POST ROADS, COMMITTEE ON THE.

There shall be appointed, at the commencement of each Congress, a Committee on the Post Office and Post Roads, to consist of eleven members.—*Rule* 74. When appointed, and number of.

"It shall be the duty of the Committee on the Post Office and Post Roads to take into consideration all such petitions and matters or things touching the post office and post roads as shall be presented, or shall come in question, and be referred to them by the House; and to report their opinion thereon, together with such propositions relative thereto as to them shall seem expedient."—*Rule* 81. Its duties.

POSTPONE, MOTION TO.

"When a question is under debate, no motion shall be received but Order in which question on, to be put.

to adjourn,
to lie on the table,
for the previous question,
to postpone to a day certain,
to commit or amend,
to postpone indefinitely;

Not to be repeated on same day and at same stage.

which several motions shall have precedence in the order in which they are arranged; and no motion to postpone to a day certain, to commit, or to postpone indefinitely, being decided, shall be again allowed on the same day and at the same stage of the bill or proposition."—*Rule* 42.

When postponed indefinitely, not to be taken up during session.

"When a question is postponed indefinitely, the same shall not be acted upon again during the session."—*Rule* 142.

Of order of business requires two-thirds vote.

"The order of business, as established by the rules, shall not be postponed or changed, except by a vote of at least two-thirds of the members present."—*Rule* 145.

Debate on.

[The motion to postpone to a day certain, under the practice, admits of but a very limited debate; but on a motion to postpone indefinitely the whole question is open to debate. When the consideration of a subject is postponed to a particular day, upon the arrival of that day it is entitled to be taken up, provided no question of privilege or other question of higher dignity be taken up. In the case of a report of a committee postponed to a day certain and a failure to consider it on that day, it becomes a report undisposed of, to be first considered when reports are in order. And where two or more reports are postponed to different days and are not reached on those days, they are to be considered in the order of the times to which they were postponed.]

Subject postponed, to be taken up when day arrives.

Reports of committees postponed, when considered.

Effect of previous question where motion to postpone is pending.

The effect of the previous question, if a motion to postpone is pending, shall be to bring the House to a vote upon such motion.—*Rule* 132.

POST ROUTES.

Bills for, not to be introduced under the rule.

A motion for leave to introduce a bill for the establishment or change of post routes and all propositions relating thereto, shall be referred under the rule, like petitions and other papers, to the appropriate committee.—*Rule* 115.

PREAMBLE.

Postponed until other parts of bill are gone through.

"When a bill is taken up in committee, or on its second reading, they postpone the preamble till the other parts of the bill are gone through. The reason is, that on consideration of the body of the bill, such alterations may therein be made as may also occasion the alteration of the preamble."—*Manual*, *p*. 90.

By *Rule* 107, in the consideration of bills committed to a Committee of the Whole House, the preamble is left to be last considered. In Committee of the Whole last considered.

[In the case of a resolution with a preamble, there is no difficulty as to the time at which the preamble is to be considered, nor in any case in Committee of the Whole; but in the House, in the case of a bill with a preamble, there is some uncertainty as to the particular stage in which the bill must be when it is proper to consider the preamble. It would seem that it might appropriately be done *after the bill has been ordered to be engrossed and read a third time, and before the third reading takes place.* By this course the bill can be engrossed either with or without the preamble, as the House shall have determined. But where a separate vote on the preamble is not asked for before the bill is read a third time, the preamble is considered as adopted.] At what particular stage of bill to be considered.

The preamble is not covered by the previous question ordered upon the passage of the resolution, but is itself subject to a separate demand of the previous question.—*Journal*, 1, 34, *p*. 1217. Subject to a separate demand of previous question.

PRESIDENT OF THE UNITED STATES.

"He shall from time to time give to the Congress information of the state of the Union, and recommend to their consideration such measures as he shall judge necessary and expedient; he may, on extraordinary occasions, convene both houses, or either of them, and, in case of disagreement between them with respect to the time of adjournment, he may adjourn them to such time as he shall think proper."—*Const.*, 2, 2, *p*. 18. Shall give information to Congress. May convene Congress. May adjourn Congress in case of disagreement.

"Every bill which shall have passed the House of Representatives and the Senate shall, before it becomes a law, be presented to the President of the United States; if he approve, he shall sign it; but if not, he shall return it, with his objections, to that house in which it shall have originated. * * * * If any bill shall not be Bills after passage to be presented to. His powers over them.

Must be returned in ten days.

returned by the President within ten days (Sundays excepted) after it shall have been presented to him, the same shall be a law, in like manner as if he had signed it, unless the Congress, by their adjournment, prevent its return, in which case it shall not be a law."—*Const.*, 1, 7, 10. There is a similar provision in regard to "every order, resolution, or vote to which the concurrence of the Senate and House of Representatives may be necessary, (except on a question of adjournment.")—*Ibid., pp.* 10, 11.

Joint orders, resolutions, and votes.

Where he fails to return a bill.

Where a House bill is allowed to become a law by the failure of the President to return it, it is usual for him to notify the House of that fact.—*Journals*, 2, 36, *pp.* 424, 480; *Stat. at Large, Vol. XII, pp.* 893, 898; *Journals*, 2, 39, *p.* 479, [and so also where he approves a bill, giving also the date of approval.] Messages from the President giving notice of bills approved shall be reported forthwith from the Clerk's desk.—*Rule* 158. And when an act has been approved by the President, the usual number of copies shall be printed for the use of the House.—*Rule* 157.

Where he approves a bill.

Where prevented by adjournment from returning a bill with his objections.

Where the President is prevented by adjournment from returning a bill with his objections, it is usual for him at the next session to communicate to the house where it originated his reasons for not approving it.—*Journals*, 2, 12, *p.* 544; 1, 30, *p.* 82; 2, 35, *p.* 151.

(See VETO.)

Bills to be enrolled before presented to.

By Joint Rule 6 it is provided that, before a bill which shall have originated in the House is presented to the President, "it shall be duly enrolled on parchment by the Clerk of the House of Representatives."

Committee present bills to.

Having been examined and signed by the Speaker and presiding officer of the Senate, the bill shall be presented by the Joint Committee on Enrolled Bills to the President for his approbation, and shall be entered on the Journal of each house. The said committee shall report the day of presentation to the President; which time shall also be carefully entered on the Journal of each house.—*Joint Rule* 9.

Time of presentation to, to be reported, &c.

No bill to be presented to, on last day of session.

"No bill or resolution that shall have passed the House of Representatives and the Senate shall be presented to the President of the United States for his approbation on the last day of the session."—*Joint Rule* 17. [This Joint Rule is necessarily suspended near the close of every session.]

Joint address to.

"When the Senate and House of Representatives shall judge it proper to make a joint address to the President, it shall be presented to him in his audience-chamber by the President of the Senate, in the presence of the Speaker and both houses."—*Joint Rule* 11.

Calls for information from.

"A proposition requesting information from the President of the United States, even where reported from a committee—*Journal*, 1, 31, *p.* 723—shall lie on the table one day for consideration, unless otherwise ordered by the unanimous consent of the House; and all such propositions shall be taken up for consideration in the order they were presented immediately after reports are called for from select committees, and when adopted, the Clerk shall cause the same to be delivered."—*Rule* 53.

To be delivered by the Clerk.

Form of call on.

[The form of resolution contemplated by this rule, as sanctioned by long usage, is: "*Resolved*, That the President of the United States be requested to inform (or communicate to) this House, if not incompatible with the public interest," &c.]

(See MESSAGES FROM THE PRESIDENT.)

Opening and counting of votes for.

Art. 12, *Amendments to the Const.*, requires that the certificate of electoral votes in the respective States for President and Vice-President shall be opened by the President of the Senate in the presence of the Senate and House of Representatives, and the votes shall then be counted. And by the act of March 1, 1792—*Stat. at Large, Vol. I, p.* 239—Congress is required to be in session on the second Wednesday in February succeeding the meeting of the electors, and said certificates shall then be opened and the votes counted.

To be opened and counted on second Wednesday in February.

Examination of electoral votes, &c.,

"The two houses shall assemble in the hall of the House of Representatives at the hour of one o'clock p. m. on the second Wednesday in February next succeeding the meeting of the electors of President and Vice-President of the United States, and the President of the Senate shall be their presiding officer; one teller shall be appointed on the part of the Senate, and two on the part of the House of Representatives, to whom shall be handed, as they are opened by the President of the Senate, the certificates of the electoral votes; and said tellers, having read the same in the presence and hearing of the two houses thus assembled, shall make a list of the votes as they shall appear from the said certificate; and the votes having been counted, the result of the same shall be delivered to the President of the Senate, who shall thereupon announce the state of the vote and the names of the persons, if any, elected, which announcement shall be deemed a sufficient declaration of the persons elected President and Vice-President of the United States, and, together with a list of the votes, be entered on the Journal of the two houses.

"If, upon the reading of any such certificate by the tellers, any question shall arise in regard to counting the votes therein certified, the same having been stated by the presiding officer, the Senate shall thereupon withdraw, and said question shall be submitted to that body for its decision; and the Speaker of the House of Representatives shall, in like manner, submit said question to the House of Representatives for its decision. And no questions shall be decided affirmatively, and no vote objected to shall be counted, except by the concurrent votes of the two houses; which being obtained, the two houses shall immediately reassemble, and the presiding officer shall then announce the decision of the question submitted; and upon any such question there shall be no debate in either house. Any other question pertinent to the object for which the two houses are assembled may be submitted and determined in like manner.

"At such joint meeting of the two houses seats shall be provided as follows: for the President of the Senate the 'Speaker's chair;' for the Speaker a chair immediately upon his left; for the Senators, in the body of the hall upon the right of the presiding officer; for the Representatives, in the body of the hall not occupied by the Senators; for the tellers, Secretary of the Senate, and Clerk of the House of Representatives, at the Clerk's desk; for the other officers of the two houses, in front of the Clerk's desk and upon either side of the Speaker's platform.

"Such joint meeting shall not be dissolved until the electoral votes are all counted and the result declared; and no recess shall be taken unless a question shall have arisen in regard to counting any of such votes, in which case it shall be competent for either house, acting separately in the manner hereinbefore provided, to direct a recess not beyond the next day, at the hour of one o'clock p. m."—*Joint Rule* 22.

[After the declaration of the persons elected President and Vice-President, a joint committee, consisting of two members of the House and one Senator, are appointed to wait on the persons elected and inform them thereof.]

Committee appointed to notify of election.

It is further provided by the 12th *Article of Amendment to Const.*, that if no person have a majority of the electoral votes for President, "then, from the persons having the highest numbers, not exceeding three, on the list of those voted for as President, the House of Representatives shall choose immediately, by ballot, the President. But in choosing the President the votes shall be taken by States, the representation from each State having one vote; a quorum for this purpose shall consist of a member or members from two-thirds of the States, and a majority of all the States shall be necessary to a choice. And if the House of Representatives shall not choose a President, whenever the right of choice shall devolve upon them, before the fourth day of March next following, then the Vice-President shall act as President, as in the case of the death or other constitutional disability of the President."

When choice of shall devolve on the House.

Votes, how taken.

Quorum.

If House does not choose before the 4th of March.

[In anticipation of the choice of President devolving upon it, the House of Representatives of the 2d session Eighteenth Congress adopted a set of rules for its government in said election.—*Journal*, 2, 18, *pp*. 212 to 215. For the subsequent proceedings of the House in conducting said election, see same *Journal*, *pp*. 220, 221, 222.]

Rules of the House in the election of.

PREVIOUS QUESTION.

Order in which motion for, to be put.

"When a question is under debate, no motion shall be received but

to adjourn,
to lie on the table,
for the previous question,
to postpone to a day certain,
to commit or amend,
to postpone indefinitely;

which several motions shall have precedence in the order in which they are arranged."—*Rule* 42.

Form of.

Must be seconded by a majority.

Its effects.

The previous question shall be in this form: "Shall the main question be now put?" It shall only be admitted when demanded by a majority of the members present; and its effect shall be to put an end to all debate, (except that the member reporting the measure under consideration may close the debate—*Journal*, 1, 31, *p*. 1056—and the every-day practice since,) and to bring the House to a direct vote upon a motion to commit, if such motion shall have been made; and if this motion does not prevail, then upon amendments reported by a committee, if any; then upon pending amendments, and then upon the main question. But its only effect, if a motion to postpone is pending, shall be to bring the House to a vote upon such motion. Whenever the House shall refuse to order the main question, the consideration of the subject shall be resumed as though no motion for the previous question had been made. The House may also, at any time, on motion seconded by a majority of the members present, close all debate upon a pending amendment, or an amendment thereto, and cause the question to be put thereon; and this shall not preclude any further amendment or debate upon the bill. A call of the House shall not be in order after the previous question is seconded, unless it shall appear, upon an actual count by the Speaker, that no quorum is present.—*Rule* 132.

May operate upon a pending amendment only.

Call of the House not in order after a second, unless no quorum present.

Right of member reporting not affected by order of.

The right of the member reporting the pending measure to close the debate is never denied him, even after the previous question is ordered.—*Journal*, 1, 31, *p.* 1056.

[But if, after having occupied part of his hour in closing the debate, he moves the previous question, he is then only entitled to occupy the floor for the remaining portion of the hour.]

"On a previous question there shall be no debate. All incidental questions of order arising after a motion is made for the previous question, and pending such motion, shall be decided, whether on appeal or otherwise, without debate."—*Rule* 133.

No debate on, nor on incidental questions of order.

It is in order, pending the demand for the previous question on the passage of a bill, to move a reconsideration of the vote on its engrossment.—*Journal*, 2, 27, *p.* 1175. [But such motion is not debatable under the practice which has prevailed for many years.]

Reconsideration of a preceding vote may be moved pending demand for.

The yeas and nays cannot be taken on seconding the demand for the previous question.—*Journal*, 2, 19, *p.* 493.

No yeas and nays on seconding.

The effect of a negative vote on the question, "Shall the main question be now put?" is to cause the House to resume the consideration of the subject as though no motion for the previous question had been made.—*Rule* 132.

Effect of negative vote on ordering main question.

A member is not debarred from moving the previous question because he has spoken once.—*Journal*, 1, 24, *p.* 1401.

Member who has already spoken may move.

Where a vote taken under the operation of the previous question is reconsidered, the question is then divested of the previous question, and is open to debate and amendment.—*Journal*, 1, 27, *p.* 129; 1, 33, *p.* 127. [These decisions apply only to cases where the previous question was fully exhausted, by votes taken on all the questions covered by it, before the motion to reconsider was made. In any other case the pendency of the previous question would preclude debate.]

Where a vote taken under the operation of, is reconsidered.

"It is not in order to move a reconsideration of the vote on ordering the main question when it is partly executed."—*Journal*, 1, 31, *pp.* 1101, 1398.

Not in order to reconsider, when partly executed.

The previous question may be moved on a resolution submitted under a call of the States, and thus prevent the debate which, under the rules, requires it to lie over. —*Journal*, 1, 26, *p.* 1067; 1, 27, *p.* 429; 1, 30, *p.* 326.

May be moved on a resolution on resolution day.

Is exhausted by an affirmative vote on reference. The previous question is exhausted by an *affirmative* vote on a motion to refer, and upon a reconsideration of said vote the question stands divested of the previous question.—*Journal*, 3, 34, *p*. 452.

Motion to recommit not in order after ordered. After the previous question is ordered, it is not in order to entertain a motion to recommit.—*Journal*, 1, 29, *p*. 643.

Motion for, cannot be laid on table. A motion for the previous question cannot be laid on the table.—*Journal*, 2, 29, *p*. 252.

Does not cut off instructions. The previous question has not the effect of cutting off instructions previously moved in connection with a motion to commit.—*Journal*, 1, 31, *p*. 1394.

Effect of, on question of order, motion to reconsider, and to postpone. [Under the practice of the House, if a question of order or a motion to reconsider is pending when the previous question is moved, when ordered it applies only to them, and is exhausted with the vote upon them; so, too, by the express language of *Rule* 132, in the case of a motion to postpone.]

No modification after second of. After the previous question has been seconded, it is not competent for the mover to modify his proposition.—

Nor withdrawal. *Journal*, 1, 31, *p*. 1397. [Nor, according to the practice, can he withdraw it after a second ;] but he may withdraw it while the House is dividing on the question of a second. —*Journal*, 2, 29, *p*. 241.

May be moved at same time with a resolution. It is competent for a member to submit a resolution, and at the same time move the previous question thereon. —*Journal*, 1, 28, *p*. 558.

Applies to questions of privilege. The previous question applies to a question of privilege equally with any other question.—*Journal*, 2, 27, *pp*. 573, 576; 1, 28, *p*. 882.

After second, not in order to go into Committee of the Whole. [After the previous question has been seconded upon a pending proposition, it is not then in order to entertain the motion to go into Committee of the Whole.]

PRINTING, PUBLIC.

Superintendent to have executed. The Superintendent of Public Printing is directed, by the joint resolution of June 23, 1860, to have executed the printing and binding authorized by the Senate and House, the executive and judicial Departments, and the Court of Claims. He is also required to take charge of, and is held responsible for, all manuscripts and other matter to be printed, engraved, or lithographed, and cause the same to be promptly executed. On and after March 4, 1861, all the printing and binding, and all blank books ordered by Congress, or by either house of Congress, shall be done and executed under said Superintendent; but no printing and binding other than that ordered by Congress or the heads of Departments, as aforesaid, shall be executed in his office. It shall be the duty of said Superintendent to receive from the Clerk of the House all matter ordered by the House to be printed or bound, and when the same is executed, see that the volumes or sheets are promptly delivered to the officer authorized to receive the same, whose receipt therefor shall be a sufficient voucher by the Superintendent of their delivery.

To be promptly executed.

None other than, to be executed in Government office.

Superintendent shall receive and deliver work.

Whenever any maps, charts, diagrams, views, or other engraving shall be required to illustrate any document ordered to be printed by either house of Congress, such engraving shall be procured by the Superintendent of Printing, under the direction and supervision of the Committee on Printing of the house ordering the same.

Engraving to be procured under the direction of said committee.

The condition of the printing, binding, and engraving, the amount and cost of paper, printing, binding, &c., a statement of the bids for materials, and other information in regard to the matters connected therewith, shall be reported to Congress on the first day of each session, or as soon as may be thereafter, by the Superintendent. —*Stat. at Large, Vol. XII, pp.* 117, 118, 119, 120.

The condition, cost, &c., of, to be reported to Congress.

By the act of March 3, 1873, it is provided that, until a contract is made, the debates shall be printed by the Congressional Printer, under the direction of the Joint Committee on Public Printing on the part of the Senate.—*Stat. at Large, Vol. XVII, p.* 510.

Debates to be printed by Congressional Printer.

Where extra copies of documents of the size of 250 pages and upwards are ordered to be printed, they shall be bound as directed by the Committee on Printing on the part of the House, at a cost not to exceed 12½ cents per volume.—*Stat. at Large, Vol. X, p.* 190. In no case shall more than 1,550 copies of any document be printed, unless extra copies be ordered; and the said regular number (1,550) shall be distributed by the officers of the house first ordering the printing of the same, to the same

What extra documents to be bound.

Not more than 1,550 copies to be printed.

How distributed.

persons and in the same manner as such numbers heretofore ordered by both houses have been distributed.—*Stat. at Large, Vol. XI, p.* 422.

Motions to print extra copies.

All motions to print extra copies of any bill, report, or other document, shall be referred to the members of the Committee on Printing from the house in which the same may be made.—*Stat. at Large, Vol. X, p.* 34.

Of extra documents, the cost of which exceeds $500.

All propositions originating in either house for printing extra copies of public documents, the cost of which shall exceed $500, shall be by concurrent resolution, and all such resolutions shall upon their transmission from either house be immediately referred to the Committee on Printing of the house to which they are sent.—*Stat. at Large, vol. XVI, p.* 233.

Bills passed in one house, and ordered to be printed in the other.

"When bills which have passed one house are ordered to be printed in the other, a greater number of copies shall not be printed than may be necessary for the use of the house making the order."—*Joint Rule* 18.

At what stage House bills are usually printed.

[The usual stage at which House bills are ordered to be printed is upon their report from a committee and their commitment to a Committee of the Whole.]

Maps not to be printed without special order.

"Maps accompanying documents shall not be printed under the general order to print, without the special direction of the House."—*Rule* 139.

Superintendent to be furnished with copies of documents accompanying reports of heads of Departments.

By the joint resolution of March 3, 1863, it is provided that, instead of furnishing manuscript copies to each house of Congress, the heads of the several Departments of Government be required to furnish the Superintendent of Public Printing with copies of the documents usually accompanying their annual reports, on or before the first day of November of each year; whose duty it shall be to print, in addition to the number now required by law, two thousand copies for the use of the Senate, and five thousand for the use of the House, in volumes (bound in the usual manner) of convenient size, and to deliver the same to the proper officers of each house, respectively, on or before the third Monday in December of each year.

Number to be printed for House, and when to be delivered.

Statement of imports and exports, when to be

The Secretary of the Treasury is required to furnish to the Superintendent of Public Printing, on or before

November 1st of each year, a condensed statement of exports and imports, who shall print and bind as soon thereafter as practicable the usual number (1,550) for the two houses, three hundred for the Treasury Department, two thousand for the Senate, and six thousand one hundred and fifty for the use of the members of the House.

furnished and printed.

The form and style in which the printing ordered by either house of Congress shall be executed, and the size of type to be used, shall be determined by the Superintendent of Public Printing, having proper regard to economy and workmanship.—*Stat. at Large, Vol. XII, pp.* 825, 826.

Form and style to be determined by Superintendent.

(See PUBLIC DOCUMENTS, BILLS, PRINTING, COMMITTEE ON.)

By the act of June 25, 1864, it is provided "that hereafter, instead of furnishing manuscript copies of the documents usually accompanying their annual reports to each house of Congress, the heads of the several Departments of Government shall transmit them, or or before the first day of November in each year, to the Superintendent of Public Printing, who shall cause to be printed the usual number, and, in addition thereto, one thousand copies for the use of the Senate and two thousand copies for the use of the House of Representatives. And that it shall be the duty of the Joint Committee on Printing to appoint some competent person, who shall edit and select such portions of the documents so placed in their hands as shall, in the judgment of the committee, be desirable for popular distribution, and to prepare an alphabetical index to the same. (See *Act of July* 27, 1866, *post.*)

Heads of Departments to send manuscript copies to Superintendent.

"That it shall be the duty of the heads of the several Departments of Government to furnish the Superintendent of Public Printing with copies of their respective reports on or before the third Monday in November in each year.

When reports to be furnished.

"That it shall be the duty of the Superintendent of Public Printing to print the President's message, the reports of the heads of Departments, and the abridge-

President's message and other documents, number and distribution of.

ment of accompanying documents prepared under the direction of the Joint Committee of Public Printing, suitably bound; and that, in addition to the number now required by law, and unless otherwise ordered by either house of Congress, it shall be his duty to print ten thousand copies of the same for the use of the Senate, and twenty-five thousand copies for the use of the House, and to deliver the same to the proper officer of each house, respectively, on or before the third Wednesday in December, following the assembling of Congress, or as soon thereafter as practicable; and further, it shall also be the duty of the said Superintendent to cause to be printed and stitched in paper covers twenty-five hundred copies of the annual reports of the executive Departments for the use of said Departments, respectively; and also one thousand copies of the reports of the Commissioner of the General Land Office, Commissioner of Pensions, Commissioner of the Internal Revenue, and such number of the report of the Commissioner of Indian Affairs, to be bound, not exceeding three thousand copies, as may be directed by the Secretary of the Interior, for their use, respectively; and also five hundred copies of the reports of the Superintendent of the Washington Aqueduct, Architect of the Capitol Extension, Metropolitan Police Board, Third Auditor of the Treasury, and of the Insane Asylum, Columbian Institute, and Commissioner of Public Buildings, respectively, for their use; and one hundred copies of the report of the Bureau of Engineers, for the use of said bureau. And he shall not print any greater number of said reports unless otherwise directed by either house of Congress.

Commercial Relations, number and distribution of.

"That seven thousand copies of the 'Commercial Relations,' annually prepared under the direction of the Secretary of State, be printed and distributed as follows, viz: the usual number (one thousand five hundred and fifty) for the houses of Congress, four hundred and fifty for the State Department, two thousand for the use of the members of the Senate, and three thousand for the use of the members of the House.

Offers for carrying mails not to be printed without special order.

"That the annual report of the Postmaster General of offers received and contracts for conveying the mails, in compliance with the twenty-fourth and twenty-fifth sections of the act of Congress approved July 2, 1836, be no longer printed, unless specially ordered by either house of Congress; and that such portion of the abovementioned act as authorized the said publication be, and the same is hereby, repealed.

Secretary of Senate to furnish copies of laws to be printed and distributed.

"That from and after the passage of this act it shall be the duty of the Secretary of the Senate to furnish the Superintendent of Public Printing with correct copies of all laws and joint resolutions as soon as possible after their approval by the President of the United States, and that the Superintendent shall immediately cause to be printed, separately, the usual number for the use of the two houses of Congress; and in addition thereto, he shall cause to be printed and bound, at the close of each session of Congress, three thousand copies thereof for the use of the Senate, and ten thousand copies for the use of the House, with a complete alphabetical index, prepared under the direction of the Joint Committee on Public Printing.

Lithographing and engraving.

"That all lithographing and engraving, where the probable total cost of the maps or plates illustrating or accompanying any one work exceeds two hundred and fifty dollars, shall be awarded to the lowest and best bidder for the interests of the Government, due regard being paid to the execution of the work, after due advertisement by the Superintendent of Public Printing, under the direction of the Joint Committee on Printing: *Provided*, That the Joint Committee on Public Printing be authorized to empower the Superintendent of Public Printing to make immediate contracts for engraving, whenever, in their opinion, the exigencies of the public service will not justify waiting for advertisement and award."—*Stat. at Large, Vol. XIII, pp.* 184–6.

Of envelopes, letter or note sheets on steel, &c., prohibited.

By the act of July 12, 1870, it is provided that hereafter no envelopes, letter or note sheets, for the use of Congress, &c., shall be printed from steel or copper plate, or by lithographing.—*Stat. at Large, Vol. XVI, p.* 233.

Where extra copies are desired by any person.

"That whenever any person may desire extra copies of any document printed at the Government Printing

Office by authority of law, and shall notify the Superintendent of Public Printing of the number of copies desired previous to its being put to press, and shall pay, in advance, the estimated cost thereof (with ten per centum added thereto—*Stat. at Large, vol. XVI, p.* 478.) to said Superintendent, the Superintendent shall be authorized, under the direction of the Joint Committee on Public Printing, to furnish such extra copies; and the money so received, together with moneys received by him from the sales of paper shavings and imperfections, shall be deposited in the Treasury of the United States to the credit of the appropriations for public printing, binding, and paper, respectively, as designated by said Superintendent; and, further, the Secretary of the Treasury is hereby directed to cause the moneys heretofore deposited by said Superintendent in the Treasury of the United States, being the proceeds of sales of paper shavings and imperfections, to be placed to the credit of the appropriations aforesaid, which said several sums of money shall be subject to the requisition of said Superintendent in the manner now prescribed by law.

Papers relating to foreign affairs.

"That whenever papers relating to foreign affairs shall be communicated to Congress accompanying the annual message of the President, it shall be the duty of the Superintendent of Public Printing to cause to be printed and bound, in addition to the usual number, four thousand copies for the use of the members of the Senate, seven thousand copies for the use of the members of the House of Representatives, and such number for the Executive Department as the President shall direct. (See *Act of July* 27, 1866, *post.*)

Form and style of printing and binding

"That the forms and style in which the printing or binding ordered by any of the Departments shall be executed, the materials and size of type to be used, shall be determined by the Superintendent of Public Printing, having proper regard to economy, workmanship, and the purposes for which the work is needed.

"That all laws or parts of laws, joint resolutions or parts of joint resolutions, conflicting with the above provisions, be, and they are hereby, repealed."—*Stat. at Large, Vol. XIII, pp.* 184, 185, 186.

By the act of March 14, 1864, it is provided that no printing or binding shall be done, or blank books procured, for the House except on the written order of the Clerk.—*Stat. at Large, Vol. XIII, p.* 25.

To be done only on written order.

By the joint resolution of February 3, 1864, it is provided that seven hundred copies of every bill or joint resolution ordered to be printed shall be furnished, unless some other number be specially required.—*Stat. at Large, Vol. XIII, p.* 402.

Number of bills to be printed.

By the joint resolution of February 14, 1865, it is provided that the Congressional Directory shall be compiled under the direction of the Joint Committee on Public Printing, and published by the Superintendent of Public Printing, the first edition of each session to be ready for distribution within one week after the commencement thereof.—*Stat. at Large, Vol. XIII, p.* 568.

Congressional Directory.

By the act of July 27, 1866, it is provided "that hereafter it shall be the duty of the Superintendent of Public Printing, in place of the reports of the executive Departments ordered by the act of June 25, 1864, to cause to be printed and bound twenty-five hundred copies of the annual reports of the executive Departments, with such accompanying documents as the heads of those Departments may respectively select, but not to exceed three hundred pages, for the use of said Departments respectively.

Annual reports of executive Departments.

Whenever papers relating to foreign affairs shall be communicated to Congress, accompanying the annual message of the President, it shall be the duty of the Superintendent of Public Printing to cause to be printed and bound, in addition to the usual number, two thousand copies for the use of the members of the Senate, four thousand copies for the use of the House, and two thousand five hundred copies for the use of the State Department, in place of the numbers ordered by the act of June 25, 1864.

Papers relating to foreign affairs.

In the publication of the report of the Secretary of the Navy, the detailed statement of the offers for supplies and of articles embraced in each class under contract shall be omitted, and in lieu thereof the Secretary of the Navy

Report of the Secretary of the Navy.

shall prepare and submit with his report a schedule embracing the offers by classes, indicating such as have been accepted.

Estimates of paper required to be submitted.

It shall be the duty of the Superintendent of Public Printing, at the commencement of each session of Congress, to submit to the Joint Committee on Printing estimates of the quantity of paper of all descriptions which will, in his opinion, be required for the execution of the public printing during the coming year. The Joint Committee on Printing shall then fix upon a standard of paper for the different descriptions of congressional and executive printing, and it shall be the duty of the Superintendent of Public Printing, under the direction of the Joint Committee on Printing, to advertise in only two newspapers published in each of the cities of New York, Cincinnati, Boston, Philadelphia, Baltimore, and Washington, for sealed proposals to furnish the Government of the United States with paper, of the quality and in the quantity specified in the advertisements, and it shall be the duty of the Superintendent to furnish samples of the standard papers adopted by the committee to applicants therefor; the said sealed proposals to be opened before, and the award of contracts to be made by, the Joint Committee on Printing, to the lowest and best bidder for the interest of the Government: *Provided*, That the advertisement for sealed proposals for furnishing paper shall designate the minimum portion of each particular quality of paper required for either three months, six months, or one year, as the Joint Committee on Printing may determine; but when the minimum portion so specified shall exceed in any case one thousand reams, the advertisement shall state that proposals will be received for one thousand reams or more: *And provided further*, That no proposals shall be considered by the Joint Committee on Printing unless accompanied by satisfactory evidence that the person or persons making said proposals are manufacturers of or dealers in the description of paper which they propose to furnish: *And provided further*, That in awarding contracts an equitable period of time for filling the same

Joint Committee to fix standard of paper.

Advertisements for proposals for paper.

Contracts to be awarded by Joint Committee.

shall be designated and allowed by the Joint Committee on Printing, without whose approval no contract shall be valid: *And provided further*, That it shall be the duty of the Superintendent of Public Printing to include in his annual report to Congress a detailed statement of all proposals made and contracts entered into for the purchase of paper.

Duty of Superintendent on delivery of paper.

It shall be the duty of the Superintendent of Public Printing to compare every lot of paper delivered by any contractor with the standard of quality, and also to see that it is of the weight contracted for, and to refuse to accept any paper from any contractor which does not conform to the standard of quality and is not of the stipulated weight. And in case of difference of opinion between the Superintendent of Public Printing and any contractor for paper with respect to its quality, the matter of difference shall be determined by the Joint Committee on Printing: *Provided*, That in default of any contractor to comply with his contract in furnishing the paper contracted for in the proper time, and of proper quality and weight, it shall be the duty of the Superintendent of Public Printing to report the same to the Joint Committee on Printing, if Congress is in session, or to the Secretary of the Interior, if during a recess of Congress, and he shall, under the direction of the Joint Committee on Printing, or of the Secretary of the Interior, as the case may be, enter into a new contract with the lowest and best bidder for the interest of the Government, among those whose proposals were rejected at the last opening of bids, or advertise for new proposals under the regulations before established; and during the interval which may thus be created, he shall, under the direction of the Joint Committee on Printing, or of the Secretary of the Interior, as above provided, purchase in open market, at the lowest market price, all such paper necessary for the public service. For any increase of cost to the Government in procuring a supply of paper for the use of the Government, the contractor or contractors in default, and his or their securities, shall be charged with and held responsible for the same, and shall be prosecuted upon their

When contractor is in default.

bond by the Solicitor of the Treasury, in the name of the United States, in the circuit court of the United States in the district in which the defaulting contractor resides; and to enable the Solicitor to do so, it shall be the duty of the Superintendent of Public Printing to report to him the default on its happening, with a full statement of all the facts in the case: *And provided further*, That the Joint Committee on Public Printing, or, during the recess of Congress, the Secretary of the Interior, be authorized to empower the Superintendent of Public Printing to make purchases of paper in open market at the lowest market price, whenever, in their opinion, the quantity is so small, or the want is so immediate, as not to justify advertisement for an award of contract therefor.

No greater number of reports to be printed, unless otherwise directed.

"All laws or parts of laws, joint resolutions or parts of resolutions conflicting with the above provisions, be, and they are hereby, repealed; nor shall the Superintendent of Public Printing print any greater number of the reports herein named, unless otherwise directed by either House of Congress."—*Stat. at Large, Vol. XIV, pp.* 305–6.

Report of the Postmaster-General.

By the joint resolution of December 20, 1867, (*Stat. at Large, Vol. XV, p.* 245,) it is provided that hereafter it shall be the duty of the Congressional Printer to cause to be printed and bound three thousand copies of the report of the Postmaster-General, instead of twenty-five hundred copies, as provided by the act approved July 27, 1866, and that so much of that act as conflicts with the above provision be, and is hereby, repealed; and this resolution shall apply to the report for the present year.

Office of Congressional Printer created, and that of Superintendent abolished.

By the act of February 22, 1867, provision is made for the election of a Congressional Printer by the Senate, upon whom are imposed the duties heretofore required of the Superintendent of Public Printing, and the latter office is thereby abolished.—*Stat. at Large, Vol. XIV, p.* 398.

Order by the executive Departments.

By the act of March 2, 1867, it is provided that all printing of any kind ordered by the executive Departments shall be executed by the Government Printer, when practicable; and if not, at such office as may be designated by the Clerk of the House of Representatives, at rates not exceeding the current rates for such printing.—*Stat. at Large, Vol. XIV, p.* 467. (See also CLERK OF THE HOUSE.)

By the act of July 20, 1868, it is provided that all necessary letter-press printing and book-binding, in all the Departments and Bureaus, shall be done and executed at the Government Printing Office, except registered bonds and written records, which may be bound as heretofore at the Departments.—*Stat. at Large, Vol. XV, p.* 111. For the Departments to be done at Government Office.

By the act of March 3, 1869, it is provided that all payments for public printing and binding not done at the Government Printing Office according to the provisions of the act of July 20, 1868, shall not be allowed by the accounting officers, and that no proposition for printing extra copies, the expense of which shall exceed the sum of $500, shall be considered by either House until the same shall have been referred to the Joint Committee on Printing, and ordered by concurrent resolution of the two Houses.—*Stat. at Large, Vol. XV, p.* 285. (See CONGRESSIONAL GLOBE.) No payments to be allowed for, where not done at Government Office. Extra copies exceeding in cost $500, must be ordered by concurrent resolution.

PRINTING, JOINT COMMITTEE ON.

"A committee, consisting of three members of the Senate and three members of the House of Representatives, shall be appointed by the President of the Senate and Speaker of the House, to be called the Joint Committee on the Public Printing. The said committee shall pass upon the accounts of the Superintendent of the Public Printing. Said committee shall have power to adopt such measures as may be deemed necessary to remedy any neglect or delay in the execution of the public printing: *Provided*, That no contract, agreement, or arrangement entered into by this committee, shall take effect until the same shall have been approved by that house of Congress to which the printing belongs, and, when the printing delayed relates to the business of both houses, until both houses shall have approved of such contract or arrangement. All motions to print extra copies of any bill, report, or other document, shall be referred to the members of the Committee on Printing To be appointed. Power and duties of. Motions to print extra copies to be referred to House, members of.

from the house in which the same may be made."—*Stat. at Large, Vol. X, p.* 34.

May cause sheets to be dry-pressed.

They may cause the printed sheets for the finer description of books authorized to be printed by either house to be dry-pressed before being bound, the cost not to exceed the sum of 50 cents per ream, medium.—*Ibid., p.* 645.

House members may direct binding of certain extra documents.

The committee on the part of the House may direct the binding of extra copies of documents, the size of which shall not be less than 250 pages; the cost not to exceed 12½ cents per volume.—*Ibid., p.* 190.

May control the order in which printing is to be done.

They may control the order in which the Superintendent shall deliver matter to be printed.—*Ibid., p.* 31.

Shall direct the procurement of engraving.

Whenever any charts, maps, diagrams, views, or other engravings shall be required to illustrate any document ordered to be printed by either house of Congress, such engraving shall be procured by the Superintendent, under the direction and supervision of the Committee on Printing of the house ordering the same.—*Stat. at Large, Vol. XII, pp.* 117 *to* 120.

To appoint person to edit and select portions of documents to be printed, and to prepare index.

By the act of June 25, 1864, it is made the duty of said committee to appoint some competent person, who shall edit and select such portion of the documents accompanying the annual reports of the heads of Departments as shall, in their judgment, be desirable for popular distribution, and to prepare an alphabetical index to the same. (See act of July 27, 1866, under head of PRINTING, PUBLIC, *ante.*)

To direct engraving and lithographing contracts.

By the same act said committee shall have the direction, after advertisement, of all lithographing and engraving where it exceeds $250 in value; and they are authorized to empower the Superintendent to make immediate contracts for engraving, whenever, in their opinion, the exigencies of the public service will not justify waiting for advertisement and award.

To direct the furnishing of extra copies of documents to any person.

By the same act the Superintendent is authorized, under the direction of said committee, to furnish extra copies of such documents as may be desired by any person.

Shall have prepared index to the laws.

By the same act said committee shall have prepared under their direction a complete alphabetical index of the laws directed to be furnished for publication by the Secretary of the Senate.—*Stat. at Large, Vol. XIII, pp.* 185, 186.

"There shall be *referred by the Clerk to the members of the Committee on Printing on the part of the House* all drawings, maps, charts, or other papers, which may at any time come before the House, for engraving, lithographing, or publishing in any way; which committee shall report to the House whether the same ought, in their opinion, to be published; and if the House order the publication of the same, that committee shall direct the size and manner of execution of all such maps, charts, drawings, or other papers, and contract by agreement, in writing, for all such engraving, lithographing, printing, drawing, and coloring, as may be ordered by the House; which agreement, in writing, shall be furnished by said committee to the Committee of Accounts, to govern said committee in all allowances for such works; and it shall be in order for said committee to report at all times."—*Rule* 100.

House members of, shall report, &c., on engraving.

"It shall be in order for the Committee on Printing to report at any time."—*Rule* 101. But by a resolution of the House (*Journal*, 2, 42, *p.* 697) it was declared "that the Committee on Printing is authorized to report at any time only upon matters of printing." And the right to report at any time carries with it the right to consider the matter when reported.—*Journal*, 1, 32, *p.* 195.

May report at any time.

(See also PRINTING, PUBLIC.)

PRIORITY OF BUSINESS.

"All questions relating to the priority of business to be acted on shall be decided without debate."—*Rule* 66.

Question relative to, not debatable.

PRIORITY OF QUESTIONS.

"When a question is under debate, no motion shall be received but to adjourn, to lie on the table, for the previous question, to postpone to a day certain, to commit or amend, to postpone indefinitely; which several motions shall have precedence in the order in which they are arranged; and no motion to commit or to postpone indefinitely, being decided, shall be again allowed on the same day and at the same stage of the bill or proposition."—*Rule* 42. [When any one of the foregoing

When a question is under debate.

motion is received, the practice is not to entertain another of lower dignity until the former is disposed of.]

On motions of reference.

"When a resolution shall be offered, or a motion made to refer any subject, and different committees shall be proposed, the question shall be taken in the following order: the Committee of the Whole House on the state of the Union; the Committee of the Whole House; a standing committee; a select committee."—*Rule* 43.

PRIVATE BILLS AND PRIVATE BUSINESS.

Private bills.

[The line of distinction between public and private bills is so difficult to be defined in many cases that it must rest on the opinion of the Speaker and the details of the bill. It has been the practice in Parliament, and also in Congress, to consider as private such as are "for the interest of individuals, public companies or corporations, a parish, city, or county, or other locality." To be a private bill, it must not be general in its enactments, but for the particular interest or benefit of a person or persons. A pension bill for the relief of a soldier's widow is a private bill; but a bill granting pensions to such persons as a class, instead of as individuals, is a public bill. Bills for the incorporation of companies, and whose operations are confined within the District of Columbia, have been treated as private; but where such companies are authorized to have agencies and transact business outside of the limits of the District, they are treated as public. Bills granting lands for railroads have always been held to be public; while a bill authorizing the extension of a railroad into the District of Columbia, or conferring certain privileges upon such an incorporation, has been held to be private.]

Relief from the test oath held to be private.

A bill relieving a person elected to the House from taking the test oath is held to be a private bill.—*Journal*, 2, 41, *pp*. 265, 266.

Take precedence on Friday and Saturday.

"Friday and Saturday in every week shall be set apart for the consideration of private bills and private business in preference to any other, unless otherwise determined by a majority of the House."—*Rule* 128. And such bills may also be considered in their order on

But may be considered on other days.

other days, notwithstanding their precedence on Friday and Saturday.—*Journal*, 1, 19, *p*. 795.

Majority may determine what to consider after disposing of.

When all private business has been disposed of on Friday or Saturday, it is competent for a majority to determine what business shall be considered.—*Journal*, 1, 26, *p*. 460.

A motion to go into a Committee of the Whole House takes precedence of motion to go into Union.

A motion to go into Committee of the Whole House on the state of the Union may be entertained on private bill day, (*Journal*, 2, 22, *p*. 212 *et passim* ;) but the motion to go into a Committee of the Whole House takes precedence, (*Journals*, 1, 29, *p*. 850; 1, 30, *p*. 775,) [unless, according to the general, although not universal practice, a special order is pending in the former.]

Bills from the Court of Claims.

"The bills from the Court of Claims shall, on being laid before the House, be read a first and second time, committed to a Committee of the Whole House, and, together with the accompanying reports, printed."—*Rule* 122.

By usage, go to a Committee of the Whole House.

[Although there is no express rule requiring it, except in the preceding case in regard to bills from the Court of Claims, it is the usage in the commitment of private bills to send them to a Committee of the Whole House, while public bills are sent to a Committee of the Whole House on the state of the Union.]—(See COMMITTEES OF THE WHOLE.)

On first and fourth Friday and Saturday, such as are not objected to are to be considered.

"On the first and fourth Friday and Saturday of each month the calendar of private bills shall be called over, (the chairman of the Committee of the Whole House commencing the call where he left off the previous day,) and the bills to the passage of which no objection shall then be made shall be first considered and disposed of. But when a bill is again reached, after having been once objected to, the committee shall consider and dispose of the same, unless it shall again be objected to by at least five members."—*Rule* 129. And this rule applies as well to the consideration of bills in the House as in Committee of the Whole.—*Journal*, 1, 31, *p*. 697. [On such days, objection, such as is indicated by the above rule, or debate arising thereon, is fatal to the further consideration of a bill, but an amendment may be entertained and voted on. And after a bill has been objected to, and on that account passed over, it cannot, without unanimous consent, be recurred to.]

PRIVATE LAND CLAIMS, COMMITTEE ON.

When appointed, and number of.

There shall be appointed at the commencement of each Congress a Committee on Private Land Claims, to consist of eleven members.—*Rule* 74.

Its duty.

"It shall be the duty of the Committee on Private Land Claims to take into consideration all claims to land which may be referred to them, or shall or may come in question, and to report their opinion thereupon, together with such propositions for relief therein as to them shall seem expedient."—*Rule* 86.

PRIVILEGE.

Privilege from arrest.

"Senators and Representatives shall, in all cases except treason, felony, and breach of the peace, be privileged from arrest during their attendance at the session of their respective houses, and in going to and returning from the same; and for any speech or debate in either house they shall not be questioned in any other place."—*Const.*, 1, 6, 9.

Not to be questioned out of House for speech or debate in House.

Privilege from arrest.

"This privilege from arrest privileges, of course, against all process the disobedience to which is punishable by an attachment of the person; as a subpœna *ad respondendum* or *testificandum*, or a summons on a jury; and with reason, because a member has superior duties to perform in another place."—*Manual, p.* 58.

House may expel its members.

"Each house may determine the rules of its proceedings, punish its members for disorderly conduct, and, with the concurrence of two-thirds, expel a member."—*Const.*, 1, 5, 8.

Penalties inflicted for breach of.

In the maintenance of what are denominated its privileges, and of the privileges of its individual members, the House, in former Congresses, has imposed various penalties.

In some cases it has directed its Speaker to reprimand the party offending.—*Journals*, 1, 4, *p.* 389; 1, 15, *p.* 154; 1, 22, *pp.* 730, 736.

In others it has committed the party to the custody of the Sergeant-at-arms.—*Journals*, 1, 4, *p*. 407; 1, 12, *p*. 280; 1, 15, *p*. 119; 234, *pp*. 277, 281, 384.

In others (where the parties were reporters of the House) it has excluded them from the hall.—*Journals*, 1, 24, *p*. 1021; 2, 33, *p*. 315.

In one case, where a witness refused to answer a question propounded to him by a select committee, it was ordered and adjudged by the House that he be committed to the common jail of the District of Columbia, to be kept in close custody until he should signify his willingness to purge himself of the contempt.—*Journal*, 1, 35, *pp*. 387 *to* 389. And after having been so imprisoned for more than three months, he was, by the further order of the House, released from jail and delivered over to the marshal of the said District to answer a presentment against him in the United States criminal court therein.—*Ibid.*, *pp*. 535 *to* 539.

In the 41st Congress, Patrick Woods having been held to answer for an assault upon a member (outside of the city) was ordered to be punished by imprisonment in the jail of the District of Columbia, as other criminals are, for three months.—*Journal*, 2, 41, *pp*. 1199, 1200. (The session terminated within a week after the order, but the order was executed.)

PRIVILEGE, QUESTIONS OF.

Take precedence of other business.

"A matter of privilege arising out of any question, or from a quarrel between two members, or any other cause, supersedes the consideration of the original question, and must be first disposed of."—*Manual*, *p*. 105. [According to the practice, not finally disposed of, but the House shall proceed to such immediate measures as it may think proper.]

Duty of the Speaker in reference to.

Whenever the Speaker is of the opinion that a question of privilege is involved in a proposition, he must entertain it in preference to any other business.—*Journal*, 1, 29, *p*. 724. [Such opinion, of course, being subject to an appeal.] And when a proposition is submitted which relates to the privileges of the House, it is his duty to entertain it, at least to the extent of submitting the question to the House as to whether or not it presents a question of privilege.—*Journals*, 3, 27, *p.* 46; 1, 29, *p.* 223; 1, 30, *p.* 712; 1, 31, *p.* 1079; 1, 35, *pp.* 376, 410.

Which have arisen. An enumeration of the various questions of privilege that may arise cannot, of course, be given, but the following list embraces nearly all that have arisen, viz:

Contested election cases—*Journals*, 1, 26, *pp.* 1283, 1300; 1, 29, *p.* 201; 1, 31, *p.* 1065; 2, 31, *p.* 119;

Failure or refusal of a witness to appear before committees of the House, or refusal to testify—*Journals*, 1, 12, *p.* 277; 2, 33, *p.* 315; 3, 34, *pp.* 241, 269; 1, 35, *pp.* 258, 371, 750, 821; 2, 35, *pp.* 411, 430, 451; 3, 40, *pp.* 226, 250, 392;

Offer to bribe a member—*Journals*, 1, 4, *p.* 389; 1, 15, *pp.* 119, 171;

Challenge of a member by a Senator—*Journal*, 1, 4, *p.* 471;

Assault by one member upon another—*Journals*, 1, 5, *p.* 154; 1, 34, *p.* 1527;

Divulging the secrets of the House—*Journal*, 1, 12, *p.* 276;

Assault upon a member—*Journals*, 1, 22, *p.* 590; 2, 23, *p.* 485; 2, 41, *pp.* 1199, 1200;

Menacing language towards a member out of the House on account of interrogatories propounded by him to a witness before the House—*Journal*, 1, 22, *p.* 740;

Disorder in the gallery—*Journal*, 1, 24, *p.* 331;

Fracas between two reporters in the presence of the House—*Journal*, 1, 24, *p.* 983;

Refusal of a member to take his seat in Committee of the Whole when ordered by the chairman to do so—*Journal*, 1, 24, *p.* 1209;

Duel between two members—*Journal*, 2, 25, *p.* 501;

Warm words and a mutual assault between two members in Committee of the Whole—*Journal*, 2, 25, *p.* 1013;

Protest by the President against certain proceedings of the House—*Journal*, 2, 27, *p.* 1459;

Proposition to impeach the President—*Journal*, 3, 27, *p.* 159; 2, 39, *p.* 121;

Alleged menance of members by a mob at the seat of Government—*Journal*, 1, 30, *p.* 712;

Charge of falsehood upon a member in a newspaper by the printer of the House—*Journal*, 1, 29, *p*. 223;

Alleged false and scandalous report of proceedings in the House by one of its reporters—*Journal*, 2, 29, *p*. 320;

Alleged mutilation of the Journal by the Speaker—*Journal*, 1, 31, *p*. 713;

Publication by the public printer of an article alleged to be for the purpose of exciting unlawful violence upon members—*Journal*, 1, 33, *p*. 965;

Charges affecting the official character of a member—*Journal*, 1, 33, *p*. 1178;

Alteration and interpolation of House bills—*Journal*, 1, 33, *p*. 1194;

Assault upon a Senator by a member of the House—*Journal*, 1, 34, *p*. 1023;

Alleged corrupt combinations on the part of certain members—*Journal*, 2, 34, *pp*. 475, 476;

Propositions to expel a member on the ground of alleged imputations resting upon him by reason of proceedings of the House at the previous Congress—*Journal*, 1, 35, *p*. 179.

Previous question applies to.

The previous question applies upon a question of privilege as well as in other cases.—*Journals*, 2, 27, *pp*. 573, 576; 1, 28, *p*. 882.

PRIVILEGE OF THE FLOOR.

(See FLOOR.)

PRIVILEGED QUESTION.

What are.

[Privileged questions are those to which precedence is given over other questions by some rule or special order of the House, and are of different grades among themselves.]

Motions to fix the day to which the House shall adjourn, and to adjourn, shall be "*always in order*."—*Rule* 44. Motions to reconsider *take precedence of all questions*, except a motion to adjourn.—*Rule* 49. Motions for an adjournment of more than three days, with the concurrence of the Senate, are privileged.—*Journal*, 2, 37, *pp*. 718 to 720. [And so, also, according to the usage, are motions to take a recess, to fix the day of final adjournment, and for a call of the House.] Motions to go into

Committee of the Whole House on the state of the Union, and to close debate in Committees of the Whole, may be made "*at any time.*"—*Rule* 104. Reports from the Committee on Enrolled Bills and the Committee on Printing may be made "*at any time.*"—*Rules* 100 and 101.

Reports of the general appropriation bills by the Committee on Appropriations, *at any time.*—*Rule* 77. Reports of the Committee of Ways and Means, *at any time.*—*Rule* 151. Motions to make any of the general appropriation bills a special order, *at any time.*—*Rule* 119. The report of a committee of conference is held to be so highly privileged as to be in order, even pending a motion for a call of the House.—*Journal*, 1, 31, *p.* 1590.

PROTEST.

Not a matter of right or privilege.

It is not a matter of right and parliamentary privilege to have received and entered upon the Journal a protest of members against the action of the House.—*Cong. Globe*, 1, 31, *pp.* 1579, 1588.

PUBLIC BUILDINGS AND GROUNDS, COMMITTEE ON.

When appointed, and number of.

There shall be appointed at the commencement of each Congress a Committee on Public Buildings and Grounds, to consist of eleven members.—*Rule* 74.

Duties of.

"It shall be the duty of the Committee on Public Buildings and Grounds to consider all subjects relating to the public edifices and grounds within the city of Washington and all the public buildings constructed by the United States which may be referred to them, and report their opinion thereon, together with such propositions relating thereto as may seem to them expedient."—*Rule* 96.

In regard to furnishing rooms.

It shall also determine the necessity of furnishing or refurnishing any of the rooms exceeding the cost of $100 per annum.—*Journal*, 3, 40, *p.* 518.

To have charge of House restaurant.

The House restaurant shall be placed in charge of said committee, with the same powers heretofore possessed by Committee on Revisal and Unfinished Business.—*Journals*, 2, 40, *p.* 111; 1, 41, *p.* 201.

PUBLIC DOCUMENTS.

What are.

Public documents are defined by the act of March 3, 1847, to be "such publications or books as have been or may be published, procured, or purchased by order of either house of Congress.—*Stat. at Large, Vol. IX, p.* 201.

"The Clerk shall have preserved for each member of the House an extra copy, in good binding, of all the documents printed by order of either house."—*Rule* 18.

Each member to receive a bound copy of.

[In addition thereto, there is deposited as soon as printed, in the document-room, a copy of each document, subject to the order of each member; and where extra copies of a document are ordered, they are sent as soon as printed to the folding-room, from whence they are distributed *pro rata* among the members.]

Additional copy of, for each member.

Extra copies of, how distributed.

"There shall be retained in the library of the Clerk's office, for the use of the members there, and not to be withdrawn therefrom, two copies of all the books and printed documents deposited in the library."—*Rule* 17.

Two copies of all to be retained in House library.

(See also PRINTING, PUBLIC, and FRANKING PRIVILEGE.)

PUBLIC EXPENDITURES, COMMITTEE ON.

There shall be appointed at the commencement of each Congress a Committee on Public Expenditures, to consist of eleven members.—*Rule* 74.

When appointed and number of.

"It shall be the duty of the Committee on Public Expenditures to examine into the state of the several public Departments, and particularly into laws making appropriations of money, and to report whether the moneys have been disbursed conformably with such laws; and also to report, from time to time, such provisions and arrangements as may be necessary to add to the economy of the Departments and the accountability of their officers."—*Rule* 85.

Its duties.

PUBLIC LANDS, COMMITTEE ON.

There shall be appointed at the commencement of each Congress a Committee on the Public Lands, to consist of eleven members.—*Rule* 74.

When appointed, and number of.

"It shall be the duty of the Committee on the Public Lands to take into consideration all such petitions and matters or things respecting the lands of the United States as shall be presented, or shall or may come in

Its duties.

question, and be referred to them by the House, and to report their opinion thereon, together with such propositions for relief therein as to them shall seem expedient."—*Rule* 80.

Allowed a clerk. By a resolution of May 27, 1862, this committee is authorized to employ a clerk, who, in addition to his usual duties, shall have charge of the land maps.—*Journal*, 2, 37, *p*. 760.

PUBLIC PRINTING.

(See PRINTING, PUBLIC, and PRINTING, COMMITTEE ON.)

QUESTIONS.

Speaker shall rise to put. "The Speaker shall rise to put a question, but may state it sitting."—*Rule* 3.

How put. Questions shall be distinctly put in this form, to wit: "As many as are of opinion that (as the question may be) say '*Aye;*'" and, after the affirmative voice is expressed, "As many as are of the contrary opinion, say '*No.*'"—*Rule* 4.

(See also TELLERS, and YEAS AND NAYS.)

Decorum of members while putting. "While the Speaker is putting any question, none shall walk out of or across the House, nor entertain private discourse."—*Rule* 65.

Division of. (See DIVISION OF QUESTIONS.)

Precedence of, &c. (See MOTIONS.)

Tie vote on. In case of an equal division on a question, the question shall be lost.—*Rule* 7.—(See also TIE VOTE.)

QUORUM.

"The House of Representatives shall be composed of members chosen every second year by the people of the several States"—*Const.*, 1, 2, 5—and "a majority of each house shall constitute a quorum to do business; but a smaller number may adjourn from day to day, and may be authorized to compel the attendance of absent members, in such manner and under such penalties as each house may provide."—*Const.*, 1, 5, 8.

Majority constitutes, for business. Power of less than.

Majority of members chosen constitutes. In view of the foregoing clauses of the Constitution, it was decided, during the 37th Congress, to which several of the States had failed to send Representatives, that *a majority of the members chosen* constituted a quorum to do business.—*Journal*, 1, 37, *p*. 117.

When, from counting the House on a division, it appears that there is not a quorum, the matter continues exactly in the state in which it was before the division.—*Manual*, *p*. 122.

Want of, on a division.

A quorum of the House for the purpose of choosing the President shall consist of a member or members from two-thirds of the States.—*Const.*, 2, 1, 16.

What constitutes, in choosing the President.

Tellers may be ordered upon motion, seconded by at least one-fifth of a quorum of the members.—*Rule* 4.

One-fifth of, may order tellers.

The Speaker each day on the meeting of the House, "and on the appearance of a quorum, shall cause the Journal of the preceding day to be read."—*Rule* 1. And it is a very common practice, when no quorum is present upon the Speaker taking the chair, for him to entertain a motion for a call of the House before causing the Journal to be read.—*Journal*, 1, 35, *p*. 840.

Journal to be read on appearance of.

Where less than a quorum is present, a motion to take a recess is not in order; and no motion is in order except for a call or to adjourn.—*Journals*, 1, 29, *p*. 356; 2, 29, *p*. 343; 2, 32, *p*. 388.

Less than, can only call House or adjourn.

"Whenever the Committee of the Whole House on the state of the Union, or the Committee of the Whole House, finds itself without a quorum, the chairman shall cause the roll of the House to be called, and thereupon the committee shall rise, and the chairman shall report the names of the absentees to the House, which shall be entered on the Journal."—*Rule* 126. And as soon (after rising for such purpose) as a quorum is ascertained to be present, the House must return into Committee.—*Journal*, 2, 27, *p*. 292.

Want of, in Committees of the Whole.

"Whenever during business it is observed that a quorum is not present, any member may call for the House to be counted, and, being found deficient, business is suspended."—*Manual*, *p*. 67; also *p*. 83.

Where not present, a member may call for count.

(See also CALLS OF THE HOUSE.)

RAILWAYS AND CANALS, COMMITTEE ON

When appointed, and number of.

There shall be appointed at the commencement of each Congress a Committee on Railways and Canals, to consist of eleven members.—*Rule* 74.

Its duties.

It shall be the duty of the Committee on Railways and Canals to take into consideration all such petitions and matters or things relating to roads and canals, and the improvement of the navigation of rivers, as shall be presented or may come in question and be referred to them by the House; and to report thereupon, together with such propositions relative thereto as to them shall seem expedient.—*Rule* 94.

READING OF PAPERS.

Right of member to insist on, where called to vote on them.

"Where papers are laid before the House or referred to a committee, every member has a right to have them once read at the table before he can be compelled to vote on them"—*Manual*, *p*. 97—and this applies to the reading of papers on a motion to refer them.—*Journal*, 1, 34, *p*. 1146. And so in regard to any proposition submitted for a vote of the House; but it being a right derived from the rules, he may at any time (when a motion to suspend the rules is in order) be deprived of it by a suspension of the rule.—*Journals*, 1, 32, *p*, 1116; 3, 34, *p*. 618; 2, 35, *p*. 572; 2, 38, *pp*. 397, 398—even after the main question is ordered to be put.—*Journal*, 3, 34, *p*. 386.

But may be deprived of it by a suspension of the rules.

Where objected to.

"When the reading of a paper is called for, and the same is objected to by any member, it shall be determined by a vote of the House."—*Rule* 141.

Construction of the 141st rule in regard to.

[The rule above recited is not construed to apply to the single reading of a paper or proposition upon which the House may be called upon to give a vote, or to the several regular readings of a bill, but to cases where a paper has been once read, or a bill has received its regular reading and another is called for, and also where a member desires the reading of a paper having relation to the subject before the House.] But it does not apply to the case of an amendment which a member, by leave, has given notice of his intention at a future time to offer. —*Journal*, 1, 31, *p*. 1149.

In case of an amendment of which notice is given.

The reading of a report relating to a pending proposition cannot be called for after the previous question is seconded, as it would be in the nature of debate.—*Journal*, 1, 23, *p*. 726. Where cannot be called for.

RECEDE, MOTION TO.

The motion to recede takes precedence of the motions to insist and ask a conference, and to adhere.—*Manual*, *pp*. 114, 115. [And even though the previous question may be pending on either of the last motions, the motion to recede may be entertained, because if it prevails the disagreement between the houses is removed and the bill is passed.] A vote to recede from a disagreement to an amendment is not equivalent to an agreement.—*Journal*, 1, 20, *pp*. 695, 697. [But in making a motion that the House recede from its disagreement to an amendment, there should be coupled with it, "*and that the House agree to the same*."] Precedence of.

(See also AMENDMENTS BETWEEN THE TWO HOUSES and CONFERENCE COMMITTEES.)

RECEPTION.

(See CONSIDERATION.)

RECESS.

Where it is convenient that the business of the House be suspended for a short time, as for a conference presently to be held, &c., it adjourns during pleasure.—*Manual*, p. 135. [The practice of the House in regard to the privileged character of the motion for a recess has varied in different Congresses, but, of late years, it has been held to be a privileged question—see *Journals*, 1, 36, *pp*. 753, 759; 2, 37, *pp*. 718, 719—and the latter practice is manifestly that contemplated in the Manual.] But it is not in order pending a motion to suspend the rules so as to take an immediate vote on a pending proposition.—*Journal*, 2, 39, *pp*. 572, 573. May be taken. Motion for, a privileged one.

It is not in order for less than a quorum to take a recess—*Journals*, 1, 29, *p*. 356; 2, 32, *p*. 388—nor, pending a call of the House, can a recess be taken unless by unanimous consent.—*Ibid*., 1, 26, *p*. 843. Less than a quorum cannot take. Not in order pending call of House.

For more than three days. Where it is proposed to take a recess, by adjournment, for more than three days, the Senate must consent before it can be taken—*Const.*, 1, 5, 9—and a resolution for that purpose is held to be privileged.—*Journal*, 2, 37, *pp.* 718 *to* 720.—(See ADJOURN, MOTION TO.)

RECOMMIT, MOTION TO.

In order at any time before passage of bill, but not if main question is ordered. "After commitment and a report thereof to the House or at any time before its passage, a bill may be recommitted."—*Rule* 124. But not after the main question is ordered to be put.—*Journal*, 1, 29, *p.* 643. [Nor, according to the practice, even pending the demand for the previous question.] "And should such recommitment take place after its engrossment, and an amendment be reported and agreed to by the House, the question shall be again put on the engrossment of the bill."—*Rule* 124.—(See COMMIT, MOTION TO.)

In case of recommitment after engrossment.

RECONSIDER, MOTION TO.

Who may make. "When a motion has been once made and carried in the affirmative or negative, it shall be in order for any member of the majority to move for the reconsideration thereof, on the same or succeeding day; and such motion shall take precedence of all other questions, except a motion to adjourn; and shall not be withdrawn after the said succeeding day without the consent of the House, and thereafter any member may call it up for consideration."—*Rule* 49.

When to be made. Precedence of. Cannot be withdrawn after the time elapsed for making. Any member may call up.

Who may make, in case of tie vote. A fair construction of this rule will permit a member who has voted with the *prevailing side* on a tie vote to move a reconsideration. Such is evidently the spirit of the rule—*Journal*, 1, 30, *p.* 1081. [So, also, it is the practice to permit any member to move a reconsideration who has voted with the *prevailing side* in a case where less than a majority prevails.]—*Cong. Globe*, 1, 39, *p.* 3892.

Who may make, when less than a majority prevails.

Any member may make, where vote has not been by yeas and nays. Where a vote is not taken by yeas and nays, and consequently no record made of each member's vote, it is the well-settled practice to permit any member to move a reconsideration.

May be entered, but not considered while another question is up.

It is in order at *any time*, even when a member is on the floor, or the highest privileged question is pending, on the same or succeeding day to move a reconsideration and have it entered, but it cannot be taken up and considered while another question is before the House.—*Journal*, 1, 34, *pp.* 1476, 1477.

May be entertained, even after papers have gone out of the possession of the House

A motion to reconsider, if made in time, may be entertained, notwithstanding the papers connected with the original proposition have gone out of the possession of the House.—*Journals*, 1, 26, *p.* 1033; 1, 28, *pp.* 1125, 1131; 1, 29, *p.* 657; 1, 33, *pp.* 336, 1199. And pending a motion to reconsider the vote on the passage of a bill, the Speaker should decline to sign the said bill if reported by the Committee on Enrolled Bills.—*Journal*, 1, 26, *p.* 1033. [When the papers have been sent to the Senate, it is usual, in case of a motion to reconsider, to send a message to that body requesting their return.]

On private bill days.

[It is not in order on a private bill day to call up and consider a motion to reconsider a vote on a public bill, if objected to, except after a postponement by a majority vote of the private business.]

[The effect of the pendency of a motion to reconsider, according to the universal usage, is to suspend the original proposition;] but "where the term of the members expires without acting on the motion to reconsider for the want of time or inclination, the motion of course fails, and leaves the original proposition operative."—(Opinion of Mr. Speaker Orr, and also of Mr. Speaker Banks, in the case of a resolution directing the payment of money out of the contingent fund of the House, where Congress adjourned *sine die*—pending a motion to reconsider the vote by which it was adopted.)

Not in order, where action has resulted which cannot be reversed.

It is not in order to move a reconsideration of a vote sustaining a decision of the Chair, after subsequent action has resulted from such decision which it is impossible for the House to reverse.—*Journal*, 1, 31, *pp.* 860, 861. Nor upon a bill introduced and referred during the first hour after the reading of the Journal on Mondays, nor upon bills introduced and referred by unanimous consent.—*Rule* 130.

Nor on bills introduced on Mondays.

Previous question is exhausted by vote on.

[Under the practice, if a motion to reconsider is pending when the previous question is ordered, such order applies to the motion to reconsider only.]

Cannot be repeated.

Where a motion to reconsider has been once put and decided, it is not in order to repeat the motion.—*Journal*, 2, 27, *p*. 1022. But it is otherwise where an amendment has been adopted since the first reconsideration.—*Journal*, 1, 31, *pp*. 1404, 1406, 1407.

Except where an amendment has been made.

Order of yeas and nays may be reconsidered.

An order that a vote be taken by yeas and nays may be reconsidered, but the question immediately recurs, subject to be decided affirmatively by one-fifth of the members present.—*Journals*, 1, 19, *p*. 796; 1, 30, *p*. 405.

So also negative vote on motion to lie on the table.

A negative vote on a motion to lie on the table may be reconsidered.—*Journal*, 2, 32, *p*. 234.

Motion to lay on table.

[It is a very common practice for the member having charge of a measure, as soon as a vote is taken upon it, "to move to reconsider the vote last taken, and also to move that the motion to reconsider be laid on the table;" and if the latter motion prevails, it is deemed a finality, so far as the vote proposed to be reconsidered is concerned. A vote to lay the motion to reconsider on the table does not carry with it the pending measure.]

If motion to reconsider be laid on table, it cannot be reconsidered.

A motion to reconsider a vote laying a motion to reconsider on the table is not in order; if entertained, it would lead to inextricable confusion, by piling up motion upon motion to reconsider.—*Journals*, 3, 27, *p*. 334; 1, 33, *p*. 357.

An amendment after engrossment.

[After a bill has been ordered to be engrossed, it is not in order to move a reconsideration of a vote on an amendment until the order of engrossment has been reconsidered; and if the motion to reconsider the engrossment is laid on the table, no reconsideration of the amendment can then be entertained.]

Engrossment pending, demand of previous question on passage.

It is in order, even pending the demand of the previous question on the passage of a bill, to move a reconsideration of the order of engrossment.—*Journal*, 2, 27, *p*. 1175. [But, of course, if moved at such a time, it is not debatable.]

Decided affirmatively, question immediately re-

According to the uniform practice, where a motion to reconsider has been passed in the affirmative, the question *immediately* recurs upon the question reconsidered. —*Journal*, 1, 31, *p*. 847. [And the House proceeds with the consideration of the subject without regard to the fact of its having been on the Speaker's table when the motion to reconsider was submitted.]

curs on original question, &c.

Where a vote taken under the operation of the previous question is reconsidered, the question is then divested of the previous question, and is open to debate and amendment.—*Journals*, 1, 27, *p*. 129; 1, 33, *p*. 127. [These decisions apply only to cases where the previous question was fully exhausted by votes taken on all the questions covered by it before the motion to reconsider was made. In any other case, the pendency of the previous question would preclude debate.]

When vote taken under previous question is reconsidered.

The previous question may be reconsidered, but not after it is partly executed.—*Journal*, 1, 35, *pp*. 1101, 1398. [And according to the usual practice, in the reconsideration of the previous question but a single vote is taken, viz: Will the House reconsider the vote on ordering the main question? Which being decided affirmatively, the question is divested of the demand for the previous question.]

Previous question may be reconsidered, if not partly executed.

Previous question, how reconsidered.

A vote on the reconsideration of a vetoed bill cannot be reconsidered.—*Journal*, 1, 28, *pp*. 1093, 1097. Nor can a vote on a motion to suspend the rules be reconsidered.—*Journal*, 2, 31, *p*. 134.

Not in order on vote refusing to pass a vetoed bill. Nor on vote on suspending the rules.

A motion to reconsider is not debatable, if the question proposed to be reconsidered was not debatable.—*Journals*, 2, 27, *p*. 331; 2, 30, *pp*. 135, 136. But the fact of a question having been decided under the operation of the previous question does not prevent debate on the motion to reconsider, if the original question was otherwise debatable.—*Journal*, 1, 33, *p*. 127. A motion to reconsider a vote on a resolution passed on resolution day, under the operation of the previous question, like the resolution, cannot be debated on that day, but must lie over.—*Journal*, 2, 30, *pp*. 135, 136.

Where not debatable.

REFER, MOTION TO.

(See COMMIT, MOTION TO.)

REPORTERS.

Admitted to gallery with permission of Speaker.

"Stenographers and reporters, other than the official reporters of the House, wishing to take down the debates, may be admitted by the Speaker to the reporters' gallery over the Speaker's chair, but not on the floor of the House; but no person shall be allowed the privilege of said gallery, under the character of stenographer or reporter, without a written permission of the Speaker, specifying the part of said gallery assigned to him; nor shall said stenographer or reporter be admitted to said gallery unless he shall state, in writing, for what paper or papers he is employed to report; nor shall he be admitted, or if admitted be suffered to retain his seat, if he shall be or become an agent to prosecute any claim pending before Congress; and the Speaker shall give his written permission with this condition.—*Rule* 135.

Must state for what paper.

Must not be claim agents.

Of Congressional Globe, occupy chairs in front of Clerk's desk, and to be furnished with printed bills, &c.

By a resolution of the House (*Journal*, 1, 32, *p.* 70) the Doorkeeper was directed to provide chairs for the reporters of the Congressional Globe, to be placed in front of the Clerk's desk. And by resolution of May 7, 1866, it is directed that the said reporters be furnished with three copies each of all bills and resolutions printed by order of the House.—*Journal*, 1, 29, *p.* 675.

Appointment of stenographic, and duties of.

By resolution of the House of January 5, 1865, the Speaker is directed to appoint a stenographic reporter, to continue in office until otherwise ordered by the House, whose duty it shall be to report in short-hand, on the order of any of the standing or special committees of the House, such proceedings as they may deem necessary, and, when ordered to be printed, properly index and supervise the publication of the same.—*Journal*, 2, 38, *pp.* 79, 80.

By resolution of the House of January 18, 1866, the foregoing resolution was modified so as to read, "that the Speaker appoint a competent stenographic reporter, to continue in office until otherwise ordered by the House, whose duty it shall be to report in short-hand, on the order of any of the standing or special committees of the House, such proceedings as they may deem necessary, and, when ordered to be printed, properly index and supervise the publication of the same; and who shall receive therefor an annual compensation at the rate now allowed by regulation for reporting court-martial proceedings: *Provided*, That all such reporting ordered by committees of the House, and all such as he shall be required to do for joint committees, shall be done by said reporter or person employed by him without extra compensation or additional expense; and the reports so taken shall be under the entire control of the committees, respectively, by which such testimony shall be taken, or of the House."—*Journal*, 1, 39, *p*. 162.

Appointment of assistant stenographer.

By resolution of the House of July 25, 1866, the Speaker was authorized to appoint a competent stenographer as assistant official reporter to the committees of the House, to be paid the same compensation as the official reporter, and whose term of service shall expire March 4, 1867.—*Journal*, 1, 39, *p*. 1117. And by resolution of the House of March 6, 1867, it was provided that the assistant stenographer of the last House be continued as such until otherwise ordered.—*Journal*, 1, 40, *p*. 13.

Of the associated press, desk assigned to.

By resolution of the House of February 26, 1866, it was provided that a desk on the floor of the House be assigned to the reporter of the associated press.—*Journal*, 1, 39, *p*. 330.

Of associated press to be subject to same rules as of Globe.

By a resolution of the House of January 11, 1867, it was provided that the reporters of the associated press, and reports made by them, should be under the same rules and regulations as the reporters and reports of the Globe.—*Journal*, 2, 39, *p*. 154.

Must be approved by the Speaker.

No person shall be appointed a reporter of the House without the approval of the Speaker.—*Stat. at Large*, *Vol*. XVII, *p*. 47.

Of Globe to furnish reports of proceedings, &c.

By resolution of the House of March 3, 1873, it is provided that the reports of the House proceedings and debates shall be furnished to the Congressional Printer by the present corps of Globe reporters, who shall hereafter, until otherwise ordered, be officers of the House, under direction of the Speaker, and shall receive the same compensation now allowed to the official reporters of committees.—*Journal*, 3, 42, *pp*. 582, 583. (See also CONGRESSIONAL GLOBE.)

Of Globe to be officers of House.

REPORTS OF COMMITTEES.

(See also COMMITTEES.)

Undetermined at end of session.

Such reports as originated in either house, and at the close of the session remain undetermined in either house, shall, after six days from the commencement of a second or subsequent session of the same Congress, be resumed as if an adjournment had not taken place. And all business before committees of the House at the end of the one session shall be resumed at the commencement of the next session of the same Congress, as if no adjournment had taken place.—*Rule* 136.

REPORTS OF COURT OF CLAIMS.

(See CLAIMS, COURT OF.)

REPORTS OF OFFICERS OF GOVERNMENT.

List of, to be made to Congress, to be prepared.

"It shall be the duty of the Clerk to make and cause to be printed, and deliver to each member, at the commencement of every session of Congress, a list of the reports which it is the duty of any officer or Department of the Government to make to Congress, referring to the act or resolution, and page of the volume of the laws or journal in which it may be contained, and placing under the name of each officer the list of reports required of him to be made, and the time when the report may be expected."—*Rule* 13.

RESIGNATION BY A MEMBER.

Right of, recognized by the House.

The right of a member to resign his seat had never been contested until the 2d session of the 41st Congress, and on that occasion the Speaker, in conformity with what seemed to be the settled authority of the House, decided that he had such right, when an appeal was taken from such decision, which on motion was laid on the table, thereby affirming the decision of the Chair.—*Cong. Globe, 2d sess. 41st Cong., Vol.* 76, *p.* 1547.

RESOLUTIONS.

Distinction between "orders" and.

"When the House commands, it is by an 'order.' But fact, principles, and their own opinions and purposes are expressed in the form of resolutions."—*Manual, p.* 86. [This distinction is not strictly kept up in the practice of the House.]

"Reports from the committees having been presented and disposed of, the Speaker shall call for resolutions from the members of each State and delegates from each Territory, beginning with Maine and the Territory last organized alternately. They shall not be debated on the very day of their being presented, nor on any day assigned by the House for the receipt of resolutions, unless where the House shall direct otherwise; but shall lie on the table, to be taken up in the order in which they were presented; and if, on that day, the whole of the States and Territories shall not be called, the Speaker shall begin on the next day where he left off the previous day: *Provided*, That no member shall offer more than one resolution, or one series of resolutions, all relating to the same subject, until all the States and Territories shall have been called."—*Rule* 52.

Daily call for.

Not to be debated.

Call for, how resumed.

Only one to be offered by a member.

"All the States and Territories shall be called for bills on leave and resolutions every Monday during each session of Congress; and, if necessary to secure the object on said days, all resolutions which shall give rise to debate shall lie over for discussion, under the Rules of the House already established; and the whole of said days shall be appropriated to bills on leave and resolutions, until all the States and Territories are called through. And the Speaker shall first call the States and Territories for bills on leave; and all bills so introduced during the first hour after the Journal is read shall be referred, without debate, to their appropriate committees: *Provided, however*, That a bill so introduced and referred shall not be brought back into the House upon a motion to reconsider."—*Rule* 130. (See MORNING HOUR ON MONDAYS.)

Call for, on alternate Mondays, and no debate thereon.

It is a common practice, when a resolution is submitted, for the mover to immediately demand the previous question, which, if ordered, will prevent debate and bring the House to a direct vote on the resolution, thus avoiding the necessity of its lying over, as would be the case if debate should arise.—*Journals*, 1, 26, *pp*. 1064, 1067; 2, 27, *p*. 429; 1, 28, *p*. 558; 1, 28, *p*. 1235; 1, 30, *p*. 326.

Debate on, may be avoided by demand of previous question.

The name of a member who offers a resolution to the

Name of member who offers, entered on Journal. consideration of the House shall be inserted on the Journals.—*Rule* 32.

Amendment of. A resolution cannot be amended so as to convert it into a joint resolution.—*Journal*, 1, 32, *p*. 679.

"No bill or resolution shall, at any time, be amended by annexing thereto, or incorporating therewith, any other bill or resolution pending before the House."—*Rule* 48. [According to the practice, an amendment containing the *substance* of a pending bill or resolution is in order.] (See AMENDMENTS.)

Where concurrence of Senate is necessary. "Every order, resolution, or vote to which the concurrence of the Senate shall be necessary, shall be read to the House and laid on the table on a day preceding that in which the same shall be moved, unless the House shall otherwise expressly allow."—*Rule* 143.

Calling for information. Such resolutions as call for information from the President or heads of Departments are required, by *Rule* 53, to lie on the table one day.—(See PRESIDENT AND EXECUTIVE DEPARTMENTS.)

RESOLUTIONS OF STATE AND TERRITORIAL LEGISLATURES.

(See JOINT RESOLUTIONS.)

RESTAURANT.

To be in charge of Committee on Public Buildings and Grounds. By resolution of the House of April 8, 1869, it is provided that the House restaurant be placed in charge of the Committee on Public Buildings and Grounds, with the same powers heretofore possessed by the Committee on Revisal and Unfinished Business.—*Journal*, 1, 41, *p*. 201. The powers above referred to are to lease the same and under such rules and regulations as to the said committee may seem expedient.—*Journal*, 2, 30, *p*. 111.

REVISION OF THE LAWS, COMMITTEE ON.

When appointed, and number of. There shall be appointed at the commencement of each Congress a Committee on the Revision of the Laws, to consist of eleven members.—*Rule* 74.

REVOLUTIONARY CLAIMS, COMMITTEE ON.

When appointed, and number of. There shall be appointed at the commencement of each Congress a Committee on Revolutionary Claims, to consist of eleven members.—*Rule* 74.

Its duties. "It shall be the duty of the Committee on Revolutionary Claims to take into consideration all such petitions and matters or things touching claims and demands originating in the revolutionary war, or arising therefrom, as shall be presented, or shall or may come in question, and be referred to them by the House; and to report their opinion thereupon, together with such propositions for relief therein as to them shall seem expedient."—*Rule* 84.

REVOLUTIONARY PENSIONS, COMMITTEE ON.

There shall be appointed at the commencement of each Congress a Committee on Revolutionary Pensions, to consist of eleven members.—*Rule* 74. When appointed, and number of.

"It shall be the duty of the Committee on Revolutionary Pensions to take into consideration all such matters respecting pensions for services in the revolutionary war, other than invalid pensions, as shall be referred to them by the House."—*Rule* 92. Its duties.

On the 26th March, 1867, upon the suggestion of the Speaker, it was ordered that all matters relating to pensions to soldiers of the war of 1812 shall be referred to the Committee on Revolutionary Pensions, instead of the Committee on Invalid Pensions, as heretofore.—*Journal*, 1, 40, *p*. 117. To take charge of pensions to soldiers of 1812.

ROADS AND CANALS, COMMITTEE ON.

(The name of this committee changed to that of "RAILWAYS and CANALS," which see.)

ROOMS IN THE CAPITOL.

"The unappropriated rooms in that part of the Capitol assigned to the House shall be subject to the order and disposal of the Speaker until the further order of the House."—*Rule* 5. Unappropriated, to be at disposal of Speaker.

RULES.

"Each house may determine the rules of its proceedings."—*Const.*, 1, 5, 8. Each house may determine its.

"No standing rule or the order of the House shall be rescinded or changed without one day's notice being given of the motion therefore, (see NOTICES;) nor shall any rule be suspended except by a vote of at least two-thirds of the members present."—*Rule* 145. But a *majority* may *at any time* suspend the rules and orders for the purpose of going into the Committee of the Not to be changed without notice. To suspend requires two-thirds, except to go into Union, or close debate in Committee of the Whole.

Whole on the state of the Union, and for closing debate in Committees of the Whole—(see DEBATE.)—*Rule* 104.

When only motions to suspend can be made.

Except during the *last ten days of the session* the Speaker shall not entertain a motion to suspend the rules of the House at any time, except on *Monday* of every week, at the expiration of one hour after the Journal is read, unless the call of States and Territories for bills on leave has been earlier concluded, when the Speaker may entertain a motion to suspend the rules.—*Rule* 145.

When motion to suspend not in order.

It is not in order to move a suspension of the rules while the House is acting under a suspension of the rules—*Cong. Globe*, 2, 27, *pp*. 58, 142; 1, 31, *p*. 1225—unless connected with the business immediately before the House—*Journal*, 2, 36, *p*. 212; nor while considering a special order, it having been made under a suspension of the rules—*Cong. Globe*, 2, 29, *pp*. 401, 439—[unless connected with the consideration of such special order;] nor while the previous question is operating.—*Journal*, 2, 33, *p*. 564.

Pending motion to suspend, motion for a recess not in order.

Pending a motion to suspend the rules, so as to take an immediate vote on a proposition, a motion for a recess is not in order.—*Journal*, 2, 39, *pp*. 572, 573. [This decision of the Speaker was sustained on appeal by the very decisive vote, by yeas and nays, of yeas 173, nays 4; and would seem to have settled the question that pending a similar motion, dilatory motions, such as had been previously tolerated, would not be entertained hereafter.]

Pending a motion to suspend, only one motion to adjourn in order.

"Pending a motion to suspend the rules, the Speaker may entertain one motion that the House do now adjourn; but after the result thereon is announced, he shall not entertain any other dilatory motion till the vote is taken on suspension."—*Rule* 161.

Motion to suspend, not debatable. Not amendable. Cannot be laid on table or postponed indefinitely.

A motion to suspend the rules is not debatable—*Cong. Globe*, 2, 27, *p*. 121; 1, 29, *p*. 343; nor is it amendable—*Cong. Globe*, 2, 30, *pp*. 319, 320; *Journal*, 2, 35, *p*. 477; nor can it be laid on the table—*Cong. Globe*, 1, 29, *p*. 343; *Journal*, 2, 35, *p*. 510; nor postponed indefinitely.—*Cong. Globe*, 1, 26, *p*. 121.

The vote on a motion to suspend the rules cannot be reconsidered.—*Journal*, 2, 31, *p*. 134. Vote on suspension cannot be reconsidered.

Where the rules are suspended to enable a member to submit a particular proposition, if he fails to submit it another member may do so.—*Journal*, 1, 23, *p*. 631. But where he submits it, and subsequently withdraws it, another member cannot renew it.—*Journal*, 2, 36, *pp*. 131 to 140. Where suspended for a particular purpose.

After the rules have been suspended to allow a proposition to be submitted, it cannot be modified.—*Cong. Globe*, 1, 31, *p*. 1727. [But it may be amended by a vote of the House.] No modification after suspension.

The rules may be suspended by a single vote for the purpose of enabling a number of bills to be reported from a committee.—*Journal*, 3, 34, *p*. 432. Motion to suspend, may embrace several bills.

A *joint* rule, so far as the House is concerned, requires a majority vote only for its suspension.—*Journal*, 2, 24, *p*. 574. Joint rule suspended by a majority.

It is not in order, under color of amendment, to move to change or rescind a rule; and where such is the *effect* of a motion, one day's notice is necessary.—*Journal*, 1, 20, *p*. 647. Not in order to change or rescind, under color of amendment.

"These rules shall be the rules of the House of Representatives of the present and succeeding Congresses, unless otherwise ordered."—*Rule* 147. To continue unless otherwise ordered.

SATURDAY.

(See Private Bills and Private Business.)

SEATS OF MEMBERS.

Previous to the 2d session of the 35th Congress each member was provided with a desk and seat within the hall, the location of which for the session has of late years been determined by lot. At that session, with a view to try the experiment of dispensing with desks, the following resolution was adopted, viz: What has been customary in regard to.

"*Resolved*, That the Superintendent of the Capitol Extension be directed, after the adjournment of the present session of Congress, to remove the desks from the hall of the House, and to make such rearrangement Desks to be removed and seats rearranged.

of the seats of members as will bring them together into the smallest convenient space."—*Journal*, 2, 35, *pp*. 580, 583.

At the next session, however, the following resolution was adopted, viz:

Restoration of the desks and seats.

"*Resolved*, That the superintendent of the Capitol Extension be directed to remove the present benches from the hall and replace the old chairs and desks, adopting substantially the original arrangements thereof, but having regard to any reduction of space occupied by them, without interfering with the convenience of the arrangement."—*Journal*, 1, 36, *p*. 351.

The following is the usual form of resolution for the selection of seats, viz:

Form of resolution for the selection of.

"*Resolved*, That the Clerk of the House (here indicate the time) place in a box the name of each member and delegate of the House of Representatives written on a separate slip of paper; that he then proceed, in the presence of the House, to draw from said box, one at a time, the said slips of paper; and, as each is drawn, he shall announce the name of the member or delegate upon it, who shall choose his seat for the present Congress: *Provided*, That before said drawing shall commence, the Speaker shall cause every seat to be vacated, and shall see that every seat continues vacant until it is selected under this order; and that every seat, after having been selected, shall be deemed vacant if left unoccupied before the calling of the roll is finished."

No second drawing in order during a Congress.

Whenever the seats of members shall have been drawn, no proposition shall be in order for a second drawing during the same Congress.—*Rule* 163.

SECRET SESSION.

When confidential communication made by President.

"Whenever confidential communications are received from the President of the United States, the House shall be cleared of all persons, except the members, clerks, Sergeant-at-arms, and Doorkeeper, and so continue during the reading of such communications, and (unless otherwise directed by the House) during all debates and proceedings to be had thereon. And when the Speaker, or any other member, shall inform the House that he has

Or upon suggestion by Speaker or member.

communications to make which he conceives ought to be kept secret, the House shall, in like manner, be cleared till the communication be made; the House shall then determine whether the matter communicated requires secrecy or not, and take order accordingly."—*Rule* 137.

House to be cleared.

The Clerk, Sergeant-at-arms, Doorkeeper, and Postmaster shall be sworn to keep the secrets of the House.—*Rule* 10.

Officers sworn to keep secrets of the House.

Such parts of the Journal of a secret session as may, in the judgment of the House, require secrecy, need not be published.—*Const.*, 1, 5, 9.

House need not publish Journal of.

SENATE.

"Every order, resolution, or vote, to which the concurrence of the Senate shall be necessary, shall be read to the House and laid on the table on the day preceding that in which the same shall be moved, unless the House shall otherwise expressly allow."—*Rule* 143. [This rule was originally adopted in 1789, but for a great many years it has been usual, in the absence of any objection, to assume that the House has allowed the immediate consideration of all such propositions.]

Orders, &c., requiring concurrence of, to lie on table one day.

Members of the Senate and their Secretary may be admitted on the floor of the House.—*Rule* 134.

Members of, and their Secretary, may be admitted within the hall.

(See MESSAGES FROM THE SENATE.)

SERGEANT-AT-ARMS.

There shall be elected at the commencement of each Congress, to continue in office until his successor is appointed, a Sergeant-at-arms, who shall take an oath "for the true and faithful discharge of the duties of his office to the best of his knowledge and abilities, and to keep the secrets of the House;" and the vote shall be taken *viva voce.*—*Rule* 10.

When to be elected, and term of office.

Oath of office.

Vote for, to be taken *viva voce.*

He is also required, by the act of July 2, 1862, to take an additional oath.—(See OATH.)

Additional oath.

"It shall be the duty of the Sergeant-at-arms to attend the House during its sittings; *to aid in the enforcement of order, under the direction of the Speaker;* to

His duties.

execute the commands of the House from time to time; together with all such process, issued by authority thereof, as shall be directed to him by the Speaker."—*Rule* 22.

Additional duty. "It shall be the duty of the Sergeant-at-arms to keep the accounts for pay and mileage of members, to prepare checks, and, if required to do so, to draw the money on such checks for the members, (the same being previously signed by the Speaker, and indorsed by the member,) and pay over the same to the member entitled thereto."—*Rule* 25.

Shall deduct excess of stationery from compensation of members. By resolution of May 4, 1842, it is made the duty of the Sergeant-at-arms to deduct the amount of excess of stationery received by members beyond their allowance from their pay and mileage.—*Journals*, 2, 27, *p*. 495, and 1, 31, *p*. 1510.—(See COMPENSATION AND MILEAGE.)

Shall give bond. "The Sergeant-at-arms shall give bond, with surety, to the United States, in a sum not less than five nor more than ten thousand dollars, at the discretion of the Speaker, and with such surety as the Speaker may approve, faithfully to account for the money coming into his hands for the pay of members."—*Rule* 26.

Symbol of office. "The symbol of his office (the mace) shall be borne by the Sergeant-at-arms when in the execution of his office."—*Rule* 23.

Fees of. "The fees of the Sergeant-at-arms shall be, for every arrest, the sum of two dollars; for each day's custody and releasement, one dollar; and for traveling expenses for himself or a special messenger, going and returning, one-tenth of a dollar per mile."—*Rule* 24. And it is provided by act of February 5, 1859, "that hereafter the mileage or traveling allowance to the officer or other person executing precepts or other summons of either house of Congress, shall not exceed ten cents for each mile necessarily and actually traveled by such officer or other person in the execution of any such precept or summons."—*Stat. at Large, Vol. XI, p*. 379.

Shall receive no fees whatever. But by the act of July 14, 1870—*Stat. at Large, Vol.*

XVI, *p.* 231—it is provided that (in addition to his regular salary) he shall receive, directly or indirectly, no fees, other compensation, or emolument whatever for performing the duties of his office, or in connection therewith.

To discharge certain duties of the Clerk.

By the act of Febuary 21, 1867—*Stat. at Large, Vol. XIV, p.* 397—it is provided that in case of a vacancy in the office of Clerk, or in the absence or inability of said Clerk to discharge the duties imposed upon him by law or custom relative to the preparation of the roll of Representatives or the organization of the House, the said duties shall devolve on the Sergeant-at-arms of the next preceding House of Representatives.

Of the two houses to appoint Capital police.

By the act of March 2, 1867—*Stat. at Large, Vol. XIV, p.* 466—it is provided that the Sergeants-at-arms of the two houses shall hereafter appoint the Capitol police. By the act of March 3, 1873, it is provided that such appointments shall be made by the Sergeants-at-arms of the two houses and the Architect of the Capitol Extension.—*Stat. at Large, Vol. XVII, p.* 488.

Also appoint watchmen, and make rules, &c., concerning the Capitol.

By the act of March 30, 1867—*Stat. at Large, Vol. XV, pp.* 11, 12—it is provided that the said Sergeants-at-arms shall appoint certain watchmen at the Capitol, and make such rules and regulations as they may deem necessary to preserve the peace and secure the Capitol from defacement, and for the protection of the public property therein; and shall have power to arrest and detain any person violating said rules until such person can be brought before the proper authorities for trial, without further order of Congress.

Also to enforce joint rule in regard to liquor.

By *Joint Rule* 19 it is made the duty of said Sergeants-at-arms, under the supervision of the presiding officers of the two houses respectively, to enforce the provisions of said rule, that "no spirituous or malt liquors, or wines, shall be offered for sale, exhibited, or kept within the Capitol, or in any room or building connected therewith, or on the public grounds adjacent thereto."

Shall make full return of Government property in his possession.

By the act of July 15, 1870, it is made his duty to make out a full and complete account of all the property belonging to the Government in his possession on the first day of each regular session, and at the expiration of his term of service.—*Stat. at Large, Vol. XVI, p.* 365.

SMITHSONIAN INSTITUTION.

By the act of August 10, 1846, three of the Regents of said Institution shall be members of the House of Representatives, to be appointed by the Speaker on the fourth Wednesday in December next after the first meeting of every Congress, to serve until the fourth Wednesday in December, the second succeeding their appointment, and vacancies shall be filled as vacancies in committees are filled.—*Stat. at Large, Vol. IX, p.* 102.

Regents of, to be appointed by the Speaker.

The Board of Regents shall submit to Congress, at each session thereof, a report of the operations, expenditures, and condition of the Institution.—*Ibid.*

Report to be made to Congress annually.

SMOKING.

Smoking is prohibited within the bar of the House or gallery.—*Rule* 65.

Prohibited in bar or gallery.

SPEAKER.

"The House of Representatives shall choose their Speaker and other officers."—*Const.*, 1, 2, 6.

House shall choose.

Upon the ascertainment of the fact that a quorum of members elect is present, and its announcement by the Clerk of the last House, it is usual for the House, on motion of some member, *immediately* to "proceed, *viva voce*, to the election of a Speaker for the —— Congress."—*Journal*, 1, 35, *p.* 8.

(See Meeting of Congress.)

By the act of June 1, 1789, it is provided that the oath or affirmation required by the 6th article of the Constitution of the United States shall be administered in the form following, to wit: "*I,* —— ——, *do solemnly swear* (or affirm, as the case may be) *that I will support the Constitution of the United States.*" And that it shall be administered to him by "any one member of the House of Representatives." *Stat. at Large, Vol. I, p.* 23. [According to the usage, the member selected for this purpose is that one who has been longest a member of the House.]—*Journal*, 1, 26, *p.* 79.

Oath.

By whom oath to be administered.

By the same act he is required to administer the fore-

Oath to be administered by, to members and Clerk, and when. going oath or affirmation "to all the members present, and to the Clerk, *previous to entering on any other business;* and to the members who shall afterward appear, *previous to taking their seats.*"—*Ibid.*

Additional oath. By the act of July 2, 1862, he is required to take an additional oath.—(See OATH.)

When, shall act as President of the United States. By the act of March 1, 1792, it is provided, "that in case of removal, death, resignation, or inability, both of the President and Vice-President of the United States, the President of the Senate *pro tempore*, and in case there shall be no President of the Senate, then the Speaker of the House of Representatives for the time being, shall act as President of the United States until the disability be removed or a President shall be elected."—*Stat. at Large, Vol. I, p.* 240.

His compensation. By the act of March 3, 1873, it is provided that the pay of the Speaker shall be ten thousand dollars per annum.—*Stat. at Large, Vol. XVII, p.* 486.

(See COMPENSATION.)

SPEAKER, HIS DUTIES, ETC.

When to call House to order. "He shall take the chair every day precisely at the hour to which the House shall have adjourned on the preceding day; shall immediately call the members to order; and, on the appearance of a quorum, shall cause the Journal of the preceding day to be read."—*Rule* 1.

Shall preserve order. Has preference in speaking to points of order. "He shall preserve order and decorum; may speak to points of order in preference to other members, rising from his seat for that purpose; and shall decide questions of order, subject to an appeal to the House by any two members; on which appeal no member shall speak more than once, unless by leave of the House."—*Rule* 2.

May speak only to matters of order. "Though the Speaker may of right speak to matters of order, and be first heard, he is restrained from speaking on any other subject except where the House have occasion for facts within his knowledge; then he may, with their leave, state the matter of fact."—*Manual, p.* 78; *Journal*, 1, 28, *p.* 1011.

He may submit question as to what shall be the practice of House. The Speaker may, in order to settle the future practice of the House under a certain state of circumstances, submit a question for its decision.—*Cong. Globe*, 1, 26, *p.* 226.

Shall rise to put a question.

"He shall rise to put a question, but may state it sitting."—*Rule* 3.

Form in which he shall put question.

"Questions shall be distinctly put in this form, to wit: 'As many as are of opinion that, (as the question may be,) say *Aye;*' and after the affirmative voice is expressed, 'As many as are of the contrary opinion, say *No.*' If the Speaker doubt, or a division be called for, the House shall divide; those in the affirmative of the question shall first rise from their seats, and afterwards those in the negative. If the Speaker still doubt, or a count be required, the Speaker shall name two members, one from each side, to tell the members in the affirmative and negative; which being reported, he shall rise and state the decision to the House. No division and count of the House by tellers shall be in order but upon motion seconded by at least one-fifth of a quorum of the members."—*Rule* 4.

When he may divide house.

When he may have tellers.

While he is putting question or addressing House.

"While the Speaker is putting any question, or addressing the House, none shall walk out of or across the House; nor in such case, or when a member is speaking, shall entertain private discourse."—*Rule* 65.

Shall decide point of order during a division peremptorily.

"If any difficulty arises in point of order during the division, the Speaker is to decide peremptorily, subject to the future censure of the House if irregular."—*Manual, p.* 122.

Breach of order by, not to put question which is in order.

"It is a breach of order for the Speaker to refuse to put a question which is in order."—*Manual, p.* 62.

When he shall vote.

"In all cases of ballot by the House, the Speaker shall vote; in other cases he shall not be required to vote unless the House be equally divided, or unless his vote, if given to the minority, will make the division equal; and, in case of such equal division, the question shall be lost."—*Rule* 7.

Has a right to vote on all questions.

[The right of the Speaker, as a member of the House, to vote on all questions, is secured by the Constitution of the United States, and was claimed and exercised by Speaker Macon, notwithstanding a then existing prohibitory rule.]

Shall name member entitled to floor.

"When two or more members happen to rise at once, the Speaker shall name the member who is first to speak."—*Rule* 59.

"If any member, in speaking or otherwise, transgress the rules of the House, the Speaker shall, or any member may, call to order."—*Rule* 61. (See ORDER.)

Shall call to order member transgressing rules in speaking.

"When a motion is made and seconded, it shall be stated by the Speaker; or, being in writing, it shall be handed to the Chair, and read aloud by the Clerk, before debated."—*Rule* 38.

When motion shall be stated by him.

"Every motion shall be reduced to writing if the Speaker or any member desire it."—*Rule* 39.

May require motion to be in writing.

"When any motion or proposition is made, the question, 'Will the House now consider it?' shall not be put unless it is demanded by some member or is deemed necessary by the Speaker."—*Rule* 41.

May put question of consideration, if he deem it necessary.

"The Speaker shall examine and correct the Journal before it is read. He shall have a general direction of the hall. He shall have a right to name any member to perform the duties of the Chair, but such substitution shall not extend beyond an adjournment."—*Rule* 5.

Shall examine Journal. Have direction of hall. Name chairman for the day.

"Where the Speaker has been ill, other Speakers *pro tempore* have been appointed."—*Manual, p.* 68; *Journals*, 1, 5, *pp.* 266, 316; 1, 30, *p.* 923.

Where ill, Speaker *pro tempore* appointed.

"A Speaker may be removed at the will of the House, and a Speaker *pro tempore* appointed."—*Manual, p.* 69.

May be removed, and Speaker *pro tempore* appointed.

"In forming a Committee of the Whole House, the Speaker shall leave his chair, and a chairman, to preside in committee, shall be appointed by the Speaker."—*Rule* 105.

Shall appoint chairman of Committee of the Whole.

"All committees shall be appointed by the Speaker, unless otherwise specially directed by the House."—*Rule* 67. [It is usual, however, for him to await the passage of an order, 'that the Speaker be authorized to appoint the regular standing committees,' before announcing them.—*Journal*, 1, 35, *p.* 55. But this would seem to be unnecessary in view of the foregoing rule.]—(See COMMITTEES.)

He shall appoint committees, unless House direct otherwise.

By the act of August 10, 1846, he is required to appoint from the members of the House on the fourth Wednesday in December of the first regular session of every Congress, three Regents of the Smithsonian Institution.—*Stat. at Large, Vol. IX, p.* 102.

He shall appoint three Regents of the Smithsonian Institution.

He shall appoint three visitors to West Point.

By the act of February 21, 1870—*Laws, 2d sess. 41st Cong., p.* 67—he is required to appoint at the next session preceding the annual examination of cadets, three members to attend the same.

He may order the galleries or lobby to be cleared.

"In case of any disturbance or disorderly conduct in the galleries or lobby, the Speaker (or chairman of the Committee of the Whole House) shall have power to order the same to be cleared."—*Rule* 9.

Shall have control and direction of petitions presented.

"Members having petitions and memorials to present may hand them to the Clerk, indorsing the same with their names, and the reference or disposition to be made thereof; and such petitions and memorials shall be entered on the Journal, subject to the control and direction of the Speaker; and if any petition or memorial be so handed in which, in the judgment of the Speaker, is excluded by the rules, the same shall be returned to the member from whom it was received."—*Rule* 131.

Estimates to be addressed to.

Estimates of appropriations, and all other communications from the executive Departments, intended for the consideration of any of the committees of the House, shall be addressed to the Speaker, and by him submitted to the House for reference.—*Rule* 159.

May admit reporters to gallery over his chair.

"Stenographers and reporters, other than the official reporters of the House, wishing to take down the debates, may be admitted by the Speaker to the reporters' gallery over the Speaker's chair, but not on the floor of the House; but no person shall be allowed the privilege of said gallery under the character of stenographer or reporter without a written permission of the Speaker, specifying the part of said gallery assigned to him; nor shall said stenographer or reporter be admitted to said gallery unless he shall state in writing for what paper or papers he is employed to report; nor shall he be so admitted, or, if admitted, be suffered to retain his seat, if he shall be or become an agent to prosecute any claim pending before Congress; and the Speaker shall give his written permission with this condition."—*Rule* 135.

Shall sign acts, writs, &c.,

"All acts, addresses, and joint resolutions shall be signed by the Speaker; and all writs, warrants, and subpœnas, issued by order of the House, shall be under his hand and seal, attested by the Clerk."—*Rule* 8.

He shall sign the checks of members for compensation, the same having been previously prepared by the Sergeant-at-arms.—*Rule* 25.

Shall sign checks of members.

The compensation which shall be due the members of each house shall be certified to by the presiding officers thereof, respectively; and the same shall be passed as public accounts and paid out of the public Treasury.—*Stat. at Large, Vol. III, p.* 404. And all certificates which may have been or may be granted by the presiding officers of the Senate and House of Representatives, respectively, of the amount due to the members of their several houses, are and ought to be deemed, held, and taken, and are hereby declared to be, conclusive upon all the Departments and officers of the Government of the United States.—*Stat. at Large, Vol. IX, p.* 523.

Amount of compensation of members to be certified by.

Certificates of, to be conclusive.

By *Rule* 26 it is provided that the bond of the Sergeant at-arms shall be in a sum not less than five nor more than ten thousand dollars, at the discretion of the Speaker, and with surety to be approved by the Speaker.

Shall fix amount and approve surety of Sergeant-at-arms' bond.

"No person shall be permitted to perform divine service in the chamber occupied by the House of Representatives, unless with the consent of the Speaker."—*Rule* 6.

Divine service in the hall only with his consent.

"The unappropriated rooms in that part of the Capitol assigned to the House shall be subject to the order and disposal of the Speaker until further orders of the House."—*Rule* 5.

Shall have disposal of rooms in Capitol.

By the act of May 2, 1828, the Speaker is authorized, jointly with the President of the Senate, to prescribe rules and regulations "for the care, preservation, orderly keeping, and police of all such portions of the Capitol, its appurtenances, and the inclosures about it, and the public buildings and property in its immediate vicinity, as are not in the exclusive use and occupation of either house of Congress," which rules, &c., shall be obeyed by the Commissioner of Public Buildings.—*Stat. at Large, Vol. IV, p.* 266.

With the President of Senate, may prescribe rules in regard to Capitol not occupied by either house exclusively.

Shall prescribe rules in regard to part of Capitol in use of House.

It shall also be the duty of said Commissioner "to obey such rules and regulations as may be, from time to time, prescribed by the presiding officer of either house of Congress, for the care, preservation, orderly keeping, and police of those portions of the Capitol and its appurtenances which are in the exclusive use and occupation of either house of Congress, respectively."—*Stat. at Large, Vol. IV, p.* 266.

With the President of Senate, shall fix pay of police.

The "necessary assistants" of said Commissioner "shall receive a reasonable compensation for their services, to be allowed by the presiding officers of the two houses of Congress;" one moiety of said sums to be paid out of the contingent fund of the House.—*Ibid.*

Duty of, on report that witness fails to testify.

By the act of January 24, 1857, it is provided that where a witness, summoned by the authority of the House to testify before the House or any of its committees, "shall willfully make default, or who, appearing, shall refuse to answer any question pertinent to the matter of inquiry in consideration, and the facts shall be reported to the House, it shall be the duty of the Speaker of the House to certify the facts under the seal of the House to the District Attorney for the District of Columbia."—*Stat. at Large, Vol. XI, p.* 156. (See WITNESS.)

Pending the election of, Clerk shall preside.

Pending the election of a Speaker, the Clerk shall preserve order and decorum, and shall decide all questions of order that may arise, subject to appeal to the House.—*Rule* 146.

SPEAKER PRO TEMPORE.

Speaker may name, for the day.

"The Speaker shall have a right to name any member to perform the duties of the Chair, but such substitution shall not extend beyond an adjournment."—*Rule* 5.

Appointed, where Speaker is ill or removed.

"Where the Speaker has been ill, other Speakers *pro tempore* have been appointed."—*Manual, p.* 64; *Journals,* 1, 5, *pp.* 266, 316; 1, 30, *p.* 923. Or where he is removed by the House.—*Manual, p.* 69.

SPEAKER'S TABLE.

(See BUSINESS ON SPEAKER'S TABLE.)

SPECIAL ORDERS.

Special orders are made under a suspension of the rules.—*Journal*, 1, 31, *p*. 1176. [And, of course, (unless unanimous consent is given for the purpose—*Journal*, 1, 30, *p*. 580)—can only be made except in the case of appropriation bills when a motion to suspend the rules is in order.] Made under a suspension of the rules.

The House may, at any time, by a vote of a majority of the members present, make any of the general appropriations bills a special order—*Rule* 119; but in all other cases it requires a two-thirds vote to make a special order, it being a change of the established order of business.—*Journals*, 1, 23, *p*. 785; 3, 27, *p*. 355; 1, 31, *p*. 1096. A majority may make general appropriation bills. It requires two-thirds to make, in other cases.

The usual form of resolution for making a special order is, "*that the* (here describe the bill or whatever else it may be) *be made the special order for the —— day of ——, and from day to day until the same is disposed of*."—*Journal*, 1, 31, *p*. 1176. [In which case, after the arrival of the time fixed, or the disposal of a special order previously made, it takes precedence of all other business until it is disposed of.] Form of resolution for making.

Sometimes the words "*Fridays and Saturdays excepted*" are inserted.—*Journal*, 1, 30, *p*. 692. [In which case the consideration of private bills may be proceeded with on those days, but it is otherwise where these words are omitted.—*Journal*, 1, 32, *pp*. 401, 433.] And sometimes the words "*and from day to day until disposed of*" are omitted.—*Journal*, 1, 31, *p*. 522. [In which case it is a special order for the day named only,] and if the matter made a special order is not taken up, or, if taken up, is left undisposed of on the day fixed, thereafter it loses its specialty.—*Journal*, 1, 31, *pp*. 631, 897. Other forms.

A special order may be postponed by a majority vote.—*Journal*, 1, 29, *p*. 1170; *Cong. Globe*, 1, 31, *p*. 1318. [And according to the usage, whenever the time arrives for the consideration of a special order in Committee of the Whole, the same may be postponed by a vote in the House.] May be postponed.

Where two special orders are made for the same time, the one first made takes precedence.—*Cong. Globe*, 1, 26, *p*. 325. [The other according to the practice, if made for Where two, on same day.

that day, and "from day to day," will come up as soon as the one first made is disposed of.]

Motion to suspend rules not in order pending. Pending a special order, it is not in order to move a suspension of the rules, the special order having been made under a suspension of the rule—*Cong. Globe*, 2, 29, *p.* 439—unless said motion be with reference to the pending special order.

Debate on, to be confined to measure. In Committee of the Whole on the state of the Union all debate on special orders shall be confined strictly to the measure under consideration.—*Rule* 114.

STATE LEGISLATURES, RESOLUTIONS OF.

(See JOINT RESOLUTIONS.)

STATIONERY.

To be procured by contract. By the act of August 26, 1842, it is provided that all stationery, of every name and nature, for the use of the House of Representatives, shall be furnished by contract by the lowest bidder. Clerk to advertise for proposals. The Clerk of the House of Representatives shall advertise, once a week for at least four weeks, in one or more of the principal papers published in the city of Washington, for sealed proposals for furnishing such articles, or the whole of any particular class of articles, specifying in such advertisement the amount, quantity, and description of each kind of articles to be furnished; and all such proposals shall be kept sealed until the day specified in such advertisement for opening the same, When proposals to be opened. when they shall be opened by or under the direction of the Clerk, in the presence of at least two persons; To whom contract to be awarded. and the person offering to furnish any class of such articles, and giving satisfactory security for the performance thereof, under a forfeiture not exceeding twice the contract price in case of failure, shall receive a contract thereof; and in case the lowest bidder shall fail to enter into such contract, and give such security within a reasonable time, to be fixed in such advertisement, then the contract shall be given to the next lowest bidder, who shall enter into such contract and give such security. Liability of contractor failing to supply. And in case of a failure to supply the articles by the person entering into such contract, he and his sureties shall be liable for the forfeiture specified in such contract, as liquidated damages, to be sued for in the name of the United States in any court having jurisdiction thereof.—*Stat. at Large, Vol. V, pp.* 526, 527.

Clerk to purchase.

By a resolution of the House of the 24th of July, 1868, (*Journal*, 2, 40, *p.* 1173,) it is provided that the Clerk be authorized as the agent of the House to purchase, in the manner provided by law, on the best terms he may find practicable, such stationery as may be requisite for the use of the House and Clerk's office, giving preference in all cases to American manufacture, provided it be equally cheap and of as good quality; that he cause to be recorded in a well-bound book, suited to that purpose, the bills and invoices of all the stationery he may so purchase from time to time; that he deliver to the members of Congress and officers hereinafter named the amounts of stationery hereinafter specified, keeping an accurate account of the same, and also of the quantity and value of that used in the Clerk's office, and that hereafter, in the annual reports now required by law to be made by the Clerk, showing the amount of expenditure from the contingent fund of the House, he be required to state, accurately and distinctly, the quantity and cost of all the stationery delivered pursuant to the provisions hereof, and that used in the Clerk's office; also the amount remaining on hand at the time of making such statement, and the amount of unexpended appropriation for stationery: *Provided*, That the amount furnished to members of Congress may be embraced in a single item.

Preference to be given to American manufacture.

Records of bills and invoices of, to be kept.

Report of, to be made annually.

Clerk to deliver to members.

And he is required to deliver to every member of the House the usual articles of stationery now furnished to members, to an amount not exceeding in value that authorized by law, at the cost price, in the stationery room, or, at the option of the members, to pay them the proper commutation in money; that he keep a true and accurate account of all stationery which he may so deliver to the several members of the House; and if in any case a member shall receive a greater amount of stationery during any session than is above provided, the

In case member receives more than his allowance.

Limitation of, not to apply to folding-paper.

Clerk shall, before the close of such session, furnish to the Sergeant-at-arms an account of such excess beyond the amounts above specified, who is hereby required to deduct the amount of such excess from the pay and mileage of such members, and refund the same into the Treasury: *Provided*, That this limitation is not intended to be made applicable to the use of wrapping-paper and envelopes which may be required in the folding-room.

Clerk also to deliver to chairmen of committees and officers of the House.

And he is also authorized and required to deliver to every chairman of the committees of the House for the use of such committees, and to the Postmaster, Sergeant-at-arms, and Doorkeeper, for the use of their respective offices, at every session of Congress, similar articles of stationery, not exceeding in value an amount which from time to time shall be fixed upon by the Committee on Accounts, and approved by the Speaker.

Increased compensation to be in lieu of allowance of.

By the act of March 3, 1873, it is provided that the increased compensation thereby allowed to Senators, Representatives, and Delegates, shall be in lieu of all pay and allowance, except actual traveling expenses to and from their homes.—*Stat. at Large, Vol. XVII, p.* 486.

STENOGRAPHERS.

(See REPORTERS.)

STRIKE OUT, MOTION TO.

And insert indivisible. Effect of negative vote on.

"A motion to strike out and insert shall be deemed indivisible; but a motion to strike out being lost, shall preclude neither amendment nor a motion to strike out and insert."—*Rule* 46.

May perfect before question is put on.

"If it is proposed to amend by striking out a paragraph, the friends of the paragraph are first to make it as perfect as they can by amendments before the question is put for striking it out."—*Manual, p.* 109.

And insert A prevailing, A cannot be struck out and B inserted.

Where it is voted affirmatively to strike out certain words and insert A, it is not afterwards in order to strike out A and insert B.—*Ibid., p.* 110.

But a portion of original paragraph comprehending A may be.

"After A is inserted, however, it may be moved to strike out a portion of the original paragraph, comprehending A, providing the coherence to be struck out be so substantial as to make this effectively a different proposition."—*Ibid.*

(See AMENDMENT.)

STRIKE OUT ENACTING CLAUSE.

(See ENACTING CLAUSE, MOTION TO STRIKE OUT.)

SUBPŒNAS.

All subpœnas issued by order of the House shall be under the hand and seal of the Speaker, attested by the Clerk.—*Rule* 8. To be under hand and seal of the Speaker, and attested by Clerk.

SUNDAY.

It is for the House, and not the Speaker, to determine whether the House shall continue in session after twelve o'clock on Saturday night.—*Journal*, 1, 24, *pp*. 577, 582. For House to determine whether session shall continue on Sunday.

SUSPENSION OF THE RULES.

(See RULES.)

TAXES.

"No motion or proposition for a tax or charge upon the people shall be discussed the day on which it is made or offered, and every such proposition shall receive its first discussion in a Committee of the Whole House."—*Rule* 110. Motion for, to be first discussed in Committee of the Whole.

"No sum or quantum of tax or duty voted by a Committee of the Whole House shall be increased in the House until the motion or proposition for such increase shall be first discussed and voted in a Committee of the Whole House; and so in respect to the time of its continuance."—*Rule* 111. So also with motion for increase of, or time of continuance.

It has been decided that the foregoing rules (110, 111) do not cover the case of a bill imposing a special duty upon national banks, to meet certain expenses to be incurred by the General Government in relation thereto.—*Journal*, 1, 38, *p*. 527; *Cong. Globe, vol.* 51, *p* 1680.

TELLERS.

On putting a question, "if the Speaker doubt, or a division is called for, the House shall divide; those in Speaker, in case of doubt on a division, or on demand of one-fifth of a quorum, may name. the affirmative of the question shall rise first from their seats, and afterwards those in the negative. If the Speaker still doubt, or a count be required by at least one-fifth of a quorum of the members, the Speaker shall name two members, one from each side, to tell the members in the affirmative and negative; which being reported, he shall rise and state the decision of the House."—*Rule* 4.

Where no quorum votes on a division. [According to the usage, whenever no quorum votes on a division, the Speaker directs the vote to be taken by tellers.]

In the election of officers. [In the election of a Speaker, it is the invariable practice of the Clerk to name four members to act as tellers of the vote; and in the election of the other officers, the same number of tellers are named by the Speaker. Such tellers are usually selected from the different political parties of which the House is composed.]

TERRITORIES, COMMITTEE ON THE.

When appointed, and number of. There shall be appointed, at the commencement of each session, a Committee on the Territories, to consist of eleven members.—*Rule* 76.

One delegate to be added to. The Speaker shall appoint from among the Delegates from the Territories an additional member of the said committee, but he shall have the same privileges only as in the House.—*Rule* 162.

Its duties. "It shall be the duty of the Committee on the Territories to examine into the legislative, civil, and criminal proceedings of the Territories, and to devise and report to the House such means as, in their opinion, may be necessary to secure the rights and privileges of residents and non-residents."—*Rule* 91.

THANKS TO THE SPEAKER.

Resolution of, in order at any time. A resolution of thanks to the Speaker is, under the practice, a privileged question, and is in order at any time.—*Journals*, 2, 20, *p*. 385; 1, 23, *p*. 879.

TIE VOTE.

In case of, Speaker shall vote; also when his vote will make. "In all cases of ballot by the House, the Speaker shall vote; in other cases he shall not be required to vote, unless the House be equally divided, or unless his vote, if given to the minority, will make the division equal; and in case of

Effect of. such equal division the question shall be lost."—*Rule* 12.

A member who has voted with the prevailing side (the negative side, according to the foregoing rule) on a tie vote, is entitled to move a reconsideration.—*Journal*, 1, 30, *p*. 1080. Who may move to reconsider, in case of.

(See RECONSIDERATION.)

UNFINISHED BUSINESS.

"The consideration of the unfinished business in which the House may be engaged at an adjournment shall be resumed as soon as the Journal of the next day is read, and at the same time each day thereafter until disposed of; and if, from any cause, other business shall intervene, it shall be resumed as soon as such other business is disposed of. And the consideration of all other unfinished business shall be resumed whenever the class of business to which it belongs shall be in order under the Rules."—*Rule* 56. When to be resumed.

"After six days from the commencement of a second or subsequent session of any Congress, all bills, resolutions, and reports which originated in the House, and at the close of the next preceding session remained undetermined, shall be resumed and acted on in the same manner as if an adjournment had not taken place. And all business before committees of the House at the end of one session shall be resumed at the commencement of the next session of the same Congress as if no adjournment had taken place."—*Rule* 136 *and Joint Rule* 21. Of the preceding session, when to be resumed.

When bills and reports from the Court of Claims to the House are left undisposed of at the end of a Congress, the bills are to be again read twice and referred to the Committee of Claims, and the adverse reports restored to the private calendar at the commencement of the next Congress.—*Journals*, 1, 35, *pp*. 134, 135; 1, 36, *p*. 247. Reports from Court of Claims undisposed of at end of Congress.

VETO.

Where a bill, having passed both houses, shall be presented to the President of the United States, "if he approve he shall sign it, but if not he shall return it, with his objections, to that house in which it shall have originated, who shall enter the objections at large on their Return of bill with objections of President. Objections to be entered on Journal. Journal and proceed to reconsider it. If, after such re-

Proceedings on veto. consideration, two-thirds of that house shall agree to pass the bill, it shall be sent, together with the objections, to the other house, by which it shall likewise be reconsidered, and if approved by two-thirds of that house

Yeas and nays on reconsideration. it shall become a law. But in all such cases the votes of both houses shall be determined by yeas and nays, and the names of the persons voting for and against the bill shall be entered on the Journal of each house respectively.

Bills must be returned within ten days. If any bill shall not be returned by the President within ten days (Sundays excepted) after it shall have been presented to him, the same shall be a law, in like manner as if he had signed it, unless the Congress by their adjournment prevent its return, in which case it shall not be a law."—*Const.*, 1, 7, 10.

Similar rules applicable to orders, resolutions, and votes. A similar provision is made in the case of orders, resolutions, or votes presented to the President for his approval.—*Ibid.*, 1, 7, *pp.* 10, 11.

Veto message read upon its being received. Whenever a bill is returned to the House with the objections of the President, it is usual to have the message containing his objections *immediately* read—*Journals*, 1, 28, *pp.* 1081, 1084; 1, 29, *pp.* 1209, 1214; 2, 33, *pp.* 397, 411; 1, 34, *p.* 1420; and for the House to pro-

And bill reconsidered or postponed. ceed to the reconsideration of the bill—*Ibid.*—or to postpone its reconsideration to a future day.—*Ibid.*, 1, 21,

But not where less than a quorum present. *p.* 742. But not where less than a quorum is present.—*Ibid.*, 33, *p.* 1341. A veto message and bill may be refer-

Bill or message may be referred, or bill laid on table. red, or the message alone, and the bill may be laid on the table.—*Journal*, 2, 27, *pp.* 1253, 1254, 1256, 1257; *Cong. Globe, same sess.*, *p.* 875.

Main question on vetoed bill. The main question in the consideration of a vetoed bill is, "Will the House on reconsideration agree to pass the bill?"—*Journals*, 2, 27, *p.* 1051; 1, 28, *p.* 1085; 1, 29, p. 1218, &c.

Two-thirds of members present necessary to pass vetoed bill. The "two-thirds" by which a vetoed bill is required to be approved before it becomes a law has been construed in both houses to mean "*two-thirds of the members present*"—*Journal*, 1, 34, *pp.* 1176, 1178, 1420, (in all of which cases one hundred and fifty-six affirmative votes would have been necessary to pass the bills if "two-thirds of the members elected" has been required,) and *Senate Journal*, 1, 34, *p.* 419.

A motion to proceed to the consideration of a vetoed bill, with the objections of the President, is a privileged question under the Constitution.—*Cong. Globe*, 2, 27, *p.* 905; 2, 28, *p.* 396. Motion to proceed to consider, a privileged question.

A vote on the passage of a vetoed bill cannot be reconsidered.—*Cong. Globe*, 1, 28, *pp.* 672, 677; *Journal, same sess.*, *p.* 1093 *to* 1098. No reconsideration of vote on vetoed bill.

Where the President does not approve a bill, and is prevented by the adjournment of Congress from returning it with his objections, it is usual for him to inform the house wherein it originated, at the next session, of his reasons for not approving it.—*Journals*, 2, 12, *p.* 544; 1, 30, *p.* 82; 2, 35, *p.* 151. Where President prevented by adjournment from returning bill with objections.

(See also PRESIDENT OF THE UNITED STATES.)

VIVA VOCE.

"In all cases of election by the House of its officers, the vote shall be taken *viva voce*."—*Rule* 10. Vote to be taken in election.

(See ELECTIONS BY THE HOUSE.)

VOTING.

"Questions shall be distinctly put in this form, to wit: 'As many as are of opinion that (as the question may be) say *Aye*;' and after the affirmative voice is expressed, 'As many as are of the contrary opinion say *No*.' If the Speaker doubt, or a division be called for, the House shall divide: those in the affirmative of the question shall first rise from their seats, and afterwards those in the negative. If the Speaker still doubt, or a count be required by at least one-fifth of a quorum of the members, the Speaker shall name two members, one from each side, to tell the members in the affirmative and negative; which being reported, he shall rise and state the decision of the House."—*Rule* 4. Different modes of, viz: By the voices. By a division, By tellers.

"And the yeas and nays of the members of either house on any question shall, at the desire of one-fifth of those present, be entered on the Journal."—*Const.*, 1, 5, 9. By yeas and nays.

(See YEAS AND NAYS.)

Point of order while engaged in.

"If any question arises in point of order during the division, the Speaker is to decide peremptorily, subject to the future censure of the House if irregular."—*Manual, p.* 122.

Every member in House shall vote, unless excused.

When motion to be excused from, to be made.

"Every member who shall be in the House when the question is put shall give his vote, unless the House shall excuse him. All motions to excuse a member from voting shall be made before the House divides, or before the call of the yeas and nays, is commenced; and the question shall then be taken without debate."—*Rule* 31.

When motion to be excused from, not in order.

[But on motions to adjourn, to fix the day to which the House shall adjourn, and for a call of the House, it has been held not to be in order to ask to be excused from voting; and for the obvious reason that nothing but a desire to consume time, and thereby delay legislation, or to prevent a majority from adjourning, could possibly influence a member in making the request.] See *Cong. Globe,* 1, 31, *p.* 376; *Journals,* 1, 31, *p.* 1538; 1, 33, *pp.* 757, 765, 854, 1243; 1, 35, *p.* 866; *Cong. Globe,* 1, 39, *p.* 945.

No member to vote where interested or without the bar, unless absent by leave.

After the roll-call is completed.

Speaker not allowed to entertain request for a member to vote or change his vote when not present when taken.

"No member shall vote on any question in the event of which he is immediately and particularly interested, or in any case where he was not within the bar of the House when the question was put. When the roll-call is completed the Speaker shall state that any member offering to vote does so upon the assurance that he was within the bar before the last name on the roll was called: *Provided, however,* That any member who was absent by leave of the House may vote at any time before the result is announced." It is not in order for the Speaker to entertain a request for a member to change his vote on any question after the result shall have been declared, nor shall any member be allowed to record his vote on any question if he was not present when such vote was taken.—*Rule* 29.

[A member of a conference committee, absent on the business of his committee, is, according to the recent practice, understood to be absent by leave of the House.]

"Upon a division and count of the House on any question, no member without the bar shall be counted."—*Rule* 30.

No member to vote if without bar.

(See BAR OF THE HOUSE.)

"In all cases of ballot by the House, the Speaker shall vote; in other cases he shall not be required to vote unless the House be equally divided, or unless his vote, if given to the minority, will make the division equal; and in case of such equal division the question shall be lost."—*Rule* 7.

Where Speaker shall vote.

Effect of a tie vote.

The names of members not voting on any call of the ayes and noes shall be recorded in the Journal immediately after those voting in the affirmative and negative, and the same record shall be made in the Congressional Globe.—*Rule* 149.

Names of members not, to be recorded.

A member has the right to change his vote before the decision of the question has been finally and conclusively pronounced by the chair.—*Journal*, 2, 20, *pp*. 357, 358. [But not afterwards.]

Member has right to change vote before decision finally pronounced.

And it is not competent for a member to have the Journal amended so as to have the record of his vote changed, upon a representation that such vote, though recorded as given, was given under a misapprehension.—*Journals*, 2, 8, *p*. 167; 2, 27, *p*. 263.

Record of vote, if correct, cannot be amended because of misapprehension of question.

WARRANTS, WRITS, ETC.

All writs, warrants, and subpœnas, issued by order of the House, shall be under the hand and seal of the Speaker, attested by the Clerk.—*Rule* 8.

To be signed by Speaker, and attested by Clerk.

WAYS AND MEANS, COMMITTEE OF.

There shall be appointed, at the commencement of each Congress, a Committee of Ways and Means, to consist of eleven members.—*Rule* 74.

When appointed, and of what number.

It shall be the duty of the Committee of Ways and Means to take into consideration all reports of the Treasury Department, and such other propositions relating to raising revenue and providing ways and means for the support of the Government as shall be presented or shall come in question and be referred to them by the House,

Its duties.

and to report their opinion thereon by bill or otherwise, as to them shall seem expedient; and said committee shall have leave to report for commitment at any time.—*Rule* 151.

Authorized to employ a clerk.

The Committee of Ways and Means is authorized, by resolution of February 18, 1856, to employ a clerk.—*Journal*, 1, 34, *p*. 557.

WEST POINT.

(See MILITARY ACADEMY.)

WITHDRAWAL OF MOTIONS.

When in order.

A motion may be withdrawn at any time before a decision or amendment—*Rule* 50—[but not after the previous question is seconded.] It may, however, be withdrawn while the House is dividing on a demand for the previous question—*Journal*, 2, 29, *p*. 241; and all incidental questions fall with such withdrawal.—*Journal*, 1, 26, *p*. 57.

WITHDRAWAL OF PAPERS.

(See PAPERS.)

WITNESS.

Summoned by order of the House.

Witnesses are summoned in pursuance of an order of the House, usually by virtue of its authority conferred upon a committee "to send for persons and papers."—*Journal*, 1, 35, *pp*. 88, 175.

Subpœnas to be under hand and seal of Speaker and attested by Clerk.

All subpœnas issued by order of the House shall be under the hand and seal of the Speaker, attested by the Clerk.—*Rule* 8.

Sergeant-at-arms shall execute subpœnas directed to him.

The Sergeant-at-arms shall execute the commands of the House from time to time, together with all such process issued by authority thereof as shall be directed to him by the Speaker.—*Rule* 22.

Who may administer oaths to.

The Speaker of the House of Representatives, a chairman of a Committee of the Whole, or a chairman of a select committee—*Stat. at Large, Vol. I, p.* 554—and the chairman of any standing committee shall be empowered to administer oaths or affirmations to witnesses in any case under their examination.—*Stat. at Large, Vol. III, p.* 345.

"The rule for paying witnesses summoned to appear before this House, or either of its committees, shall be as follows: For each day a witness shall attend, the sum of four dollars; for each mile he shall travel in coming to or going from the place of examination, the sum of five cents each way; but nothing shall be paid for traveling when the witness has been summoned at the place of trial."—*Rule* 138. Fees of.

The failure or refusal of a witness to appear, or refusal to testify, is a breach of the privileges of the House, and has been punished by commitment to the custody of the Sergeant-at-arms, by expulsion from the floor as a reporter, and by commitment to the common jail of the District of Columbia.—*Journals*, 1, 12, *pp*. 276, 277; 2, 33, *pp*. 315, 318; 2, 34, *pp*. 269, 277, 281, 384, 567; 1, 35, *pp*. 371, 387 *to* 389, 535 *to* 539. Failure of, to appear or testify. Penalty for failure of, to appear or testify.

Any person summoned as a witness by authority of the House to give testimony or to produce papers upon any matter before the House or any committee thereof, who shall willfully make default, or who, appearing, shall refuse to answer any question pertinent to the matter of inquiry in consideration before the House or committee by which he shall be examined, shall, in addition to the pains and penalties now existing, be liable to indictment as for a misdemeanor. And when a witness shall fail to testify, as above, and the facts shall be reported to the House, it shall be the duty of the Speaker to certify the fact under the seal of the House, to the district attorney for the District of Columbia.—*Stat. at Large, Vol. XI, pp*. 155, 156. Additional penalty for failure of, to testify. Duty of Speaker on failure of, to testify.

The testimony of a witness examined and testifying before either house of Congress, or any committee of either house of Congress, shall not be used as evidence in any criminal proceeding against such witness in any court of justice: *Provided, however*, That no official paper or record produced by such witness on such examination shall be held or taken to be included within the privilege of said evidence so as to protect such witness from any criminal proceeding as aforesaid; and no witness shall hereafter be allowed to refuse to testify to any Testimony of, not to be used against. Official paper produced by.

fact or to produce any paper touching which he shall be examined by either house of Congress, or any committee of either house, for the reason that his testimony touching such fact, or the production of such paper, may tend to disgrace him, or otherwise render him infamous: *Provided*, That nothing in this act shall be construed to exempt any witness from prosecution and punishment for perjury committed by him in testifying as aforesaid.—*Stat. at Large, Vol. XII, p.* 333.

May be punished for perjury.

WRITING.

Motions to be reduced to.

"Every motion shall be reduced to writing if the Speaker or any member desire it."—*Rule* 39.

Words excepted to, to be taken down in.

"If a member be called to order for words spoken in debate, the person calling him to order shall repeat the words excepted to, and they shall be taken down in writing at the Clerk's table."—*Rule* 62.

YEAS AND NAYS.

May be taken if desired by one-fifth of those present.

"The yeas and nays of the members of either house on any question shall, at the desire of one-fifth of those present, be entered on the Journal."—*Const.*, 1, 5, 9.

Must be taken on passage of a vetoed bill.

"And in all cases" (on the passage of a vetoed bill) "the votes of both houses shall be determined by yeas and nays, and the names of the persons voting for and against the bill shall be entered on the Journal of each house respectively."—*Ibid.*, 1, 7, 10. The yeas and nays may be called for while a vote on a division by tellers is being taken—*Cong. Globe*, 2, 28, *p.* 121—or while the Speaker is announcing the result of such vote—*Ibid.*, 1, 29, *p.* 420—or even after the announcement, and before passing to any other business—1, 31, *p.* 277—but not after the result is announced, if delayed until the Speaker shall be in the act of putting another question—*Journal*, 1, 32, *p.* 254.

When demand for may be made.

A quorum not necessary on ordering.

["One-fifth of those present" has always been construed to mean *one-fifth of those who vote* on the question of ordering the yeas and nays, regardless of the fact as to whether or not a quorum is present.]

It is not in order to repeat a demand for the yeas and nays which has been once refused.—*Cong. Globe*, 1, 29, *p.* 304; 2, 30, *p.* 623; *Journal*, 1, 33, *p.* 939. After refusal of, not in order to repeat demand.

An order of the yeas and nays—*Journals*, 1, 19, *p.* 796; 1, 30, *p.* 405—or a refusal of the yeas and nays—*Cong. Globe*, 2, 30, *p.* 623—may be reconsidered. Order of, or refusal of, may be reconsidered.

The yeas and nays cannot be demanded on seconding a demand for the previous question.—*Journal*, 2, 19, *p.* 493. Nor can they be taken on any question in Committee of the Whole.—*Cong. Globe*, 1, 28, *p.* 618. Not in order on seconding previous question. Nor in Committee of the Whole.

"In taking the yeas and nays on any question the names of the members shall be called alphabetically."—*Rule* 35. And while they are being taken, no member or other person shall visit or remain by the Clerk's table.—*Rule* 65. In taking, names to be called alphabetically. No person to visit Clerk's desk while being taken.

After the yeas and nays are ordered and a member has answered to his name, the roll-call must progress without debate.—*Cong. Globe*, 1, 31, *p.* 1686. No debate after one response on call of.

"Every member who shall be in the House when the question is put shall give his vote, unless the House shall excuse him. All motions to excuse a member from voting shall be made before the House divides, or before the call of the yeas and nays is commenced; and the question shall then be taken without debate."—*Rule* 42. Every member in House shall vote, unless excused. When motion to be excused from voting to be made.

"No member shall vote on any question in the event of which he is immediately and particularly interested, or in any case where he was not within the bar of the House when the question was put. When the roll-call is completed the Speaker shall state that any member offering to vote does so upon the assurance that he was within the bar before the last name on the roll was called: *Provided, however*, That any member who was absent by leave of the House may vote at any time before the result is announced."—*Rule* 29. No member to vote where interested, or without the bar. After the roll-call is completed.

But the Speaker shall not entertain the request of a member to change his vote after announcement or to vote if not present when the vote was taken.—*Rule* 29. After result announced.

[A member of a committee of conference, according to the recent practice, is understood to have leave of the House to be absent on the duties of his committee.] Member of conference committee has privilege of one absent by leave.

No member to vote if without bar.

"Upon a division and count of the House on any question no member without the bar shall be counted."—*Rule* 41.

(See BAR OF THE HOUSE.)

Names of members not voting on call of, to be recorded.

The names of members not voting on any call of the yeas and nays shall be recorded in the Journal immediately after the names of those voting in the affirmative and negative, and the same record shall be made in the Congressional Globe.—*Rule* 149.

Member has right to change vote before decision finally pronounced.

A member has the right to change his vote before the decision of the question has been finally and conclusively pronounced by the Chair.—*Journal*, 2, 20, *pp.* 357, 358. [But not afterwards.]

Record of vote, if correct, cannot be amended because of misapprehension of question.

And it is not competent for a member to have the Journal amended, so as to have the record of his vote changed, upon a representation that such vote, though recorded as given, was given under a misapprehension.—*Journals*, 2, 8, *p.* 167; 2, 27, *p.* 263.

Erroneous record of vote may be corrected after result is declared.

A member has a right to have an erroneous record of his vote corrected after the announcement of the result of a vote.—*Journal*, 1, 38, *pp.* 586, 587.

INDEX TO BARCLAY'S DIGEST.

A.

E.

F.

M.

Q.

R.

o

www.ingramcontent.com/pod-product-compliance
Lightning Source LLC
LaVergne TN
LVHW021301110826
845150LV00003B/454

* 9 7 8 1 4 2 5 5 5 9 9 2 2 *